European Soccer

European Soccer

Edited by L. N. Bailey

PELHAM BOOKS

First published in Great Britain by
PELHAM BOOKS LTD
52 Bedford Square
London, W.C.1
1970

Set and printed in Great Britain by Tonbridge Printers Ltd,
Peach Hall Works, Tonbridge, Kent, in Times ten on eleven point,
on paper made by P. F. Bingham Ltd, and bound by James Burn
at Esher, Surrey

Contents

Contents

Illustrations

Introduction

While the main object of this book was to give a record of European football during the 1969–1970 season, with a list of previous winners of championships and cups for various countries it was felt that the World Cup could not be ignored.

More than half the countries who competed in the Mexico finals came from Europe and their progress which resulted in the failure of England to retain the Jules Rimet Cup, and the success of Italy – who wiped out the bitter 1966 memories of defeat by North Korea in reaching the final – have been recorded by my colleague Donald Saunders, who was in Mexico.

His summing up of the organisation is that while Mexico may never again have the opportunity to demonstrate what a colourful fiesta the World Cup can be, it is to be hoped their example will not be quietly ignored.

While every effort has been made with the help of various football associations and clubs to make the records as complete and accurate as possible, the magnitude of such an undertaking is unlikely to pass without an omission of some sort and one offers apologies in advance for any errors of omission or commission.

It is just hoped that the book will fill a long vacant spot on the soccer bookshelves.

L. N. BAILEY
London

Foreword

By Sir Stanley Rous, President of F.I.F.A.

My 'parish' as president of the Federation Internationale de Football Association consists of 135 countries scattered all over the globe and I spend as much of my time as possible visiting them to show them they are all members of one great family whose interests are not forgotten. I mention this to show that the 33 countries who form the *Union des Associations Européennes de Football* are but a part, even so an important part, of the main association. Nevertheless, I welcome this attempt to give a word and statistical picture of the European scene over the past season, particularly as during the last decade or so European countries and clubs have come into so much closer contact chiefly through the three main club competitions, the European Champions Clubs' Cup, the Cup-Winners' Cup and the European Fairs' Cup which provide players with the great opportunity of studying the styles of play and techniques operating in various countries. Furthermore it brings them into contact with different referees which is also important. As an old referee I am a great believer in a uniform standard of refereeing and much of my work as president of F.I.F.A. is devoted to this aim because through this the standard of football will be maintained at a high level. Football is the world's greatest sport; I hope it always remains so.

1 How The World Cup Was Won

by DONALD SAUNDERS

Shortly after two o'clock on the afternoon of Sunday, June 21, 1970, the ninth World Soccer Championships came to a rousing climax beneath leaden skies, with Gustavo Diaz Ordaz, the President of Mexico, presenting the Jules Rimet Trophy to Carlos Alberto, Brazil's handsome captain.

As Carlos Alberto led his merry men on a lap of honour round Mexico City's Aztec Stadium, amid a blizzard of multi-coloured confetti, most of the 110,000 spectators rose from their seats to roar their approval of the Brazilians' third great triumph in this competition in 12 years.

None of those lucky enough to be at the Aztec Stadium that afternoon would have disputed Brazil's right to take home the golden cup as a keepsake. During the three previous weeks, Carlos Alberto's men had proved themselves more accomplished than their successful 1962 predecessors and had touched heights not far below those scaled by the Brazilian heroes of 1958. Apart from the luckless Hungarians of 1954, there have been no greater teams than those three in international soccer history.

From the moment they opened their campaign against Czechoslovakia, in Guadalajara, on Wednesday, June 3, to the dying seconds of their 4–1 victory over Italy in the final, Brazil played adventurous football, the like of which had not been seen since their success in Chile eight years earlier.

They set out to score more often than the other side. With the notable exception of Peru and West Germany, the other finalists concentrated on conceding fewer goals than their opponents did. And, therein, lies the true reason for Brazil's well deserved triumph.

During the most colourful and entertaining of all world championships, six Brazilians became household names. Pele, Tostao, Jairzinho, Rivelino, Gerson and Clodoaldo brought delight to millions of television watchers who long ago must have concluded that soccer was neither art nor entertainment.

Pele, of course, had been famous since, as a lad of 17, he scored twice against Sweden in the 1958 final. Tostao, Jairzinho, Gerson and Rivelino were not unknown to students of international football.

Clodoaldo underlined Brazil's unique ability to 'find' a world class player during these tournaments.

Between them, these six 'carried' one of the most vulnerable defences in the competition. And in the process they struck a savage blow at those who would have us believe soccer is a military-style exercise based on sound defensive tactics.

Brazil usually lined up at the start in 4–3–3 formation but, thereafter, they rarely had fewer than four men up front. Indeed, Pele, Jairzinho, Tostao and Rivelino were often joined, deep inside enemy territory, by Gerson and Clodoaldo.

But it was not formation that won them the cup. There are far better tacticians in Europe than there are in Brazil. Dazzling artistry, superb ball control, perfect balance, graceful athleticism, almost telepathic understanding and sheer love of the game combined to lift these Latin Americans back on the throne.

In almost every match they were in danger of defeat. On each occasion they cheerfully thrust aside the threat and swept boldly to victory. Some coaches might have frowned at seven goals conceded in six games. Mario Zagalo, Brazil's team chief, was delighted with the nineteen his men scored.

No doubt, it will be argued, especially in Europe, that Zagalo could afford this adventurous approach because he had six of the world's greatest attacking players on call. But there were other teams in Mexico, too, who possessed gifted forwards. Instead of allowing these men freedom of expression, most coaches kept them on the tightest rein or asked two of them at a time to do the job for which Brazil employed a minimum of four.

Italy and Uruguay were particularly guilty of this sin. Had the Italians employed against Brazil the all-out policy they were obliged to use during extra-time in their semi-final with West Germany, they might have halted the merry dance of Pele and his companions.

Instead, they kept the talented, experienced Rivera on the substitutes' bench until the closing minutes, played the thrustful Domenghini deep, asked Riva and Boninsegna to run themselves into the ground and stumbled to humiliating defeat.

Uruguay, it is true, suffered the severe handicap of losing Rocha, their Bobby Charlton, for good after only thirteen minutes of their first group match. Even so, when they lined up against Brazil in the semi-final in Guadalajara, they possessed, in Cubilla, Morales and Fontes, forwards capable of wrecking Brazil's flimsy defence, had Montero Castillo, Maneiro and Cortes not been under orders to play defensively behind them.

Having snatched an early lead, the Uruguayans concentrated on containing Pele and company, gave away an equaliser in first-half injury time and ultimately collapsed under late and heavy pressure.

Equally, England could be justly accused of being over-cautious, not only during their 1–0 defeat by Brazil, but in their other three games.

In the late sixties, Sir Alf Ramsey evolved the 4–4–2 system, which he believed best suited the players available to him. It worked none too well, even before the squad left for Mexico, and may well have been replaced by the 4–3–3 formation that brought success in 1966 had England survived to the semi-final.

Indeed, Ramsey used three men up during the first half hour of the quarter-final against West Germany and the plan worked so well that, with Mullery and Peters moving through from mid-field to score, England were leading 2–0 early in the second half.

Then they and Ramsey began to think about the next match. As concentration slackened, over-confidence took root and the Germans were allowed to gain control of a match they must have thought they had lost.

Beckenbauer halved the lead in the 70th minute, with a shot from outside the penalty box, then the veteran Seeler backheaded the equaliser over the badly-positioned Bonetti eleven minutes later. Finally, Mueller, Germany's ace marksman, brought his total of World Cup goals to eight, by volleying home a cross Labone or Bonetti might have cut off.

No one will ever be able to explain adequately why England lost this match and, with it, all hopes of retaining the trophy. The immediate reaction was to blame Bonetti and Ramsey. Both did make mistakes that hot Sunday noon, but these were no worse, even if more obvious, than errors committed by the team as a whole.

It has been argued that if Banks had not been struck down by a stomach complaint the night before, England would not have been beaten. Possibly this great goalkeeper would have dealt firmly with Seeler's header. Perhaps he would have reached the ball before Mueller. Whether he would have saved England is another matter.

The attitude of the team midway through the second half was all wrong. They concluded, much too soon, that, for the second consecutive time, they had tamed the old foe from Germany in a World Cup tie. Instead of maintaining, or even increasing, pressure on a defence that was falling apart, they began to push the ball around arrogantly in midfield, partly to conserve energy for future battles but largely, I suspect, to let a hostile crowd know who were the masters.

Even Ramsey allowed his mind to stray momentarily from present to future. Some minutes before Beckenbauer's goal, he had ordered Bell to get ready to replace Bobby Charlton. At the time it was a sensible plan, aimed at keeping the ageing Charlton fresh for the semi-final that then seemed highly likely. The mistake Ramsey made was not to change his mind when Germany scored and that next match receded to the far horizon.

Once the Germans had moved back into the game, it would have been wiser to keep Charlton in mid-field, where he was playing well and showing no sign of distress, and to send on Clarke in place of Lee, who was struggling up front.

Clarke had made a promising World Cup debut in the previous match against Czechoslovakia and his skill in and around the penalty box might have helped Hurst keep the wilting German defence under pressure. Bell, always a slow starter, merely added to the confusion in which England found themselves after Charlton's departure.

Worse still, Ramsey next sent on Hunter in place of the faltering Peters. This, again, was a logical move – as long as there was a lead to protect. Alas, shortly after Hunter's arrival on the pitch, Seeler equalised.

So England were left with only two attacking mid-field players – Bell and Ball – and two tired strikers – Lee and Hurst – at the moment when another goal was essential. Moreover, their will to win had been sapped, along with their stamina.

Meanwhile, the Germans, so weary midway through the second half, had been revitalised by two goals. And, with Schulz taking over from Hottges in defence, and Grabowski replacing Libuda up front, they still had a nicely balanced team to take into extra-time.

It was Grabowski who proved to be manager Helmut Schoen's trump card. This tall, powerful winger had caused England enough trouble during the last 20 minutes of normal time. During the additional half hour he tore apart the tightest defence in the world.

In contrast, Bell, the only England forward who could raise a gallop during extra time, was unable to carry on his young shoulders the heavy burden thrust upon them. So, once Mueller's volley had beaten Bonetti, we all knew England's reign as world champions was over.

'This should never have happened,' said Ramsey, with some justification, afterwards. 'No international team, especially England, should give away two goals.' One can understand his bewilderment. Never before, during his management, had the team been beaten after leading by such a margin.

But even had this disaster – it could be called a fluke – not befallen them, England still might have come home empty handed. Assuming they had beaten the Germans 2–0, as they should have, they then would have faced Italy in the semi-finals. After a hard battle they might have reached the final, where, I fear, the Brazilians, this time, would have taken good care of them.

From their first match against Rumania, right to the bitter moment of collapse against West Germany, England had been obliged to work much harder for survival than had Brazil. Though they had shown themselves to be resilient, I doubt whether they could have played better in this second Mexico clash with Pele and his colleagues than they had when losing the first one.

On the other hand, there is every reason to believe that Brazil, having improved with each appearance, would have scaled heights they had not approached a fortnight earlier.

The 4–4–2 system was not the direct cause of England's failure against West Germany. It may well have become the reason for ultimate disappointment had they reached the final. The formation made unreasonable demands, first physically, eventually mentally as well, on the front runners, Lee and Hurst, on Ball in mid-field and on Moore at the back. Lee had shown clear signs of strain by the quarter finals; the other three probably would have run out of stamina by the final.

The system had always seemed a risky one for employment in a long, hard tournament staged in the heat and high altitude of Mexico. Presumably, Ramsey stuck to it throughout the group matches because he considered he did not have enough top-class attacking strength to justify a switch to 4–3–3.

Yet, in the squad were Osgood and Clarke, both men of deft skill and sound scoring record. Had they been groomed for internatioual football a couple of years earlier, they might have been experienced enough to employ as front line troops, instead of being used infrequently as reserves.

Possibly it was a mistake, too, to omit Thompson, who was in the original party of 28, from the World Cup 22. Conventional wingers are out of fashion in England. But in Mexico their retention by such countries as Brazil, Italy, Uruguay, West Germany and Peru was wholly justified.

In many cases they helped their teams progress further than expected and in none were they luxuries. Had Thompson been given the place allocated to Astle, England might have caused opposing defences more trouble and improved on their meagre haul of four goals from four games.

Searching for reasons for failure, one also must raise doubts about England's preparation. Possibly too much emphasis was placed on altitude, too little on heat. While Ramsey's men were straining their lungs in the lofty cities of Bogota and Quito during the middle of May, most of their opponents were becoming accustomed to the high temperatures of Mexico. In the long run, the sun, not the thin air, posed the greater problem.

The eight-day visit to Colombia and Ecuador, of course, was not arranged purely for the purpose of acclimatisation. Ramsey's intention also was to give his players competitive practice and to counter boredom, which inevitably raised its ugly head during a month-long wait for battle to commence.

No doubt, the 'A' and 'B' teams enjoyed their victories over Colombia and Ecuador but the boost to morale was probably more than offset by irritating, long and tiring air trips and by the disruption of routine. Morale is always a difficult quality to gauge, but it seemed to me that this sagged a little after a difficult 'A' match in Quito and the events of the next few days.

It was on the return from Quito that Moore was detained in Bogota for questioning in connection with an emerald bracelet a jeweller said had been stolen. This great player is a man of such strong character that he survived the ordeal so well that no member of the sixteen teams reached a higher standard of football more consistently than he did. Yet, the incident may well have had an adverse effect on his colleagues, who, for the better part of a week, did not know for sure whether he would be free to lead them into action.

Even so, this affair could have been exploited in England's favour. Such was the wave of sympathy in Mexico for Moore, that much of the hostility England had been obliged to withstand, since their original arrival in the country, might have disappeared – if a public relations expert had been there to help it on its way.

I doubt whether England would ever have been really popular. But it is possible that Mexico would not have been so wholeheartedly against them, if one or two gestures of friendship towards Press and public had been attempted. And, who knows, a little less support for the Germans when England were up against it during the quarter-final might have made all the difference.

Ramsey, however, does not regard public relations as an important part of his job. Two days after Moore's return to the fold, England's manager was making it quite clear that he did not consider the Jalisco Stadium pitch in Guadalajara to be as good as he had found it during the team's reconnaissance 12 months earlier. No other manager or coach found cause for complaint about the surface.

So, as they emerged from the tunnel 48 hours later, for their opening game against Rumania, England were greeted with jeers that would have frightened lesser men. The jeers did not die until Sir Alf and his former champions were *en route* for home a fortnight later.

Despite this sad departure, however, the 1970 World Cup finals will still be remembered as the best of the nine. The football, certainly, was more skilful and exciting than it had been in England in 1966. And the behaviour was infinitely better. Indeed, Sir Stanley Rous, president of F.I.F.A., emphasising that not one player had been sent off during the entire tournament, praised all 16 nations for their excellent conduct.

Yet, many of us had expected this to be the most violent championships of all time. Why were we so wrong? Principally because the referees, having been carefully chosen and thoroughly prepared, reached a higher standard than ever before.

Whether they came from Europe or Latin America, most of the officials did their job firmly enough to deter even the most determined potential delinquent. Moreover, to the surprise of most of us, interpretation of the laws, for the first time, came within striking distance of being universal.

Players from Europe soon learned that tackling from behind simply was not 'on'. The Latin Americans decided to employ body checking only when no alternative readily presented itself.

With players such as Pele, Jairzinho, Mueller, Seeler, Byshovets, Riva, the Uruguayan Cubilla, and Cubillas of Peru, receiving far greater protection than any forwards enjoyed in 1966, goals came regularly enough to satisfy the most demanding spectator.

These goals, and the flowing moves that led to many of them, more than compensated for the 'walking football' that fear of high altitude persuaded some teams to play during the closing stages of their group matches.

Consequently, F.I.F.A.'s decision to stage the tournament in Mexico, roundly criticised during the previous six years, ultimately was justified. The Mexicans put on a gay, colourful show that did much to restore soccer's somewhat tarnished image. What's more they turned up in their thousands to support it. Let us hope West Germany, indeed Europe, will be as successful, in 1974.

2 European Teams in a Classic

by DONALD SAUNDERS

England's early exit from the World Cup left some 5,000 British visitors to Mexico with a deep sense of loss. Many had forfeited half a dozen summer holidays to pay for the trip of a lifetime, truly believing that it would culminate in their cheering their heroes to victory in the final. Now all seemed pointless.

No longer were they chanting 'England, England' in the British pub at the Fenix Hotel in Guadalajara. Nor were they making daily pilgrimages to the Hilton to seek autographs. With Sir Alf Ramsey's troops *en route* for home, the champions' World Cup headquarters had reverted to a businessman's hotel, and Northern, Midlands and Cockney dialects had been replaced by a lazy Texas drawl.

But within a few days, the feeling of anti-climax, even of despair, had been swept away by the most exciting semi-final in the history of this competition. Italy and West Germany fought each other with such good-tempered tenacity, at the Aztec Stadium, on Wednesday, June 17, that the World Cup, again, was proved bigger than the most illustrious of its competitors. As Europe's last two survivors came to grips, England's demise was forgotten.

The Italians had come down from the lofty heights of Pueblo to Mexico City with a modest haul of five goals from four ties, and four of those had been scored against Mexico in the quarter-final. The Germans had moved up from the torrid heat of the pretty, shoe-making town of Leon with a formidable goals aggregate of thirteen. And, for good measure, they had England's highly-prized scalp tucked into their belt.

So, said the experts, this would be a battle of wits between the enterprising marksmen of Germany and the cautious stonewallers from Italy. Within eight minutes those forecasts were being revised.

After repulsing a couple of early raids, the Italians broke up field and Boninsegna drove home a 20-yarder to put them in front. Though not unaccustomed to such set-backs, the Germans took half an hour to get over this one. Then these great competitors fought for the equaliser with the spirit that had almost won them the championship at Wembley in 1966 and had earned them revenge over England in the 1970 quarter-final.

Their reward came as the last minutes of injury-time ticked away, with full-back Schnellinger lunging desperately to prod a pass from Held past the prostrate Albertosi. So began the most dramatic half hour of the entire tournament.

No doubt Italians among the 90,000 crowd must have wondered, as extra time began, whether their heroes would collapse, just as England had in similar circumstances at Leon. Their fears were heightened four minutes later, when Mueller snapped up a half chance to put Germany in front for the first time in the game.

That should have been the end of Italy, whose poor record in post-war tournaments had earned them a reputation as poor travellers possessing little combative spirit. Yet, within five minutes, the over-lapping Burgnich had put them level.

Before the Germans could recover, Riva had rammed the ball past Maier and Italy were back in front. So, we all said complacently, Germany had met their match at last. England's conquerors refused to believe such nonsense. And they were right. Early in the second period of extra-time, Mueller popped in his 10th World Cup goal to square the battle.

But the Germans flags did not flutter for long. One minute later Rivera, who had spent much of the tournament seated on the substitutes' bench, scored the most important goal of his life and Italy were in the final for the first time since their second consecutive World Cup triumph in 1938. Henceforth, surely no one will dare to call them spineless.

The Italians' problem, now they had outlasted the most determined battlers in the world, was to recover in time for the final in four days' time. While they stumbled, exhausted, to the dressing room, the Brazilians were driving happily through cheering crowds that lined the route to their hotel in the suburbs of Guadalajara.

Mario Zagalo's men had needed no extra time to dispose of their near neighbours and bitter rivals from Uruguay. Moreover, their 3–1 semi-final victory at the Jalisco Stadium had earned them sweet revenge for the still-resented humiliation of defeat by Uruguay in the 1950 final in Rio.

Brazil, however, had not danced comfortably into the 1970 final. The Uruguayans had surprised them by moving boldly into the attack, after the early skirmishing, and had shocked them by jumping into an early lead with a softish goal, which Cubilla swept in front of the mesmerised Felix into the far corner of the net.

Most of us who had watched Brazil's group matches had long been certain that their slack defence and patently nervous goalkeeper would one day let them down. The question we now asked was whether their six great attacking stars could steer them out of trouble.

For a long, long time the answer looked like being 'No'. As these Latin American rivals began to make skilful use of blindside tripping and bodychecking, there were distinct signs that the Brazilians were becoming edgy.

Rivelino, master of the 'bent' free-kick, put two straight into the wall and another into the crowd. Even the great Pele once hit an intended shot into the barrier near the corner flag.

But Uruguay failed to see or take their chance to nudge their opponents nearer disintegration. Instead of piling on the pressure, they withdrew further and further into the shell they thought would protect their slender lead. And, as Czechoslovakia, England and Rumania had discovered, even the soundest defence will eventually slip up when Pele and his troupe of artists are allowed to move forward.

The moment of truth for Uruguay came two minutes after the stadium clock, which moved backwards from 45, had reached zero. Clodoaldo raced on to a pass from Tostao and thumped the ball so hard and accurately that even Mazurkiewicz, the most accomplished goalkeeper in Latin America, could not halt its progress.

Though the Uruguayans complained bitterly that the clock had made this goal invalid, Senor Mendebil, the Spanish referee, waved aside their protests, presumably because he had decided to add two and a half minutes for first-half stoppages.

So, Brazil came out after the interval smiling broadly, while Uruguay were still fuming. For another 25 minutes the battle remained hard and tense, though one now felt Brazil would find the answer. That view was handsomely justified in the 76th minute, when a lilting move between Pele and Tostao ended with Jairzinho gliding through to place the ball in the corner of the net.

As Jairzinho went leaping into the arms of his colleagues on the substitutes' bench, we all knew Brazil had reached their fourth final in 20 years and their third in the last 12. A few minutes before time, Rivelino confirmed this, by scoring their third goal, seconds after Felix had wiped out his many earlier errors by leaping athletically to hold a close-range header from Cubilla.

The Uruguayans never will agree that Brazil should have entered the final. They argued, with some justification, that they had been unfairly treated by F.I.F.A., when ordered to travel to Guadalajara for the semi-final. This meant they had been obliged to play at four different grounds – Puebla, Toluca, Mexico City and Guadalajara – while the Brazilians had been allowed to make a home from home for themselves at the Jalisco Stadium, where they had played five consecutive ties.

Uruguay also were convinced that Clodoaldo's injury-time goal should have been disallowed. And finally they pointed out that Rocha, their mid-field general, had been unable to help their cause after being injured in the thirteenth minute of their opening match. Yet, in the long run foolish tactics, not misfortune, cost Uruguay their chance to become the first outright owners of the trophy. From their first match to the later stages of their semi-final, they were guilty of being the most negative team in the competition.

Only when they lined up against the West Germans, in the third-place match at the Aztec Stadium the following Saturday, did they throw caution to the winds and let us see how accomplished were their forwards.

This fixture is one many would like to see withdrawn from the World Cup programme. It brings together two bitterly disappointed teams who, having narrowly failed to reach the final, usually are not greatly concerned whether they come third or fourth. The 1970 match was the exception.

It was clear from the start that Uruguay and West Germany wanted to wind up their campaign with victory. So the crowd were treated to 90 minutes of attacking soccer that made nonsense of fears that footballers from low level countries would never surmount the problems posed by the Mexican climate.

Uruguay had played three of their previous five games in the Puebla-Toluca centres, which at 8,000 ft plus, were the highest of the lot, then they had been obliged to battle on into extra-time to beat Russia in the quarter-final in Mexico City, which is 7,500 ft above sea level. The Germans had withstood the grilling heat of Leon (approximately 6,000 ft) on four occasions and had suffered the strain of extra-time in their quarter- and semi-finals.

Yet, from kick-off to final whistle, both teams drove themselves to the limit on this, their somewhat pointless last appearance in Mexico.

Eventually the Germans triumphed, thanks to a first-half goal by Overath and the agility and good fortune of Wolter, their reserve goalkeeper. But so bravely did the Uruguayans try to win this match that they at least earned the satisfaction of being cheered off the pitch, by a crowd that had jeered them long and loud when they first had emerged from the tunnel.

So, at last, we came to the final, which, from the moment the draw was made the previous January, had promised to produce a great confrontation between Latin America and Europe. Most experts had pictured Brazil lining up, at the Aztec Stadium on June 21, against England. Instead, the Italians enjoyed the privilege of trying to uphold the old world's prestige.

Ironically, the cool, damp weather would have been ideal for England, had they been out on the pitch instead of crouching round their television sets back home. No doubt the Italians appreciated the drop in temperature and the absence of sunshine. European conditions offered some compensation for the bias of the crowd, who, almost to a man, were waving green and yellow flags and chanting 'Brazil, Brazil'.

Not that there was much to shout about until a cat-and-mouse affair had reached its 18th minute. Then the stands erupted, as Pele leapt above a tightly packed defence to head home what is likely to be the last of his many World Cup goals.

The Italians took this nasty jolt in their stride, continued to play thoughtfully, added a little aggression to their customary caution and, shortly before half-time, gratefully accepted the inevitable gift from Brazil's defence. The honour of tapping the ball into the empty net fell to Boninsegna.

For the next ten minutes, Brazil were in grave danger of losing their cool. A Brazilian was booked for kicking the prostrate Bertini, Pele was lucky not to join him in the notebook, when he complained bitterly, and unreasonably, because the half-time whistle had blown seconds before he put the ball into the net for the second time.

But, by the time the battle had been rejoined, Brazil had regained their composure and their rhythm. Though the Italians held on grimly, they slowly but surely were subjected to pressure even they could not withstand.

The collapse came mid-way through the second half, with Gerson blasting home the tournament's most spectacular goal in the 67th minute, and Jairzinho running in number three four minutes later.

Italy probably would have been glad to concede victory and reach the sanctuary of the dressing-room there and then. But Brazil had not yet finished with them. Minutes from time, Pele, Gerson, Rivelino and Tostao joined in a lilting samba that ended with Carlos Alberto, their captain, sprinting upfield to drive in a goal that made absolutely sure no one would forget that Latin America was back on top of the world.

3 England Show Their Discipline

by DONALD SAUNDERS

When England look back on their disappointing 1970 World Cup campaign, they may recall two games with reasonable satisfaction. They exercised commendable self-discipline when beating Rumania 1–0 in their opening fixture at the Jalisco Stadium, and deserved better fortune when losing 1–0 to Brazil on the same pitch in their next match.

Sir Alf Ramsey had long declared that the game he feared most in Mexico was the first one. We discovered just how right he was on Tuesday, June 2. Though England always looked superior to the Rumanians, they might well have been provoked into throwing the match away.

To their credit, they kept the tightest rein on their tempers, while Mocanu, the most ruthless tackler seen in Mexico, brought down Newton, his substitute Wright, Lee and Peters in 20 hair-raising second-half minutes. Their refusal to be ruffled enabled them to clinch hard-earned victory with a 65th minute goal by Hurst.

Newton did not recover in time to line up against Brazil four days later. The Brazilians, however, were more severely handicapped, since they were without Gerson, who had strained a muscle during their 4–1 win against Czechoslovakia.

The Jalisco Stadium was packed for this Sunday lunchtime clash between the holders of the trophy and the team most fancied to succeed them. And though some of the spectators may have gone home vaguely disappointed by the shortage of goals, most found the struggle between Europe's finest defence and Latin America's most gifted forwards absorbingly rewarding.

There was never a moment during 90 tense minutes when one side was clearly on top. With Mullery tracking Pele's every step, Cooper battling grimly to hold Jairzinho, Labone keeping a firm grip on Tostao and Moore plugging every gap that appeared, Brazil's master craftsmen had to work as perhaps never before.

But although England were superb at the back, and workmanlike in the middle, they did not reach Brazil's penalty box often enough, or in sufficient numbers, to upset a defence that everyone in the stadium knew could not withstand heavy pressure. All too often,

England moved across the pitch, as though afraid to push forward, in case they should lose the ball – and with it the match.

True, they had good reason to fear Brazil's striking power. As early as the 10th minute Banks had been obliged to make the save of the tournament to push a close-range header from Pele round the corner.

Even Banks, however, could not prevent Jairzinho completing a brilliant move with Pele and Rivelino with a fine angled shot in the 60th minute. Nor could England close that narrow gap. Astle, substituting for Lee, should have done so moments after he arrived on the pitch – but he dragged the ball wide of the unguarded net from six yards. Then Ball missed two chances he normally would have snapped up. And, finally, Bell hammered the day's hardest shot against the bar.

So England met with World Cup defeat for the first time since they had gone down 3–1 in the 1962 quarter-final in Chile – to Brazil. Though the consequences this time were not as disastrous as they had been eight years earlier, they still were serious. Failure to beat Brazil meant that, almost certainly, they now would have to settle for second place in the group and would have to travel to Leon to meet West Germany in the quarter-final. They did not need telling that a Guadalajara match with the bold but naive Peruvians would have been less taxing.

As expected, Brazil won their last match with Rumania, collected maximum points, finished as leaders of the group and earned a 'home' quarter-final with Peru. This left England to scramble a 1–0 victory over Czechoslovakia, clinched by a penalty by Clarke, and move into the last eight as runners-up.

Meanwhile, Peru's early gallop had been halted by the West Germans in their last match in Group Four. The gay Latin Americans, coached by Didi, a Brazilian star in 1958, had previously outgunned Bulgaria 3–2, after being two goals down, and had thrashed the inexperienced Moroccans 3–0.

When Didi's men lined up against the Germans, however, they came face to face with World Cup reality for the first time. With Mueller scoring a hat-trick inside 38 minutes, the Peruvians discovered that no team can hope to succeed at this level unless they pay some attention to defence.

Even so, Peru went happily off from Leon to Guadalajara, the following Sunday, to take on the might of Brazil and kept bravely searching for goals until they went down 4–2 with all guns blazing. With a little more experience and some stiffening at the back, they could cause rather greater trouble in Munich in 1974.

Compared with Leon and Guadalajara, the entertainment

provided in the other two groups was modest. As hosts, Mexico were allowed the privilege of opening the tournament against Russia, at the Aztec Stadium, on Sunday, May 31. A goalless draw persuaded most of us that we had been right to think this would be the most boring World Cup in history. The dreariest and one of the toughest matches of the competition was notable only for the booking of four Russians and one Mexican.

Fortunately, things livened up when the Belgians swept to a 3–0 victory over El Salvador, the following Wednesday, to move unexpectedly to the top of the table. Not that these dark horses from Western Europe retained their lofty position for long. Three days later, they crashed 4–1 to the Russians, who suddenly remembered that attack is often the best form of defence.

The Belgians still had a chance of qualifying for the quarter-finals when they lined up against Mexico in Group One's last match. But this time their luck was right out and a hotly disputed penalty by Pena earned the Mexicans a place among the last eight for the first time in 40 years of patient striving.

Small wonder, then, that thousands of youngsters ran riot through the streets of Mexico City that night. Well into the small hours they disrupted traffic, climbed on cars and buses, hauled themselves to the tops of statues and went tramping round the boulevards chanting 'Mexico, Mexico'.

Delight turned to anger at noon next day. Russia also had qualified for the quarter-finals – with the same number of points and an identical goal difference. So F.I.F.A. were obliged to draw lots to see which country should travel to Toluca to meet Italy and which should remain at the Aztec to tackle Uruguay.

Mexico lost the toss and soon F.I.F.A.'s headquarters in the city were besieged by screaming protesters, all convinced that their heroes had been cheated.

This must have come as glad tidings to Italy, who, possibly over-conscious of the high altitude, had exerted the minimum of effort to reach the quarter-finals. A 1–0 win over Sweden and goalless draws with Uruguay and Israel steered them to the top of the table.

Uruguay could not match this meagre total of four points. They started off with a 2–0 victory over Israel shared the spoils of that goal-less affair with Italy, then slipped up 0–1 against Sweden. They could scarcely have run things closer. If Sweden, surprisingly beaten 1–0 by Israel, had managed just one more goal somewhere along the road, Uruguay could have been eliminated on a drawing of lots.

Yet, these Latin Americans failed to heed the warning. The following Sunday, they again refused to move out of their shell and were lucky indeed to scrape into the semi-finals at the expense of the Russians.

Russia had every reason to curse their luck. Early in extra-time what looked like a perfectly good goal by Byshovets was ruled offside, then four minutes from the end Uruguay won the match with a goal by Esparrago that the television cameras clearly indicated should not have been allowed. Cubilla, according to the cameras, took the ball yards over the by-line before crossing it to Esparrago.

Italy reached the semi-finals with much less difficulty. Though the Toluca stadium was packed with Mexicans and thousands more chanted ceaselessly outside, the European champions swept the host nation contemptuously out of the World Cup by scoring four times after conceding a 12th minute goal.

This victory must have been greeted with some relief even by the most patriotic Mexican policeman. For two weeks they had laboured hard and late to keep their boisterous compatriots under control in the streets of Mexico City, Guadalajara, Puebla, Toluca and Leon. Now, at last, there was nothing left to celebrate – or so they thought.

One week later, the streets of the capital were thronged again. Even a 12-hour downpour failed to prevent thousands of young Mexicans linking up with their deliriously happy cousins from Brazil.

Only when dawn approached did the tumult and the shouting die. And by then Latin America's great triumph over Europe had been well and truly celebrated.

Never again, perhaps, will Mexico have the opportunity to demonstrate what a colourful fiesta the World Cup finals can be. Let us hope the example they have set the world will not now be quietly ignored.

4 Brazil's Path to Victory

After 40 years the Jules Rimet Cup went out of circulation at the Aztec Stadium, Mexico City, on June 21 when Brazil beat Italy 4–1 in the final of the World Cup. This was Brazil's third victory—they won in Sweden in 1958 and in Chile in 1962—and the trophy thus became their own property. In Munich in 1974 clubs will compete for a new trophy supplied by F.I.F.A., to be known as the Association Football World Cup.

Over those 40 years there had been nine competitions for the Jules Rimet trophy, which was named after a Frenchman who did much for soccer before and after the first world war. After helping to get the French League started in 1910 he became President of the French Football Federation in 1919.

He was also President of F.I.F.A., a post he held for 36 years, and it was his work for the world organisation and the institution of the world cup, which led to the trophy being named after him.

The 1970 competition was problably the greatest of all, and the cleanest, with not one player being sent off the field. This was due to the hard work put in before the competition started to impress upon coaches, players and referees, the necessity for a uniform interpretation of the laws. Furthermore, referees knew they had the full backing of F.I.F.A. for any action they took on the field. Obviously the message got through to the players.

On the playing side Gerd Mueller, 24, the West German striker, took the goalscoring honours with 10, failing by three to equal the 1958 feat of France's Just Fontaine, but going into third place in the all-time list behind Hungary's Kocsis, who scored 11 in 1954.

Mueller, who was born in Nordlingen, Bavaria, and played in youth soccer in his home town, was signed by Bayern Munich in August 1964 when he was 18. He helped the club to gain promotion to the Federal League, and to three German Cup successes as well as a League championship.

'Player of the Year' in 1967 and 1969—he helped his club with the European Cup-Winners' Cup by beating Glasgow Rangers in 1967 —he was leading goalscorer in 1966 and 1967 and last season set a record for the League with 33 goals. He is the League's leading scorer with 123 goals.

GROUP ONE—Mexico City

May 31	Russia 0	Mexico 0
June 3	Belgium 3	El Salvador 0
6	Russia 4	Belgium 1
7	Mexico 4	El Salvador 0
10	Russia 2	El Salvador 0
11	Mexico 1	Belgium 0

FINAL TABLE

	P	W	D	L	Goals F	A	Pts
Russia	3	2	1	0	6	1	5
Mexico	3	2	1	0	5	0	5
Belgium	3	1	0	2	4	5	2
El Salvador	3	0	0	3	0	9	0

May 31 1970: MEXICO (0) 0   RUSSIA (0) 0.   112,504
MEXICO: Calderon; Pena, Perez, Hernandez, Lopez, Vantolra, Guzman Pulido, Velarde (Munguia 66 mins), Valdivia, Fragoso.
RUSSIA: Kavazashvili; Kaplichny, Lochev, Logofet, Shesternev, Asatiani, Muntyan, Serebryanikov (Puzach 46 mins), Byshovets, Yevryuzhikhin, Nodiya (Khmelnitsy 65 mins).
Referee: K. Tschenscher (West Germany).

June 3 1970: BELGIUM (1) 3 (Van Moer 2, Lambert 1, pen.) EL SALVADOR (0) 0
BELGIUM: Piot; Heylens, Thissen, Dewalque, Dockx, Semmeling, Van Moer, Devrindt, Van Himst, Puis, Lambert.
EL SALVADOR: Magana; Rivas, Mariona, Osorio, Manzano (Mendez Cortez 65 mins), Quintanilla, Vasquez, Cabezas, Rodriquez, Martinez, Aparicio.
Referee: A. Radulescu (Rumania).

June 6 1970: RUSSIA (1) 4 (Byshovets 2, Asatiani, Khmelnitsy) BELGIUM (0) 1 (Lambert)
RUSSIA: Kavazashvili; Kaplichny (Lovchev 33 mins), Afonin, Dzodzuashvili (Kisselev 74 mins) Shesternev, Asatiani, Muntyan, Khurtsilava, Byshovets, Yevryuzhikhin, Khmelnitsky.
BELGIUM: Piot; Heylens, Thiessen, Dewalque, Dockx, Van Moer, Semmeling, Van Himst, Jeck, Lambert, Puis.
Referee: R. Scheurer (Switzerland).

June 7 1970: MEXICO (1) 4 (Valdivia 2, Fragoso, Basaguren); EL SALVADOR (0)
MEXICO: Calderon; Pena, Perez, Munguia, Borja (Lopez 46 mins, Basaguren 77 mins), Padilla, Vantolra, Guzman, Gonzalez, Valdivia, Fragoso.

EL SALVADOR: Magana; Rivas, Mariona, Mendez Cortes, Osorio, Quintanilla, Rodriquez, Vasquez, Martinez, Cabezas, Aparicio (Mendez 57 mins).
Referee: Aly Kandil (United Arab Republic).

June 10 1970: EL SALVADOR (0) 0   RUSSIA (0) 2 (Byshovets 2)
EL SALVADOR: Magana; Rivas, Mariona, Osorio, Rodriquez (Sermeno, 60 mins), Vasquez, Cabezas (Aparicio 46 mins), Monge, Portillo, Castro, Sergio Mendez.
RUSSIA: Kavazashvili; Afonin, Dzodzuashvili, Khurtsilava, Shesternev, Kiselev (Asatiani 50 mins), Muntyan, Serebryanikov, Byshovets, Puzach (Yevryuzhikhin 46 mins), Khmelnitsky.
Referee: R. Hormazabel (Chile).

June 11 1970: MEXICO (1) 1 (Pena pen.) BELGIUM (0) 0.
MEXICO: Calderon; Pena, Perez, Vantolra, Guzman, Munguia, Gonzalez, Pulido, Valdivia (Basaguren 46 mins), Fragoso, Padilla.
BELGIUM: Piot; Heylens, Thiessen, Dewalque, Jeck, Dockx, Van Moer, Semmeling, Van Himst, Puis, Polleunis (Devrindt).
Referee: A. Coeregga (Argentina).

GROUP TWO—Toluca and Puebla

June	12	Uruguay 2	Israel 0	Toluca
	3	Italy 1	Sweden 0	Puebla
	6	Uruguay 0	Italy 0	Puebla
	7	Israel 1	Sweden 1	Toluca
	10	Uruguay 0	Sweden 1	Puebla
	11	Israel 0	Italy 0	Toluca

FINAL TABLE

					Goals		
	P	W	D	L	F	A	Pts
Italy	3	1	2	0	1	0	4
Uruguay	3	1	1	1	2	1	3
Sweden	3	1	1	1	2	2	3
Israel	3	0	2	1	1	3	2

June 2 1970: URUGUAY (1) 2 (Maneiro, Mujuica) ISRAEL (0) 0. Puebla
URUGUAY: Mazurkiewicz; Ancheta, Matosas, Ubinas, Montero Mujica, Cubilla, Rocha (Cortes 10 mins), Esparrago, Maneiro, Lozada.
ISRAEL: Vissoker; Primo, Rosen, Rozenthal, Shum, Spiegel, Feigenbaum, Spigler, Schwager, Rom (Vollach 57 mins), Talbi (Bar 46 mins).
Referee: R. Davidson (Scotland).

June 3 1970: ITALY (1) 1 (Domenghini) SWEDEN (0) 0. Toluca
ITALY: Albertosi; Burgnich, Facchetti, Cera, Niccolai (Rosato 36 mins), Bertini, Riva, Domenghini, Mazzola, De Sisti, Boninsegna.
SWEDEN: Hellstroem; Axelsson, Nordqvist, Grip, Svensson, Larsson,

Bo. (Nicklasson), Eriksson (Ejderstadt 57 mins), Kindvall, Grahn, Cronqvist, Olsson, Jan.
Referee: J. Taylor (England).

June 6 1970: URUGUAY (0) 0   ITALY (0) 0.   Puebla
URUGUAY: Mazurkiewicz; Ancheta, Matosas, Ubinas, Mujica, Montero, Cortes, Cubilla, Esparrago, Maneiro, Bareno (Zubia 72 mins).
ITALY: Albertosi; Burgnich, Facchetti, Bertini, Rosato, Cera, Domenghini (Furino 46 mins), Riva, Mazzola, De Sisti, Boninsegna.
Referee: R. Glockner (East Germany).

June 7 1970: SWEDEN (0) 1 (Turesson) ISRAEL (0) 1 (Spigler).
Toluca
SWEDEN: Larsen, S. G.; Selander, Axelsson, Grip, Svensson, Larsson, Bo. Kindvall, Persson (Palsson), Nordahl, Turesson, Olsson, J.
ISRAEL: Vissoker; Bar, Primo, Rosen, Rozenthal, Shum, Spiegel, Feigenbaum, Spigler, Schwager, Vollach.
Referee: S. Tareken (Ethiopia).

June 10 1970: SWEDEN (0) 1 (Grahn) URUGUAY (0) 0.   Puebla.
SWEDEN: Larsen, S. G.; Selander, Axelsson, Nordqvist, Grip, Svensson, Larsson, Bo., Eriksson, Kindvall (Turesson 56 mins), Nicklasson (Grahn 84 mins), Persson.
URUGUAY: Mazurkiewicz; Ancheta, Matosas, Ubinas, Montero, Mujica, Esparrago (Fontes 62 mins), Maneiro, Zubia, Cortes, Lozada.
Referee: H. Landbauer (United States).

June 11 1970: ISRAEL (0) 0   ITALY (0) 0.   Toluca
ISRAEL: Vissoker; Bar, Bello, Primo, Rosen, Rozenthal, Shum, Spiegel, Feigenbaum (Rom), Spigler, Schwager.
ITALY: Albertosi; Burgnich, Facchetti, Cera, Rosato, Bertini, Riva, Domenghini (Rivera), Mazzola, De Sisti, Boninsegna.
Referee: A. de Moraes (Brazil).

GROUP THREE—Guadalajara

June	2	Rumania 0 England 1
	3	Czechoslovakia 1 Brazil 4
	6	Rumania 2 Czechoslovakia 1
	7	England 0 Brazil 1
	10	Rumania 2 Brazil 3
	11	England 1 Czechoslovakia 0

FINAL TABLE

	P	W	D	L	Goals F	A	Pts
Brazil	3	3	0	0	8	3	6
England	3	2	0	1	2	1	4
Rumania	3	1	0	2	4	5	2
Czechoslovakia	3	0	0	3	2	7	0

Above: The President of Mexico, Gustavo Diaz Ordaz, and Sir Stanley Rous, President of F.I.F.A., at the opening in Mexico City of what proved to be the most successful of all World Cup competitions. *Below:* Manchester United's Bobby Charlton, who made his record 106th appearance for England while in Mexico, being presented with a 'Sportsman of the Year' medal by the Governor of the state of Jalisco, Francisco Medina Ascensio, in Guadalajara

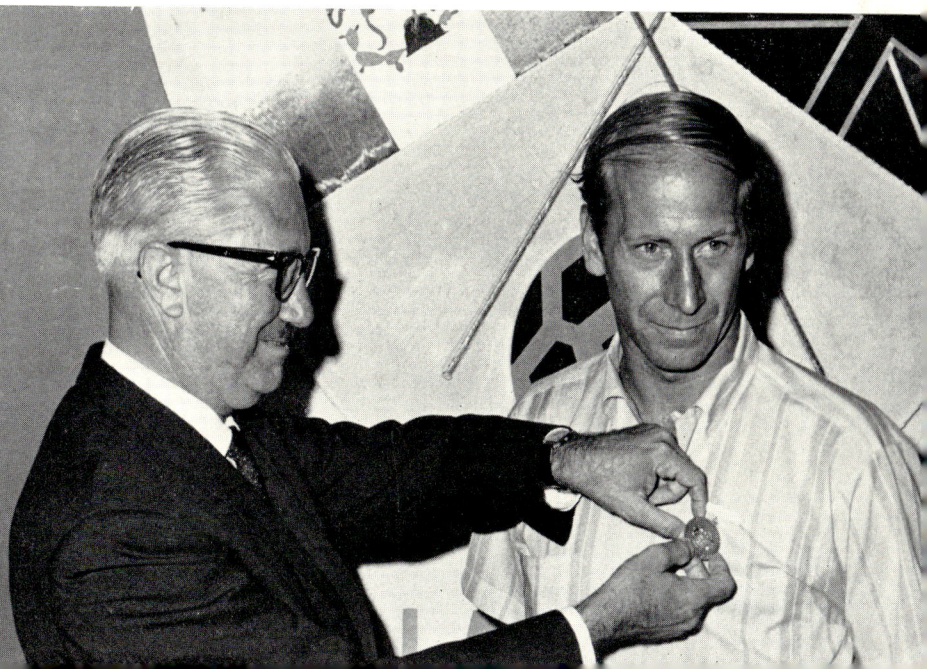

Moment of triumph. Brazil's captain, Carlos Alberto, holds aloft the Jules Rimet trophy which his team won outright for Brazil by defeating Italy 4–1 in the World Cup Final in Mexico City

June 2 1970: RUMANIA (0) 0   ENGLAND (0) 1 (Hurst)
RUMANIA: Adamache; Satmareanu, Lupescu, Dinu, Mocanu, Dumitru, Nunweiler, Dembrovski, Tataru (Neagu 75 mins), Dumitrache, Lucescu.
ENGLAND: Banks; Newton (Wright 53 mins), Cooper, Mullery, Labone, Moore, Lee (Osgood 77 mins), Ball, Charlton R., Hurst, Peters.
Referee: V. Loraux (Belgium).

June 3 1970: CZECHOSLOVAKIA (1) 1 (Petras) BRAZIL (1) 4 (Rivelino, Pele, Jairzinho 2)
CZECHOSLOVAKIA: Viktor; Dobias, Horvath, Migas, Hagara, Hrdlicka (Kvasnak 46 mins), Kuna, Vesely F., (Vesely B. 86 mins), Petras, Adamec, Jokl.
BRAZIL: Feliz; Britto, Piazza, Carlos Alberto, Clodoaldo, Jairzinho, Gerson (Paulo Cesar 76 mins), Tostao, Pele, Rivelino, Everaldo.
Referee: R. Barreto (Uruguay).

June 6 1970: RUMANIA (0) 2 (Neagu, Dumitrache pen.) CZECHO-SLOVAKIA (1) 1 (Petras).
RUMANIA: Adamache; Satmareanu, Lupescu, Dinu, Mocanu, Dumitru (Gherchely), Nunweiler, Neagu, Dembrovski, Dumitrache, Lucescu (Tataru).
CZECHOSLOVAKIA: Vencel; Dobias, Migas, Horvath, Zlocha, Kvasnak, Kuna, Vesely B., Jurkanin (Adamec), Petras, Jokl (Vesely F.).
Referee: Diege De Leo (Mexico).

June 7 1970: ENGLAND (0) 0   BRAZIL (0) 1 (Jairzinho).
ENGLAND: Banks; Wright, Cooper, Mullery, Labone, Moore, Lee (Bell 62 mins), Ball, Charlton R. (Astle 62 mins), Hurst Peters.
BRAZIL: Felix; Brito, Piazza, Carlos Alberto, Clodoaldo, Jairzinho, Tostao (Roberto 66 mins), Pele, Rivelino, Everaldo, Paulo Cesar.
Referee: Abrahm Klein (Israel).

June 10 1970: BRAZIL (2) 3 (Pele 2, Jairzinho) RUMANIA (1) 2 (Dumitrache, Dembrovski).
BRAZIL: Felix; Carlos Alberto, Brito, Fontana, Everaldo (Marco Antonio 57 mins), Clodoaldo (Edu 72 mins), Paulo Cesar, Piazza, Jairzinho, Pele, Tostao.
RUMANIA: Adamache (Raducanu 29 mins); Satmareanu, Lupescu, Dinu, Mocanu, Dumitru, Nunweiler, Neagu, Dembrovski, Dumitrache (Tataru 70 mins), Lucescu.
Referee: F. Marschall (Austria).

June 11 1970: ENGLAND (0) 1 (Clarke pen 49 mins) CZECHO-SLOVAKIA (0) 0
ENGLAND: Banks; Newton, Charlton J., Moore, Cooper, Mullery, Bell, Charlton R. (Ball 65 mins), Clarke, Astle (Osgood 60 mins), Peters,
CZECHOSLOVAKIA: Viktor; Dobias, Hrivnak, Migas, Hagara, Pollak. Kuna, Vesely F., Petras, Adamec, Capkovic, Jan (Jokl 70 mins).
Referee: R. Machin (France).

B

GROUP FOUR—Leon

June	2	Peru 3	Bulgaria 2
	3	Morocco 1	West Germany 2
	6	Peru 3	Morocco 0
	7	Bulgaria 2	West Germany 5
	10	Peru 1	West Germany 3
	11	Bulgaria 1	Morocco 1

FINAL TABLE

				GOALS		
	P	W	D	L	F	A	Pts
West Germany	3	3	0	0	10	4	6
Peru	3	2	0	1	7	5	4
Bulgaria	3	0	1	2	5	9	1
Morocco	3	0	1	2	2	6	1

June 2 1970: PERU (0) 3 (Gallardo, Chumpitaz, Cubillas)   BULGARIA (1) 2 (Dermendjiev, Bonev).
PERU: Rubinos; Campos (Gonzalez J. 27 mins), De La Torre, Chumpitaz, Fuentes, Mifflin, Challe, Baylon (Sotil 49 mins), Leon, Cubillas, Gallardo.
BULGARIA: Simeonov; Shalamanov, Dimitrov, Penev, Aladjov, Davidov, Bonev, Yakimov, Popov (Marachliev 66 mins), Jekov, Dermendjiev.
Referee: A. Sbardella (Italy).

June 3 1970: WEST GERMANY (0) 2 (Seeler, Mueller)   MOROCCO (1) 1 (Houmane)
WEST GERMANY: Maier; Vogts, Schultz, Fichtel, Hottges (Loehr 46 mins), Seeler, Beckenbauer, Overath, Haller (Grabowski 46 mins), Mueller, Held.
MOROCCO: Kassou; Lamrani, Khanoussi, Slimani, Benkrif, Maaroufi, Said Ghandi, Bamous (Farks 72 mins), Ghazouani (Elkhiatti 54 mins), Houmane, Jarir, El Filali.
Referee: L. A. Van Raven (Holland).

June 6 1970: PERU (0) 3 (Cubillas 2, Challe)   MOROCCO (0) 0
PERU: Rubinos; Gonzalez, Chumpitaz, Fuentes, De La Torre, Mifflin, Challe, Sotil, Leon, Cubillas, Gallardo.
MOROCCO: Kassou; Marani, Khanoussi, Slimani, Benkrif, Maaroufi, Bamous, Ghandi (Alloui 80 mins), Houmane Jarir, E. Filali (Fadili 67 mins), Ghazouani.
Referee: T. Bachramov (Russia).

June 7 1970: WEST GERMANY (2) 5 (Mueller 3 (1 pen), Libuda, Seeler) BULGARIA (1) 2 (Nikodimov, Kolev).
WEST GERMANY: Maier; Schultz, Schnellinger, Fichtel, Hottges, Seeler, Beckenbauer (Weber 71 mins), Overath, Libuda, Mueller, Loehr (Grabowski 57 mins).
BULGARIA: Simeonov; Gaidarski, Jetchev, Penev, Gaganelov (Shal-

amanov 58 mins), Kolev, Bonev, Nikodimov, Dermendjiev (Mitkov 46 mins), Asparoukhov, Marachliev.
Referee: Ortiz Mendebil (Spain).

June 10 1970: WEST GERMANY (3) 3 (Mueller 3) PERU (1) 1 Cubillas)
WEST GERMANY: Maier; Vogts, Hottges, Schnellinger, Fichtel, Seeler, Beckenbauer, Overath, Libuda (Grabowski), Mueller, Loehr.
PERU: Rubinos; Gonzalez, Chumpitaz, De La Torre, Fuentes, Mifflin (Cruzado), Challe, Leon (Ramirez), Sotil, Cubillas, Gallardo.
Referee; A. Aguilar (Mexico)

June 11 1970: MOROCCO (0) 1 (Ghazouani); BULGARIA (1) 1 (Jetchev).
MOROCCO: Hazzaz; Fadili, Khanoussi, Slimani, Benkrif, Maaroufi, Bamous, El Filali, Ghandi, Alloui (Faras), Ghazouani (Choukri).
BULGARIA; Yordanov; Shalamanov, Jetchev, Penev, Gaidarski, Nikodimov, Kolev, Popov, Asparoukhov, Yakimov (Bonev), Mitkov.
Referee: S. Ribeiro (Portugal).

QUARTER FINALS—June 14
URUGUAY (0) 1   RUSSIA (0) 0 (after textra time).   Mexico City
ITALY (1) 4   MEXICO (1) 1.   Toluca
WEST GERMANY (0) 3   ENGLAND (1) 2 (after extra time).   Leon
BRAZIL (2) 4   PERU (1) 2.   Guadalajara
WEST GERMANY (0) 3 (Beckenbauer, Seeler, Mueller) ENGLAND (1) 2 (Mullery, Peters). After extra time. 90-minute score 2–2.   Leon
WEST GERMANY: Maier; Hottges (Schultz 46 mins), Schnellinger, Beckenbauer, Vogts, Seeler, Fichtel, Overath, Meuller, Libuda (Grabowski 58 mins), Loehr.
ENGLAND: Bonetti; Newton, Mullery, Labone, Cooper, Moore, Lee, Ball, Charlton R. (Bell 69 mins), Hurst, Peters (Hunter 80 mins).
Referee: A. Coregga (Argentina).
RUSSIA (0) 0   URUGUAY (0) 1 (Esparrago). After extra time. 90-minute score 0–0
RUSSIA: Kavazashvili; Afonin, Dzodzuashvili, Kaplichny, Shesternev, Khurtsilava, Asatiani (Kiselev 84 mins), Muntyan, Byshovets, Yevryuszhiskin, Khmelnitsky.
URUGUAY: Mazurkiewicz; Ancheta, Matosas, Ubinas, Montero, Mujica, Maneiro, Morales, Cortes, Cubilla (Rocha 91 mins), Fontes (Esparrago 104 mins).
Referee: L. Van Ravens (Holland).
BRAZIL (2) 4 (Tostao 2, Jairzinho, Rivelino)   PERU (1) 2 (Gallardo, Cubillas).
BRAZIL: Felix; Carlos Alberto, Brito, Piazza, Marco Antonio, Gerson (Paulo Cesar 76 mins), Clodoaldo, Rivelino, Jairzinho (Roberto 78 mins), Tostao, Pele.
PERU: Rubinos; Campos, Fernandez, Chumpitaz, Fuentes, Mifflin. Challe, Baylon (Sotil 52 mins), Leon (Reyes 60 mins), Cubillas, Gallardo, Referee: V. Lauraux (Belgium).

ITALY (1) 4 (Riva 2, Rivera, Guzman o.g.)　MEXICO (1) 1 (Gonzalez).

ITALY: Albertosi; Burgnich, Facchetti, Cera, Rosato, Bertini, Riva, Domenghini (Gori 85 mins), Mazzola (Rivera 46 mins), De Sisti, Boninsegna.

MEXICO: Calderon; Pena, Perez, Munguia (Diaz 60 mins), Padilla, Vantolra, Guzman, Pulido, Gonzalez (Borja 70 mins), Valdivia, Fragoso.

Referee: R. Scheurer (Switzerland).

SEMI-FINALS—June 17

ITALY (1) 4　WEST GERMANY (0) 3. After extra time. 90-minute score 1–1. Mexico City

BRAZIL (1 3　URUGUAY (1) 1. Guadalajara

ITALY (1) 4 (Boninsegna, Burgnich, Riva, Rivera)　WEST GERMANY (0) 3 (Schnellinger, Mueller 2). After extra time. 90-minute score 1–1. Mexico City

ITALY: Albertosi; Burgnich, Facchetti, Cera, Rosato (Poletti 90 mins), Bertini, Riva, Domenghini, Mazzola (Rivera 46 mins), De Sisti, Boninsegna.

WEST GERMANY: Maier; Schnellinger, Beckenbauer, Schultz, Vogts, Seeler, Overath, Mueller, Patzke (Held 66 mins), Loehr (Libuda 53 mins), Grabowski.

Referee: A. Yamasaki (Peru).

BRAZIL (1) 3 (Clodoaldo, Jairzinho, Rivelino)　URUGUAY (1) 1 (Cubilla). Guadalajara

BRAZIL: Felix; Carlos Alberto, Brito, Piazza, Everaldo, Gerson, Clodoaldo, Rivelino, Jairzinho, Tostao, Pele.

URUGUAY: Mazurkiewicz; Ubinas, Ancheta, Matosas, Mujica, Montero, Maneiro (Esparrago 74 mins), Cortes, Cubilla, Fontes, Morales.

Referee: J. de Mendebil (Spain).

FINAL—June 21 1970. Mexico City

BRAZIL (1) 4 (Pele, Gerson, Jairzinho, Carlos Alberto)　ITALY (1) 1 (Boninsegna)

BRAZIL: Felix; Carlos Alberto, Brito, Piazza, Everaldo, Gerson, Clodoaldo, Rivelino, Jairzinho, Tostao, Pele.

ITALY: Albertosi; Burgnich, Cera, Rosato, Facchetti, Domenghini, De Sisti, Bertini (Juliano 75 mins), Mazzola, Boninsegna (Rivera 84 mins), Riva.

Referee: Rudi Glockner (East Germany).

THIRD AND FOURTH PLACE—June 20 1970. Mexico City

WEST GERMANY (1) 1 (Overath)　URUGUAY (0) 0

WEST GERMANY: Wolter; Weber, Schnellinger (Lorenz 46 mins), Vogts, Fichtel, Patzke, Seeler, Overath, Held, Libuda (Loehr 74 mins), Mueller.

URUGUAY: Mazurkiewicz; Ancheta, Matosas, Ubinas, Montero (Sandoval 67 mins), Mujica, Cubilla, Maneiro, Morales, Fontes (Esparrago 46 mins), Cortez.

Referee: Antonio Sbardella (Italy).

PLAYERS' APPEARANCES

BELGIUM (13 players, 3 matches)
3—Nicolas Dewalque, Jan Baptist Dockx, Georges Heylens, Christian Piot, Wilfrid Puis, Leon Semmeling. Jean Thiessen, Paul Van Himst, Wilfrid Van Moer; 2—Leon Jeck, Raoul Lambert; 1 (and 1 sub)—Johannes Devrindt, Odilon Polleunis.

BRAZIL (16 players, 6 matches)
6—Hercules Ruas Brito, Carlos Alberto, Clodoaldo, Felix, Jairzinho, Pele, Piazza, Tostao; 5—Everaldo, Rivelino; 4—Gerson; 2 (and 2 sub) —Paulo Cesar; 1 (and 1 sub)—Marco Antonio; 1—Fontana; 1 as sub —Edu, Roberto.

BULGARIA (20 players, 3 matches)
3—Dimitar Penev; 2 (and 1 sub)—Khristo Bonev, Alexander Shalamanov; 2—Georgi Asparoukhov, Dinko Dermendjiev, Milko Gaidarski, Dorbromir Jetchev, Todor Kolev, Asparoukh Nikodimov, Fueorgui Popov, Simeon Simeonov, Dimitov Yakimov; 1 (and 1 sub)—Dimitar Marachliev, Vassil Mitkov; 1—Stefan Aladjov, Ivan Davidov, Ivan Dimitrov, Boris Gaganelov, Petar Jekov, Stoyan Yordanov.

CZECHOSLOVAKIA (19 players, 3 matches)
3—Karol Dobias, Ladislav Kuna, Vaclav Migas, Ladislav Petras; 2 (and 1 sub)—Josef Adamec, Karel Jokl, Frantisek Vesely; 2—Alexander Horvath, Vladimir Hagara, Ivo Viktor; 1 (and 1 sub)—Andrej Kvasnak, Bohumil Vesely; 1—Jan Capkovic, Ivan Hrdlicka, Vladimir Hrivnak, Josef Jurkanin, Jaroslav Pollak, Alexander Vencel, Jan Zlocha.

EL SALVADOR (17 players, 3 matches)
3—Salvador Cabezas, Raul Magana, Salvador Mariona, Saturnino Osorio, Lindo Rodriquez, Jorge Vasquez, Roberto Rivas; 2 (and 1 sub) —Ernesto Aparicio; 2—Juan Martinez, Jose Quintanilla; 1 (and 1 sub) —Mendez Cortez, Mendez Sergio; 1—Guillermo Castro, Raul Manzano, Mario Monge, Jaime Portillo; 1 (as sub)—Genaro Sermenco.

ENGLAND (19 players, 4 matches)
4—Bobby Charlton, Terry Cooper, Bobby Moore, Alan Mullery, Martin Peters; 3 (and 1 sub)—Alan Ball; 3—Gordon Banks, Geoff Hurst, Brian Labone, Francis Lee, Keith Newton; 1 (and 2 sub)—Colin Bell; 1 (and 1 sub)—Jeff Astle, Tommy Wright; 1—Peter Bonetti, Jack Charlton, Allan Clarke; 2 as sub—Peter Osgood; 1 as sub—Norman Hunter.

WEST GERMANY (19 players, 6 matches)
6—Gerhard Mueller, Wolfgang Overath, Uwe Seeler; 5—Franz Beckenbauer, Klaus Fichtel, Josef Maier, Karl-Heinz Schnellinger, Hans-Hubert Vogts; 4 (and 2 sub)—Johannes Loehr; 4 (and 1 sub)—Reinhard Libuda; 4—Horst Hottges; 3 (and 1 sub)—Willi Schultz; 2 (and 1 sub) —Siegfried Held; 2—Bernd Patzke; 1 (and 4 sub)—Jurgen Grabowski; 1 (and 1 sub)—Wolfgang Weber; 1—Helmut Haller, Horst Wolter; 1 as sub—Max Lorenz.

ISRAEL (14 players, 3 matches)
3—Jehochua Feigenbaum, David Primo, Sri Rosen, Shmuel Rozenthal, Jeshaayahu Schwager, Itzchak Shum, Giora Spiegel, Mordecai Spigler,

Itzchak Vissoker; 2 (and 1 sub)—Feiwel Bar; 1 (and 1 sub)—O. Daniel Rom, Yochanan Vollach; 1—Menachem Bello, Rachamin Talbi.

ITALY (17 players, 6 matches)
6—Enrico Albertosi, Mario Bertini, Roberto Boninsegna, Tarcisio Burgnich, Pier Luigi Cera, Giancarlo De Sisti, Angelo Domenghini, Giacimto Facchetti, Alessandro Mazzola, Luigi Riva; 5 (and 1 sub)— Roberto Rosato; 1—Comunardo Nicolai; 4 as sub—Gianni Rivera; 1 as sub—Giuseppe Furino, Sergio Gori, Antonio Juliano, Fabrizio Poletti.

MEXICO (17 players, 4 matches)
4—Ignacio Calderon, Favier Guzman, Javier Fragoso, Gustavo Pena, Mario Perez, Javier Valdivia, Jose Vantolra; 3 (and 1 sub)—Antonio Munguia; 3—Jose Gonzalez, Aaron Padilla, Hector Pulido; 1 (and 1 sub)—O. Enrique Borja, Horacio Lopez; 1—Guillermo Hernandez, Mario Velardo; 2 as sub—Juan Basaguren; 1 as sub—Isidoro Diaz.

MOROCCO (17 players, 3 matches)
3—Bamous Driss, Benkrif Boujemaa, Mohamed El Filali, Ghandi Said, Mouhob Ghazouani, Khanoussi Moulay Driss, Maaroufi Mohamed, Slimani Kacem; 2—Jarir Mohamed Houmane, Kassou Allal, Lamrani Abdallah; 2 (and 1 sub)—Alloui Agmed, Fadili Jilali; 1—Hazzaz Mohamed; 2 as sub—Faras Ahmed; 1 as sub—Choukri Mustapha, Elkhiatti Abdelkader.

PERU (17 players, 4 matches)
4—Roberto Challe, Hector Chumpitaz, Teofilo Cubillas, Nicolas Fuentes, Alberto Gallardo, Pedro Leon, Ramon Mifflin, Luis Rubinos; 3— Orlando De La Torre; 2 (and 1 sub)—Javier Gonzalez; 2 (and 2 sub)— Hugo Sotil; 2—Julio Baylon, Eloy Campos; 1—Jose Fernandez; 1 as sub—Luis Cruzado, Oswaldo Ramirez, Eladio Reyes.

RUMANIA (14 players, 3 matches)
3—Steriea Adamache, Emeric Dembrovski, Cornel Dinu, Florea Dumi- trache, Ioan Dumitru, Mircea Lucescu, Niculae Lupescu, Mihai Mocanu, Radu Nunweiler, Ludovic Satmareanu; 2 (and 1 sub)—Alexandru Neagu; 1 (and 2 sub)—Gheorghe Tataru; 1 as sub—Laszlo Gherchely, Necula Raducanu.

RUSSIA (17 players, 4 matches)
4—Anatoli Byshovets, Anzor Kavazashvili, Vladimir Muntyan, Albert Shesternev; 3 (and 1 sub)—Kakhi Asatiani, Vitali Khmelnitsky, Gennady Yveryuzhikhin; 3—Valentin Afonin, Revaz Dzodzuashvili, Vladimir Kaplichny, Murtaz Khurtsilava; 2—Victor Serebryanikov; 1 (and 1 sub)—Nikolai Kiselev, Anatoli Puzach, Yevgeny Lovchev; 1—Gennady Logofet, Givi Nodya.

SWEDEN (19 players, 3 matches)
3—Kurt Axelsson, Roland Grip, Ove Kindvall, Bo Larsson, Tommy Svensson; 2—Leif Eriksson, Sven-Gunnar Larsson, Bjorn Nordqvist, Jan Olsson, Orjan Persson, Hans Selander; 1 (and 1 sub)—Ove Grahn, Goran Nicklasson, Tom Turesson; 1—Claes Cronqvist, Ronnie Hellstrolm, Thomas Nordahl; 1 as sub—Inge Ejderstadt, Sten Palsson.

URUGUAY (17 players, 6 matches)
6—Atilio Ancheta, Roberto Matosas, Ildo Maneiro, Ladislao Mazurkie-wicz, Julio Montero, Juan Mujica, Ignacio Luis Ubinas; 5 (and 1 sub)
—Julio Cortes; 5—Luis Cubilla; 3 (and 3 sub)—Victor Esparrago;
3 (and 1 sub)—Dagoberto Fontes; 3—Julio Morales; 2—Julio Lozada;
1 (and 1 sub)—Pedro Rocha, Oscar Zubia; 1—Ruben Bareno; 1 as sub
—Rodolfo Sandoval.

GOALSCORERS

BELGIUM (4)—Van Moer 2, Lambert 2 (1 penalty).
BRAZIL (19)—Jairzinho 7, Pele 4, Rivelino 3, Tostao, 2, Carlos Alberto, Clodoaldo and Gerson 1 each.
BULGARIA (5)—Bonev, Dermendjiev, Jetchev, Kolev, Nikodimov 1 each.
CZECHOSLOVAKIA (2)—Petras 2.
EL SALVADOR (0).
ENGLAND (4)—Hurst, Mullery, Peters, Clarke (pen), 1 each.
WEST GERMANY (17)—Mueller 10, Seeler 3, Beckenbauer, Libuda, Overath, and Schnellinger 1 each.
ISRAEL (1)—Spigler.
ITALY (10)—Riva 3, Boninsegna 2, Rivera 2, Burgnich, Domenghini, Guzman (Mexico o.g.), 1 each.
MEXICO (6)—Valdivia 2, Basaguren, Fragoso, Gonzalez and Pena (pen) 1 each.
MOROCCO (2)—Houmane, Ghazouani, 1 each.
PERU (9)—Cubillas 5, Gallardo 2, Challe and Chumpitaz 1 each.
RUMANIA (4)—Dumitrache 2 (1 pen), Dembrovski and Neagu 1 each.
RUSSIA (6)—Byshovets 4, Asatiani and Khmelnitsky 1 each.
SWEDEN (2)—Grahn and Turesson 1 each.
URUGUAY (4)—Cubilla, Esparrago, Maneiro and Mujica 1 each.

PREVIOUS FINALS

1930—MONTEVIDEO (URUGUAY)
URUGUAY (1) 4 (Scarone, Castro, Cea, Iriarte) ARGENTINA (2) 2 (Peucelle, Stabile).
URUGUAY: Ballesteros; Mascheroni, Nasezzi; Andrade, Fernandez, Gestido; Dorado, Scarone, Castro, Cea, Iriarte.
ARGENTINA: Botasso; Della Torre, Paternoster; Evaristo J., Monti, Suarez; Peucelle, Varallo, Stabile, Ferreira, Evaristo M.

1934—ROME (ITALY)
ITALY (0) 2 (Schiavio, Orsi) CZECHOSLOVAKIA (0) 1 (Puc). After extra time. 90-minute score 1–1.
ITALY: Combi; Monzeglio, Allemandi; Ferraris IV, Monti, Bertolini; Guaita, Meazza, Schiavio, Ferrari, Orsi.
CZECHOSLOVAKIA: Planika; Zenicek, Cytroky; Kostalek, Cambal, Krcil; Junek, Svoboda, Sobotka, Nejedly, Puc.

1938—PARIS (FRANCE)
ITALY (3) 4 (Colaussi 2, Piola 2)   HUNGARY (1) 2 (Sarosi, Titkos).
ITALY: Oliveiri; Foni, Rava, Serantoni, Andreolo, Locatelli, Biavatti, Meazza, Pila, Ferrari, Colaussi.
HUNGARY: Szabo; Polgar, Biro, Szalay, Szucs, Lazar, Sas, Vincze Sarosi, Zsengeller, Titkos.

1950—BRAZIL
The final stages were played on a league system with four teams, with Uruguay winning from Brazil, Sweden and Spain.

1954—BERNE (SWITZERLAND)
WEST GERMANY (2) 3 (Morlock, Rohn 2)   HUNGARY (2) 2 (Puskas, Czibor).
WEST GERMANY: Turke; Posipal, Kohlmeyer, Eckel, Liebrich, Mai, Rahn, Morlock, Walter O., Walter F., Schafer.
HUNGARY: Grosics; Buzansky, Lantos, Bozsik, Lorant, Zakarias, Czibor, Kocsis, Hidegkuti, Puskas, Toth, M.

1958—STOCKHOLM (SWEDEN)
BRAZIL (2) 5 (Vava 2, Pele 2, Zagalo)   SWEDEN (1) 2 (Liedholm, Simonsson).
BRAZIL: Gilmar; Santos D., Santos, N., Zito, Bellini, Orlando, Garincha, Didi, Vava, Pele, Zagalo.
SWEDEN: Svensson K.; Bergmark, Axbom, Boerjesson, Gustavsson, Parling, Hamrin, Gren, Simonsson, Liedholm, Skoglund.

1962—SANTIAGO (CHILE)
BRAZIL (1) 3 (Amarildo, Zito, Vava)   CZECHOSLOVAKIA (1) 1 (Masopust).
BRAZIL: Gilmar; Santos D., Santos N., Zito, Mauro, Zozimo, Didi, Garincha, Vava, Amarildo, Zagalo.
CZECHOSLOVAKIA: Schroif; Tichy, Novak, Pluskal, Popluhar, Masopust, Pospichal, Scherer, Kvasnak, Kadraba, Jelinek.

1966—WEMBLEY (ENGLAND)
ENGLAND (1) 4 (Hurst 3, Peters)   WEST GERMANY (1) 2 (Haller, Weber). After extra time.
ENGLAND: Banks; Cohen, Wilson, Stiles, Charlton J., Moore, Ball, Hurst, Hunt, Charlton R., Peters.
WEST GERMANY: Tilkowski; Hottges, Schultz, Weber, Schnellinger, Haller, Beckenbauer, Overath, Seeler, Held, Emmerich.

5 The Road to Mexico

Seventy-one countries entered for the 16 places in the final stages of the World Cup, and 69 of them had to play through the qualifying stages. The countries accepted by F.I.F.A. were as follows:

Africa (12): Algeria, Camerouns, Ethiopia, Ghana, Libya, Morocco, Nigeria, Rhodesia, Senegal, Sudan, Tunisia and Zambia.

America, North, Central and Caribbean (13): Bermuda, Canada, Costa Rica, Guatemala, Haiti, Honduras, Jamaica, Mexico, Netherlands Antilles, El Salvador, Surinam, Trinidad and United States of America.

America, South (10): Argentina, Bolivia, Brazil, Chile, Colombia, Ecuador, Paraguay, Peru, Venezuela and Uruguay.

Asia (4): Israel, Japan, North Korea and South Korea.

Europe (30): Austria, Belgium, Bulgaria, Czechoslovakia, Cyprus, Denmark, England, Finland, France, East Germany, West Germany, Greece, Holland, Hungary, Northern Ireland, Republic of Ireland, Italy, Luxemburg, Norway, Poland, Portugal, Rumania, Russia, Scotland, Spain, Sweden, Switzerland, Turkey, Wales and Yugoslavia.

Oceania (2): Australia and New Zealand.

Entries from Albania, Guinea and Congo Kinshasa were received after the closing date, Dec. 15 1967, and could not be considered, while Cambodia, Nationalist China, Hongkong, Indonesia, Malaysia, Mauritius, Papua and New Guinea were not in a position to enter teams. Only one of the countries accepted for competition refused to take part; that was North Korea, who objected to Israel being placed in the Asian group.

With two of the 16 final places going to the holders and the host country the committee allotted eight of the remaining 14 places to European teams, three to South America, and one each to North, Central and Caribbean America, Asia-Oceania and Africa.

This left 69 countries to battle through the qualifying competition and they played 173 matches—one was abandoned because of fog after 50 minutes—before they completed the qualifying competition in the middle of Dec. 1969. Six play-offs were needed, with El Salvador and Morocco each being concerned in two of them.

41

The first country to qualify for the finals, of course, was Mexico as hosts, on Oct. 8 1964, when they were granted the finals at F.I.F.A. congress in Tokyo. England were next when they won the World Cup at Wembley on July 30 1966. The first country to qualify by playing were Belgium, who made sure of their place on Feb. 23 1969, when they beat Spain 2–1 in Liege.

Belgium were followed by West Germany (May 21), Uruguay (July 20), Brazil (Aug. 24), Peru (Aug. 31), El Salvador (Oct. 8), Sweden (Oct. 15), Morocco (Oct. 26), Rumania and Russia (Nov. 16), Italy (Nov. 22), Czechoslovakia (Dec. 3), Bulgaria (Dec. 7), Israel (Dec. 14).

All former holders of the Jules Rimet Cup took part in the final stages—Uruguay (1930 and 1950), Italy (1934 and 1938), West Germany (1954), Brazil (1958 and 1963) and England (1966).

GROUP ONE

Rumania qualified from Group One for the final stages in Mexico, but when the groupings were made known it looked as though Portugal would be the favourites. It was a big surprise when the country who had played so well in the 1966 World Cup, to take third place, finished at the foot of the group with a victory over Rumania as their only reward.

After that victory it seemed that Portugal might make it, but gradually their standard declined. The more experienced players like Eusebio failed to sustain their form and successive defeats to Greece and Switzerland—the latter at home—practically ended their hopes.

Greece were the shock team of the group and only a goal stopped them displacing Rumania at the top of the table. Everything depended on the final match in the group between these two countries which was played in the August Twenty Third Stadium in Bucharest before a crowd of 100,000. A draw meant Rumania went to Mexico —a Greek win and the place went to Greece.

Not until the Greeks had missed a couple of easy chances did Dembrovski head Rumania into a 38-minute lead. Four minutes after the interval Domazos with a 20-yard shot put the Greeks on level terms and with all to play for the Greeks subjected the Rumanian defence to a heavy bombardment.

However, the Rumanians, with home advantage, survived and set up their own offensive, but were glad to settle for the draw which gave them their passport to Mexico.

GROUP ONE RESULTS

Oct. 12 1968   Switzerland 1   Greece 0   Basle

Oct. 27		Portugal 3	Rumania 0	Lisbon
Nov. 23		Rumania 2	Switzerland 0	Bucharest
Dec. 11		Greece 4	Portugal 2	Athens
April 16	1969	Portugal 0	Switzerland 2	Lisbon
		Greece 2	Rumania 2	Athens
May 4		Portugal 2	Greece 2	Oporto
May 14		Switzerland 0	Rumania 1	Lausanne
Oct. 12		Rumania 1	Portugal 1	Bucharest
Oct. 15		Greece 4	Switzerland 1	Salonika
Nov. 2		Switzerland 1	Portugal 1	Berne
Nov. 16		Rumania 1	Greece 1	Bucharest

FINAL TABLE

	P	W	D	L	F	A	Pts
Rumania	6	3	2	1	7	6	8
Greece	6	3	1	2	13	9	7
Switzerland	6	1	3	2	5	8	5
Portugal	6	1	2	3	8	10	4

Oct. 12 1968: SWITZERLAND (1) 1 (Quentin) GREECE (0) 0. Basle. 35,778

SWITZERLAND: Grob; Ramseier, Tacchella, Michaud, Pirmin, Stierli, Odermatt (sub Guggisberg), Durr, Kuhn, Vuilleumier, Kunzli, Quentin.

GREECE: Ikonomopoulius; Kamaras, Gaitatzis, Zanderoglou, Balopoulos, Karafeskos, Domazos, Chaltas, Sideris, Papaioannou, Dedes (sub Youlsos).

Oct. 27 1968: PORTUGAL (2) 3 (Jacinto 2, Jacinto Joao) RUMANIA (0) 0. Lisbon. 32,222

PORTUGAL: Americo; Jacinto, Ruiz (sub Humberto), Jose Carlos, Hilario, Jaime Gracia, Coluna, Jose Agusto, Eusebio, Figueiredo, Simoes (sub Jacinto Joao).

RUMANIA: Coman (sub Cornelio); Satmareanu, Nicolae, Dinu, Mocanu, Ghergheli, Petescu, Pircliab, Dembrovski (sub Grojeja), Dobrin, Lucescu.

Nov. 23 1968: RUMANIA (0) 2 (Dumitrache, Domide) SWITZERLAND (0) 0. Bucharest. 18,854

RUMANIA: Gornea; Satmareanu, Boc, Dinu, Mocanu, Ghergheli, Nunweiler, Matrinovici D (sub Dembrovski), Domide, Dumitrache, Lucescu (sub Kalio).

SWITZERLAND: Grob; Ramseier, Michaud, Tacchella, Stierli, Citherlet (sub Brenna), Durr, Kuhn, Vuilleumier, Kunzli, Quentin.

Dec. 11 1968: GREECE (2) 4 (Papaionnaou, Dedes, Torres o.g., Sideris) PORTUGAL (1) 2 (Agusto, Eusebio). Athens. 36,750

GREECE: Oskenomoncules; Kamaras, Zanderoglou, Balopoulos, Gaitatzis, Haitas, Domazos (sub Koudas), Sideris, Papaionnaou, Botanis.

PORTUGAL: Americo; Jacinto, Armando, Jose Carlos, Hilario, Rolando, Coluna, Agusto (sub Jacinto Joao), Torres, Eusebio, Simoes.

April 16 1969: PORTUGAL (0) 0 SWITZERLAND (2) 2 (Vuilleumier 2). Lisbon. 9,321
PORTUGAL: Damas; Conceipao, Humberto, Jose Carlos (sub Jacinto), Hilario, Rolando, Peres, Simoes, Torres (sub Manuel Antonio), Eusebio, Jacinto Joao.
SWITZERLAND: Prosperi; Ramseier, Michaud, Tacchella, Stierli, Kuhn, Signorelli, Quentin (sub Desbiolles), Odermatt, Kunzli, Vuilleumier.

April 16 1969: GREECE (0) 2 (Sideris, Dedes) RUMANIA (0) 2 (Dumitrache 2). Athens. 37,039
GREECE: Oskenomoncules; Kamaras, Balopoulos, Zanderglou (sub Kremydas), Gaitatzis, Haitas, Dedes, Papaionnaou, Karafeskos (sub Ghioutsos), Sideris, Botinos.
RUMANIA: Raducanu; Satmareanu, Bok, Deleanu, Coe, Ghergheli, Dinu, Dumitrache, Dembrovski, Ioanescu, Lucescu.

May 4 1969: PORTUGAL (0) 2 (Eusebio, Peres) GREECE (0) 2 Botinos, Efetheakis). Oporto. 6,221
PORTUGAL: Damas; Conceicao, Pinto, M., Jorge, J., Carrico, Jacinto (sub Manuel Antonio), Rolando, Peres, Eusebio, Jacinto Joao (sub Figueireo).
GREECE: Ikonomopoulus; Intzogiou (sub Dedes), Gaitatzis, Balopoulos, Kremydas, Chaitas, Efetheakis, Kondas (sub Botinos), Sideris, Domazos, Papaionnou.

May 14 1969: SWITZERLAND (0) 0 RUMANIA (1) 1 (Michaud o.g.). Lausanne. 28,466
SWITZERLAND: Prosperi; Ramseier, Michaud, Tacchella, Chapuisat, Odermatt, Signorelli (sub Stierli), Kuhn, Vuilleumier, Kunzli, Quentin.
RUMANIA: Raducanu; Deleanu, Coe (sub Halmageanu), Boc, Satmareanu, Nunweiler, Dinu, Lucescu, Tufan, Dumitrache, Dembrovski.

Oct. 12 1969: RUMANIA (1) 1 (Dobrin) PORTUGAL (0) 0. Bucharest. 58,573
RUMANIA: Raducanu; Satmareanu, Halmageanu, Coe, Deleanu, Dinu, Nunweiler, Dembrovski, Dumitrache, Dobrin, Lucescu.
PORTUGAL: Damas; Gomez, Batista, Humberto, Hilario, Gonsalves, Jose Maria (sub Toni), Nelson, Torres (sub Jacinto), Eusebio, Simoes.

Oct. 15 1969: GREECE (3) 4 (Botinos 2, Sideris, Koudas) SWITZERLAND (0) 1 (Kunzli). Salonika. 47,458
GREECE: Ikonomopoulos; Gaitatzis, Kamaras, Spyridon, Statopoulos, Haitas, Koudas, Domazos, Sideris (sub Dedes), Papaionnou, Botinos (sub Sarafis).
SWITZERLAND: Prosperi; Ramseier, Michaud (sub Belmer), Tacchella, Perraud, Odermatt, Chapuisat, Kuhn, Kunzli, Blatter, Wegner (sub Vuilleumier).

Nov. 2 1969: SWITZERLAND (0) 1 (Kunzli) PORTUGAL (1) 1 (Eusebio). Berne. 28,807

SWITZERLAND: Prosperi; Chapuisat, Guyot, Perroud, Ramseier, Guiggisberg, Ruegg (sub Odermatt), Kuhn, Jeandupeux (sub Brenna), Kunzli, Vuilleumier.

PORTUGAL: Damas; Conceicao, Humberto, Rodriquez, Hilario, Tome, Rolando (sub Concalves), Simoes, Eusebio, Peres (sub Marinho).

Nov. 16 1969: RUMANIA (1) 1 (Dembrovski) GREECE (0) 1 (Domazos). Bucharest. 62,577

RUMANIA: Raducanu; Satmareanu, Halmageanu, Coe, Deleanu, Dinu, Nunweiler, Dembrovski, Dobrin (sub Ghergheli), Dumitrache, Lucescu.

GREECE: Ikonomopoulos; Gaitatzis, Kamaras, Spyridon, Dimitriou, Domazos, Haitas, Roudas (sub Botinos), Sideris (sub Dedes), Papaionnou, Elefterekis.

GROUP TWO

Although a play-off, the only one in Europe, was necessary before Czechoslovakia qualified for Mexico in Group Two, the fate of the group was really decided nearly six months before when Hungary slumped to a shock 3–2 defeat against Denmark in Copenhagen.

'If we can't beat Denmark, then we don't deserve to go to Mexico,' was the cry of disappointed followers of the Olympic champions who, for the first time in their history, failed to reach the final stages of the World Cup.

Although this was their only defeat in the scheduled games, they finished the series with a similar record to Czechoslovakia, being level on points but having a slightly superior goal average. They had beaten the Czechs and also drawn with them. As goal average is not taken into account in the qualifying competition, a play-off was necessary between Hungary and Czechoslovakia.

For some time the two countries could not agree on a neutral ground but finally settled to play this decider at the Velodrome in Marseilles in December.

A draw would have been sufficient to send Hungary to Mexico, but weakened by the absence of such experienced players as Albert, Szucs and Pancsics, they were overwhelmed by some fine attacking football from the Czechs, who were runners-up to Brazil in the 1962 World Cup finals.

It was a penalty taken by Kvasnak which put Czechoslovakia in the lead just before the interval, and they added three more goals in the space of 25 minutes in the second half through Veseley, Adamec and Krol before the Hungarians got their consolation goal from a penalty taken by Kocsis in the final minute of the game.

There was plenty of criticism in Hungary at the failure of the national team, with the result that the board of the Football

Association, together with Karol Sos, the national team manager, all resigned. Sos has been succeeded by Josef Offer, who will hope to build up a new team for the European championship and for the Olympic Games in Munich in 1972.

GROUP TWO RESULTS

Sept. 25 1968	Denmark 0	Czechoslovakia 3	Copenhagen
Oct. 20	Czechoslovakia 1	Denmark 0	Bratislava
Dec. 4	Republic of Ireland 1	Denmark 1	Dublin
	(Abandoned after 50 minutes, fog)		
May 4 1969	Republic of Ireland 1	Czechoslovakia 2	Dublin
May 25	Hungary 2	Czechoslovakia 0	Budapest
May 27	Denmark 2	Republic of Ireland 0	Copenhagen
June 8	Republic of Ireland 1	Hungary 2	Dublin
June 15	Denmark 3	Hungary 2	Copenhagen
Sept. 14	Czechoslovakia 3	Hungary 3	Prague
Oct. 7	Czechoslovakia 3	Republic of Ireland 0	Prague
Oct. 15	Republic of Ireland 1	Denmark 1	Dublin
Oct. 22	Hungary 3	Denmark 2	Budapest
Nov. 5	Hungary 4	Republic of Ireland 0	Budapest

FINAL TABLE

	P	W	D	L	F	A	Pts
Hungary	6	4	1	1	16	7	9
Czechoslovakia	6	4	1	1	12	6	9
Denmark	6	2	1	3	6	10	5
Republic of Ireland	6	0	1	5	3	14	1

PLAY-OFF

Dec. 3 1969	Czechoslovakia 4	Hungary 1	Marseilles

Sept. 25 1968: DENMARK (0) 0 CZECHOSLOVAKIA (2) 3 (Jokl, Kuna, Hagara) Copenhagen. 30,258

DENMARK: Engadahl; Larsen, Yde, Lund, Jensen, H. M., Enemark, Mortensen, Jensen, B., Le Fevre, Wiberg-Larsen, Printzlau.

CZECHOSLOVAKIA: Viktor; Dobias, Plass, Hagara, Horvath, Szikora, Vesely, B., Jokl, Kuna, Adamec, Capkovic Jan.

Oct. 20 1968: CZECHOSLOVAKIA (0) 1 DENMARK (0) 0. Bratislava. 14,249.

CZECHOSLOVAKIA: Viktor; Dobias, Hagara, Plass, Horvath, Szikora, Vesely, Jokl, Kuna, Adamec, Kabat.

DENMARK: Engadahl; Larsen, Sorensen, Yde, Jensen, H. M., Enemark, Mortensen, Wiberg-Larsen, Jensen, B., Steffensen, Le Fevre.

Dec. 4 1968: REPUBLIC OF IRELAND (1) 1 (Giles, pen.) DENMARK (1) 1 (Wiberg-Larsen). Dublin. 23,555.
(Abandoned after 50 minutes, fog)

REPUBLIC OF IRELAND: Kelly; Carroll, Dunne, Dempsey, Hurley, Fullam, O'Neill, Dunphy, Hale, Giles, Rogers.

DENMARK: Engadahl; Larsen, Christiansen, Sorensen, Jensen, H. M., Sandvad, Praest, Jensen, B., Holstroem, Wiberg-Larsen, Le Fevre.

May 4 1969: REPUBLIC OF IRELAND (1) 1 (Rogers) CZECHOSLO-VAKIA (0) 2 (Kabat, Adamec). Dublin. 32,002.
REPUBLIC OF IRELAND: Kelly; Brennan, Mulligan, Finucane, Hurley, Dempsey, O'Neill, Leech (sub Hand), Treacy, Giles, Rogers.
CZECHOSLOVAKIA: Vencel; Dobias, Plass, Horvath, Hagara, Szikora, Kvasnak, Jurkanin, Adamec, Kabat.

May 25 1969: HUNGARY (1) 2 (Dunai, Albert) CZECHOSLOVAKIA (0) 0. Budapest. 72,938.
HUNGARY: Szentimihalyi; Kaposzta, Meszoly, Pancsics, Nosko (sub Farkas), Szoeke, Szucs (sub Fazekas), Albert, Bene, Dunai, Zambo.
CZECHOSLOVAKIA: Vencel; Dobias (sub Pivarnik), Plass, Zlocha, Szikora, Horvath, Vesely, Jokl, Kuna, Adamec, Kabat.

May 27 1969: DENMARK (1) 2 (O. Soerensen 2) REPUBLIC OF IRELAND (0) 0. Copenhagen. 26,195.
DENMARK: Engadahl; Larsen, Nielsen, Andersen, Jensen, H. M., Moeller, Jensen, B., Soerensen, Madsen, Soerensen, L., Le Fevre.
REPUBLIC OF IRELAND: Kelly; Brennan, Mulligan, Finucane, Dempsey, O'Neill (sub Newman), Treacy, Leech, Givens, Dunphy, Rogers.

June 8 1969: REPUBLIC OF IRELAND (0) 1 (Givens) HUNGARY (1) 2 (Dunai, Bene). Dublin. 17,286.
REPUBLIC OF IRELAND: Kelly; Brennan, Dunne, Conway, Finucane, Mulligan, Dunphy, Leech, Hurley (sub O'Neill), Rogers, Givens.
HUNGARY: Szentimihalyi; Kaposzta, Meszoly, Ihasz, Zambo, Szucs, Bene, Albert, Gorocs, Dunai II, Kozma (sub Farkas).

June 15 1969: DENMARK (2) 3 (O. Soerensen, Le Fevre, O. Madsen) HUNGARY (2) 2 (Bene, Farkas). Copenhagen. 29,957.
DENMARK: Engadahl; Larsen, Nielsen, Michaelsen, Jensen, H. M., Moeller, Jensen, B., Soerensen, O., Madsen, Soerensen, L., Le Fevre.
HUNGARY: Fater; Kaposzta, Pancsics, Meszoly, Juhasz, Szucs, Bene, Albert (sub Farkas), Gorocs, Dunai, A. (sub Fazekas), Zambo.

Sept. 14 1969: CZECHOSLOVAKIA (1) 3 (Hagara, Kvasnak, Kuna) HUNGARY (2) 3 (Bene, Dunai, Fazekas). Prague. 33,907.
CZECHOSLOVAKIA: Viktor; Pivernak, Plass (sub Hrivnak), Horvath, Hagara, Kvasnak, Szikora (sub Pollak), Kuna, Vesely, Adamec, Capokovic, Jan.
HUNGARY: Szentimihalyi; Kaposzta, Pancsics, Ihasz, Meszoly (sub Juhasz), Szucs, Fazekas (sub Puskas), Gorocs, Bene, Dunai II, Zambo.

Oct. 7 1969: CZECHOSLOVAKIA (3) 3 (Adamec 3) REPUBLIC OF IRELAND (0) 0. Prague. 32,879.
CZECHOSLOVAKIA: Viktor; Pivarnak, Migas (sub Hrivnak), Horvath, Hagara, Kvasnak, Kuna, Vesely, Jurkanin (sub Jokl), Adamec, Kuna.
REPUBLIC OF IRELAND: Fitzpatrick; Brennan, Carroll, Finucane,

Mulligan, Kinnear, Conway, Conroy, Givens (sub Fullam), Hale, Conmy.

Oct. 15 1969: REPUBLIC OF IRELAND (1) 1 (Givens) DENMARK (1) 1 (Jensen, B.). Dublin. 19,603.
REPUBLIC OF IRELAND: Kelly; Kinnear, Brennan, Mulligan, Byrne, Conway, Dunphy, Rogers, Conroy, Givens, Treacy.
DENMARK: Pulsen; Larsen, Nielsen, Thorsy, Jensen, H. M., Moeller, Praest, Michaelsen, Jensen, B., Andersen, Roemer.

Oct. 22 1969: HUNGARY (2) 3 (Benez 2, Szucs) DENMARK (0) 0. Budapest. 37,558.
HUNGARY: Szentimihalyi; Keleman, Pancsics, Ihasz, Halmosi, Szucs, Fazekas, Kocsis, Bene, Kozma, Zambo.
DENMARK: Poulsen; Larsen, Jensen, H. M., Moeller, Nielsen, T., Michaelsen, Nielsen, E., Thorst, Madsen, Jensen, B., Roemer-Jensen.

Nov. 5 1969: HUNGARY (1) 4 (Halmosi, Bene, Puskas, Kocsis) REPUBLIC OF IRELAND (0) 0. Budapest. 23,620.
HUNGARY: Tamas; Kelemen, Pancsics, Ihasz, Halmosi, Szucs, Fazekas, Gorocs (sub Kocsis), Bene, Dunai, Zambo.
REPUBLIC OF IRELAND: Kelly; Brennan, Dunne, Mulligan, Dempsey, Kinnear, Conroy, Conway, Givens, Dunphy (sub Treacy), Rogers.

PLAY-OFF

Dec. 3 1969: CZECHOSLOVAKIA (1) 4 (Kvasnak pen., Vesely, Adamec, Jokl) HUNGARY (0) 1 (Kocsis pen.). Marseilles. 7,857.
CZECHOSLOVAKIA: Viktor (sub Vencel); Pivarnik, Migas, Hagara, Horvath, Kuna (sub Pollak), Kvasnak, Vesely, Petras, Adamec, Jokl.
HUNGARY: Tamas; Kelemen, Meszoly, Ihasz, Halmosi, Nosko, Gorocs (sub Puskas), Fazekas (sub Kocsis), Bene, Farkas, Zambo.

GROUP THREE

Italy, smarting under criticism that followed their shock defeat by North Korea, the surprise finalists in the 1966 World Cup, quickly regained their form and rhythm to make sure of winning the three-country Group Three, in which they dropped only one point—to East Germany in Dresden.

They had won the European Championship in 1968 and had a proud home record of not having been beaten since 1961 when England were successful in Rome. Under their new coach, Ferruccio Vercareggi, they were showing they could be a threat to the best in the world.

The big threat in the group were the much improved East German side, but the fact that Italy had held them to a draw in the away fixture was in their favour for the return in Naples, which was the final game in the group.

Such was the interest in this match that more than 84,000 packed the stadium that Saturday afternoon to greet the East Germans. They saw the Italians put up one of their best displays, scoring three first-half goals through Mazzola, Domenghini and Riva in the space of 30 minutes to make sure of their tickets for Mexico.

Wales unfortunately finished at the foot of the group with four defeats in four matches, a record which might have been better if they had had a little more co-operation from English league clubs.

GROUP THREE RESULTS

Oct. 23 1968	Wales 0 Italy 1	Cardiff
Mar. 29 1969	East Germany 2 Italy 2	East Berlin
April 16	East Germany 2 Wales 1	Dresden
Oct. 22	Wales 1 East Germany 3	Cardiff
Nov. 4	Italy 4 Wales 1	Rome
Nov. 22	Italy 3 East Germany 0	Naples

FINAL TABLE

	P	W	D	L	F	A	Pts
Italy	4	3	1	0	10	3	7
East Germany	4	2	1	1	7	7	5
Wales	4	0	0	4	3	10	0

Oct. 23 1968: WALES (0) 0 ITALY (1) 1 (Riva). Cardiff. 18,072.
WALES: Millington; Thomas, Williams, Burton, Powell, Hole, Rees, Davies, W., Davies, R., Green, Jones.
ITALY: Zoff; Burgnich, Facchetti, Rosato, Salvadore, Castano, Domenghini, Rivera, Anastasi, De Sisti, Riva.

March 29 1969: EAST GERMANY (1) 2 ((Vogel, Kreitsche) ITALY (0) 2 (Riva 2). East Berlin. 52,177.
EAST GERMANY: Croy; Fraesdorf, Urbanczyk, Seehaus, Bransom, Bransch, Koerner, Noeldner, Loewe, Frenzel, Kreitsche, Vogel.
ITALY: Zoff; Burgnich, Salvadore, Castano, Facchetti, Rivera, De Sisti, Bertini, Prati, Mazzola, Riva.

April 16 1969: EAST GERMANY (1) 2 (Loewe, Rock) WALES (0) 1 (England). Dresden. 38,198.
EAST GERMANY: Croy; Fraesdorf, Urbanczyk, Bransch, Seehaus, Koerner, Loewe (sub Rock), Stein, Frenzel, Kreitsche, Vogel.
WALES: Millington; Rodriques, Burton, Hennessey, England, Hole, Jones, Durban, Mahoney, Toshack, Rees.

Oct. 22 1969: WALES (0) 1 (Powell) EAST GERMANY (0) 3 (Vogel, Loewe, Frenzel). Cardiff. 22,104.
WALES: Sprake; Rodriques, Thomas, Hennessey, England, Powell, Durban, Krzywicki, Davies, W., Toshack, Rees.
EAST GERMANY: Croy; Fraesdorf, Urbanczyk, Seehaus, Bransch, Koerner, Stein, Loewe, Frenzel, Irmscher, Vogel.

Nov. 4 1969: ITALY (1) 4 (Riva 3, Mazzola) WALES (0) 1 (England). Rome. 67,841.

ITALY: Albertosi; Burgnich, Facchetti, Bertini (sub Juliano), Puja, Salvadore, Domenghini, Rivera, Anastasi (sub Mazzola), De Sisti, Riva.
WALES: Sprake; Thomas, Derrett, Durban, England, Moore, Yorath, Toshack, Hole, Krzywicki, Rees (sub Reece).

Nov. 22 1969: ITALY (3) 3 (Mazzola, Domenghini, Riva) EAST GERMANY (0) 0. Naples. 84,293.
ITALY: Zoff; Burgnich, Facchetti, Cera (sub Juliano), Puja, Salvadore, Chiarugi, Mazzola, Domenghini, De Sisti, Riva.
EAST GERMANY: Croy; Fraesdorf (sub Rock), Urbanczyk, Seehaus, Bransch, Koerner, Stein, Loewe (sub Ducke), Frenzel, Irmscher, Vogel.

GROUP FOUR

Although the Russians went into their qualifying matches with a poor international record, having lost away to East Germany and lost at home to Sweden and drawn with Poland also at home, they went through their four matches without defeat, thanks to their national coach Gavril Kachalin, who brought them to peak fitness at the right time.

Probably their key match was their first when they drew with Northern Ireland in Belfast. The Irish, under Billy Bingham, had won both their games with Turkey and a victory over Russia in this match would have given them at least a play-off and at most a ticket to Mexico if they could have avoided defeat in the return in Russia.

Northern Ireland and Russia met during the political troubles in Ulster and only after long diplomatic exchanges the day before—involving the Irish F.A., the Northern Ireland Ministry of Home Affairs, who wanted the matched called off, the Russian Football Federation, and the Russian Embassy—did it take place, with the kick-off changed from 8 p.m. to 6 p.m.

Even though the Irish had one of their strongest sides available, including Best and Dougan, they failed to take their big chance, and could not pierce a solid Russian defence. Best was shadowed by Dzodzuashvili and Dougan closely watched by Kaplichny. Both were unable to make much impression on the game, which ended in a goalless draw.

Without Best Ireland had little hope of winning in Russia, so their only chance after the 2–0 defeat in Moscow was that Turkey would beat the Russians in Istanbul, but the miracle did not materialise.

GROUP FOUR RESULTS

Oct. 23 1968	Northern Ireland 4 Turkey 1	Belfast
Dec. 11	Turkey 0 Northern Ireland 3	Istanbul
Sept. 10 1969	Northern Ireland 0 U.S.S.R. 0	Belfast
Oct. 15	U.S.S.R. 3 Turkey 0	Kiev

Oct. 22   U.S.S.R. 2 Northern Ireland 0   Moscow
Nov. 16   Turkey 1 U.S.S.R. 3   Istanbul

FINAL TABLE

	P	W	D	L	F	A	Pts
U.S.S.R.	4	3	1	0	8	1	7
Northern Ireland	4	2	1	1	7	3	5
Turkey	4	0	0	4	2	13	0

Oct. 23 1968: NORTHERN IRELAND (1) 4 (Best, McMordie, Dougan, Campbell) TURKEY (1) 1 (Ogun). Belfast. 38,363
NORTHERN IRELAND: Jennings; Craig (sub Stewart), Harvey, Nicholson, Neill, Clements, Campbell, McMordie, Dougan, Irvine, Best.
TURKEY: Nihat; Sukru, Necdet, Ismail, Ercan, Vilmaz, Mesut (sub Abdullah), Santi, Ogun, Can Bartu, Ender.

Dec. 11 1968: TURKEY (0) 0 NORTHERN IRELAND (1) 3 (Harkin 2, Nicholson). Istanbul. 19,110.
TURKEY: Ali; Talat, Husseyin, Ercan, Ergun, Ayhan, Santi, Ogun, Fevzi, Metin, Faruk.
NORTHERN IRELAND: Jennings; Craig, Harvey, Nicholson, Neill, Stewart, Hamilton, McMordie, Dougan, Harkin, Clements.

Sept. 10 1969: NORTHERN IRELAND (0) 0 U.S.S.R. (0) 0. Belfast. 35,138.
NORTHERN IRELAND: Jennings; Rice, Elder, Todd, Neill, Nicholson, Campbell, McMordie, Dougan, Clements, Best.
U.S.S.R.: Rudakov; Shesternev, Kaplichny, Dzodzuashvili, Lovchev, Afonin, Muntyan, Kiselev, Khmelnitsky, Puzsch, Husainov.

Oct. 15 1969: U.S.S.R. (1) 3 (Muntyan 2, Nodiya) TURKEY (0) 0. Kiev. 71,115.
U.S.S.R.: Rudakov (sub Kavazashvili); Dzodzuashvili, Shesternev, Lovchev, Kaplichny (sub Khurtsilava), Serebryanikov, Muntyan, Asatiani, Ghershkovich, Byshovets, Nodiya.
TURKEY: Sabri; Mehmet, Ergun, Kamuran, Ercan, Vilmaz, Metin, Ayhan, Can Bartu (sub Mesut), Santi, Ender.

Oct. 22 1969: U.S.S.R. (1) 2 (Nodiya, Byshovets) NORTHERN IRELAND (0) 0. Moscow. 83,057.
U.S.S.R.: Rudakov; Dzodzuashvili, Shesternev, Lovchev, Kaplichny, Serebryanikov, Muntyan, Asatiani, Ghershkovich, Byshovets, Nodiya.
NORTHERN IRELAND: Jennings; Craig, Harvey, Hunter, Neill, Nicholson, Hegan, Jackson, Dougan, Harkin, Clements.

Nov. 16 1969: TURKEY (1) 1 (Ender) U.S.S.R. (2) 3 (Asatiani 2, Khmelitsky) Istanbul. 29,642.
TURKEY: Ali; Ayhan, Ergun, Kamuran, Ercan, Vilmaz, Metin, Elmastanhoglu, Nihat, Can Bartu, Ender.
U.S.S.R.: Kavazashvili; Dzodzuashvili, Shesternev, Lovchev, Khurtsilava, Serebryanikov, Muntyan, Asatiani, Byshovets, Khmelnitsky, Nazisha.

GROUP FIVE

Sweden, beaten finalists by Brazil in 1958 when they were the host country for the World Cup, romped through Group Five, scoring 12 goals in their first three games, and then, as something of an anticlimax when their final place was assured, losing to France whom they had previously beaten 2–0.

It was this latter victory over France in Stockholm which took Sweden to Mexico. Both goals were scored by their striker, Ove Kindvall, a professional with the Dutch club Feyenoord, who had been released for this match. So delighted were his colleagues at his performance that they carried him shoulder high from the field at the conclusion of the game and later he was chosen as Sweden's 'Footballer of the Year.'

With the aid of professionals with other European clubs, Orvar Bergmark had been able to build up a useful Swedish squad, and he has since been putting his players through simulated altitude tests to fit them for Mexico.

The big failure of the group was the performance of France, who never recovered from the shock home defeat they suffered from Norway in their opening match. Although they fully avenged that loss by going to Oslo for the return game and winning 3–1, the ground lost could not be recovered by their new coach, Georges Boulogne.

GROUP FIVE RESULTS

Oct. 9 1968	Sweden 5	Norway 0	Stockholm
Nov. 6	France 0	Norway 1	Strasburg
June 19 1969	Norway 2	Sweden 5	Oslo
Sept. 10	Norway 1	France 3	Oslo
Oct. 15	Sweden 2	France 0	Stockholm
Nov. 1	France 3	Sweden 0	Paris

FINAL TABLE

	P	W	D	L	F	A	Pts
Sweden	4	3	0	1	12	5	6
France	4	2	0	2	6	4	4
Norway	4	1	0	3	4	13	2

Oct. 9 1968: SWEDEN (1) 5 (Kindvall 3, Larsson 2) NORWAY (0) 0. Stockholm. 29,087.
SWEDEN: Hellstroem; Selander, Axelsson, Nordquist, Grip, Svensson, Larsson, Grahn, Eriksson, Kindvall, Persson.
NORWAY: Olsen, S.B.; Rodvang, Spydevold, Eggen, Mathiesen, Borno, Nilsen, Olsen, O. D., Berg, Iversen, Sunde (sub Pressberg).

Nov. 6 1968: FRANCE (0) 0 NORWAY (0) 1 (Iversen). Strasburg. 16,320.

FRANCE: Carnus; Lemerre, Quittet, Busquier, Djorkaeff, Gress (sub Louchet), Michel, Szepaniak, Blanchet, Guy, Bereta.

NORWAY: Olsen, S. B.; Rodvang, Spydevold, Eggen, Mathiesen, Bornoe, Nilsen, Johannessen, Olsen, O. D., Iversen, Sunde.

June 19 1969: NORWAY (0) 2 (O. D. Olsen 2) SWEDEN (3) 5 (Persson, Eriksson, Kindvall, Grahn, Grip). Oslo. 26,284.

NORWAY: Olsen, S. B.; Mathiesen, Eggen, Spydevold, Borno, Seemann, Nilsen, Berg, Jensen, Iversen (sub Sunde), Johannessen (sub Olsen, O. D.).

SWEDEN: Peterson; Selander, Axelsson, Nordquist, Grip, Eriksson, Svensson, Larsson (sub Olsson), Grahn, Kindvall, Persson.

Sept. 10 1969: NORWAY (0) 1 (O. D. Olsen) FRANCE (1) 3 (Revelli 2, Michel). Oslo. 22,445.

NORWAY: Kasperen; Eggen, Olafsen, Thorsen, Slinning, Borno, Seemann, Olsen, O. D., Berg, Iversen, Jensen.

FRANCE: Carnus; Djorkaeff, Novi, Bosquier, Rostagni, Broissart, Michel, Loubet, Revelli, Chiesa (sub Larou), Bras.

Oct. 15 1969: SWEDEN (1) 2 (Kindvall 2) FRANCE (0) 0. Stockholm. 48,518.

SWEDEN: Hellstroem; Selander, Axelsson, Nordquist, Grip, Svensson, Eriksson (sub Magnusson), Larsson, Grahn, Kindvall, Persson.

FRANCE: Carnus; Djorkaeff, Novi, Bosquier, Rostagni, Broissart, Michel, Loubet, Chiesa, Revelli, Bereta.

Nov. 1 1969: FRANCE (3) 3 (Bras 2, Djorkaeff) SWEDEN (0) 0. Paris. 17,916.

FRANCE: Carnus; Djorkaeff, Novi, Bosquier, Rostagni, Michel, Broissard, Bras, Loubet, Lech, Bereta.

SWEDEN: Hellstroem; Eriksson, Kristensson, Nordquist, Grip, Svensson (sub Nicklasson), Larsson, Magnusson, Grahn, Turesson, Johansson (sub Eklund).

GROUP SIX

Belgium became the first country in Europe to qualify for Mexico as a result of a six-month campaign which brought them nine points from five games, with Yugoslavia, runners-up to Italy in the 1968 European Championship, Spain, finalists in the 1966 World Cup, and Finland the also-rans.

Belgium's place became secure when Yugoslavia failed to beat Spain in Yugoslavia and the last threat was removed. With players like Van Himst, Devrindt and Van Moer—who was chosen Player of the Year—to spearhead the attack, and Heylens, Dewalque, Jeck and Thiessen to protect a class goalkeeper in Trappeniers, Raymond Goethals was able to build up a good, strong, all-round side capable of playing attacking football.

The failure of Spain resulted in a shake-up at the top, and the appointment in July 1969 of the former Hungarian centre-forward Ladislas Kubala as the sole selector of the national team—the first time the job had been handed to one man.

The man who had played international football for three countries —Hungary, Czechoslovakia and Spain—had made his home in Spain for the last twenty years, and has had experience there as player and manager. He has been given three years to make Spain a power in Europe once again.

GROUP SIX RESULTS

June 19 1968	Finland 1	Belgium 2	Helsinki
Sept. 25	Yugoslavia 9	Finland 1	Belgrade
Oct. 9	Belgium 6	Finland 1	Waregem
Oct. 27	Yugoslavia 0	Spain 0	Belgrade
Nov. 16	Belgium 3	Yugoslavia 0	Brussels
Dec. 11	Spain 1	Belgium 1	Madrid
Feb. 23 1969	Belgium 2	Spain 1	Liege
April 30	Spain 2	Yugoslavia 1	Barcelona
June 4	Finland 1	Yugoslavia 5	Helsinki
June 25	Finland 2	Spain 0	Helsinki
Oct. 15	Spain 6	Finland 0	La Linea
Oct. 19	Yugoslavia 4	Belgium 0	Skopje

FINAL TABLE

	P	W	D	L	F	A	Pts
Belgium	6	4	1	1	14	8	9
Yugoslavia	6	3	1	2	19	7	7
Spain	6	2	2	2	10	6	6
Finland	6	1	0	5	6	28	2

June 19 1968: FINLAND (1) 1 (Flinck) BELGIUM (0) 2 (Devrindt, Polleunis). Helsinki. 10,578.

FINLAND: Heinonen; Makipaa, Jalonen, Syrjavaara, Numilla, Kilponen, Nuorpanen, Flinck, Tolsa, Toivanen, Lindholm.

BELGIUM: Trappeniers; Heylens, Thissen, Dewalque, Plaskie, Beurlet, Polleunis, Pitzen, Van Himst, Dockx, Devrindt.

Sept. 25 1968: YUGOSLAVIA (2) 9 (Musemic 4, Zambata 2, Dzajic 2, Osim) FINLAND (0) 1 (Tolsa). Belgrade. 6,810.

YUGOSLAVIA: Curkovic; Cvek, Jetvic, Belin, Holcer, Pavlovic, Petkovic, Zambata, Musemic, Osim, Dzajic.

FINLAND: Nasman; Makipaa, Jalonen, Kilponen, Makkonen, Numilla, Heikila, Nuorpanen, Tolsa, Toivanen, Lindholm.

Oct. 9 1968: BELGIUM (3) 6 (Polleunis 3, Puis 2, Semmeling) FIN-LAND (0) 1. (Tolsa) Waregem. 8,052.

BELGIUM: Boone; Heylens, Dewalque (sub Dockx), Peeters, Beurlet, Thissen, Van Moer, Bettens, Semmeling, Van Himst, Puis.

FINLAND: Heinonen; Makipaa, Kilponen, Jalonen, Flinck, Numelin,

Aikkala (sub Toivanen), Nuorpanen, Tolsa, Nikkonen (sub Toivola), Lindholm.

Nov. 16 1968: BELGIUM (1) 3 (Devrindt 2, Polleunis) YUGOSLAVIA (0) 0. Brussels. 20,233.
BELGIUM: Trappeniers; Heylens, Dewalque, Peeters, Thissen, Van Moer, Polleunis, Semmeling, Devrindt, Van Himst, Puis.
YUGOSLAVIA: Curkovic; Cvek, Pavlovic, Holcer, Jetvic, Trivic, Hasinovic, Petkovic, Osim, Zambata, Dzajic.

Oct. 27 1968: YUGOSLAVIA (0) 0 SPAIN (0) 0 Belgrade. 23,963.
YUGOSLAVIA: Curkovic; Cvek, Jetvic, Pavlovic, Dojcinovski, Holcer, Petkovic (sub Bukal), Belin, Zambata, Vardic, Rora (sub Antic).
SPAIN: Iribar; Torres, Eladio, Pirri, Zabalza, Ufarte, Amancio, Luis (sub Perada), Germano, Marcial (sub Gallego), Tonono.

Dec. 11 1968: SPAIN (0) 1 (Garate) BELGIUM (1) 1 (Devrindt). Madrid. 11,906.
SPAIN: Sadurni; Torres, Tonono, Zabalza, Eladio, Pirri, Germano, Pirri, Claramunt, Amancio, Garate, Grosso.
BELGIUM: Trappeniers; Jeck, Hanon, Dewalque, Thissen, Van Moer, Dockx, Semmeling, Devrindt, Polleunis, Verheyen.

Feb. 23 1969: BELGIUM (1) 2 (Devrindt 2) SPAIN (0) 1 (Asensi). Liege. 31,668.
BELGIUM: Trappeniers; Heylens, Jeck, Dewalque, Thissen, Van Moer (sub Dockx), Polleunis, Semmeling, Devrindt, Van Himst, Puis.
SPAIN: Iribar; Martin (sub Torres), Eladio, Glaria, Gallego, Zoco, Claramunt (sub Asensi), Grosso, Vava, Amancio, Velasquez.

April 30 1969: SPAIN (2) 2 (Bustillo, Amancio) YUGOSLAVIA (0) 1 (Pavlovic). Barcelona. 9,914.
SPAIN: Sadurni; Martin, Tonono, Videgany, Glaria, Zabalza, Grosso (sub Fuste), Amancio, Bustillo, Velasquez, Rexach.
YUGOSLAVIA: Curkovic; Bajic, Paunovic, Gracanin, Pavlovic, Holcer, Bjekovic, Trivic, Osim (sub Katic), Acimov (sub Povric), Dzajic.

June 4 1969: FINLAND (1) 1 (Tolsa) YUGOSLAVIA (3) 5 (Bukal 2, Dzajic, Piric, Sprecco). Helsinki. 8,740.
FINLAND: Naesman (sub Patrikainen); Makipaa, Kilponen, Kautonen, Haikonen, Toivanen, Maekelelse, Andelmin, Tolsa (sub Talaslahti), Peltonen, Lindholm.
YUGOSLAVIA: Mulbaric; Gracanin, Jetvic, Piric, Holcer, Pavlovic, Hlevnjak, Bukal, Sprecco, Dzajic.

June 25 1969: FINLAND (2) 2 (Lindholm, Tolsa) SPAIN (0) 0. Helsinki. 11,838.
FINLAND: Naesman; Makipaa, Kilponen, Saviomaa, Kautonen, Numelin, Makela, Andelmin, Tolsa, Nuorpanen, Lindholm.
SPAIN: Sadurni; Martin, Glaria, Tonono, Videgany, Zabalza (sub Fuste), Amancio (sub Ballester), Grosso, Bustillo, Velasquez, Asensi.

Oct. 15 1969: SPAIN (5) 6 (Garate 2, Pirri, Velasquez, Amancio, Quino) FINLAND (0) 0. La Linea. 21,003.

SPAIN: Reina; Gaztelu, Eladio, Pirri, Barrachini, Violeta, Amancio, Velasquez, Garate (sub Quino), Asensi, Gento (sub Pujol).

FINLAND: Naesman (sub Makela); Makipaa, Forsell, Ranta, Kilponen, Lamberg, Avlomaa, Peltonen, Tolsa, Toivanen, Lindholm.

Oct. 19 1969: YUGOSLAVIA (3) 4 (Spasovski 2, Belin, Dzajic) BELGIUM (0) 0. Skopje. 21,583.

YUGOSLAVIA: Mulbaric; Holcer, Paunovic, Ramijak, Gracanin, Pavlovic, Belin, Spasovski, Bukal, Acimovic, Dzajic.

BELGIUM: Piot; Heylens, Jeck, Hanon, Thissen, Beurlet, Polleunis, Van Moer, Lambert, Van Himst, Puis.

GROUP SEVEN

Only Scotland presented any considerable threat to West Germany who qualified in Group Seven, but the Scots do not seem able to rise to the occasion. They really lost their chance when they allowed the Germans to get away with a draw at Hampden in the first match. Only a late goal from Murdoch saved them from defeat.

The Scots still had an outside chance of an appearance in Mexico when they went to Hamburg for the return encounter with West Germany and their supporters' hopes were raised when they took an early lead. Although they managed to raise the standard of their play and put up a better show than in previous matches, they were finally beaten by the odd goal in five by Helmut Schoen's well-drilled German side, and also had the misfortune to have Gemmell sent off three minutes from the end.

West Germany, who had taken England into extra time in the World Cup final at Wembley in 1966, still had the nucleus of that team on which to build and with the discovery of the exciting Gerd Mueller to add power to the attack. The young Bayern Munich striker scored at least once in all Germany's six matches.

GROUP SEVEN RESULTS

May 19 1968	Austria 7 Cyprus 1	Vienna
Oct. 13	Austria 0 West Germany 2	Vienna
Nov. 6	Scotland 2 Austria 1	Glasgow
Nov. 23	Cyprus 0 West Germany 1	Nicosia
Dec. 11	Cyprus 0 Scotland 5	Nicosia
April 16 1969	Scotland 1 West Germany 1	Glasgow
April 19	Cyprus 1 Austria 2	Nicosia
May 10	West Germany 1 Austria 0	Nuremburg
May 17	Scotland 8 Cyprus 0	Glasgow
May 21	West Germany 12 Cyprus 0	Essen
Oct. 22	West Germany 3 Scotland 2	Hamburg

Nov. 5   Austria 2   Scotland 0   Vienna

FINAL TABLE

	P	W	D	L	F	A	Pts
West Germany	6	5	1	0	20	3	11
Scotland	6	3	1	2	18	7	7
Austria	6	3	0	3	12	7	6
Cyprus	6	0	0	6	2	35	0

May 19 1968: AUSTRIA (3) 7 (Hoff I 5, 2 pens., Redl, Siber) CYPRUS (0) 1 (Kanzilieris). Vienna. 27,171.
AUSTRIA: Harreither; Gebhardt, Glechner, Stamm, Froehlich, Sturmberger, Hoff II, Paritz, Hoff I, Siber, Redl.
CYPRUS: Alkiviadis; Christou, Iakovou, Panajotou, Kavasis, Krystallis, Pitharas, Kantzilieris, Papadopoulos, Christodoulo, Stylianou.

Oct. 13 1968: AUSTRIA (0) 0 WEST GERMANY (1) 2 (Mueller, Eigenstiller o.g.). Vienna. 67,115.
AUSTRIA: Harreither; Pumm, Sturmberger, Eigenstiller, Fak, Hasil, Starek, Ettmeyer, Fritsch, Kogelberger, Metzler.
WEST GERMANY: Maier; Vogts, Schultz, Weber, Hottges, Beckenbauer, Netzer, Doerfel, Ulpass, Mueller, Held.

Nov. 6 1968: SCOTLAND (1) 2 (Law, Bremner) AUSTRIA (1) 1 (Starek). Glasgow. 79,982.
SCOTLAND: Simpson; Gemmell, McCreadie, Bremner, McKinnon, Greig, Johnstone, Cooke, Law, Lennox, Hughes.
AUSTRIA: Fuchsbichler; Gebhardt, Sturmberger, Eigenstiller, Pumm, Starek, Ettmeyer, Metzler, Hasil, Siber, Redl.

Nov. 23 1968: CYPRUS (0) 0 WEST GERMANY (0) 1 (Mueller). Nicosia. 6,080.
CYPRUS: Alkiviadis; Iakovou, Theodorou, Stephanou, Kourous, Panayiouyou, Koundis, Marcos, Melis, Pakkos, Stylianou.
WEST GERMANY: Maier; Vogts, Schultz, Weber, Hottges, Overath, Lorenz, Doerfel, Wimmer, Mueller, Held.

Dec. 11 1968: CYPRUS (0) 0 SCOTLAND (5) 5 (Gilzean 2, Stein 2, Murdoch). Nicosia. 5,895.
CYPRUS: Alkiviadis; Iakovou, Theodorou, Kourous, Panayiouyou, Michaeil, Efumiades, Krystallis (sub Xipolitas), Asprou, Pakkos (sub Marcov), Stylianou.
SCOTLAND: Heriot; Fraser, McCreadie, Bremner, McKinnon (sub McNeill), Greig, McLean, Murdoch, Gilzean, Cooke, Stein (sub Lennox).

April 16 1969: SCOTLAND (0) 1 (Murdoch) WEST GERMANY (1) 1 (Mueller). Glasgow. 96,292.
SCOTLAND: Lawrence; Gemmell, McCreadie, Greig, McKinnon, Bremner, Johnstone, Murdoch, Law, Gilzean, Lennox (sub Cooke).
WEST GERMANY: Wolter (sub Maier); Schnellinger, Vogts, Beckenbauer, Schultz, Patzke, Doerfel, Haller, Mueller, Overath, Held (sub Lorenz).

April 19 1969: CYPRUS (0) 1 (Efumiades) AUSTRIA (1) 2 (Kreuz, Redl). Nicosia. 5,247.
CYPRUS: Alkiviadis; Christou, Kattou, Kavasis, Kourous, Panayiouyou, Michaeil (sub Asprou), Krystallis, Efumiades, Pakkos, Stylianou.
AUSTRIA: Harreither; Linhart, Sturmberger, Eigenstiller, Fak, Hof, Eisele (sub Ettmeyer), Kreuz, Buzek, Flogel, Redl.

May 10 1969: WEST GERMANY (0) 1 (Mueller) AUSTRIA (0) 0. Nuremburg. 56,613.
WEST GERMANY: Maier; Patzke, Hottges, Schultz, Vogts, Beckenbauer, Overath, Doerfel, Mueller, Held, Brenninger.
AUSTRIA: Fraydl; Pumm, Eigenstiller, Sturmberger, Fak, Starek, Ettmeyer, Kogelberger, Siber, Redl.

May 17 1969: SCOTLAND (3) 8 (Stein 4, Gray, McNeill, Henderson, Gemmell pen.) CYPRUS (0) 0. Glasgow. 38,263.
SCOTLAND: Herriot; McCreadie, Gemmell, Bremner, McNeill, Greig, Henderson, Cooke, Stein, Gilzean, Gray.
CYPRUS: Alkiviadis; Mertakis, Sarakis (sub Fokis), Stephanou, Kourous, Sotirakis (sub Constantus), Panicos, Marcos, Krystallis, Mellos, Stylianou.

May 21 1969: WEST GERMANY (7) 12 (Mueller 4, Overath 3, Haller 2, Lorenz, Hottges, Held) CYPRUS (0) 0. Essen. 36,036.
WEST GERMANY: Maier; Vogts, Hottges, Beckenbauer, Schultz, Lorenz, Libuda, Haller, Mueller, Overath, Held.
CYPRUS: Alkaviadis; Mertakis, Sarakis, Sotirakis, Kourous, Stephanou, Kettenis, Fokis, Krystallis, Mellos, Stylianou.

Oct. 22 1969: WEST GERMANY (1) 3 (Fichtel, Mueller, Libuda) SCOTLAND (1) 2 (Johnstone, Gilzean). Hamburg. 70,448.
WEST GERMANY: Maier; Hottges, Vogts, Beckenbauer, Schultz, Fichtel, Haller, Overath, Mueller, Seeler, Libuda.
SCOTLAND: Herriott; Greig, Gemmell, Bremner, McKinnon, McNeill, Johnstone, Cormack, Gilzean, Gray, Stein.

Nov. 5 1969: AUSTRIA (1) 2 (Redl 2) SCOTLAND (0) 0. Vienna. 10,091.
AUSTRIA: Harreither; Waliner, Sturmberger, Schmidradner, Fak, Geyer, Hof, Ettmeyer, Paritz, Kaiser, Redl.
SCOTLAND: McGarr; Greig, McKinnon, Stanton, Burns, Murdoch, Cooke, Bremner, Gilzean, Curran, Gray.

GROUP EIGHT

Bulgaria and Poland had a good fight for the qualifying spot in Group Eight, which finally went by a point to Bulgaria, who reached the last stages for the third successive time.
    Poland kept their chances alive by beating an injury-hit Bulgaria 3–0 in Warsaw in November 1969, which meant that Bulgaria had

to beat Luxemburg in their final game or, if they only drew, face a play-off with Poland.

The Warsaw failure was Bulgaria's first, and only, defeat. Despite their attempts to play a tight defensive game in order to get a draw, the Poles were not to be denied and three times they found a way through for a good victory.

A month later the Bulgarians took on Luxemburg, the chopping blocks of the group, on a bone-hard and show-covered pitch, and stamped their superiority on a closely fought game with a 3–1 victory which gave them their passport to Mexico.

Bulgaria's coach, Stefan Bozhkov, relied mainly on experienced players like Asparoukhov and Yakimov, the forwards, and Zhechev, a defender, who had played in the 1962 and 1966 finals. Another five, Shalamanov, Penev, Dermendjiev, Gaganelov and the goal-keeper, Simeonov, were in the 1966 finals, while Dimitrov played in Chile, but did not go to England.

GROUP EIGHT RESULTS

Sept.	4 1968	Holland 2	Luxemburg 0	Rotterdam
Oct.	27	Bulgaria 2	Holland 0	Sofia
Mar.	26 1969	Luxemburg 0	Holland 4	The Hague
April	20	Poland 8	Luxemburg 1	Cracow
April	23	Bulgaria 2	Luxemburg 1	Sofia
May	7	Holland 1	Poland 0	Rotterdam
June	15	Bulgaria 4	Poland 1	Sofia
Sept.	7	Poland 2	Holland 1	Chorzow
Oct.	12	Luxemburg 1	Poland 5	Luxemburg
Oct.	22	Holland 1	Bulgaria 1	Rotterdam
Nov.	9	Poland 3	Bulgaria 0	Warsaw
Dec.	7	Luxemburg 1	Bulgaria 3	Luxemburg

FINAL TABLE

	P	W	D	L	F	A	Pts
Bulgaria	6	4	1	1	12	7	9
Poland	6	4	0	2	19	8	8
Holland	6	3	1	2	9	5	7
Luxemburg	6	0	0	6	4	24	0

Sept. 4 1968: HOLLAND (1) 2 (Jansen, van Hanegem) LUXEMBURG (0) 0. Rotterdam. 48,188.

HOLLAND: Van Beveren; Suurbier, Israel, Laseroms, Van Duivenbode, Veenstra, Jansen, Swart, Van der Kuylen, Van Hanegem, Moulijn.

LUXEMBURG: Hoffman, R.; Kuffer, Jeitz, Ewen, Hoffman, J., Hoffmann, N., Konter, Schmit, Dublin, Pilot, Kirchens.

Oct. 27 1968: BULGARIA (1) 2 (Bonev, Asparoukhov) HOLLAND (0) 0. Sofia. 18,073.

BULGARIA: Simeonov; Shalamanov, Dimitrov, Jetchev, Gaganelov,

Penev, Popov, Bonev, Asparoukhov, Yakimov, Dermendjiev (sub Kolkov).
HOLLAND: Van Beveren; Suurbier, Israel, Eykenbroek, Van Duivenbode, Groot, Muller, Boumeester, Klijnan, Van Hanegem, Rensenbrink.

March 26 1969: HOLLAND (2) 4 (Palplatz 2, Cruyff, Van Dijk) LUXEMBURG (0) 0. The Hague. 47,207.
HOLLAND: Van Beveren; Suurbier, Israel, Eykenbroek, Van Duivenbode, Groot, Jansen, Palplatz, Van Dijk, Cruyff, Rensenbrink.
LUXEMBURG: Hoffman, R.; Konter, Jeitz, Leszinski, Hoffmann, J., Hoffmann, N., Pilot, Klein, Schmit, Phillipe, Dublin.

April 20 1969: POLAND (3) 8 (Lubanski 4, Dejna 2, Wilim 2) LUXEMBURG (0) 1 (Leonard). Cracow. 28,327.
POLAND: Gomola; Szadkowski, Winkler, Anczok, Wilczek, Dejna, Blaut, Szoltysik, Lubanski, Bryshezy, Wilim.
LUXEMBURG: Hoffmann, R.; Kuffer, Konter, Jeitz, Leszinski, Hoffmann, N., Schmit, Dublin, Leonard, Phillipe, Kirchens.

April 23 1969: BULGARIA (1) 2 (Asparoukhov 2, 1 pen.) LUXEMBURG (0) 1 (Leonard, pen.). Sofia. 18,998.
BULGARIA: Simeonov; Aladjov, Penev, Gaganelov, Jetchev, Yakimov, Popov (sub Jekov), Bonev, Asparoukhov, Dermendjiev, Mitkov.
LUXEMBURG: Standebach; Kuffer, Jeitz, Leszinski, Hoffmann, J., Konter, Hoffmann, N., Dublin, Leonard, Schmit, Kirchens.

May 7 1969: HOLLAND (0) 1 (Roggeveen) POLAND (0) 0. Rotterdam. 43,658.
HOLLAND: Van Beveren; Suurbier, Israel, Eykenbroek, Van Duivenbode, Pronk, Rijnders (sub Jansen), Palplatz, Van Dijk, Van Hanegem (sub Roggeveen), Rensenbrink.
POLAND: Kostka; Anczok, Winkler, Szadkowski, Latocha, Wilczek, Dejna, Blaut, Szoltysik, Lubanski, Wilim.

June 15 1969: BULGARIA (2) 4 (Bonev, Dermendjiev, Penev, Asparoukhov) POLAND (1) 1 (Dejna). Sofia. 38,313.
BULGARIA: Simeonov; Peshev, Ivkov, Gaganelov, Jetchev, Penev, Dermendjiev, Bonev, Asparoukhov, Kolev, Kotov.
POLAND: Kostka; Piechniczek, Oslislo, Anczok, Szadowski, Winkler, Szoltysik, Dejna, Wilczek (sub Markx), Lubanski, Blaut.

Sept. 8 1969: POLAND (0) 2 (Jarosik, Lubanski) HOLLAND (1) 1 (Wery). Chorzow. 70,220.
POLAND: Kostka; Latocha, Szadkowski, Wrazy, Anczok, Szmidt, Dejna, Szoltysik, Markx, Lubanski, Hfaber (sub Jarosik).
HOLLAND: Van Beveren; Suurbier, Israel, Eykenbroek, Strik, Groot, Van Dijk, Van Hanegem (sub Veenstra), Wery, Cruyff, Moulijn (sub Roggeveen).

Oct. 12 1969: LUXEMBURG (1) 1 (Kirchens) POLAND (0) 5 (Dejna 2, Jaroski pen., Bula, Lubanski). Luxemburg. 5,431.
LUXEMBURG: Hoffmann, R.; Kuffer, Leszinski, Jeitz, Hoffmann, J., Schartz, Hoffmann, N., Dublin, Phillipe, Schmit, Kirchens.

POLAND: Kostka; Stachurski, Strazalkowski, Winkler, Anczok, Bula, Blaut (sub Gadocha), Zmijewski, Lubanski, Dejna, Jarosik.

Oct. 22 1969: HOLLAND (1) 1 (Veenstra) BULGARIA (0) 1 (Bonev). Rotterdam. 63,304.

HOLLAND: Treijtel; Suurbier, Israel, Rijnders, Strik, Eykenbroek, Wery, Van der Kuylen, Van Hanegem, Veenstra, Moulijn.

BULGARIA: Simeonov; Shalamanov, Jetchev, Penev, Dimitrov, Aladjov, Dermendjiev, Bonev, Asparoukhov, Georgiev, Kolev.

Nov. 9 1969: POLAND (1) 3 (Jarosik 2, Dejna) BULGARIA (0) 0. Warsaw. 61,278.

POLAND: Kostka, Latocha, Winkler, Oslizlo, Anczok, Szoltysik, Dejna, Bula, Zmijewski, Lubanski, Jarosik.

BULGARIA: Simeonov (sub Filopov); Jetchev, Shalamanov, Dimitrov, Aladjov, Dermendjiev, Bonev, Jekov, Kolev, Marashlijev.

Dec. 7 1969: LUXEMBURG (0) 1 (Philippe pen.) BULGARIA (2) 3 (Dermendjiev, Yakimov, Bonev). Luxemburg. 4,929.

LUXEMBURG: Hoffmann, R.; Kuffer, Pilot, Leszinski, Hoffmann, J., Schartz, Zangerlie, Phillipe, Hoffmann, N.

BULGARIA: Simeonov; Shalamanov, Dimitrov, Jetchev, Gaganelov, Penev, Yakimov, Dermendjiev, Bonev, Asparoukhov, Jekov.

GROUP NINE

England, as holders of the Jules Rimet Cup, qualified automatically for the final stages in Mexico.

GROUP TEN

Peru's success in Group Ten at the expense of the more fancied Argentina was really a triumph for the well-prepared plans of their coach Waldir Pereira Didi, who played in Brazil's winning World Cup sides of 1958 and 1962, and who was assisted by his Uruguayan coach, Roberto Scarone.

Didi set out months before the opening matches to build a team to tackle Argentina and Bolivia. Their opening match was against Argentina, an important one, as Argentina had been beaten by Bolivia. A single goal gave them victory, but a week later they crashed to Bolivia in the high altitude of La Paz.

This left Bolivia leading the group, but in the return match in Lima Peru made no mistake and with Argentina beating Bolivia and Peru holding Argentina to a draw in a tough final game the Peruvians reached the final for the first time in their history.

Nine of Peru's 22-squad were from one team, Universitario de Deportes, who are coached by Scarone, and it was generally agreed that, although there were many good individual players in the side, success was due to the way this talent had been blended into teamwork.

If Argentina had taken their preparations more seriously they might have done better. They started badly and, although improvement was shown later, it was too late to stage the necessary recovery.

GROUP TEN RESULTS

July 27 1969	Bolivia 3 Argentina 1	La Paz
Aug. 3	Peru 1 Argentina 0	Lima
Aug. 10	Bolivia 2 Peru 1	La Paz
Aug. 17	Peru 3 Bolivia 0	Lima
Aug. 24	Argentina 1 Bolivia 0	Buenos Aires
Aug. 31	Argentina 2 Peru 2	Buenos Aires

FINAL TABLE

	P	W	D	L	F	A	Pts
Peru	4	2	1	1	7	4	5
Bolivia	4	2	0	2	5	6	4
Argentina	4	1	1	2	4	6	3

July 27 1969: BOLIVIA (1) 3 (Diaz, Blacutt, Alvarez) ARGENTINA (1) 1 (Tarabini). La Paz. 21,267.

BOLIVIA: Issa; Maldonado, Agreda, Alvarez, Rojas, Herbas, Blacutt, Gonzalez, Diaz, Rada, Farias.

ARGENTINA: Cejas; Sune, Marzolini, Brindisi, Perfumo, Albrecht, Marcos, Rattin (sub Pachame), Onega, Cocco, Tarabini.

Aug. 3 1969: PERU (0) 1 (Leon) ARGENTINA (0) 0. Lima. 43,147.

PERU: Rubinas; Gonzalez, Fuentes, Mifflin, de la Torre, Chumpitaz, Baylon, Challe, Leon, Cubillas, Gallardo.

ARGENTINA: Cejas (sub Santoro); Gallo, Marzolini, Brindisi, Perfumo, Basile, Bernao, Rulli, Yazalde (sub Onega), Pachame, Tarabini.

Aug. 10 1969: BOLIVIA (0) 2 (Alvarez, Chumpitaz o.g.) PERU (0) 1 (Challe). La Paz. 20,670.

BOLIVIA: Issa; Maldonado, Agreda, Alvarez, Rojas, Herbas, Blacutt, Gonzalez (sub Cabrera), Diaz, Rada, Farias.

PERU: Rubinas; Gonzalez (sub Fernandez), Fuentes, Mifflin, de La Torre,, Chumpitaz, Baylon, Challe, Leon, Cubillas, Gallardo.

Aug. 17 1969: PERU (0) 3 (Cubillas, Challe, Gallardo) BOLIVIA (0) 0. Lima. 43,148.

PERU: Rubinos; Gonzalez, Risco, Challe, de la Torre, Chumpitaz, Baylon, Cruzado, Leon, Cubillas, Gallardo (sub Zagarra).

BOLIVIA: Issa; Maldonado, Diaz, Julio, Rada, Rojas, Herbas, Blacutt, Diaz, Juan, Torres, Alvarez, Cabrera (sub Hertado).

Aug. 24 1969: ARGENTINA (0) 1 (Albrecht) BOLIVIA (0) 0. Buenos Aires. 47,069.

ARGENTINA: Cejas; Sune, Perfumo, Albrecht, Marzolini, Rulli, Pachame, Bernao, Yazalde, Onega, Mas.

BOLIVIA: Cobo; Maldonado, Rojas, Herbas, Agreda, Blacutt, Rada, Alvarez, Gonzalez, Diaz, Juan, Cabrera.

Aug. 31 1969: ARGENTINA (0) 2 (Albrecht, Rendo) PERU (0) 2 (Ramires 2). Buenos Aires. 53,627.

ARGENTINA: Cejas; Gallo, Perfumo, Albrecht, Marzolini, Rulli (sub Rendo), Brindisi, Pachame, Marcos, Yazalde, Tarabini.

PERU: Rubinos; Campos, de la Torre, Chumpitaz, Risco, Challe, Cruzado, Baylon, Leon, Cubillas, Ramirez.

GROUP ELEVEN

The man of a few thousand words, Joao Soldanha—who took over the Brazil team in February 1969 and was dismissed in March 1970 —produced an attacking side that averaged nearly four goals a game to head Group Eleven and finish with a 100 per cent record, and an almost cast-iron defence.

Critics were comparing the side with the winning combination of 1958 and 1962 and even suggesting that it was superior. But such was the play of the side that Soldanha was able to use an unchanged eleven throughout the tournament.

The individuality of such players as Carlos Alberto in defence, Gerson in midfield, and Jairzinho, Tostao, Pele and Edu in the forward line was neatly blended into the side to produce a very workmanlike machine.

After the tournament, Tostao, the 22-year-old centre-forward, said to be the successor of Pele, had the misfortune to be hit on an eye by the ball, which necessitated a trip to the United States for a serious operation. He was said to have recovered well.

Paraguay, Colombia and Venezuela, the other runners in Group Eleven, had little chance of stopping the progress of that powerful Brazilian side.

GROUP ELEVEN RESULTS

July 27 1969	Colombia 3	Venezuela 0	Bogota
Aug. 2	Venezuela 1	Colombia 1	Caracas
Aug. 7	Colombia 0	Brazil 2	Bogota
Aug. 7	Venezuela 0	Paraguay 2	Caracas
Aug. 10	Venezuela 0	Brazil 5	Caracas
Aug. 10	Colombia 0	Paraguay 1	Bogota
Aug. 17	Paraguay 0	Brazil 3	Asuncion
Aug. 21	Paraguay 1	Venezuela 0	Asuncion
Aug. 21	Brazil 6	Colombia 2	Rio de Janeiro
Aug. 24	Brazil 6	Venezuela 0	Rio de Janeiro
Aug. 24	Paraguay 2	Colombia 1	Asuncion
Aug. 31	Brazil 1	Paraguay 0	Rio de Janeiro

FINAL TABLE

	P	W	D	L	F	A	Pts
Brazil	6	6	0	0	23	2	12
Paraguay	6	4	0	2	6	5	8
Colombia	6	1	1	4	7	12	3
Venezuela	6	0	1	5	1	18	1

July 27 1969: COLOMBIA (2) 3 (Gonzalez 2, Segrera pen.) VENEZU-
ELA (0) 0. Bogota. 47,898.
COLUMBIA: Largacha; Segovia, Hernandez, Garcia, Segrera, Lopez,
Brand, Agudelo, Gallego, Gonzalez, Ortiz.
VENEZUELA: Colmenares; David, Chico, Pedrito, Freddy, Sanchez,
Mendoza, Antonio, Iriarte, Tortolero, Nitti.

Aug. 2 1969: VENEZUELA (0) 1 (Mendoza) COLOMBIA (0) 1 (Tom-
ayo). Caracas. 17,101.
VENEZUELA: Fasano; David, Chico, Pedrito, Freddy, Sanchez,
Mendoza, Antonio, Iriarte, Nitti (sub Salcedo), Rafa.
COLOMBIA: Largacha; Segovia, Castro, Garcia, Segrera, Lopez,
Brand (sub Tamayo), Agudelo, Gallego (sub Lobaton), Gonzalez,
Ortiz.

Aug. 6 1969: COLOMBIA (0) 0 BRAZIL (2) 2 (Tostao 2). Bogota·
51,131.
COLOMBIA: Largacha; Sanchez, Segrera, Lopez, Castro, Segovia,
Agudelo, Tamayo, Garcia, Gallego, Ortiz.
BRAZIL: Felix; Carlos Alberto, Djalma Diaz, Joel, Rildo, Piazza, Gerson,
Jairzinho, Pele, Tostao, Edu.

Aug. 6 1969: VENEZUELA (0) 0 PARAGUAY (1) 2 (P. Rojas, Sosa).
Caracas. 9,110.
VENEZUELA: Fasano; Marin, Chico, Pedrito, Freddy, Sanchez, Ravelo,
Useche, Mendoza, Tortolero, Nitti.
PARAGUAY: Aguilera; Molina, Bobadilla, Valdez, Rojas, S., Mendoza,
Rojas, P., Sosa, Ocampo, Martinez, Godoy.

Aug. 10 1969: VENEZUELA (0) 0 BRAZIL (0) 5 (Pele 2, Tostao 3).
Caracas. 30,063.
VENEZUELA: Garcia; David, Freddy, Sanchez, Chico, Pedrito, Useche,
Iriarte, Antonio, Mendoza, Nitti.
BRAZIL: Felix; Carlos Alberto, Djalma Diaz, Joel, Rildo, Piazza,
Gerson, Jairzinho, Tostao, Pele, Edu.

Aug. 10 1969: COLOMBIA (0) 0 PARAGUAY (0) 1 (Martinez).
Bogota. 51,049.
COLOMBIA: Largacha; Segovia, Segrera, Lopez, Castro, Garcia,
Agudelo, Santa, Brand, Gallego, Ortiz.
PARAGUAY: Aguilera; Molina, Rojas, S., Bobadilla, Mendoza, Sosa,
Rojas, P., Martinez, Ocampo, Valdez, Giminez.

Aug. 17 1969: PARAGUAY (0) 0 BRAZIL (0) 3 (Edu 2, Jairzinho)
Asuncion. 44,850.

Above: Jairzinho exultant as he scores Brazil's third goal in the World Cup Final against Italy. The European champions were decisively beaten by a great Brazilian side. *Below:* Mexican-hatted, Pele is carried shoulder-high after Brazil's victory in the Final

Above: Top scorer in Mexico, West Germany's Gerd Mueller scores his side's third goal against Italy in the semi-final, a match described as the finest in the competition's history. *Below:* Italy's fourth goal against West Germany, which clinched her place in the final. It was the fifth goal scored in extra time

PARAGUAY: Aguilera; Molina, Mendoza, Valdez, Bobadilla, Rojas, S., Colman (sub Arrua), Rojas, P., Ferreira, Martinez, Giminez (sub Mora).

BRAZIL: Feliz; Carlos Alberto, Rildo, Piazza, Djalma Diaz, Joel, Jairzinho, Gerson, Tostao, Pele, Edu.

Aug. 21 1969: BRAZIL (2) 6 (Tostao 2, Jairzinho 2, Edu, Pele) COLOMBIA (1) 2 (Gallego 2). Rio de Janeiro. 94,977.

BRAZIL: Felix; Carlos Alberto, Rildo, Piazza, Djalma Diaz, Joel, Jairzinho, Gerson, Tostao, Pele, Edu.

COLOMBIA: Largacha; Segovia, Castro, Alvarez, Segrera, Soto, Ramirez, Agudelo, Gallego, Mesa, Santa.

Aug. 21 1969: PARAGUAY (1) 1 (Giminez) VENEZUELA (0) 0. Asuncion. 11,059.

PARAGUAY: Villanueva; Molina, Bobadilla, Rojas, S., Mendoza, Arrua, Rojas, P., Ivaldi, Martinez, Ocampo (sub Ferreira), Giminez.

VENEZUELA: Garcia; David, Freddy, Sanchez (sub Surcalejo), Torres, Useche, Pedrito, Nitti, Antonio, Rafa, Chico.

Aug. 24 1969: PARAGUAY (1) 2 (Arrua 2) COLOMBIA (0) 1 (Segrera). Asuncion. 15,744.

PARAGUAY: Villaneuva; Molina, Bobadilla, Rojas, S., Mendoza, Rojas, P., Ivaldi, Mora (sub Ferreira), Arrua, Ocampo, Giminez.

COLOMBIA: Quintana; Segovia, Soto, Segrera, Castro, Alvarez, Agudelo, Ramirez, Gallego, Mesa, Gonzalez.

Aug. 24 1969: BRAZIL (5) 6 (Tostao 3, Pele 2 (1 pen.), Jairzinho) VENEZUELA (0) 0. Rio de Janeiro. 122,841.

BRAZIL: Felix (sub Lula); Carlos Alberto, Djalma Diaz, Joel (sub Brito), Rildo, Piazza, Gerson, Jairzinho, Pele, Tostao, Pele, Edu.

VENEZUELA: Fasano; Chico, Sanchez, Freddy, David, Useche, Naranjo, Curo, Iriarte, Antonio, Nitti.

Aug. 31 1969: BRAZIL (0) 1 (Pele) PARAGUAY (0) 0. Rio de Janeiro. 183,341.

BRAZIL: Felix; Carlos Alberto, Santos, Joel, Rildo, Piazza, Gerson, Jairzinho, Pele, Tostao, Edu.

PARAGUAY: Aguilera; Molina, Rojas, S., Bobadilla, Mendoza, Sosa Rojas, P., Ivaldi (sub Valdez), Ocampo, Ferreira, Giminez.

GROUP TWELVE

Uruguay, who qualified from Group Twelve, looked the least impressive of the South American winners, but at least they had the satisfaction of being the only team that did not give away a goal in the qualifying competition.

This was a tribute to their excellent defence, behind which is Ladislao Mazurkiewicz, a world class goalkeeper who showed his fine talents against England at Wembley in the 1966 finals.

Uruguay began with a win over Ecuador, a draw against Chile and

C

another victory over Ecuador which put the pressure on their rivals. When Chile were held to a draw by Ecuador, who scored first at Guayaquil, Chile needed to beat Uruguay in the final match to stop the Uruguayans going to Mexico.

With home advantage in Montevideo, Uruguay scored a convincing victory over their rivals to satisfy Juan Hohberg, a naturalised Uruguayan who had played for Argentina in the 1954 World Cup that he had the backbone of a useful side for Mexico.

GROUP TWELVE RESULTS

July	9 1969	Ecuador 0	Uruguay 2	Guayaquil
July	13	Chile 0	Uruguay 0	Santiago
July	20	Uruguay 1	Ecuador 0	Montevideo
July	27	Chile 4	Ecuador 1	Santiago
Aug.	3	Ecuador 1	Chile 1	Guayaquil
Aug.	10	Uruguay 2	Chile 0	Montevideo

FINAL TABLE

	P	W	D	L	F	A	Pts
Uruguay	4	3	1	0	5	0	7
Chile	4	1	2	1	5	4	4
Ecuador	4	0	1	3	2	8	1

July 6 1969: ECUADOR (0) 0 URUGUAY (1) 2 (Bareno, Ubinas). Guayaquil. 55,783.

ECUADOR: Ordenna; Quinjano, Portilla, Tovar, Quinteros, Tapia, Cardenas, Munoz, Lasso, Bolanos, Espinoza.

URUGUAY: Mazurkiewicz; Anchetta, Matosas, Ubinas, Montero, Caetano, Rocha, Cubilla, Zubia, Cortes, Bareno.

July 13 1969: CHILE (0) 0 URUGUAY (0) 0. Santiago. 68,882.

CHILE: Neff; Rodriques, Dias, Hodge, Quintano, Valdes, Araya, Reinoso, Olivares, Fouilloux, Yavar.

URUGUAY: Mazurkiewicz; Ubinas, Caetano, Montero, Castilo, Anchetta, Matosas, Cubilla, Cortes, Zubia, Rocha (sub Forte), Bareno.

July 20 1969: URUGUAY (0) 1 (Anchetta) ECUADOR (0) 0. Monte. video. 39,387.

URUGUAY: Mazurkiewicz; Ubinas, Caetano, Montero, Castillo, Anchetta, Matosas, Silva, S., Cortes, Silva, H., Cubilla, Bareno.

ECUADOR: Maldonado; Lecaro, Macias, Tovar, Quinteros, Munoz, Noriega, Bolanos, Tapia (sub Rodriquez), Espinoza (sub Malagon).

July 27 1969: CHILE (0) 4 (Olivares 2, Valdes 2) ECUADOR (0) 1 (Macias). Santiago. 68,857.

CHILE: Neff; Rodriques, Diaz, Valdes, Laube, Quintano, Araya, Hodge, Olivares, Reinoso, Velia.

ECUADOR: Maldonado; Echenique, Macias, Tovar, Portilla, Quinteros, Munoz, Noriega, Lasso, Tapia, Bolanos.

Aug. 3 1969: ECUADOR (1) 1 (Rodriquez) CHILE (0) 1 (Olivares). Guayaquil. 11,547.
ECUADOR: Maldonado; Quinjano, Lecaro, Macias, Tovar, Noriega, Tapia, Munoz, Rodriquez, Bolanos, Espinoza.
CHILE: Neff; Rodriques, Quintano, Laube, Diaz, Hodge, Reinoso, Araya, Marcos, Olivares, Velia.
Aug. 10 1969: URUGUAY (1) 2 (Cortes, Rocha) CHILE (0) 0. Montevideo. 62,693.
URUGUAY: Mazurkiewicz; Ubinas, Caetano, Montero, Castillo, Anchetta, Matosas, Cubilla, Rocha, Silver, S. (sub Acuna), Cortes, Bareno.
CHILE: Neff; Rodriques, Dias, Hodge, Laube, Quintano, Velia (sub Araya), Reinoso, Olivares, Yavar, Hoffman.

GROUP THIRTEEN

Group Thirteen, which comprised the countries in the North, Central America and Caribbean zone, needed 32 matches from the 12 nations engaged to produce a qualifier for Mexico. And it also produced a minor 'war' which was something unique in the history of the World Cup.

El Salvador, who finally qualified after a long struggle, was concerned in the 'war.' After they had beaten Honduras in a semifinal to force a play-off in San Salvador, it was claimed that their nationals living in Honduras had been beaten up. As a result diplomatic relations were broken off.

After moves by neighbouring countries, peace was restored and the play-off took place in Mexico City with the crowd limited to 20,000 in case of trouble between rival supporters. After a two-hour match, extra time having been necessary, El Salvador reached the final for a meeting with Haiti.

Again they needed a play-off, and again they had to go into extra time before they qualified to reach the finals—the first occasion that they had entered for the competition, taking the CONCAF place which in past years has usually gone to the more experienced Mexico side, as the strongest in that part of the world.

This time, of course, Mexico did not have to play through the qualifying rounds.

GROUP THIRTEEN RESULTS

First Preliminary Round: Sub Group 13.1

Nov. 27 1968	Costa Rica 3	Jamaica 0	San Jose
Dec. 1	Jamaica 1	Costa Rica 3	San Jose
Dec. 5	Honduras 3	Jamaica 1	Tegucigalpa
Dec. 8	Jamaica 0	Honduras 2	Tegucigalpa

Dec. 22　　　　Honduras 1　Costa Rica 0　Tegucigalpa
Dec. 29　　　　Costa Rica 1　Honduras 1　San Jose

FINAL TABLE

	P	W	D	L	F	A	Pts
Honduras	4	3	1	0	7	2	7
Costa Rica	4	2	1	1	7	3	5
Jamaica	4	0	0	4	2	11	0

Nov. 27 1968: COSTA RICA (0) 3 JAMAICA (0) 0. San Jose. 14,940.
COSTA RICA: Gutierrez; Estupinan, Eiizohdo, Grant McDonald, Vela, Calvo, Vaughus, Chavarria, Saenz, Ganilz, Hernandez.
JAMAICA: Rowe; Simmons, Scott, Brown, F., Pearce, Brown, L., Hamilton, Cole, Dunkley, Largie, Welsh, A.

Dec. 1 1968: JAMAICA (1) 1 COSTA Rica (2) 3. San Jose. 11,273.
JAMAICA: Rowe; Scott, Brown, F., Pearce, Brown, L., Hamilton, Cole, Dunkley, Largie, Welsh, Williams.
COSTA RICA: Umana; Estupinan, Elizohdo, Palomino, Grand McDonald, Rojas, Neza, Hernandez, F., Chavarria, Hernandez, L., Nunez.

Dec. 5 1968: HONDURAS (2) 3 JAMAICA (0) 1. Tequcigalpa. 7,441.
HONDURAS: Avila; Deras Manzanares, Warrier, Connor, Mairet, Abate, Fajardo, Arevalo, Murillo, Elvir, Guevara.
JAMAICA: Constantine; Pearce, Largie, H., Scott, Brown, F., Brown, L., Hamilton, Mason, Largie, D., Dunkley, Welsh.

Dec. 8 1968: HONDURAS (1) 2 JAMAICA (0) 0. Tegucigalpa. 3,577.
HONDURAS: Avila; Manzanares, Maibet, Warrier, Connor, Coello, Abate, Fajardo, Murillo, Elvir, Guevara.
JAMAICA: Constantine; Dawkins, Largie, H., Scott, Brown, F., Brown, L., Dwaes, Cole, Largie, D., Dunkley, Welsh.

Dec. 22 1968: HONDURAS (0) 1 COSTA RICA (0) 0. Tegucigalpa. 8,724.
HONDURAS: Avila; Manzanares, Warrier, Welch, Bulnes, Mendoza, Rosales, Gomez, Urquia, Bran, Ferrera.
COSTA RICA: Umana; Estupinan, Elizohdo, Rojas, Calvo, Quiroz, Vega, Martin, Saenz, Hernandez, Lopez.

Dec. 29 1968: COSTA RICA (1) 1 HONDURAS (1) 1. San Jose. 21,636.
COSTA RICA: Gutierrez; Quiroz, Gomez, Rojas, Grant McDonald, Vega, Salas, Levy, Hall, Acuna, Hernandez.
HONDURAS: Avila; Matamoros, Warrier, Zelaya, Welch, Mendoza, Rosales, Ferrera, Gomez, Elvir, Guevara.

First Preliminary Round: Sub Group 13.2

Nov. 17 1968	Guatemala 4　Trinidad 0	Guatemala City
Nov. 20	Trinidad 0　Guatemala 0	Guatemala City
Nov. 23	Trinidad 0　Haiti 4	Port au Prince
Nov. 25	Haiti 2　Trinidad 4	Port au Prince
Dec. 8	Haiti 2　Guatemala 0	Port au Prince
Feb. 23 1969	Guatemala 1　Haiti 1	Guatemala City

FINAL TABLE

	P	W	D	L	F	A	Pts
Haiti	4	2	1	1	9	5	5
Guatemala	4	1	2	1	5	3	4
Trinidad	4	1	1	2	4	10	3

Nov. 17 1968: GUATEMALA (1) 4 TRINIDAD (0) 0. Guatemala City 26,845.
GUATEMALA: Garcia: Oliva, Camposeco, De Leon, Melgar, A., Montoya, Torres, Melgar, N., Pena, Valdez, Stokes.
TRINIDAD: Mouttet; Steadman, Murren, De La Bastide, David, Areey, De Leon, Cummins, Haynes, Cave, Archibald.

Nov. 20 1968: TRINIDAD (0) 0 GUATEMALA (0) 0. Guatemala City. 16,215,
TRINIDAD: Mouttet; Roijdon, Murren, De La Bastide, Steadman, Butcher, De Leon, Aimey, Cummins, Haynes, Archibald.
GUATEMALA: Garcia; Oliva, Camposeco, Melgar, A., Villavicencio, Torres, Slusher, Melgar, N., Chacon, Valdez, Stokes.

Nov. 23 1968: TRINIDAD (0) 0 HAITI (1) 4. Port au Prince. 6,368.
TRINIDAD: Mouttet; Rondon, Steadman, Butcher, Murren, De La Bastide, Cummins, De Leon, Haynes, Cave, Archibald.
HAITI: Franciolln; Argelus, Legros, Gilles, Ducoste, Vorbe, Barthelmy, Guillaume, Obas, St Vil, Francois.

Nov. 25 1968: HAITI (2) 4 TRINIDAD (1) 2. Port au Prince. 2,233.
HAITI: Francillon; Argelus, Ducoste, Legros, Gilles, Vorbe, Barthelmy, Guillaume, Obas, St Surin, Francois.
TRINIDAD: Mouttet; David, Rondon, Murren, Butcher, Murren, De La Bastide, Cummins, De Leon, Haynes, Cave, Archibald.

Dec. 8 1968: HAITI (2) 2 GUATEMALA (0) 0. Port au Prince. 7,755.
HAITI: Francillon; Argelus, Ducoste, Legros, Gilles, Obas, Barthelmy, St Surin, Desier, Guillaume, Francois.
GUATEMALA: Garcia; Oliva, Camposeco, Leon, Melgar, A., Torres, Roldan, Stokes, Valdez.

Feb. 23 1969: GUATEMALA (1) 1 HAITI (0) 1. Guatemala City. 31,728.
GUATEMALA: Gonzales, J.; Lopez, Camposeco, De Leon, Ochoa, Montoya, Roldan, Torres, Melgar, N., Pena, Gonzales, E.
HAITI: Francillon; Argelus, Ducoste, Legros, Formose, Phillipe, Obas, Barthelmy, Desier, St Vil, Francois.

First Preliminary Round: Sub Group 13.3

Nov. 24 1968	Surinam 6	N. Antilles 0	Paramaribo
Dec. 1	El Salvador 6	Surinam 0	San Salvador
Dec. 5	N. Antilles 2	Surinam 0	Aruba
Dec. 12	El Salvador 1	N. Antilles 0	San Salvador
Dec. 15	N. Antilles 1	El Salvador 2	San Salvador
Dec. 22	Surinam 4	El Salvador 1	Paramaribo

FINAL TABLE

	P	W	D	L	F	A	Pts
El Salvador	4	3	0	1	10	5	6
Surinam	4	2	0	2	10	9	4
N. Antilles	4	1	0	3	3	9	2

Nov. 24 1968: SURINAM (3) 6 NETHERLANDS ANTILLES (0) 0. Paramaribo. 4,140.

SURINAM: Barron; Boschman, Elliot, Wong Swie Sang, Purperhart, Hoft, Waterval, Schal, Vanenburg, Schoonhoven, Corte.

NETHERLANDS ANTILLES: Diaz; Pablo, Constancia, E., Flores, Dubero, Loefstok, J., Martina, Constancia, J., Luydema, Loefstok, M., Brokke.

Dec. 1 1968: EL SALVADOR (1) 6 SURINAM (0) 0. San Salvador. 10,037.

EL SALVADOR: Fernandez; Rivas, Castro, Vasquez, Mena, Cabezas, Quintanilla, Azucar, Martinez, Barraza, Estrada.

SURINAM: Barron; Hoff, Boschman, Elliot, Wong Swie Sang, Purperhart, Schal, Schoonhoven, Waterval, Bosthwizen, Corte.

Dec. 5 1968: NETHERLANDS ANTILLES (0) 2 SURINAM (0) 0. Aruba. 1,592.

NETHERLANDS ANTILLES: Diaz; Pablo, Flores, Wernet, Loefstok, J., Loefstok, M., Dubero, Martina, Driksz, Brokke, Luydens.

SURINAM: Barron; Wong Swie Sang, Boschman, Hoft, Elliot, Corte, Purperhart, Schoonhoven, Waterval, Schal, Oosthuizen.

Dec. 12 1968: EL SALVADOR (0) 1 NETHERLANDS ANTILLES (0) 0. San Salvador. 12,205.

EL SALVADOR: Fernandez; Rivas, Castro, Vasquez, Mena, Quintanilla, Bucaro, Azucar, Martinez, Barraza, Valiente.

NETHERLANDS ANTILLES: Diaz; Loefstok, J., Pablo, Bikker, Constancia, Wernet, Driksz, Dubero, Loefstok, M., Martina, Luydens.

Dec. 15 1968: NETHERLANDS ANTILLES (0) 1 EL SALVADOR (0) 2. San Salvador. 13,059.

NETHERLANDS ANTILLES: Diaz; Flores, Constancia, E., Pablo, Loefstok, J., Wernet, Dubero, Victoria, Martina, Driksz, Luydens, Loefstok, M., Constancia, J.

EL SALVADOR: Fernandes; Rivas, Castro, Vasquez, Mena, Cabezas, Quintanilla, Rodriuez, Barraza, Valiente.

Dec. 22 1968: SURINAM (3) 4 EL SALVADOR (1) 1. Paramaribo. 4,327.

SURINAM: Barron; Hoft, Wong Swie Sang, Elliot, Corte (sub Schoonhoven), Weidum, Vanenburg (sub Waterval), Schal, Lagadeau, Purperhart, Oosthuizen.

EL SALVADOR: Fernandes; Rivas (sub Mejia), Castro, Vasquez, Mena, Quintanilla (sub Cabezas), Bucaro, Azucar, Monge, Gonzalez, Aceredo.

First Preliminary Round: Sub Group 13.4

Oct. 6 1968   Canada 4 Bermuda 0   Toronto

Oct. 13	Canada 4	United States 2	Toronto
Oct. 20	Bermuda 0	Canada 0	Hamilton
Oct. 26	United States 1	Canada 0	Atlanta
Nov. 3	United States 6	Bermuda 2	Kansas City
Nov. 11	Bermuda 0	United States 2	Hamilton

FINAL TABLE

	P	W	D	L	F	A	Pts
United States	4	3	0	1	11	6	6
Canada	4	2	1	1	8	3	5
Bermuda	4	0	1	3	2	12	1

Oct. 6 1968: CANADA (1) 4 (Vigh, Zenatta, Papadakis 2) BERMUDA (0) 0. Toronto. 3,432.
CANADA: Greco; Berry, Lenarduzzi, Kerr, Lecce, Di Luca, McPate, Papadakis, Vigh, Harvey, Zenatta.
BERMUDA: Nusum; Simons, Minors, Smith, R., Cann, Cholmondley (sub Smith, L.), Hunt, Ming, Darrell (sub Armstrong), Romaine, Lewis.

Oct. 13 1968: CANADA (1) 4 (McPate 2, Patterson, Vigh) UNITED STATES (1) 2 (Roy, Stritzel). Toronto. 5,959.
CANADA: Greco; Berry, Lenarduzzi, Kerr, Lecce, Di Luca, McPate, Papadakis ((sub Patterson), Vigh, Harvey, Zenatta.
UNITED STATES: De Long; Kofler, Clear, Bachmeier, Gansler, Krat, Millar, Baker, Roy, Stritzel, Albrecht.

Oct. 20 1968: BERMUDA (0) 0 CANADA (0) 0. Hamilton. 5,324.
BERMUDA: Nusum; Minors, Simons, Romaine, Cann, K., Ming, Cann, W., Smith, Hunt, Darrell, Trott.
CANADA: Greco; Berry, Lenarduzzi, Lecce, Di Luca, Harvey, Kerr, McPate, Vigh, Papadakis, Zenatta.

Oct. 26 1968: UNITED STATES (0) 1 (Albrecht) CANADA (0) 0. Atlanta. 2,727.
UNITED STATES: Feher; Gansler, Murphy, Krat, Gentile, Bachmeier, Stritzel, Albrecht, Millar, Baker, Roy.
CANADA: Harper; Berry, Lecce, Di Luca, Lenarduzzi, Kerr, Harvey, Hansen, McPate, Vigh, Papadakis.

Nov. 3 1968: UNITED STATES (2) 6 (Millar 3, Baker 2, Roy) BERMUDA (1) 2 (Trott, Best). Kansas City. 2,235. Approx. 500.
UNITED STATES: Feher (sub De Long); Gansler, Krat, Gentile, Bachmeier, Murphy, Millar, Baker, Roy, Stritzel, Albrecht.
BERMUDA: Nusum (sub Jennings); Simons, Minors, Ming, Cann, Dowling, Daniels, Romaine, Best, Darrell, Trott.

Nov. 11 1968: BERMUDA (0) 0 UNITED STATES (2) 2 (Smith, H., o.g., Roy). Hamilton. 2,942.
BERMUDA: Jennings; Daniels, Minors, Smith, H., Cann, Dowling, Hunt, Smith, L., Best, Trott, Lewis.
UNITED STATES: De Long; Gentile, Krat, Benedek, Bachmeier, Murphy, Millar, Baker, Roy, Stritzel, Albrecht.

GROUP THIRTEEN RESULTS

Second Preliminary Round: Sub Group 13.5

June 8 1969	Honduras 1 El Salvador 0	Tegucigalpa
June 15	El Salvador 3 Honduras 0	San Salvador

PLAY-OFF

June 27	El Salvador 3 Honduras 2	Mexico City

June 8 1969: HONDURAS (0) 1 EL SALVADOR (0). Tegucigalpa. 17,827.

HONDURAS: Avila; Bulnes, Dick, Welch, Metcalfe, Mendoza, Marshal, Rosales, Cardona, Gomez, Bran.

EL SALVADOR: Fernandez; Rivas, Castor, Meridua, Osorio, Quintanilla, Vasquez, Barraza, Rodriquez, Martinez, Estrada.

June 15 1969: EL SALVADOR (3) 3 (Martinez 2, Acevedo) HONDURAS (0) 0. San Salvador. 36,470.

EL SALVADOR: Fernandez; Acevedo, Monge, Rodriquez, Quintanilla, Flamenco, Manzane (Osorio), Vasquez, Marions, Martinez, Rivas.

HONDURAS: Avila; Matamoros, Wells, Bulnes, Marshal (Rivera), Mendoza, Urquilla (sub Roxica), Gomez, Cardona, Bran, Rosales.

PLAY-OFF

June 27 1969: EL SALVADOR (2) 3 (Martinez 2, Rodriquez) HONDURAS (2) 2 (Cordona, Gomez) (after extra time; 90-minute score 2–2). Mexico City. 15,326.

EL SALVADOR: Fernandez; Rivas, Ansano, Cabezas, Marions, Vasquez, Quintanilla, Monge, Rodriquez, Acevedo, Martinez.

HONDURAS: Avila; Deras, Welch, Mendoza, Bulnes, Dick, Cardenas, Marshal, Gomez, Rosales, Bran.

Sub Group 13.6

April 20 1969	Haiti 2 United States 0	Port au Prince
May 11	United States 0 Haiti 1	San Diego, Cal.

April 20 1969: HAITI (2) 2 (Barthelmy, Millar o.g.) UNITED STATES (0) 0. Port au Prince. 6,917.

HAITI: Francillon; Argelus, Legros, Ducoste, Formose, Vorbe, Obas, Barthelemy, Desier, St Vil, Francois.

UNITED STATES: Banach; Mata, Cameron, Murphy, Krat, Stritzel, Bachmeier, Abouza (sub McBride), Miller, Roy, Albrecht.

May 12 1969: UNITED STATES (0) 0 HAITI (1) 1 (St Vil). San Diego, Cal. 4,274.

UNITED STATES: Banach; Bachmeier, Krat, Murphy, Mata, Stritzel, Hausmann, Maliszewski, Millar, Baker, Albrecht.

HAITI: Francillon; Argelus, Gilles, Ducoste, Obas, Desier, Barthelemy, St Vil, Francois, Vorbe, Lecros.

GROUP THIRTEEN RESULTS

Third Preliminary Round

Sept. 21 1969	Haiti 1 El Salvador 2	Port au Prince

Sept. 28	El Salvador 0	Haiti 3	San Salvador
PLAY-OFF			
Oct. 8	El Salvador 1	Haiti 0	Kingston, Jamaica
	(after extra time)		

Sept. 21 1969: HAITI (0) 1 (Obas) EL SALVADOR (1) 2 (Acevedo, Rodriguez). Port au Prince. 10,415.

HAITI: Francillon; Formose, Argelus, Desier, Legros, Ducoste, Obas, Barthelemy, St Vil, Vorbe, Francois.

EL SALVADOR: Suarez; Rivas, Ansano, Cabezas, Mariana, Vasquez, Martinez, Rodriguez, Monge, Quintanilla, Acevedo.

Sept. 28 1969: EL SALVADOR (0) 0 HAITI (3) 3 (Desier, Francois, Barthelemy). San Salvador. 36,403.

EL SALVADOR: Suarez; Rivas, Ansano, Cabezas, Mariana, Vasquez, Rodriguez, Martinez (sub Torres), Monge, Quintanilla, Acevedo.

HAITI: Francillon; Argelus, Guillal, Vorbe, Legros, Ducoste, Barthelemy, Francois, Desier, Obas, St Vil.

PLAY-OFF

Oct. 8 1969: HAITI (0) 0 EL SALVADOR (0) 1 (Martinez) (after extra time; 90-minute score 0–0). Kingston, Jamaica. 6,742.

HAITI: Francillon; Argelus, Guillal, Legros, Ducoste, Vorbe, Bayonnen, Barthelemy, Francois, Desier, St Vil.

EL SALVADOR: Fernandez; Rivas, Mariana, Vasquez, Mongano, Flamenco, Quintanilla, Rodriquez, Monge, Martinez, Acevedo.

GROUP FOURTEEN

Mexico, as host country, qualified automatically for the finals.

GROUP FIFTEEN

The Asian and Oceania Group Fifteen provided F.I.F.A. with more headaches than any of the other groups. First of all, they had to tackle the complaint of North Korea, surprise finalists in the 1966 World Cup and shock winners over Italy. Drawn with New Zealand and Israel, they refused to play against Israel. Consequently they took no part in the competition, which left New Zealand and Israel to play off in one sub-group.

Next came the problem of Rhodesia, who were drawn with South Korea, Australia and Japan in another sub-group which was to be played at Seoul. But the South Koreans were not prepared to grant visas for the Rhodesians to enter the country.

F.I.F.A. decided to make another sub-group, putting Rhodesia in with the winners of the Seoul tournament, with the winners to meet the winners of the Israel v. New Zealand matches!

Australia, with the help of nine players from England who had emigrated, won the Seoul tournament, which led to a protest from

South Korea about the eligibility of the players, but this was over-ruled by F.I.F.A., who said they had Australian passports.

Israel twice beat New Zealand, the matches being played in Tel Aviv to cut down travelling expenses. The problem now was where to play the Rhodesia v. Australia tie with so many countries closed to the Rhodesians. Finally, Lourenço Marques in Mozambique was agreed, and the Australians once again had to make a long journey for their matches. But after two drawn ties they won a play-off and qualified to meet Israel for the right to go to Mexico.

The first match took place in Tel Aviv and the Israelis, through Giora Spiegel, won by a single goal. The margin might, however, have been more if Spiegel had not missed a penalty. Ten days later the two countries met again on the Sydney Sports ground and Australia's hopes disappeared when Mordecai Spigler put Israel ahead ten minutes from the end. Although Watkiss equalised seven minutes later, Israel went into the final stages for the first time in their history.

The man responsible for their success was Emanuel Schaefer, 45, a tough German-born ex-player of Polish parentage, who played the game in Poland and Israel and graduated through the youth team to take charge of the Israel national side two years ago. He believes in German football and has tried to model the side on that style of play.

GROUP FIFTEEN RESULTS

First Preliminary Round: Sub Group 15.1

Oct. 10 1969	Japan 1 Australia 3	Seoul
Oct. 12	South Korea 1 Japan 2	Seoul
Oct. 14	Australia 2 South Korea 1	Seoul
Oct. 16	Japan 1 Australia 1	Seoul
Oct. 18	South Korea 2 Japan 0	Seoul
Oct. 20	Australia 1 South Korea 1	Seoul

FINAL TABLE

	P	W	D	L	F	A	Pts
Australia	4	2	2	0	7	4	6
South Korea	4	1	2	1	6	5	4
Japan	4	0	2	2	4	8	2

Oct. 10 1969: JAPAN (1) 1 (Watanabe) AUSTRALIA (1) 3 (McColl, Ogi o.g., Baartz). Seoul. 2,513.

JAPAN: Yokoyama; Katayama, Onishi, Mori, Yamaguchi, Kamata, Watanabe (sub Kimura), Ogi (sub M. Miyamoto), Kuwahara, Miyamoto, T., Sugiyama.

AUSTRALIA: Corry; Keith, Ackerley, Warren, Schaefer, Marnoch, McColl, Abonyi, Baartz, Watkiss, Perin (sub Vojtek).

Oct. 12 1969: JAPAN (1) 2 (Miyamoto, T., Kuwahara) SOUTH KOREA (2) 2 (Kim Ki-Bok, Park Soo II). Seoul. 16,520.

JAPAN: Yokoyama; Kikukawa, Katayama, Yamaguchi, Kamata, Ogi, Matsumoto, Mori, Kuwahara, Miyamoto, T., Sugiyama.

SOUTH KOREA: Lee Sae Yun; Seo Toon Chan, Kim Yoon Chan, Kim Jung Suk, Lim Kook Cham (sub Park Lee Chun), Kim Ho, Kim Jung Nam, Park Soo II, Lee Lee Woo, Lee Hae Tak, Kim Ki-Bok, Yung Byung Taik (Hong In Woong).

Oct. 14 1969: AUSTRALIA (1) 2 (Watkiss, McColl) SOUTH KOREA (1) 1 (Lee Woo). Seoul. 10,250.

AUSTRALIA: Corry; Keith, Marnoch, Ackerley, Schaefer, Watkiss, McColl, Abonyi, Warren, Baartz, Vojtek.

SOUTH KOREA: So Cho Myung; Kim Jung Suk, Chu Chung So, Seo Yoon Chan, Kim Ho, Kim Jung Nam, Park Lee Chan, Lee Hae Tak, Lee Lee Woo, Kim Ki-Bok (sub Hong In Woong), Park Soo II.

Oct. 16 1969: AUSTRALIA (1) 1 (McColl) JAPAN (1) 1 (Miyamoto, T.). Seoul. 1,359.

AUSTRALIA: Corry; Keith, Ackerley, Warren, Schaefer, Marnoch, McColl, Abonyi, Baartz, Watkiss, Vojtek.

JAPAN: Yokoyama; Katayama, Mori (sub Kawano), Kunieda, Yamaguchi, Kamata, Kuwahara, Ogi, Matsumoto (sub Watanabe), Miyamoto, T., Sugiyama.

Oct. 18 1969: SOUTH KOREA (2) 2 (Chung Kang Chi 2) JAPAN (0) 0. Seoul. 9,264.

SOUTH KOREA: Lee Sae Yun; Seo Toon Chan, Lim Kook Cham, Kim Jung Suk, Jim Ho, Kim Jung Nam, Chung Kang Chi, Lee Hae Tak (sub Park Lee Chan), Lee Lee Woo (sub Park Soo II), Hong In Wong, Yung Byung Taik.

JAPAN: Funamoto; Katayama, Kunieda, Mori, Yamaguchi, Kikukawa (sub Kamata), Watanabe, Yaguichi (Miyamoto, M.), Kuwahara, Ogi, Sugiyama.

Oct. 20 1969: SOUTH KOREA (1) 1 (Park Soo II) AUSTRALIA (1) 1 (Baartz). Seoul. 9,675.

SOUTH KOREA: So Cho Myung; Kim Jung Suk, Chu Chung So, Seo Yoon Chan, Kim Ho, Kim Jung Nam, Lee Lee Woo, Park Soo II, Kim Ki-Bok, Park Lee Chan, Lee Hae Tak.

AUSTRALIA: Corry; Keith, Ackerley, Warren, Schaefer, Marnoch (sub Zeman), McColl, Abonyi (Rutherford), Baartz, Perin, Vojtek.

First Preliminary Round: Sub Group 15.2

Sept. 28 1969	Israel 4 New Zealand 0	Tel Aviv
Oct. 1	New Zealand 0 Israel 2	Tel Aviv
	North Korea withdrew.	

Sept. 28 1969: ISRAEL (0) 4 (Spigler, Spiegel, Feigenbaum 2) NEW ZEALAND (0) 0. Tel Aviv. 26,669.

ISRAEL: Vissoker; Bar, Bello, Rozen, Primo, Rozenthal, Spiegel, Spigler, Talbi, Feigenbaum, Shum.

NEW ZEALAND: Phillips; Latimour, Moyes, Griffiths, Hunter, De Graaf, Bilby, Bland, Guilden, Thomas, Mears.

Oct. 1 1969: ISRAEL (2) 2 (Spiegel, Spigler).

ISRAEL: Vissoker; Bar, Bello, Primo, Shum, Shuruk, Spiegel, Spigler, Talbi, Feigenbaum, Vollavh.

NEW ZEALAND: Phillips; Latimour, Moyes, Griffiths, Hunter, Bilby, Mears, Bruce, Guilden, Bland, Legg.

GROUP FIFTEEN RESULTS

Second Preliminary Round

Nov. 23 1969	Australia 1	Rhodesia 1	Lourenco Marques, Mozambique
Nov. 27	Rhodesia 0	Australia 0	Lourenco Marques, Mozambique
PLAY-OFF			
Nov. 29	Australia 3	Rhodesia 1	Lourenco Marques, Mozambique

Nov. 23 1969: AUSTRALIA (0) 1 (McColl) RHODESIA (0) 1 (Thompson). Lourenco Marques. 3,540.

AUSTRALIA: Corry; Keith, Ackerley, Schaefer, Murdoch, Walsh, Rutherford (sub Vojtek), Abonyi, Alston, Baartz, McColl.

RHODESIA: Jordan; Knowles, Togere, Haddon, Chibaya, Siranda, Nxumado, Chalmers, Robertson, Grainger, Shaya.

Nov. 27 1969: RHODESIA (0) 0 AUSTRALIA (0) 0. Lourenco Marques. 2,512.

RHODESIA: Jordan; Knowles, Chieza, Haddon, Siranda, Togere, Nxumado, Robertson, Grainger, Chalmers, Marapa.

AUSTRALIA: Corry; Ackerley, Keith, Schaefer, Murdoch, Walsh, Abonyi, Baartz, Warren, Watkiss (sub Rutherford), Vojtek.

Nov. 29 1969: AUSTRALIA (2) 3 (Rutherford 2, Tigere o.g.) RHODESIA (0) 1 (Chalmers). Lourenco Marques. 1,066.

AUSTRALIA: Corry; Terryn, Keith, Schaefer, Marnoch, Walsh, Abonyi, Baartz, Warren, Rutherford, Vojtek.

RHODESIA: Jordan (sub Gilbert); Knowles, Chieza, Haddon, Siranda, Tigere, Nxumado, Marapa, Grainger, Chalmers, Shaya.

GROUP FIFTEEN RESULTS

Third Preliminary Round

Dec. 4 1969	Israel 1	Australia 0	Tel Aviv
Dec. 14	Australia 1	Israel 1	Sydney

Dec. 4 1969: ISRAEL (1) 1 (Spiegel) AUSTRALIA (0) 0. Tel Aviv· 26,666.

ISRAEL: Vissoker; Bar (sub Lubetski), Bello, Rosenthal, Shuruk, Rosen, Talki, Spigler, Fiegenbaum, Spiegel, Schum.

AUSTRALIA: Corry; Keith, Ackerley, Watkiss, Schaefer, Zeman, Abonyi, Rutherford, Baartz, Warren, McColl (sub Vojtek).

Dec. 14 1969: AUSTRALIA (0) 1 (Watkiss) ISRAEL (0) 1 (Spigler). Sydney. 10,898.

AUSTRALIA: Corry; Keith, Ackerley, Schaefer, Marnoch, Walsh, Abonyi, Watkiss, Warren, Baartz, Vojtek.

ISRAEL: Vissoker; Bar, Bello, Primo, Rosen, Rosenthal, Talbi, Spiegel, Feigenbaum, Spigler, Schum.

GROUP SIXTEEN

The eleven nations in the African Group Sixteen, who are clamouring for more places in the final stages of the World Cup, were finally reduced after 24 matches to one—Morocco, who went to Mexico threatening not to compete because they might have to meet Israel, almost a repetition of their attitude in the 1968 Olympics.

Ghana received a bye in the first round of games which consisted of five groups, and joined Tunisia, Morocco—who needed a play-off with Senegal—Ethiopia, Sudan—who won by scoring most goals in the second game with Zambia—and Nigeria in the second round.

Again Morocco had a struggle to get through their second round tie. Following two goalless draws with Tunisia, a third draw followed in the play-off in Marseilles and only by winning the toss of the disc did they progress. Even the toss brought a protest from Tunisia, which was overruled. Ghana were surprisingly eliminated by Nigeria, who, with Sudan, joined Morocco for the third and final round.

This round was played on a League basis with the countries meeting home and away after a Moroccan proposal for a three match tournament in a neutral country, Spain, Italy or Algeria, had been rejected. Once again Morocco won through, although beaten in their final match by Nigeria. That, however, was Nigeria's only victory.

GROUP SIXTEEN RESULTS

First Preliminary Round: Sub Group 16.1

Nov. 17 1968	Algeria 1	Tunisia 2	Algiers
Dec. 29	Tunisia 0	Algeria 0	Tunis

Sub Group 16.2

Nov. 3 1968	Morocco 1	Senegal 0	Casablanca
Jan. 5 1969	Senegal 2	Morocco 1	Dakar
PLAY-OFF			
Feb. 17 1969	Morocco 2	Senegal 0	Las Palmas

Sub Group 16.3

Jan. 26 1969	Libya 2	Ethiopia 0	Benghazi
Feb. 9	Ethiopia 5	Libya 1	Addis Ababa

Sub Group 16.4
Oct. 27 1968   Zambia 4   Sudan 2   Lusaka
Nov. 8   Sudan 4   Zambia 2   Khartoum
                 (after extra time; Sudan won most goals in second game)

Sub Group 16.5
Dec. 7 1968   Nigeria 1   Camerouns 1   Lagos
Dec. 22   Camerouns 2 Nigeria 3   Douala

Sub Group 16.6
                 Ghana a bye.

Sub Group 16.1
Nov. 17 1968: ALGERIA (1) 1 (Amirouche, pen.) TUNISIA (0) 2 (Chakroun 2). Algiers. 13,419.

ALGERIA: Krimo; Aulkhler, Khiari, Attoul, Amar, Djemas, Hadefi, Amircouhe (sub Hachouf), Lalmas, Soukhane, Achour.

TUNISIA: Attouga; Zouaoul, Habacha, Douiri, M'Ghirbi, Laroussi (sub Kechra), Mahdi, Chaibi (sub Fendri), Trabel, Cheman, Chakroun.

Dec. 29 1968: TUNISIA (0) 0 ALGERIA (0) 0. Tunis. 36,814.

TUNISIA: Attouga; Zouaoul, Habacha, M'Ghirbi, Benzarti, Laroussi, Douiri, Chaibi, Cheman, Belbhith, Chakroun.

ALGERIA: Abrouk; Belloueif, Tayer (sub Tahar), Hadefi, Haddi, Salem, Mekloufi, Lalmas, Natouri, Lekkak, Ben Tahar (sub Salimi).

Sub Group 16.2
Nov. 3 1968: MOROCCO (0) 1 SENEGAL (0) 0. Casablanca. 2,582.

MOROCCO: Kassou; Boujemaa, Filali, Fadila, Malhi, Hajjami, Tazi, Bamous, Zarouil, Faras, Zahid.

SENEGAL: Thiam; Diagne, Gueye, M'Baye, Dieng, Gomis, Dieme, Ba, Cisse, Diarra, Diop.

Jan. 5 1969: SENEGAL (2) 2 MOROCCO (1) 1. Dakar. 11,487.

SENEGAL: Thiam; Gueye, Diagne, M'Baye, Dieng, Gomis, Dieme, Cisse, Diop, Toure, Saar.

MOROCCO: Kassou; Filali, Boujemaa, Maaroufi, Sahraoui, Lamrani, Tazi, Akesbi, Bamous, El Kayati, Chinoune.

PLAY-OFF
Feb. 17 1969: MOROCCO (0) 2 SENEGAL (0) 0. Las Palma. 7,924.

MOROCCO: Kassou; Lamrani, Boujemaa, Hafnapui, Maaroufi, Bamous, Khezzar, Bouassa, Sarir, Ghazouani.

SENEGAL: Thiam; Diagne, Gueye, M'Baye, Dieng, Gomis, Coulibaly, Cisse, Ba, Diarra, Saar.

Sub Group 16.3
Jan. 26 1969: LIBYA (1) 2 ETHIOPIA (0) 0. Benghazi. 5,687.

LIBYA: Mohamed, M.; Abdessalom, Azddin, Mortar, Hachmi, Naggur, Mohamed, R., Ali, Mohamed, K., Mahmoud, Admed.

ETHIOPIA: Abebe Getachew; Booreziom, Ismael, Awad, Aberaha, Abdo Getachew, Germa, Mengstu, Esha, Geremew, Wolde Getachew.

The Road to Mexico 79

Feb. 9 1969: ETHIOPIA (2) 5 LIBYA (1) 1. Addis Ababa. 6,759.
LIBYA: Abebe Getachew; Bekursion, Ismael, Aberaha, Awad, Worku,
Germa, Feseha, Abdo Getachew, Geremew, Solomon.
ETHIOPIA: Abouahoud Ali; Abdessalom, Azddin, Mortar, Hachemi,
Mohammed, A., Mohammed, R., Baski Ali, Mohamed, K., Mahmoud,
Admed.

Sub Group 16.4
Oct. 27 1968: ZAMBIA (2) 4 SUDAN (1) 2. Lusaka. 11,714.
ZAMBIA: Malama; Musamali, Musonda, Chama, Mwila, Stephenson,
Simutowe, Kapengwe, Makinaza, Chitalu, Kaposa.
SUDAN: Abdelhziza; Mabrouk, Salim, Abdelgadir, Hassan, Elmar,
Bushra, Abbarer, Ismael, El Fadil, Gadalla.

Nov. 8 1968: SUDAN (1) 4 ZAMBIA (1) 2. Khartoum. 17,083.
SUDAN: Abdelhziza; Abdelgadir, Awad Rora, Kawarti, Samir, Bushra,
Rafi, Gagdoul, Santo, Ismael, Hassabou.
ZAMBIA: Malama; Stephenson, Musonda, Chama, Makinaza, Sokazwe,
Simutowe, Mwila, Chitalu, Kapengwe, Kaposa.

Sub Group 16.5
Dec. 7 1968: NIGERIA (0) 1 CAMEROUNS (0) 1. Lagos. 7,201.
NIGERIA: Fregene; Igwe, Ofuokwu, Obojemene, Olumobeji, Opone,
Aghoghokia, Olayombo, Brodick, Sava, Salami.
CAMEROUNS: Alangama; Moukoko, Owona, P., Naaumbe, Oyono,
Mbappe, Bassanguen, Mangana, Owona, N., Essomba, Montassie.

Dec. 22 1968: CAMEROUNS (2) 3 NIGERIA (1) 2. Douala. 6,988.
CAMEROUNS: Alangama; Moukoko, Owona, P., Naaumbe, Epete,
Mbappe, Bassanguen, Ayo, Montasse, Atangama, Owona, N.
NIGERIA (not in line-up order): Opone, Osode, Olayombo, Andrew,
Energuie, Salami, Obojemene, Ofuokwu, Anieke, Nuhri, Olumobeji.

Second Preliminary Round: Sub Group 16.1a
April 26 1969   Tunisia 0   Morocco 0   Tunis
May 18   Morocco 0   Tunisia 0   Casablanca
PLAY-OFF
June 13   Morocco 2   Tunisia 2   Marseilles
                (Morocco won on toss of disc)

Sub Group 16.2b
May 4 1969   Ethiopia 1   Sudan 1   Addis Ababa
May 11   Sudan 3   Ethiopia 1   Khartoum

Sub Group 16.3c
May 10 1969   Nigeria 2   Ghana 1   Ibadan
May 18   Ghana 1   Nigeria 1   Accra

Sub Group 16.1a
April 26 1969: TUNISIA (0) 0 MOROCCO (0) 0. Tunis. 26,706.
TUNISIA: Sassi; Benzarti, Douiri, M'Ghirbi, Habacha, Zouaoul,
Halila, Chaibi, Belghit, Cheman, Chakroun.

MOROCCO: Hazzae; Lamrani, Boujemaa, Khannoussi, Slimani, El Fillali, Ayach, Haaroufi, Moumane, Bamous, Ghazouani.

May 18 1969: MOROCCO (0) 0 TUNISIA (0) 0. Casablanca. 9,781.

MOROCCO: Hazzae; El Filali, Boujemaa, Idriss, Slimani, Abdallah, Said, Maaroufi, Houmane, Bamous, Ghazouani.

TUNISIA: Sassi; Benzarti, Douiri, M'Ghirbi, Habacha, Zouaoul, Chaibi, Laroussi, Madhi, Cheman, Chakroun.

PLAY-OFF

June 13 1969: MOROCCO (1) 2 (Idriss, Houmane) TUNISIA (1) 2 (Chaibi, Cheman). Marseilles. 4,185.

MOROCCO: Hazzae; Lamrani, Slimani, Idriss, Boujemaa, Maaroufi, El Fillali, Said, Maghour, Houmane, Farras.

TUNISIA: Attouga; Benzarti, Kiribi, Habacha, Douiri, Trabelsi, Belghit, Chaibi, Telloum, Nourredine, Cheman.

Sub Group 16.2b

May 4 1969: ETHIOPIA 1 SUDAN 1. Addis Ababa. 9,015.

May 11 1969: SUDAN (1) 3 ETHIOPIA (0) 1. Khartoum. 22,373.

SUDAN: Aziz; Ibraham Yahra, Negm El-Div, Mahmoud Salim, Meni, Elvin, Bushra Wahba, Gad Ella, Nesr El-Din Abas, Hider Hassan Abdel Wahar, Samir Salih.

ETHIOPIA: Arebe; Bekuresion, Asthw Kebede, Abataha Araya, Awade Mohamed, Getachew Abdo, Germa Asmaton, Italo Vasalo, Luchan Vasalo, Geremew Zargan, Asefaw Tewlale.

Sub Group 16.3c

May 10 1969: NIGERIA (1) 2 GHANA (0) 1. Ibadan. 25,118.

NIGERIA: Fregene; Igwe, Ofuokwu, Garba, Olumobeji, Opone, Olubode, Olayombo, Sessi, Anieke, Oshode.

GHANA: Mensah; Ankrah, O., Allotey, Amarteifio, Eshun, Christian, Foley, Attaquayefio, Ghartey, Ankrah, A., Al Hassan, Laryea.

May 18 1969: GHANA (1) 1 NIGERIA (1) 1. Accra. 22,386.

GHANA: Addoquaye; Ankrah, O., Allotey, Amarteifio, Eshun, Attaquayefio, Foley, Ankrah, A., Ghartey, Amusa, Ola.

NIGERIA: Fregene; Igwe, Ofuokwu, Brodrick, Olumobeji, Opone, Olubode, Oshode, Garba, Anieke, Lawal.

GROUP SIXTEEN RESULTS

Third Preliminary Round

Sept. 13 1969	Nigeria 2	Sudan 2	Lagos
Sept. 21	Morocco 2	Nigeria 1	Casablanca
Oct. 3	Sudan 3	Nigeria 3	Khartoum
Oct. 10	Sudan 0	Morocco 0	Khartoum
Oct. 26	Morocco 3	Sudan 0	Casablanca
Nov. 8	Nigeria 2	Morocco 0	Ibadan

FINAL TABLE

	P	W	D	L	F	A	Pts
Morocco	4	2	1	1	5	3	5
Nigeria	4	1	2	1	8	7	4
Sudan	4	0	3	1	5	8	3

Sept. 13 1969: NIGERIA (2) 2 SUDAN (2) 2. Lagos. 20,651.
NIGERIA: Fregene; Igwe, Ofuokwu, Obojemene, Olumobeji, Opone, Osode, Eke, Okoye, Anieke, Lawal.
SUDAN: Aziz; Mahmoud Salim, Awad Mesr Musa, Amin Zaki, Gafer Hassan, Bushra Wahba, Ibrahim Yahra, Hider Hassan, Nesr El-Din Abas, Aiz El-Din Osman, Kheir El-Seed.

Sept. 21 1969: MOROCCO (0) 2 NIGERIA (0) 1. Casablanca. 3,600.
MOROCCO: Kassou; Lamrani, Slimani, Idriss, Boujemaa, El Fillali, Maaroufi, Said, Houmane, Faras, Ghazouani.
NIGERIA: Fregene; Adigun, Olumobeji, Dediare, Ofuokwu, Opone, Okoye, Babaloga, Aryee, Line, Lawal.

Oct. 3 1969: SUDAN (1) 3 NIGERIA (0) 3. Khartoum. 26,502.
SUDAN: Aziz; Gafer Hassan, Mahmoud Said, Amin Zaki, Awad Nasr, Ibrahim Yahya, Bushra Wahba, Aiz El-Din Osman, Nasr El-Din Abas, Mohamed El-Beshir, Kheir El-Seed.
NIGERIA: Fregene; Igwe, Ofuokwu, Brodrick, Olumobeji, Opone, Babaloga, Ine, Garba, Eke, Sessi.

Oct. 10 1969: SUDAN (0) 0 MOROCCO (0) 0. Khartoum. 18,020.
SUDAN: Aziz; Mahmoud Said, Awad Wasr, Amin Zaki, Gafer Hassan, Ibrahim Yahya, Bushra Wahba, Mohamed El-Beshir, Aiz El-Din Osman, Babekir Osman, Kheir El-Seed.
MOROCCO: Kassou; Lamrani, Boujemaa, El Fillali, Idriss, Maaroufi, Slimani, Faras, Houmane, Bamous, Said.

Oct. 26 1969: MOROCCO (1) 3 SUDAN (0) 0. Casablanca. 19,600.
MOROCCO: Kassou; Lamrani, Boujemaa, Khannoussi, Slimani, Maaroufi, Said, El Fillali, Houmane, Bamous, Faras.
SUDAN: Aziz; Mahmoud Said, Awad Nasr, Amin Zaki, Gafer Hassan, Noir Awad Abdh, Mohamed El-Beshir, Aiz El-Din Osman, Bushra Wahba, Hassabu Omar.

Nov. 6 1969: NIGERIA (0) 2 MOROCCO (0) 0. Ibadan. 11,156.
NIGERIA: Fregene; Nze, Ofuokwu, Broderick, Olumobeji, Dediare, Osode, Okoye, Aryee, Lawal, Salami.
MOROCCO: Khalidi; Lamrani, Babay, El Filalli, Khalifa, Aniny, El Khiati, Zeghrari, Zarouil, Tazi, El Maghraoui.

6 The World Club Battle of Buenos Aires

Once again the matches for the World Club championship—an unofficial competition which is contested every year between the winners of the European Cup and the winners of the South American Club Championship, the Libertadores de America Cup—raised the question of whether football would be better served if they were discontinued.

Year after year the games produce brawls. The 1969 meeting between A.C. Milan, of Italy, and Estudiantes de la Plata of Argentina—which the Italians won 4–2 on aggregate for the two-legged tie—seemed to go even further away from the skills of football than the previous meetings of Estudiantes and Manchester United, and Racing Club of Buenos Aires and Glasgow Celtic, which had both developed into rough houses.

This time, however, the Argentina Football Association came down heavily on the culprits and handed out tough suspensions right and left, a tacit admission that the style of football played by their representatives was bringing the game into disrepute. This made one wonder why there was all the fuss when Rattin was sent off the field at Wembley during their World Cup match with England in 1966, a game which caused the usual taciturn Sir Alf Ramsey to make his now famous 'animals' reference.

To take the 1969 events in sequence: Estudiantes, who had won the South American championship and the World Club championship the previous year by beating Manchester United, had again qualified to take on the European winners. As part of their preparation they made a summer tour of Spain, playing in various tournaments without any great success but gaining valuable European experience and not showing any signs of violence.

The first leg of the World Club championship against A.C. Milan was set for October 8 in Milan's splendid San Siro Stadium, where an excited crowd of 80,000 saw Milan gain a 3–0 lead through two South American expatriates, the ex-Brazilian Angelo Sormani, 29, who scored two of their goals, and Nestor Combin, the Argentine born ex-French international who had played for France in the World Cup in England in 1966. Milan had snapped up Combin for

£300,000 from Torino just before the league season opened to take the place of their Swedish international, Kurt Hamrin.

Estudiantes gained very few friends by their display in the San Siro stadium and Italian writers were very critical of their play. One said that although Estudiantes had a team of great players they reflected some of the worst evils of Argentine soccer; another accused them of insulting and intimidating the referee, and a third wrote 'The British were right. Estudiantes do not know how to play soccer. They merely aim at the legs.'

How right the critics were was amply born out when the return game came to be played in the Boca Juniors Stadium in Buenos Aires on October 22, when Estudiantes won 2–1, which was not enough to pull back A.C. Milan's first leg lead and force a play-off.

This match was marked by some of the worst fouls seen on a football field with fighting, kicking, spitting and jersey pulling—not unknown in South American football. Two Estudiantes players were sent off by the Chilean referee, Domingo Massaro Conley, and two Italian players carried off on stretchers.

No doubt the Estudiantes players were frustrated by Milan's tactics in putting up their well-known defensive wall in order to protect their three-goal lead, and this was further increased when the Italians went further ahead after half-an-hour through a goal by Gianni Rivera.

Now four goals down the Estudiantes players completely lost their heads as they threw everything into attack. First of all they attacked Milan's left winger Prati, who had to be carried off on a stretcher, and he was replaced by Rognoni. Not surprisingly, under constant pressure the Italian defence cracked and just before half-time Conigliaro got a goal back for Estudiantes, Suarez following immediately with another to make the score at half-time Estudiantes 2–1 in the lead but 4–2 down on aggregate.

A foul by Suarez on Combin in the second half saw the Italian player become the second to need a stretcher to reach the dressing room; the referee requested Suarez also to make for the dressing room and take an early bath. The fighting and the feuding continued and just before the end Manero, of Estudiantes, was sent off to join his colleague Suarez, to complete an unpleasant game of football in which there had been no further scoring but plenty of incident as the game ended.

To their credit the Argentine Football Association acted very quickly. The following day they dealt severely with three Estudiantes players. The goalkeeper, Alberto Poletti, was banned for life for allegedly kicking a Milan player and clashing with Italian supporters after the match; Ramon Aguire Suarez, the centre-half, who was sent off, was banned from 30 league games and from international matches for five years; and Eduardo Manero, the defender also sent off, was banned from 20 league games and from internationals for three years.

The President of Argentina, General Juan Carlos Organta, who watched the match on TV, said that 'some of the Estudiantes players violated the most elementary standards of sporting ethics.'

As if all the incidents on the field were not enough the Argentine police decided to add to them. Apart from arresting the three Estudiantes players for causing a breach of the peace, they also decided to arrest the Milan player, Combin, as he was carried off on the stretcher—were they frightened he might get away?—and charge him with evading military service.

The Milan team refused to fly home without their colleague and finally he was released when it was found that Combin, who left Argentina when he was 17, had done his military service in France. This was all in order with the Argentine military authorities under an agreement between the two countries.

WORLD CLUB CHAMPIONS

1960	Real Madrid (Spain)
1961	Penarol (Uruguay)
1962	Santos (Brazil)
1963	Santos (Brazil)
1964	Inter-Milan (Italy)
1965	Inter-Milan (Italy)
1966	Penarol (Uruguay)
1967	Racing Club Buenos Aires (Argentina)
1968	Estudiantes de la Plata (Argentina)
1969	A.C. Milan (Italy)

July 3 1960: PENAROL (Uruguay) 0 REAL MADRID (Spain) 0. Montevideo.

PENAROL: Maidena; Martinez, Aguerre, Pino, Salvador, Goncalves, Cubilla, Linazza, Hohberg, Spencer, Borges.

REAL MADRID: Dominquez; Marquitos, Santamaria, Pachin, Zarraga, Vidal, Canario, Del Sol, Di Stefano, Puskas, Bueno.

Sept. 4 1960: REAL MADRID 5 (Puskas 2, Di Stefano, Hererra, Gento) PENAROL 1 (Borges). Madrid.

REAL MADRID: Dominquez; Marquitos, Santamaria, Pachin, Vidal, Zarraga, Herrera, Del Sol, Di Stefano, Puskas, Gento.

PENAROL: Maidena; Pino, Mayewski, Martinez, Aguerre, Salvador, Cubilla, Linazza, Hohberg, Spencer, Borges.

Real Madrid won.

Sept. 4 1961: BENFICA (Portugal) 1 (Coluna) PENAROL (Uruguay) 0. Lisbon.

BENFICA: Costa Pereira; Angelo, Sariva, Joao, Neto, Cruz, Augusto, Santana, Aguas, Coluna, Cavem.

PENAROL: Maldena; Gonzales, Martinez, Cano, Aguerre, Goncalves, Spencer, Cubilla, Cabrera, Sasia, Ledesma.

Sept. 17 1961: PENAROL 5 (Sasia pen., Joya 2, Spencer 2) BENFICA 0. Montevideo.

PENAROL: Maldena; Gonzales, Martinez, Cano, Aguerre, Goncalves, Cubilla, Ledesma, Sasia, Spencer, Joya.

BENFICA: Costa Pereira; Angelo, Sariva, Joao, Neto, Cruz, Augusto, Santana, Mendes, Coluna, Cavem.

Sept. 19 1961: PENAROL 2 (Sasia 2, 1 pen.) BENFICA 1 (Eusebio). Montevideo.

PENAROL: Maldena; Gonzales, Martinez, Cano, Aguerre, Goncalves, Cubilla, Ledesma, Sasia, Spencer.

BENFICA: Costa Pereira; Angelo, Humberto, Cruz, Neto, Coluna, Augusto, Eusebio, Aguas, Cavem, Simoes.

Penarol won.

Sept. 19 1962: SANTOS (Brazil) 3 (Pele 2, Coutinho) BENFICA (Portugal) 2 (Santana 2). Rio de Janeiro.

SANTOS: Gilmar; Lima, Mauro, Zito, Calvet, Dalmo, Dorval, Mengalvio, Coutinho, Pele, Pepe.

BENFICA: Rita; Angelo, Humberto, Raul, Cavem, Cruz, Augusto, Santana, Eusebio, Coluna, Simoes.

Oct. 11 1962: BENFICA 2 (Eusebio, Santana) SANTOS 5 (Pele 3, Coutinho, Pepe). Lisbon.

BENFICA: Costa Pereira; Jacinto Joao, Paul, Humberto, Cruz, Cavem, Coluna, Augusto, Santana, Eusebio, Simoes.

SANTOS: Gilmar; Olavo, Mauro, Calvet, Dalmo, Lima, Zito, Dorval, Coutinho, Pele, Pepe.

Santos won.

Oct. 18 1963: A.C. MILAN (Italy) 4 (Trapattoni, Amarildo 2, Mora) SANTOS (Brazil) 2 (Pele 2, 1 pen.). Milan.

A.C. MILAN: Ghezzi; David, Maldini, Trebbi, Pelagalli, Trapattoni, Mora, Lodetti, Altafini, Rivera, Amarildo.

SANTOS: Gilmar; Lima, Haroldo, Calvet, Geraldino, Zito, Mengalvio, Dorval, Coutinho, Pele, Pepe.

Nov. 14 1963: SANTOS 4 (Pepe 2, Mengalvio, Lima) A.C. MILAN 2 (Altafini, Mora). Rio de Janeiro.

SANTOS: Gilmar; Ismael, Mauro, Haroldo, Dalmo, Lima, Mengalvio, Dorval, Coutinho, Almir, Pepe.

A.C. MILAN: Ghezzi; David, Maldini, Trebbi, Pelagalli, Trapattoni, Mora, Lodetti, Altafini, Rivera, Amarildo.

Nov. 16 1963: SANTOS 1 (Dalmo) A.C. MILAN 0. Rio de Janeiro.

SANTOS: Gilmar; Ismael, Mauro, Haroldo, Dalmo, Lima, Mengalvio, Dorval, Coutinho, Almir, Pepe.

A.C. MILAN: Balzarini (sub Barluzzi), Pelagalli, Maldini, Trebbi, Benitez, Trapattoni, Mora, Lodetti, Altafini, Amarildo, Fortunato.
Santos won.

Sept. 9 1964: INDEPENDIENTE (Argentina) 1 (Rodriquez) INTER-MILAN (Italy) 0. Buenos Aires.
INDEPENDIENTE: Santoro; Ferreiro, Guzman, Maldonado, Rolan, Mura, Acevedo, Barnao, Prospitti, Rodriquez, Savoy.
INTER-MILAN: Ghezzi; Burgnich, Guarneri, Facchetti, Tagnin, Picchi, Jair, Mazzola, Milani, Suarez, Corso.
Sept. 23 1964: INTER-MILAN 2 (Mazzola, Corso) INDEPENDIENTE 0. Milan.
INTER-MILAN: Sarti; Burgnich, Guarneri, Facchetti, Malatrasi, Picchi, Jair, Mazzola, Milani, Suarez, Corso.
INDEPENDIENTE: Santoro; Ferreiro, Paflik, Decaria, Acevedo, Maldonado, Suarez, Mura, Prospitti, Rodriquez, Savoy.
Sept. 23 1964: INTER-MILAN 1 (Corso) INDEPENDIENTE 0. (After extra time.) Madrid.
INTER-MILAN: Sarti; Malatrasi, Guarneri, Facchetti, Tagnin, Picchi, Domenghini, Peiro, Milani, Suarez, Corso.
INDEPENDIENTE: Santoro; Guzman, Paflik, Decaria, Acevedo, Maldonado, Bernao, Prospitti, Suarez, Rodriquez, Savoy.
Inter-Milan won.

Sept. 8 1965: INTER-MILAN (Italy) 3 (Peiro, Mazzola 2) INDEPEND-IENTE (Argentina) 0. Milan.
INTER-MILAN: Sarti; Burgnich, Guarneri, Facchetti, Bedin, Picchi, Jair, Mazzola, Peiro, Suarez, Corso.
INDEPENDIENTE: Santoro; Pavoni, Guzman, Navarro, Acevedo, Ferreiro, Bernao, De La Mata, Avalay, Rodriquez, Savoy.
Sept. 15 1965: INDEPENDIENTE 0 INTER-MILAN 0. Buenos Aires.
INDEPENDIENTE: Santoro; Navarro, Pavoni, Ferreiro, Rolan, Guzman, Bernao, Mura, Avalay, Mori, Savoy.
INTER-MILAN: Sarti; Burgnich, Guarneri, Facchetti, Bedin, Picchi, Jair, Mazzola, Peiro, Suarez, Corso.
Inter-Milan won.

Oct. 12 1966: PENAROL (Uruguay) 2 (Spencer 2) REAL MADRID (Spain) 0. Montevideo.
PENAROL: Mazurkiewcz; Forlas, Gonzales, Lescano, Gonsalves, Varela, Abbadie, Cortes, Spencer, Rocha, Joya.
REAL MADRID: Betancourt; Pachin, Sanchis, De Filipe, Ruiz, Zoco, Serena, Amancio, Pirri, Velasquez, Bueno.
Oct. 26 1966: REAL MADRID 0 PENAROL 2 (Rocha pen., Spencer).
REAL MADRID: Betancourt; Calpe, Sanchis, Pirri, De Filipe, Zoco, Serena, Amancio, Grosso, Velasquez, Gento.
PENAROL: Mazurkiewcz; Gonzales, Caetano, Lescano, Gonsalves, Vacla, Abbadie, Cortes, Spencer, Rocha, Joya.
Penarol won.

Oct. 18 1967: GLASGOW CELIC (Scotland) 1 (McNeill) RACING CLUB, BUENOS AIRES (Argentina) 0. Glasgow.
GLASGOW CELTIC: Simpson; Craig, Gemmell, Murdoch, McNeill, Clark, Johnstone, Lennox, Wallace, Auld, Hughes.
RACING CLUB: Cejas; Martin, Perfumo, Basile, Diaz, Mori, Rulli, Maschio, Raffo, Cardenas, Rodriques.
Nov. 1 1967: RACING CLUB 2 (Raffo, Cardenas) GLASGOW CELTIC 1 (Gemmell pen.). Buenos Aires.
RACING CLUB: Cejas; Perfumo, Chabay, Martin, Rulli, Basile, Cardenas, Raffo, Cardoso, Rodriques, Maschio.
GLASGOW CELTIC: Fallon; Greig, Gemmell, Murdoch, McNeill, Clark, Johnstone, Wallace, Chalmers, O'Neill, Lennox.
Nov. 4 1967: RACING CLUB 1 (Cardenas) GLASGOW CELTIC 0. Montevideo.
RACING CLUB: Cejas; Perfumo, Basile, Martin, Rulli, Chabay, Cardoso, Maschio, Cardenas, Rodriques, Raffo.
GLASGOW CELTIC: Fallon; Craig, Gemmell, Murdoch, McNeill, Clark, Johnstone, Lennox, Wallace, Auld, Hughes.
Racing Club won.

Sept. 25 1968: ESTUDIANTES DE LA PLATA (Argentina) 1 (Conigliaro) MANCHESTER UNITED (England) 0. Buenos Aires.
ESTUDIANTES DE LA PLATA: Poletti; Malbernat, Suarez, Madero, Medino, Pachame, Togneri, Bilardo, Ribaudo, Conigliaro, Veron.
MANCHESTER UNITED: Stepney; Dunne, Foulkes, Sadler, Burns, Crerand, Charlton, Stiles, Morgan, Law, Best.
Oct. 16 1968: MANCHESTER UNITED 1 (Morgan) ESTUDIANTES DE LA PLATA 1 (Veron). Old Trafford, Manchester.
MANCHESTER UNITED: Stepney; Brennan, Dunne, Foulkes, Crerand, Sadler, Morgan, Kidd, Charlton, Law, Best.
ESTUDIANTES DE LA PLATA: Poletti; Malbernat, Suarez, Madero, Medino, Bilardo, Pachame, Ribaudo, Conigliaro, Togneri, Veron.
Estudiantes de la Plata won.

Oct. 8 1969: A.C. MILAN (Italy) 3 (Sormani 2, Combin) ESTUDIANTES DE LA PLATA (Argentina) 0. Milan.
A.C. MILAN: Cudicini; Anquiletti, Schnellinger, Rosato, Malatrasi, Fogli, Sormani, Lodetti, Combin (sub Rognoni), Rivera, Prati.
ESTUDIANTES DE LA PLATA: Poletti; Suarez, Manero, Malbernat, Togneri, Medina, Echecopar (Ribaudo), Bilardo, Conigliaro, Flores, Veron.
Oct. 22 1969: ESTUDIANTES DE LA PLATA 2 (Conigliaro, Suarez) A.C. MILAN 1 (Rivera). Buenos Aires.
ESTUDIANTES DE LA PLATA: Poletti; Manero, Suarez, Madero, Malbernat, Bilardo (sub Echecopar), Romero, Togneri, Conigliaro, Taverna, Veron.
A.C. MILAN: Cudicini; Malatrasi (Fogli), Anquiletti, Schnellinger,

Rosato, Maldera, Lodetti, Rivera, Sormani, Combin, Prati (sub Rognoni).
A.C. Milan won.

SOUTH AMERICAN CLUB CHAMPIONSHIP

1960   Penarol (Uruguay) beat Olimpia (Paraguay)
1961   Penarol (Uruguay) beat Palmeiras (Brazil)
1962   Santos (Brazil) beat Penarol (Uruguay).
1963   Santos (Brazil) beat Boca Juniors (Argentina)
1964   Independiente (Argentina) beat Nacional (Uruguay)
1965   Independiente (Argentina) beat Penarol (Uruguay)
1966   Penarol (Uruguay) beat River Plate (Argentina)
1967   Racing Club (Argentina) beat Nacional (Uruguay)
1968   Estudiantes (Argentina) beat Palmeiras (Brazil)
1969   Estudiantes (Argentina) beat Nacional (Uruguay)
1970   Estudiantes (Argentina) beat Penarol (Uruguay).

7 Feyenoord Shock Celtic to Take European Cup

Although the decline of the Latin clubs like Real Madrid and Benfica had been noted as had the dominance of British teams in European competitions, the rise of the Dutch clubs had tended to be overlooked. Holland had failed to qualify for the World Cup finals and Ajax of Amsterdam had been rather overwhelmed by A.C. Milan in the 1968–1969 European Cup final in Madrid so that when Feyenoord of Rotterdam reached the final with the redoubtable Celtic as opponents in the 1969–1970 competition they were very much the underdogs.

Feyenoord were not new to European competition but their past record inspired no confidence. They had been beaten by Tottenham Hotspur in the European Cup in 1961 and by Newcastle United in the Inter-Cities Fairs' Cup as recently as 1968. But no allowance for progress had been made and Celtic, winners of the Cup in 1967 and conquerors of Leeds United on their way to the final, were confidently expected to have little trouble in disposing of the Dutch upstarts in the San Siro Stadium in Milan on May 6 and so bring off a British treble of European Cup, European Cup-Winners' Cup and European Fairs' Cup.

But it was the Dutch champions who played the better football and fully deserved their 2–1 victory even though their winning goal did not come until four minutes from the end of extra time. Even Celtic were forced to admit that on the night they were beaten by a better and superior team as their dream of a treble—European Cup, Scottish League Championship and Scottish League Cup—ended.

Feyenoord, formed in 1908, the first Dutch club to win the trophy, had previously reached the semi-finals in 1963 when they were beaten by Benfica. But this time they set out with a plan 12 months earlier when they won the Dutch League championship by three points from their great rivals Ajax under their Austrian coach, Ernst Happel. They knew they had one or two weak positions, mainly in midfield, and they set about strengthening them by looking around for the right players.

They persuaded Ajax to part with their midfield international, Theo van Duivenbode, 26, who had played a big part in helping the club into the European Cup final, knowing that his experience of this type of football would be extremely useful. Looking south they signed Franz Hasil, 25, an Austrian international with 11 caps and another midfield player from the German club, Schalke 04, who had been finalists to Bayern Munich for the German Cup. Both players fitted so well in Happel's scheme of things that Feyenoord became the surprise club of the competition.

One player, however, who had had much to do with their successful run in the competition was missing from the Milan final. He was Holland's number one goalkeeper, Eddy Treijtel who, following a loss of form towards the end of the season was replaced by the veteran Pieter Graafland, 36, who had made many appearances in the past for his country. He had also played in the Feyenoord side that reached the European Cup semi-final in 1963.

But with Rinus Israel, 28, van Duivenbode, Hasil and Theo Laseroms, 30, forming a strong all-international defence, and Ove Kindvall, 26, the Swedish international striker up front supported by Wim van Hanegem, 26, and Coen Moulijn, 32, also internationals in support—Moulijn also played in the 1963 semi-final—Feyenoord had a side in which it was really difficult to pinpoint a weakness.

It would be easy to dismiss Celtic on the strength of one poor performance, but the fact must not be forgotten that Jock Stein has got together a class team who can still come back, once over the disappointment of this unexpected defeat. Though the experienced players like Bobby Murdoch, Billy McNeill, Bertie Auld, and the mercurial Jimmy Johnstone are getting older there are younger players coming along like David Hay, 20, a brilliant full-back, and George Connelly, who is only 19. Hay, an Under-23 international, has already been called up for full Scottish internationals.

Happel's one big fear in the final was that if Celtic scored first in the opening half-hour the morale of his team might suffer; but in fact the reverse happened, and as Happel said afterwards Tommy Gemmell's goal seemed to give them more heart and help put them on top. While agreeing that Feyenoord were the better side Stein admitted that too many of the Celtic players were off form, but true to tradition he refused to name them. 'I will tell them privately,' he said.

There were 80,000 in Milan's San Siro Stadium—a quarter from Scotland and a quarter from Holland—for the final which for 48 hours had been threatened by strikes by municipal and hotel workers, but thanks to efforts by the Mayor of Milan, Aldo Aniasi, and the Italian Football League, the match was played as scheduled.

As expected Celtic's more physical approach to the game threw pressure on the Feyenoord defence in the early stages, but they held out well, and were even able to go forward with Kindvall getting a couple of chances which he was unable to convert. Bobby Lennox did get the ball in the net for Celtic but an infringement had occurred. Then Celtic got ahead after 29 minutes.

Gemmell went up-field for a free kick taken by Murdoch and from the edge of the penalty area he shot low into the net past the unsighted Graafland to the surprise of the Dutch fans—and so gave Celtic the lead as he had done against Inter-Milan in the 1967 final. But it was not for long. Within two minutes Feyenoord were on level terms.

Another free kick led to the goal. This was taken on the right wing, the ball being sent high into the Celtic goalmouth. The ball was headed from player to player until finally Israel, like Gemmell a full-back, headed past Williams. Feyenoord were now beginning to control the game, slowing the pace to the discomfort of Celtic, Jansen, Hasil and Van Hanegem being the masters in midfield.

With the middle of the field in their hands Feyenoord were able to offer a tight defence which caused Italian critics to liken their style of play to their own, with the exception they gave the Dutch team credit for more imagination in their attacking methods and their ability to make the quick opening and profit by it.

Celtic could make little of the seven-man line Feyenoord defence up against them while their own back line always looked vulnerable when the Dutch were on the attack, with Kindvall a dangerous raider although he could not turn his talents into goals before the scheduled ninety minutes were up.

For the third time in a final extra time was needed and when both players and spectators had become resigned to a replay two days later—which would have been the first in the competition's history—the winning goal came four minutes from the end. A free-kick to Feyenoord was taken quickly. The ball went over the head of McNeill who, falling backwards desperately, threw up his hands to try and stop it but failed. Kindvall ran round him and as Williams came out of his goal the Swede just got a toe-end to the ball in front of the goalkeeper's hands and pushed it over his head into the net.

Although McNeill had handled the ball, the Italian referee, Concetto Lo Bello, played the advantage rule and allowed play to continue. Williams was probably a split second late in coming out of his goal to meet Kindvall's challenge but it was the goal which settled the match and there was little doubt that it was the right team who were the winners.

The game was televised live to twenty countries.

Feyenoord had a very easy start on their path to success. Drawn at home to the champions of Iceland, K.B. Reykjavik, they were able to play both matches in Rotterdam to cut down expenses. After winning the first leg by 12–2 in which Ruud Geels was their top scorer with four goals after coming on as a substitute for Moulijn, they eased up in the return and won 4–0 to give them a 16–2 aggregate success.

Celtic should have heeded the warning when Feyenoord put out A.C. Milan, the holders and World Club champions, in the second round. A nine-minute goal by Nestor Combin, the Argentine expatriate who played for France, gave A.C. Milan a 1–0 first-leg lead which they were expected to hold. But Feyenoord had other ideas. A home crowd of 65,000 saw Jansen wipe out the deficit in five minutes with a long shot which Milan's goalkeeper, Cudicini, fumbled and eight minutes from time Van Hanegem headed the winning goal.

Once again drawn away in the quarter-final Feyenoord again found themselves a goal down after the first leg against the East German champions, F.C. Vorwaerts in East Berlin. But two more goals at home, second-half efforts by Kindvall—surprisingly he missed a penalty—and Wery, qualified them for a semi-final meeting with the Polish Army side, Legia Warsaw, when once again they were drawn away for the first leg.

A goalless draw on a muddy pitch in Poland however gave them an excellent chance for the second leg at home and they took this to gain a 2–0 victory. Again Feyenoord had the advantage of a quick goal, Van Hanegem heading in after three minutes. It was Hasil who made the game safe inside half an hour from a pass by Kindvall after a fine solo run by the Swede.

Here are the marksmen who scored Feyenoord's 24 goals to win the Cup—Kindvall and Geels six each, Van Hanegem four, Wery and Jansen two each, and Romeyn, Van Duivenbode, Hasil and Israel one each.

Celtic opened their fourth successive season in the European Cup by being held rather surprisingly to a goalless draw by Basle in Switzerland but they made no mistake against the Swiss champions at home winning 2–0 with goals by Hood and Gemmell. This was followed by a 3–0 home victory over Benfica, Gemmell, Wallace and Hood scoring, a lead considered sufficient to end the run of the Lisbon Eagles in the competition.

But even though Benfica were going through a difficult period at that time, struggling to find their form, they still had fight left in them and when Celtic got to the Estadio Da Luz they were shaken by two first-half goals. Still fighting hard to stay in the competition

Benfica reaped reward of persistent attacks against a solid Celtic defence with a goal one minute from time and forced the tie into extra time with an aggregate of 3–3. No further goals were scored, and progress depended upon the toss of the disc. This went to Celtic, the toss being made ironically by a Dutch referee.

Fiorentina, the Italian champions, provided less tough opposition in the quarter-final stage. They were well beaten 3–0 in Glasgow, Auld and Wallace goals being helped by one from Fiorentina's defender Carpentti, and in the return leg in Florence the Italians managed only one goal. With Leeds also in the last four, prospects of an all-British final for the first time loomed but the two British clubs were drawn to clash in a semi-final with the first leg at Elland Road. This was regarded as a battle of giants, the best of British football and the best of Scottish football in opposition.

But Leeds conceded a first-minute goal to Connelly and Celtic took that 1–0 lead into the second leg and, although a Scot, Billy Bremner, neutralised it 14 minutes after the start at Hampden Park, Celtic came back with two second-half goals by Hughes and Murdoch to qualify for the final on a 3–1 aggregate.

Celtic's 12 goals in the competition were scored by Gemmell three, Hood and Wallace two each, Auld, Connelly, Hughes, Murdoch and Fiorentina's Carpentti (own goal) one each.

The big surprise of the competition was the elimination of Real Madrid who had competed in every European Cup since its inception in 1955, but who will be missing from the 1970–71 line-up. And the knock-out blow was delivered in their own magnificent Bernabeu Stadium by the Belgian champions, Standard Liege, in the second round. Having held the Belgians to a single goal in Liege it was thought the six-time winners of the trophy would be able to wipe out this deficit and win on their own ground.

But times have changed, styles have changed and players have changed. No longer were Real Madrid the power in Europe, a team to be feared. They could not match the Belgians. Louis Pilot, the Luxemburg international, put Standard Liege two up before Real Madrid had settled down in the second leg. Velasquez reduced the lead after 20 minutes only for Depireux to restore it four minutes later. Three minutes after the interval Dewalque brought down Amancio and Gento made it three-two on aggregate with a penalty but in the 69th minute the Jugoslav Galic made the match score 3–2 and the aggregate 4–2 in favour of Standard and so it remained to the end to send 85,000 disappointed Spanish fans streaming away from the stadium.

Admittedly Real Madrid were not at full strength being without four of their regular players, but usually their reserve strength is equal to any occasion. It was a mistake by their number two goal-keeper, Jonquera deputising for the injured Betancourt which let in the first Standard goal. They also missed their Paraguayan-born winger Fleitas who was well repaying the £60,000 they had paid Malaga for his services before the start of the season.

Standard were not allowed to bask in their glory for long. They came up against Leeds United in the following round and were beaten in both legs but they held the English champions to a single goal on each occasion.

U.E.F.A. seeded ten clubs in the draw for the first round to make sure they did not meet each other early in the competition. Nine of them won but the tenth, Bayern Munich, were beaten by the un-seeded French champions, Saint Etienne, who recovered from a 2–0 defeat in Munich to win 3–0 at home.

Preliminary Round
Aug. 21 1969: PALLOSEURA TURKU (Finland) (0) 0 K.B. COPEN-HAGEN (Denmark) (0) 1 (Skouborg).
Aug. 28 1969: K.B. COPENHAGEN (2) 4 (Skouborg 2, Brage, Praest) PALLOSEURA TURKU (0) 0.

First Round
Sept. 24 1969: REAL MADRID (Spain) (3) 8 (Georgiou o.g., Gento 2, Grosso, Fleitas 2, Grande, Pirri) OLYMPIAKOS (Cyprus) (0) 0.
REAL MADRID: Betancourt; Calpe, De Felipe, Zoco, Sanchis, Pirri, Grosso, Velasquez (Jose Luis), Fleitas, Amancio (Grande), Gento.
OLYMPIAKOS: Filotas; Argyrou M., Georgiou (Argyrou D.), Partasides, Constantinou, Ashiotis (Avraamides), Katsis, Xypolytas, Kettenis, Efthimiades, Markou.
Oct. 1 1969: REAL MADRID (3) 6 (Diego 2, Planelles, Grande, Avra-mides o.g., Fleitas) OLYMPIAKOS (1) 1 (Kettenis).
REAL MADRID: Jonquera; Espildora, Babiloni, Zunzunegui, Benito, Jesus Luis, Planelles, Fleitas, Grande, De Diego, Bueno.
OLYMPIAKOS: Filotas; Argyrou M., Partasides, Xpolytas, Savakis, Ashiotis, Katsis, Avraamides, Kettenis, Efthimiades, Markou.
Real Madrid won 14–1 on aggregate.

Sept. 10 1969: A.C. MILAN (Italy) (1) 5 (Prati 2, Rivera, pen., Rognoni, Combin) AVENIR BEGGEN (Luxemburg) (0) 0.
A.C. MILAN: Cudicini; Anquilletti, Rosato, Maldera, Schnellinger, Fogli (Fontana), Sormani, Lodetti (Rognoni), Combin, Rivera, Prati.
AVENIR BEGGEN: Moes; Schiltz (Cattani), Schmit, C., Wohlfart, Giardin, Kutten (Adams, F.), Wagener, Kremer, Heger, Schmit, J., Bamberg.
Sept. 24 1969: AVENIR BEGGEN (0) 0 A.C. MILAN (1) 3 (Combin, Sormani, Rivera)
AVENIR BEGGEN: Moes; Schiltz, Wagener, Giardin, Wohlfart,

Franocis, Adams (Kollwelter), Kremer (Catani), Schmit, J., Heger, Bamberg.
A.C. MILAN: Cudicini; Santin, Rosato, Malatrasi, Schnellinger, Trapattoni, Lodetti (Fontana), Sormani, Combin (Golin), Rivera, Prati.
A.C. Milan won 11–0 on aggregate

Sept. 17 1969: BAYERN MUNICH (W. Germany) (1) 2 (Brenninger, Roth) SAINT ETIENNE (France) (0) 0.
BAYERN MUNICH: Maier; Koppenhoffer, Beckenbauer, Pumm, Schwarzenbeck, Ohlhauser, Michi, Roth, Muller, Schmidt, Brenninger.
SAINT ETIENNE: Carnis; Durkovic, Mitoraj, Bosquier, Polny, Broissart, Jacuet, Keita, Revelli, Larque, Bereta.
Oct. 1 1969: SAINT ETIENNE (1) 3 (Revelli 2, Keita) BAYERN MUNICH (0) 0
SAINT ETIENNE: Carnis; Durkovic, Mitoraj, Bosquier, Camerini, Broissart, Herbin, Samardzic, Revelli, Keita, Bereta.
BAYERN MUNICH: Maier; Koppenhoffer, Beckenbauer, Schwarzenbeck, Pumm, Ohlhauser, Roth, Schmidt, Michi, Muller, Brenninger.
Saint Etienne won 3–2 on aggregate

Sept. 17 1969: BENFICA (Portugal) (2) 2 (Eusebio 2) K.B. COPENHAGEN (Denmark) (0) 0.
BENFICA: Henrique; Malta, Humberto, Zeca, Adolfo, Toni (Jose Augusto), Coluna, Simoes (Graca), Torres, Eusebio, Diamantino.
K.B. COPENHAGEN: Haguenau; Juhrgenfren, Sorensen, A., Lindhy, Petersen, Skovgaard, Moller, Sorensen J., Praest, Brage, Krogdahl.
Oct. 1 1969: K.B. COPENHAGEN (1) 2 (Skouborg 2 (1 pen.)) BENFICA (3) 3 (Eusebio, Diamantino 2).
K.B. COPENHAGEN: Haguenau; Jorgensen, Petersen, Sorensen A., Moller, Ravn, Praest, Sorensen J., Brage, Skouburg, Krogdahl.
BENFICA: Henrique (Nacimento); Malta, Humberto, Zeca, Adolfo (Jacinto), Toni, Coluna, Simoes, Torres, Eusebio, Diamantino.
Benfica won 5–2 on aggregate.

Sept. 17 1969: BASLE (Switzerland) (0) 0 GLASGOW CELTIC (0) 0.
BASLE: Kunz; Kiefer, Michaud, Siegenthaler, Fischli, Odermatt, Benthaus, Ramseier (Rahmen), Blamer, Hauser, Wenger.
CELTIC: Fallon; Hay, Brogan, McNeill, Gemmell, Clark, Lennox, Johnstone, Wallace, Chalmers (Hood), Hughes.
Oct. 1 1969: GLASGOW CELTIC (1) 2 (Hood, Gemmell) BASLE (0) 0.
CELTIC: Fallon; Hay, Gemmell, Clark, McNeill, Callaghan T., Johnstone, Wallace, Chalmers, Hood, Lennox.
BASLE: Kunz; Kiefer, Michaud, Ramseier, Siegenthaler, Fischli, Blamer, Odermatt, Hauser, Benthaus, Wenger.
Glasgow Celtic won 2–0 on aggregate.

Sept. 17 1969: FEYENOORD (Holland) (7) 12 (Kindvall 3, Geels 4, Van Hanegem 2, Romeyn, Wery, van Duivenbode) K.B. REYKJAVIK (Iceland) (0) 2 (Baldvinsson, Bjoernsson).

FEYENOORD: Treijtel; Romeyn, Israel, Haak, Duivenbode, Hasil, Jansen, Wery (Veldhoen), Kindvall, Van Hanegem, Moulijn.

REYKJAVIK: Petersson; Kjartansson, Armaalon, Jonsson, Schramm, Bjoernsson, Felixsson, Baldvinsson, Larisson, Hofsteinsson, Jakobson.

Sept. 30 1969: FEYENOORD (2) 4 (Geels 2, Kindvall, Wery) K.B. REYKJAVIK (0) 0.

FEYENOORD: Treijtel; Haak, Israel, Laseroms, van Duivenbode, Hasil, Jansen, Geels, Kindvall, Wery, Moulijn.

REYKJAVIK: Petersson; Armaalon, Schraam, Jonsson, Qlarson, Hofsteinsson, Kasperson, Bjoernsson, Baldvinsson, Larisson, Frinizsson.

Both matches in Rotterdam by arrangement
Feyenoord won 16–2 on aggregate.

Sept. 17 1969: C.S.K.A. SOFIA (Bulgaria) (1) 2 (Jekov 2) FERENC-VAROS (Hungary) (0) 1 (Rakosi).

C.S.K.A.: Filipov; Zafirov, Gaganelov, Marintchov, Sztankov B., Penev, Sztankov K., Marachilev, Jekov, Yakimov, Nikodimov.

FERENCVAROS: Geczi; Balint, Pancsics, Megezi, Juhasz, Horvath, Szucs, Branikovic, Nemeth (Tatral), Rakosi, Katona.

Oct. 1 1969: FERENCVAROS (2) 4 (Szoeke 2 (1 pen.), Branikovic, Rakosi) C.S.K.A. SOFIA (1) 1 (Marosliev).

FERENCVAROS: Geczi; Balint, Pancsics, Megezi, Horvath, Szucs, Szoeke, Brantikovic, Juhasz, Rakosi, Katona.

C.S.K.A.: Fiipov; Zafirov, Gaganelov, Marintchov, Sztankov B., Penev, Parasliev, Sztankov K., Jekov, Yakimov, Nicodimov.

Ferencvaros won 5–3 on aggregate

Sept. 17 1969: AUSTRIA VIENNA (Austria) (1) 1 (Riedl) DINAMO KIEV (U.S.S.R.) (0) 2 (Serber, Muntyan).

AUSTRIA VIENNA: Stanwald; Froelich, Frank, Sara, Kuntz, Geyer, Pariz, Hickersberger, Kogelberger, Fiala, Riedl.

DINAMO KIEV: Rudakov; Medvid, Sosnichin, Lechenko, Szabo, Gruilikovski, Muntyan, Bogovik, Peach, Serebryanikov, Byshovets.

Oct. 1 1969: DINAMO KIEV (0) 3 (Muntyan, Byshovets, Puzack) AUSTRIA VIENNA (1) 1 (Pariz).

DINAMO KIEV: Rudakov; Medvid, Sosnichin, Gruilikovski, Lechenko, Szabo, Muntyan, Serebryanikov, Puzach, Byshovets, Khmelnitsky.

AUSTRIA VIENNA: Schneider; Sara (Pakach), Frank, Prolix, Geyer, Kriger, Fiala, Kouna, Pariz, Hickersberger, Kogelberger.

Dinamo Kiev won 5–2 on aggregate.

Sept. 17 1969: VORWAERTS (E. Germany) (0) 2 (Piepenberg 2) PANA-THINAIKOS (Greece) (0) 0.

VORWAERTS: Sulkovski; Fraesdorf, Muller, Withulz, Hamann Koerner, Struebing, Noeldner, Wruck, Begerard, Piepenberg.

PANATHINAIKOS: Ekonomapoulos; Tomazas, Athanassopoulos, Dimitriou, Kamezas, Souzpis, Filacourts, Eleftazakis, Grammos, Dumazos, Fratzis.

Two of Italy's stars who had contrasting roles in Mexico— Riva, who played in all their matches, and the temperamental Rivera, who was used as a second half substitute

Captains in action in the Third Place play-off in Mexico City: Uruguay's Luis Ubinas (*left*) and West Germany's Uwe Seeler

Allan Clarke sends the Czechoslovakian goalkeeper Ivo Viktor the wrong way with a penalty kick to give England a 1–0 victory

Oct. 1 1969: PANATHINAIKOS (1) 1 (Antoniades) VORWAERTS (0)
1 (Laslop).
Vorwaerts won 3–1 on aggregate.

Sept. 17 1969: FIORENTINA (Italy) (0) 1 (Maraschi) OESTER
VAEXJOE (Sweden) (0) 0.
FIORENTINA: Superchi; Rogora, Longoni, Esposito, Ferrante, Brizi,
Chiarugi, Merlo (Rizzo), Maraschi, De Sisti, Amarildo.
OESTER VAEXJOE: Hegberg; Lindberg, Bild P. O., Blomqvist, Blom,
Svensson, Bergstrand, Bild H. (Fransson), Ejderstedt, Ljunggren,
Fjordestam.
Oct. 1 1969: OESTER VAEXJOE (1) 1 (Fjordestam) FIORENTINA (1)
2 (Amarildo, Esposito).
OESTER VAEXJOE: Hegberg G.; Hegberg A., Lindberg, Bild P. O.,
Blomqvist, Blom, Bergstrand, Karlsson, Svensson, Ejderstadt, Ljuond-
berg, Fjordestam.
FIORENTINA: Superchi; Facchetti, Rogora, Ferrante, Brizi, Esposito,
De Sisti, Amarildo, Maraschi, Rizzo, Chiarugi.
Fiorentina won 3–1 on aggregate.

Sept. 17 1969: LEEDS UNITED (5) 10 (Jones 3, Clark 2, Giles 2,
Bremner 2, O'Grady) LYN OSLO (Norway) (0) 0.
LEEDS UNITED: Sprake; Reaney, Cooper, Bremner, Charlton, Hunter,
Madeley, Clarke, Jones, Giles, O'Grady.
LYN OSLO: Olsen S.; Rodvang, Oestvold, Morisbak, Kolle, Guilden,
Boerrehaug, Christopherson, Berg, Olsen O., Austnes.
Oct. 1 1969: LYN OSLO (0) 0 LEEDS UNITED (3) 6 (Belfitt 2, Hibbitt 2,
Jones, Lorimer).
LYN OSLO: Olsen S.; Rodvang, Oestvold, Boerrehaug, Kolle, Morisbak,
Berg, Christopherson, Hovdan, Olsen O., Birkeland.
LEEDS UNITED: Sprake; Reaney, Cooper, Bremner, Madeley, Gray,
Lorimer, Belfitt, Jones, Bates, Hibbitt.
Leeds United won 16–2 on aggregate.

Sept. 17 1969: HIBERNIAN (Malta) (0) 2 (Cassar, Bonnello) SPARTAK
TRNAVA (Czechoslovakia) (0) 2 (Adamec, Martinkovic).
Oct. 1 1969: SPARTAK TRNAVA (1) 4 (Adamec 2, Hrusecky, Azzopardi
o.g.) HIBERNIAN (0) 0.
SPARTAK TRNAVA: Kozinka (Varadin); Majernik, Jarabek, Hagara,
Hrusecky, Kuna, Martinkovic, Svec, Farkas, Adamec, Kabat.
HIBERNIAN: Mizzi; Privitera, Azzopardi, Garuana, Malita, Delia,
Theobald, Micalief, Aquilina (Buckel), Barello, Young.
Spartak Trnava won 6–2 on aggregate.

Sept. 17 1969: RED STAR BELGRADE (Yugoslavia) (5) 8 (Karasi 2,
Lazarevic 2, Dzajic 2, Klenkovski, Acimovic) LINFIELD (N. Ireland)
(0) 0.
RED STAR BELGRADE: Dujikovoc; Krivokuca, Jetvic, Pavlovic,

D

Dojcinovsky, Klenkovski, Antonijevic, Karasi, Lazarevic, Acimovic, Dzajic.
LINFIELD: McGonegall; Gilliland, Atterson, Andrews, Hatton, Bowyer, Viollet, Millen, McGraw, Hamilton, Pavis (Feeney).
Oct. 1 1969: LINFIELD (2) 2 (McGraw 2) RED STAR BELGRADE (1) 4 (Antonijevic 4)
LINFIELD: McGonegall; Gilliland, White, Millen, Hatton, Bowyer, Viollet, Hamilton, McGraw, Pavis, Feeney.
RED STAR BELGRADE: Racic; Keri, Krivokuca, Pavlovic, Dojcinovsky, Klenkovski, Antonijevic, Karasi, Aruejcic, Acimovic, Perazic.
Red Star Belgrade won 12–2 on aggregate.

Sept. 17 1969: STANDARD LIEGE (Belgium) (2) 3 (Depireux 3) NENDURI TIRANA (Albania) (0) 0.
STANDARD LIEGE: Piot; Beurlet, Dewalque, Jeck, Thiessen, Takac, Pilot, Semmeling, Kostedde (Blaise), Depireux, Galic.
NENDURI TIRANA: Tafay; Mema A., Kasmi, Bytisi, Dhales, Meme K., Pano, Bukoviku, Hyka, Hazanxbia (Ceta).
Oct. 1 1969: NENDURI TIRANA (0) 1 (Kozonska) STANDARD LIEGE (0) 1 (Galic).
NENDURI TIRANA: Tafay; Mema A., Kasmi, Bytisi, Dhales, Meme K., Pano, Bukoviku, Hyka, Kozonska, Ishkas.
STANDARD LIEGE: Piot; Beurlet, Dewalque, Jeck, Thiessen, Depireux, Takac, Pilot, Cvetler, Kostedde, Galic.
Standard Liege won 4–1 on aggregate.

Sept. 17 1969: GALATSARAY (Turkey) (2) 2 (Gokman 2) WATERFORD (Rep. of Ireland) (0) 0.
GALATSARAY: Nihat; Ali, Ergun, Muzaffer, Talat, Turan, Ugur, Ayhan, Gokmen, Mehmet, Muhlis.
WATERFORD: Thomas; Bryan, Morrisey, McGeogh, Morley, Maguire, Casey, Hale, O'Neill, Buck, Matthews.
Oct. 1 1969: WATERFORD (0) 2 (Buck, Morley) GALATSARAY (1) 3 (Ugur, Gokman, Ayhan).
WATERFORD: Thomas; Bryan, Morrisey, Maguire, Morley, McGeough, Casey, Hale, O'Neill (Trainor), Buck, Matthews.
GALATSARY: Nihat; Ergun, Akin, Muzaffer, Talat, Turan, Ugur, Mehmet (Muhlis), Gokman, Ayhan (Seridun), Ali.
Galatsaray won 5–2 on aggregate.

Sept. 17 1969: U.T. ARAD (Rumania) (1) 1 (Domide) LEGIA WARSAW (Poland) (0) 2 (Zmijewski, Godocha).
U.T. ARAD: Gornea; Birau, Bacos, Pojont, Brandescu, Petrescu, Brosovschi, Lereter (Dumitrescu), Sima (Schopu), Domide, Axente.
LEGIA WARSAW: Grotinschy; Stachurski, Niedzolka, Zygmunt, Traskowski, Dejna, Brycheczy, Blaut, Zmijewski, Piesko, Godocha.
Oct. 1 1969: LEGIA WARSAW (0) 8 (Godocha 2, Blaut, Brycheczy, Stachurski, Dejna, Zmijewski, Piesko) U.T. ARAD (0) 0.
Legia Warsaw won 10–1 on aggregate.

Second Round

Nov. 12 1969: SPARTAK TRNAVA (Czechoslovakia) (0) 1 (Kabat) GALATSARAY (Turkey) (0) 0.

SPARTAK TRNAVA: Geryk; Varadin, Majernik, Jarabek, Hagara, Hrusecky, Kuna, Martinkovic (Kostial), Juska, Adamec, Kabat.

GALATSARAY: Nihat; Ali, Ergun (Feridun), Muzaffer, Talat, Akin, Mehmet, Ayhan, Gokman, Muhlis, Ugur.

Nov. 26 1969 GALATSARAY (0) 1 (Ercun) SPARTAK TRNAVA (0) 0.

GALATSARAY: Nihat; Ali, Muzaffer, Talat, Akin, Ergun, Turan, Mehmet, Ayhan, Gokman, Ugur.

SPARTAK TRNAVA. Geryk; Varadin, Majernik, Jarabek, Hagara, Hrusecky, Martinkovic, Svec, Kuna, Juska, Adamec.

Galatsaray won on toss of disc.

Nov. 12 1969: GLASGOW CELTIC (Scotland) (2) 3 (Gemmell, Wallace, Hood) BENFICA (Portugal) (0) 0.

GLASGOW CELTIC: Fallon; Craig, Gemmell, Murdoch, McNeill, Clark, Johnstone, Hood, Wallace, Auld, Hughes.

BENFICA: Henrique; Malta, Humberto C., Zeca, Humberto F., Graca, Coluna, Simoes, Torres, Eusebio (Augusto), Diamantino (Jorge).

Nov. 26 1969: BENFICA (0) 3 (Eusebio, Graca, Diamantino) GLASGOW CELTIC (0) 0. After extra time.

BENFICA: Henrique; Malta, Da Silva, Messias, Coluna, Adolfo, Graca, Toni, Aguas (Diamantino), Jorge, Eusebio, Simoes.

GLASGOW CELTIC. Fallon; Craig, Gemmell, Murdoch, McNeill, Brogan, Johnstone, Callaghan, Wallace, Auld, Hughes.

Celtic won on the toss of a disc.

Nov. 16 1969: A.C. MILAN (Italy) (1) 1 (Combin) FEYENOORD (Holland) (0) 0.

A.C. MILAN: Cudicini; Anquiletti, Schnellinger, Trapattoni, Rosato, Santin, Sormani (Fontana), Lodetti, Combin, Rivera (Rognoni), Prati.

FEYENOORD: Treijtel; Romeyn, Israel, Laseroms, van Duivenbode, Hasil, Jansen, Wery, Kindvall, Van Hanegem, Moulijn.

Nov. 26 1969: FEYENOORD (1) 2 (Jansen, Van Hanegem) A.C. MILAN (0) 0.

FEYENOORD: Treijtel; Romeyn, Israel, Laseroms, van Duivenbode, Hasil, Jansen, Van Hanegem, Wery, Kindvall, Moulijn.

A.C. MILAN: Cudicini; Schnellinger, Anquiletti, Maldera, Rosato, Santin, Fogli, Sormani, Lodetti, Combin, Prati.

Feyenoord won 2-1 on aggregate.

Nov. 12 1969. F.C. VORWAERTS (East Germany) (1) 2 (Fraesdorf, Begerard) RED STAR BELGRADE (Yugoslavia) (1) 1 (Antonijevic).

F.C. VORWAERTS. Sulkovski; Fraesdorf, Muller, Hamann, Withulz, Wruck, Noeldner, Koerer, Nachtigall, Begerard, Piepenberg.

RED STAR BELGRADE. Dujkovic; Djoric, Jetvic, Pavlovic, Dojcinovsky, Krivokuca, Antonijevic, Ostojic, Arnejic, Acimovic, Dzajic.

Nov. 26 1969: RED STAR BELGRADE (1) 3 (Karasi 2, Acimovic) F.C.
VORWAERTS (1) 2 (Begerard 2).
RED STAR BELGRADE: Dujkovic; Djoric, Jetvic, Pavlovic, Dojcinovsky, Krivokuca, Aontonijevic, Ostojic, Arnejic, Acimovic, Dzajic.
F.C. VORWAERTS: Sulkovski; Fraesdorf, Muller, Withulz, Wruck, Noeldner, Koerner, Nachtigall, Begerard, Meyer, Stribling.
F.C. Vorwaerts won on away goals rule.

Nov. 12 1969: LEEDS UNITED (England) (3) 3 (Giles, Jones 2)
FERENCVAROS (Hungary) (0) 0.
LEEDS UNITED: Sprake; Reaney, Madeley, Bremner, Charlton, Hunter, Lorimer, Bates, Jones, Giles, Gray.
FERENCVAROS: Geczi; Novak, Pancsics, Balint, Horvath, Megezi, Szucs, Juhasz, Branticovic, Szoeke, Katona.
Nov. 26 1969: FERENCVAROS (0) 0 LEEDS UNITED (1) 3 (Jones 2, Lorimer).
FERENCVAROS: Geczi; Novak, Balint, Megyesi, Johasz, Szucs, Szoeke, Branticovic, Horvath (Vajda), Nemeth, Katona.
LEEDS UNITED: Sprake; Reaney, Cooper, Bremner, Charlton, Hunter, Lorimer, Madeley, Jones, Giles, Gray (Galvin).
Leeds United won 6–0 on aggregate.

Nov. 12 1969: DINAMO KIEV (Russia) (0) 1 (Serebryanikov) FIORENTINA (Italy) (1) 2 (Chiarugi, Maraschi)
DINAMO KIEV: Rudakov; Mediid, Sosnichin, Lechenko, Szabo (Bogovik), Gruilikovski, Muntyan, Puzach, Byshovets, Serebryanikov, Troshkin.
FIORENTINA: Superchi; Rogora, Longoni, Esposito, Ferrante, Brizi, Chiarugi, Merlo, Maraschi, De Sisti, Amarildo.
Nov. 26 1969: FIORENTINA (0) 0 DINAMO KIEV (0) 0.
FIORENTINA: Superchi; Rogora, Longoni, Esposito, Ferrante, Brizi, Chiarugi, Merlo, Maraschi, De Sisti, Amarildo.
DINAMO KIEV: Ridakov; Medvid, Sosnichin, Lechenko, Trochi, Gruilikovski, Muntyan, Puzach, Byshovets, Serebryanikov, Khmelnitsky.
Fiorentina won 2–1 on aggregate.

Nov. 12 1969: LEGIA WARSAW (Poland) (0) 2 (Piezko, Dejna) SAINT
ETIENNE (France) (1) 1 (Revelli).
LEGIA WARSAW: Grotinschy; Foltyn, Stachurski, Niedzolka, Zygmunt, Traskowski, Dejna, Brycheczy, Blaut, Zmijewski, Godocha.
SAINT ETIENNE: Carkus; Durkovic, Mitoraj, Bosquier, Herbin, Smardzic, Brossart, Revelli, Keita, Bereta, Largue.
Nov. 26 1969: SAINT ETIENNE (0) 0 LEGIA WARSAW (0) 1 (Dejna).
SAINT ETIENNE: Camerini; Bereta, Herbin, Bosquier, Keita, Carnus, Mitoraj, Revelli, Brossart, Durkovic, Largue.
LEGIA WARSAW: Grotinschy; Stachurski, Niedzolka, Zygmunt, Traskowski, Dejna, Brycheczy, Blaut, Piesko, Zmijewski, Godocha.
Legia Warsaw won 3–1 on aggregate.

Nov. 19 1969: STANDARD LIEGE (Belgium) (1) 1 (Depireux) REAL MADRID (Spain) (0) 0.

STANDARD LIEGE: Piot; Beurlet, Dewalque, Pilot, Thiessen, Van Moer, Takac, Galic, Kostedde, Depireux, Cvetler.

REAL MADRID: Betancourt; Sanchis, Zoco, Babiloni, Benito, Pirri, Grosso, Velasquez, Fleitas, Mancio, Gento.

Dec. 3 1969: REAL MADRID (1) 2 (Velasquez, Gento) STANDARD LIEGE (2) 3 (Pilot, Depireux, Galic).

REAL MADRID: Junquera; Calpe, Zunzunegui (Babiloni), Benito, Pirri, Zoco, De Diego, Amancio, Grosso, Velasquez, Gento.

STANDARD LIEGE: Piot; Beurlet, Jeck, Thiessen, Dewalque, Pilot, Takac, Van Moer, Kostedde (Galic), Depireux, Cvetler.

Standard Liege won 4–2 on aggregate.

Quarter-Finals

Mar. 4 1970: GLASGOW CELTIC (Scotland) (1) 3 (Auld, Carpentti o.g., Wallace) FIORENTINA (Italy) (0) 0.

GLASGOW CELTIC: Williams; Hay, Gemmell, Murdoch, McNeill, Brogan, Johnstone, Lennox, Wallace, Auld, Hughes.

FIORENTINA: Superchi; Rogora, Longoni, Carpentti, Ferrante, Brizi, Esposito, Merlo, Maraschi, De Sisti, Amarildo.

Mar. 18 1970: FIORENTINA (1) 1 (Chiarugi) GLASGOW CELTIC (0) 0.

FIORENTINA: Superchi; Rogora, Longoni, Esposito, Ferrante, Brizi, Chiarugi, Merlo, Maraschi, De Sisti, Amarildo.

GLASGOW CELTIC: Williams; Hay, Gemmell, Connelly, Brogan, Johnstone, McNeill, Murdoch, Wallace, Lennox, Auld.

Glasgow Celtic won 3–1 on aggregate.

Mar. 4 1970: GALATSARAY (Turkey) (0) 1 (Ayhan) LEGIA WARSAW (Poland) (0) 1 (Brycheczy).

GALATSARAY: Nihat; Ergun, Ekrem, Muzaffer, Talat, Akin, Mehmet (Mazlum), Turan, Celovic (Ali), Ayhan, Ugur.

LEGIA WARSAW: Grotinschy; Stachurski, Zygmunt, Blaut II, Traskowski, Brycheczy, Dejna, Blaut I, Piesko, Godocha.

Mar. 18 1970: LEGIA WARSAW (1) 2 (Brycheczy 2) GALATSARAY (0) 0.

LEGIA WARSAW: Grotinschy; Stachurski, Blaut II, Zygmunt, Traskowski, Brycheczy, Deyna, Blaut I, Zmijewski, Piesko, Godocha.

GALATSARAY: Nihat; Ekrem, Ergun, Ali, Muzaffer, Talat, Akin, Mehmet, Turan, Ayhan, Ugur.

Legia Warsaw won 3–1 on aggregate.

Mar. 4 1970: STANDARD LIEGE (Belgium) (0) 0 LEEDS UNITED (England) (0) 1 (Lorimer).

STANDARD LIEGE: Piot; Beurlet, Thiessen, Dewalque, Jeck, Pilot, Semmeling, Van Moer, Galic, Depireux, Takac.

LEEDS UNITED: Sprake; Reaney, Cooper, Bremner, Charlton, Hunter, Lorimer, Clarke, Jones, Giles, Madeley.

Mar. 18 1970: LEEDS UNITED (0) 1 (Giles pen.) STANDARD LIEGE (0) 0.

LEEDS UNITED: Sprake; Reaney, Cooper, Bremner, Charlton, Hunter, Lorimer, Clarke, Jones, Giles, Madeley.

STANDARD LIEGE: Piot; Beurlet, Thiessen, Dewalque, Jeck, Pilot, Semmeling, Van Moer, Galic, Depireux, Takac.

Leeds United won 2–0 on aggregate.

Mar. 4 1970: F.C. VORWAERTS (East Germany) (0) 1 (Piepenburg) FEYENOORD (Holland) (0) 0.

F.C. VORWAERTS: Sulkovski; Fraesdorf, Muller, Hamann, Withulz, Koerner, Noeldner (Wruck), Struebling, Nachtigall, Begerard, Piepenburg.

FEYENOORD: Treijtel; Romeyn, Laseroms, Israel, Veldoen, Van Duivenbode (Vrauwdeunt), Hasil, Jansen, Van Hanegem, Wery, Kindvall.

Mar. 18 1970: FEYENOORD (0) 2 (Kindvall, Wery) F.C. VORWAERTS (0) 0.

FEYENOORD: Treijtel; Geels, Israel, Laseroms, Van Duivenbode, Hasil, Jansen, Wery, Kindvall, Van Hanegem, Moulijn.

F.C. VORWAERTS: Sulkovski; Fraesdorf, Muller, Hamann, Withulz, Struebling, Koerner, Nachtigall, Noeldner, Begerard, Piepenburg.

Feyenoord won 2–1 on aggregate.

Semi-Finals

April 1 1970: LEEDS UNITED (England) (0) 0 GLASGOW CELTIC (Scotland) (0) 1 (Connelly).

LEEDS UNITED: Sprake; Reaney, Cooper, Bremner (Bates), Charlton, Madeley, Lorimer, Clarke, Jones, Giles, Gray.

GLASGOW CELTIC: Williams; Hay, Gemmell, Murdoch, McNeill, Brogan, Johnstone, Connelly, Wallace, Lennox, Auld.

April 15 1970: GLASGOW CELTIC (0) 2 (Hughes, Murdoch) LEEDS UNITED (1) 1 (Bremner).

GLASGOW CELTIC: Williams; Hay, Gemmell, Murdoch, McNeill, Brogan, Johnstone, Connelly, Hughes, Auld, Lennox.

LEEDS UNITED: Sprake (Harvey); Madeley, Cooper, Bremner, Charlton, Hunter, Lorimer, Clarke, Jones, Giles, Gray.

Glasgow Celtic won 3–1 on aggregate.

April 1 1970: LEGIA WARSAW (Poland) (0) 0 FEYENOORD ROTTERDAM (Holland) (0) 0.

LEGIA WARSAW: Grotinschy; Stachurski, Traskowski, Dejna, Brycheczy, Zmijewski, Piesko (Malkiewicz), Zygmunt, Blaut II, Blaut I, Godocha.

FEYENOORD: Treijtel; Haak, Laseroms, van Duivenbode, Hasil (Geels), Jansen, Van Hanegem, Wery, Kindvall, Moulijn.

April 15 1970: FEYENOORD (2) 2 (Van Hanegem, Hasil) LEGIA WARSAW (0) 0.

FEYENOORD: Treijtel; Haak, Laseroms, Israel, Van Duivenbode, Hasil, Jansen, Wery, Kindvall, Van Hanegem, Moulijn.

LEGIA WARSAW: Grotinschy; Stachurski, Blaut II, Zygmunt, Traskowski, Brycheczy, Blaut I, Dejna, Zmijewski, Piesko, Godocha. *Feyenoord won 2–0 on aggregate.*

Final—Milan
May 6 1970: FEYENOORD (Holland) (1) 2 (Israel, Kindvall) CELTIC (Scotland) (1) 1 (Gemmell).
(After extra time. 90-minute score 1–1)
FEYENOORD: Graafland; Romeyn (Haak 105 min.), Israel, Laseroms, Van Duivenbode, Jansen, Van Hanegem, Hasil, Wery, Kindvall, Moulijn.
CELTIC: Williams; Hay, Gemmell, Murdoch, McNeill, Brogan, Johnstone, Hughes, Wallace, Auld (Connelly 77 min.), Lennox.
Note: Players who were brought on as substitutes are given in brackets after the names of players they replaced.

Results of Finals
1955–56	Real Madrid 4	Rheims 3	Paris
1956–57	Real Madrid 2	Fiorentina 0	Madrid
1957–58	Real Madrid 3	A.C. Milan 2*	Brussels
1958–59	Real Madrid 2	Rheims 0	Stuttgart
1959–60	Real Madrid 7	Eintracht Frankfurt 3	Glasgow
1960–61	Benfica 3	Barcelona 2	Berne
1961–62	Benfica 5	Real Madrid 3	Amsterdam
1962–63	A.C. Milan 2	Benfica 1	Wembley
1963–64	Inter-Milan 3	Real Madrid 1	Vienna
1964–65	Inter-Milan 1	Benfica 0	Milan
1965–66	Real Madrid 2	Partizan Belgrade 1	Brussels
1966–67	Glasgow Celtic 2	Inter-Milan 1	Lisbon
1967–68	Manchester United 4	Benfica 1*	Wembley
1968–69	A.C. Milan 4	Ajax Amsterdam 1	Madrid
1969–70	Feyenoord 2	Glasgow Celtic 1*	Milan

* After extra time.

Teams in Finals
1955–56
June 12 1956: REAL MADRID (2) 4 (Rial 2, Marquitos, Di Stefano) RHEIMS (2) 3 (Leblond, Tremplin, Hidalgo). Paris. 40,000
REAL MADRID: Alonzo; Atienza, Marquitos, Lesmes, Munoz, Zarraga, Joseito, Marcal, Di Stefano, Rial, Gento.
RHEIMS: Jacquet; Zimny, Jonquet, Giraudo, Leblond, Siatka, Hidalgo, Giovacki, Kopa, Bliard, Tremplin.
1956–1957
May 30 1957: REAL MADRID (0) 2 (Di Stefano pen., Gento) FIOREN-TINA (0) 0. Madrid. 125,000
REAL MADRID: Alonzo; Torres, Marquitos, Lesmes, Munoz, Zarraga, Kopa, Mateos, Di Stefano, Rial, Gento.

FIORENTINA: Sarti; Magnini, Orzan, Cervato, Scaramucci, Segato, Julinho, Montmori, Virgili, Gratton, Bizzari.

1957–1958

May 29 1958: REAL MADRID (0) 3 (Di Stefano, Rial, Gento) A.C. MILAN (0) 2 (Schiaffino, Grillo). Brussels. 70,000

(After extra time. 90-minute score 2–2)

REAL MADRID: Alonzo; Atienza, Santamaria, Lesmes, Santisteban, Zarraga, Kopa, Joseito, Di Stefano, Rial, Gento.

A.C. MILAN: Soldan; Fontana, Maldini, Beraldo, Bergamaschi, Radice, Danova, Lindholm, Schiaffino, Grillo, Cucchiaroni.

1958–1959

June 3 1959: REAL MADRID (1) 2 (Mateos, Di Stefano) RHEIMS (0) 0. Stuttgart. 70,000

REAL MADRID: Dominguez; Marquitos, Santamaria, Zarraga, Santisteban, Ruiz, Kopa, Mateos, Di Stefano, Rial, Gento.

RHEIMS: Colonna; Rodzik, Jonquet, Giraudo, Penverne, Leblond, Lamartine, Bliard, Fontaine, Piantoni, Vincent.

1959–1960

May 18 1960: REAL MADRID (3) 7 (Di Stefano 3, Puskas 4) EINTRACHT FRANKFURT (1) 3 (Kress, Stein 2). Glasgow. 127,621.

REAL MADRID: Dominquez; Marquitos, Santamaria, Pachin, Zarraga, Vidal, Canario, Del Sol, Di Stefano, Puskas, Gento.

EINTRACHT FRANKFURT: Loy; Lutz, Eigenbrodt, Hofer, Weilbacher, Stinka, Kress, Lindner, Stein, Pfaff, Meier.

1960–1961

May 31 1961: BENFICA (2) 3 (Aguas, Ramallets o.g., Coluna) BARCELONA (1) 2 (Kocsis, Czibor). Berne. 26,732

BENFICA: Costa Perreira; Joao, Germano, Angelo, Neto, Cruz, Augusto, Santana, Aguas, Coluna, Cavem.

BARCELONA: Ramallets; Foncho, Gensana, Gracia, Verges, Garay, Kubala, Kocsis, Evaristo, Suarez, Czibor.

1961–1962

May 2 1962: BENFICA (2) 5 (Eusebio 2, Aguas, Cavem, Coluna) REAL MADRID (3) 3 (Puskas 3). Amsterdam. 61,257

BENFICA: Costa Perreira; Joao, Germano, Angelo, Cavem, Cruz, Augusto, Eusebio, Aguas, Coluna, Simoes.

REAL MADRID: Araguistain; Cassado, Santamaria, Miera, Felo, Pachin, Tejada, Del Sol, Di Stefano, Puskas, Gento.

1962–1963

May 22 1963: A.C. MILAN (0) 2 (Altafina 2) BENFICA (1) 1 (Eusebio). Wembley. 45,715

A.C. MILAN: Ghezzi; David, Maldini, Trebbi, Benitez, Trapattoni, Pivatelli, Sani, Altafina, Rivera, Mora.

BENFICA: Costa Perreira; Cavem, Humberto, Raul, Cruz, Santana, Coluna, Augusto, Torres, Eusebio, Simoes.

1963–1964

May 27 1964: INTER-MILAN (1) 3 REAL MADRID (0) 1. Vienna. 71,333

INTER-MILAN: Sarti; Burgnich, Guarneri, Facchetti, Tagnin, Picchi, Jair, Mazzola, Milani, Suarez, Corso.

REAL MADRID: Vicente; Isidro, Santamaria, Pachin, Zoco, Muller, Amancio, Felo, Di Stefano, Puskas, Gento.

1964–1965

May 27 1965: INTER-MILAN (1) 1 (Jair) BENFICA (0) 0. Milan. 89,000

INTER-MILAN: Sarti; Burgnich, Guarneri, Facchetti, Bedin, Picchi, Jair, Mazzola, Peiro, Suarez, Corso.

BENFICA: Costa Perreira; Cavem, Germano, Raul, Cruz, Neto, Coluna, Augusto, Torres, Eusebio, Simoes.

1965–1966

May 11 1965: REAL MADRID (0) 2 (Amancio, Serena) PARTIZAN BELGRADE (0) 1 (Vasovic). Brussels. 46,745

REAL MADRID: Araguistain; Pachin, De Felipe, Zoco, Sanchis, Pirri, Velasquez, Serena, Amancio, Grosso, Gento.

PARTIZAN BELGRADE: Soskic; Jusufi, Rasovic, Vasovic, Mihajlovic, Becejac, Kovacevic, Bajic, Hasanagic, Galic, Pirmajer.

1966–1967

May 25 1967: GLASGOW CELTIC (0) 2 (Gemmell, Chalmers) INTER-MILAN (1) 1 (Mazzola pen.). Lisbon. 45,000

GLASGOW CELTIC: Simpson; Craig, McNeill, Clark, Gemmell, Murdoch, Auld, Johnston, E, Wallace, Chalmers, Lennox.

INTER-MILAN: Sarti; Burgnich, Guarneri, Picchi, Facchetti, Bedin, Bicicli, Domenghini, Mazzola, Cappellini, Corso.

1967–1968

May 29 1968: MANCHESTER UNITED (0) 4 (Charlton 2, Best, Kidd) BENFICA (0) 1 (Graca). Wembley. 92,225

(After extra time. 90-minute score 1–1)

MANCHESTER UNITED: Stepney; Brennan, Dunne, Crerand, Foulkes, Stiles, Best, Kidd, Charlton, Sadler, Aston.

BENFICA: Henrique; Adolfo, Humberto, Jacinto Joao, Cruz, Graca, Coluna, Augusto, Torres, Eusebio, Simoes.

1968–1969

May 28 1969: A.C. MILAN (2) 4 (Prati 3, Sormani) AJAX AMSTERDAM (0) 1 (Vasovic pen.). Madrid. 50,000

A.C. MILAN: Cudicini; Anquilletti, Schnellinger, Rosato, Malatrasi, Trapattoni, Hamrin, Lodetti, Sormani, Rivera, Prati.

AJAX AMSTERDAM: Bals; Suurbier, Vasovic, Van Duivenbode, Hulshoff, Pronk (Muller), Groot (Nuninga), Swart, Danielsen, Cruyff, Keizer.

8 European Cup-Winners' Cup Goes to Manchester City

Manchester City became the second English League club to win a European trophy when they won the European Cup-Winners' Cup by beating Gornik Zabrze, the team from Poland's coal-mining centre, by two goals to one at the rainswept Prater Stadium of Vienna on April 29—the day following Arsenal's success in the Fairs' Cup. This was Manchester City's fourth major success in three seasons following the Football League championship, the F.A. Cup and the Football League Cup—a tribute to the hard work and devotion of their manager, Joe Mercer, the former Everton and Arsenal player, to make up for the disappointments he had suffered at Aston Villa, who had been ably assisted by the volatile Malcolm Allison as coach.

Together they had fashioned a sound all-round side of youth and experience. Even though without Mike Summerbee in their forward line against Gornik because of calf trouble which failed to respond to treatment, they were still able to master the Poles in the style which had carried them through the competition. And they survived the loss of their experienced defender Mick Doyle after 22 minutes when he was carried off with an ankle injury.

Tony Book, the man Allison found in Southern League football when he was with Plymouth and later persuaded to join him at Maine Road, proved an inspiring captain in conditions which must not have been unfamiliar to Manchester players, Francis Lee put up one of his greatest performances, 18-year-old Tony Towers, one of the discoveries of the season played like a veteran and with the rest of the team backing them up so well, City for once pushed their local Manchester United rivals into the background.

But while City officials were delighted with their success they were more than disappointed at the small crowd of only 10,000 who turned up for the match and were critical of U.E.F.A. for choosing the Austrian capital for the final. Apart from the weather which kept away the fans there was a live TV broadcast of the game.

That Manchester City were full value for their victory was fully acknowledged by the Polish critics who agreed they were faster on the ball, adopted more modern tactics, and marshalled their defence much better when Gornik threw everything into attack in the second half. But it was generally thought that three exhausting semi-final ties lasting five and a half hours with A.S. Roma had taken some of the sting from Gornik.

City soon stamped their authority on the game when Neil Young pounced on a rebound of a Glyn Pardoe shot off the goalkeeper Hubert Kostka to give them the lead just seven minutes before Doyle was carried off to take no further part in the game.

Even so they managed to contain the Poles and three minutes before half-time they went further ahead. Young was racing through and looked a certain scorer. There was only one thing that Kostka could do to stop him—and he did it. He brought him down with a rugby tackle. The Austrian referee, Paul Schiller, immediately awarded a penalty, and Lee's spot-kick went into the net off Kostka's boot.

In the second half Gornik knew their only chance was to throw everything into attack and even their captain, Stanislaw Oslizlo, usually a strong man in defence, was up among the forwards, and it was he who, taking advantage of a rare mix up by City's defenders, reduced Gornik's arrears in the 68th minute. But City managed to hold out for the rest of the game and finished good winners. Five minutes from the end Gornik also lost a defender, Stefan Florenski, injuring a leg after falling heavily.

It was away back in September that Manchester City began their first season in the competition in Bilbao's San Manes Stadium where they hit back from 3–1 down to gain a 3–3 draw against Atletico Bilbao, which put them in good heart for the second leg at Maine Road where they ran out easy 3–0 winners. Their next opponents were Lierse S.K. of Belgium and once again they were away for the first leg. But the Belgians offered little opposition and were beaten by three first-half goals at home. They conceded another five when they went to Manchester.

The quarter-final took Manchester City away for the third successive time and they held the students of Academica Coimbra of Portugal to a goalless draw—achieving what they had set out to do—but they had a struggle to win the second leg, being forced into extra time and only a goal by the teenager Towers, who substituted for Heslop in the second half, one minute from the end put them into the semi-final.

Again City had an away draw, and this time a visit to Germany to meet Schalke 04, who were in the competition as losing finalists because Bayern Munich had won the German double of League and Cup. Mercer was disappointed when City were beaten by a 75th minute Reinhard Libuda goal in the first leg in Gelsenkirchen, which had upset City's obvious plan to play for a draw. But they quickly ended any hopes the Germans had in the second leg with three goals in the first 27 minutes to run out winners by 5–1.

Gornik's path to the final was tougher than that of their opponents and included a victory on away goals and also the only play-off necessary in the campaign. They began with an easy victory over the Greek club, Olympiakos, winning 5–0 at home after gaining a 2–2 draw in Athens. Drawn against Glasgow Rangers, who had been beaten by Scottish League champions Celtic in the Scottish Cup final, they expected stronger opposition than they received.

The first leg was played in Chorzow, and Gornik, with a 100 per cent home record against British clubs, quickly showed their skill by taking a two-goal lead inside nine minutes to the delight of the 60,000 crowd. The first came when their international striker Wlodzimierz Lubanski cleverly beat two defenders and shot past Neef after only four minutes. Five minutes later a fierce drive from Zygfryd Szoltysik hit the underside of the bar from the edge of the penalty area and bounced down. Although Neef gathered the ball and cleared the Belgian referee ruled it had crossed the line and awarded a goal, which Rangers hotly disputed.

Rangers got a goal back eleven minutes after the interval when their Swedish international, Orjan Persson swept the ball first time with his left foot into the net from a pass by Willie Henderson. This goal inspired Rangers who began to hold Gornik but a defensive slip by the Dane, Kai Johansen, in the last two minutes cost them a third goal—Lubanski nipping in to score again and given Gornik a 3–1 victory.

In the second leg Rangers again showed they were capable of fighting back and a crowd of 70,000 at Ibrox Park were cheered when Jim Baxter put them back in the game with a goal after 17 minutes. But after the interval Rangers fell away and the Poles took command. Goals by Alfred Olek, Lubanski and Skoweronek, who had gone on as substitute for Wladyslaw Szardynski after half-time in 17 minutes sent Rangers crashing to another 3–1 defeat—which had a sequel the following morning when they sacked their manager, David White.

Two goals in Sofia by Szoltysik and Lubanski, which later were to count double, enabled Gornik to win their quarter-final tie with Levski Spartak. They were beaten 3–2 by the Bulgarian side in Sofia, and managed to win only by 2–1 at home which meant that the scores were level on aggregate at 4–4. So the away goals rule had to be called into operation to decide the winners.

And in their semi-final with A.S. Roma only the toss of the disc in the dressing-room after 330 minutes football took them to the final in Vienna. Roma had qualified for the semi-final on winning the toss against P.S.V. Eindhoven, the Dutch side for whom Willi Van Der

Kuylen had converted a penalty to give them a 1–0 victory after a similar defeat in Rome.

Gornik went to Rome for the first leg and centre-forward Jan Banas gave them the lead from a pass by Lubanski after 23 minutes only for Elvio Salvori to send an 80,000 crowd wild with delight with an equaliser eight minutes after the interval. The Poles seemed satisfied with the result but to their surprise and that of 100,000 people in the Chorzow Stadium for the second leg the Italians went ahead Fabio Capello scoring from a penalty after 10 minutes.

With Roma massing nine men in defence the Gornik forwards had a frustrating time and it was not until the final minute of the game that they equalised when they were awarded a penalty and Lubanski managed to beat Alberto Ginulfi to the relief of the crowd and his fellow players. So the match went into extra time and within three minutes Lubanski had scored again. Now it was Roma's turn to struggle and not until 15 seconds from the end did they equalise when Giacomo La Rosa, who had been brought on as substitute for Cappellini for the extra time period, managed to score.

So ended what must have been one of the most up-and-down matches ever seen in the stadium, and one of the most exciting, which sent the teams to a play-off in France at Strasbourg. Floodlight problems delayed the kick-off for an hour, and when the match was played yet another inconclusive result was obtained. Lubanski gave Gornik the lead after 42 minutes but Capello equalised from a penalty 14 minutes later. Again extra time was played, and so after five and a half hours football it was left to the referee to toss the disc in the dressing-room to decide which team went into the final, the most unsatisfactory way of deciding a match. Gornik won the toss. Well, perhaps they deserved it. They had been slightly the better football side, even if they had not been able to score that extra goal which would have proved it.

Although U.E.F.A. seeded four teams for the draw for the first round it was necessary, with the holders being qualified for the next season's competition, to have one preliminary round match. That produced an anomaly of two strong teams like Rapid Vienna of Austria and Torpedo Moscow of Russia having to meet while weaker sides such as Mjoendalen, the Norwegian amateurs, Apoel of Nicosia, and Reykjavik, the Iceland Cup holders, all went straight into the first round where they were well beaten.

One feels it would have been better to have had Rapid and Torpedo in the first round as more attractive sides. As it was, Rapid disposed of their Russian rivals and then went out in the first round to P.S.V. Eindhoven, being beaten in both legs.

Mjoendalen were crushed by Cardiff City 7–1 and 5–1, Lierse

S.K., the Belgian part-timers, dismissed Apeol 10–1 and 1–0, and Reykjavik went out 4–0 and 4–0 to Levski Spartak of Sofia—which suggests a preliminary round for the weaker sides in the competition.

Two other strong sides, Atletico Bilbao and Manchester City, were drawn together in the first round, a pairing which proved Bilbao's new English manager, Ronnie Allen, the former Wolves chief, to be either psychic or just a lucky forecaster. When Bilbao won the Spanish Cup for the 21st time in 31 finals the previous season he looked forward to the draw and said 'Manchester City first and then the others can take their turn to be beaten.' Unfortunately for Allen, Bilbao did not get over their first hurdle.

It is often said that clubs taking part in European competitions are greedy because they want two-legged ties, but matches are not always as successful as they seem. For instance the West German side Schalke 04, visited Norkoping in Sweden to play I.F.K. in a second round tie and found that only 2,346 people had turned up to see them get a goalless draw. But there were 15,000 in Gelsenkirchen's Gluckauf stadium for the return which Schalke won 1–0.

Preliminary Round
Aug. 27 1969: RAPID VIENNA (0) 0 MOSCOW TORPEDO (Russia) (0) 0.
Sept. 3 1969: MOSCOW TORPEDO (0) 1 (Ghershkovich) RAPID VIENNA (0) 1.
Rapid Vienna qualified on away goal.

First Round
Sept. 17 1969: GLASGOW RANGERS (Scotland) (2) 2 (Johnston 2) STEAUA BUCHAREST (Rumania) (0) 0.
GLASGOW RANGERS: Neef; Johansen, Provan, Greig, McKinnon, Baxter, Henderson, Jardine, Stein, Johnston, Persson.
STEAUA BUCHAREST: Suciu; Cristache, Satmareanu, Vigu, Dumitriu, Halmageanu, Pantea, Tataru, Voinea, Negrea, Creiniceanu.
Oct. 1 1969: STEAUA BUCHAREST (0) 0 GLASGOW RANGERS (0) 0.
STEAUA BUCHAREST: Suciu; Cristache, Satmareanu, Halmageanu, Vigu, Dumitriu, Negrea, Pantea, Tataru, Voinea, Pantea.
GLASGOW RANGERS: Neef; Johansen, Provan, Greig, McKinnon, Baxter, Henderson, Watson, Stein, Jardine, Johnston.
Glasgow Rangers won 2–0 on aggregate.

Sept. 17 1969: SHAMROCK ROVERS (Rep. of Ireland) (0) 2 (Barber 2) SCHALKE 04 (W. Germany) (1) 1 (Pirkner).
SHAMROCK ROVERS: Smith; Gregg, Canavan, Keiran, Mulligan, Richardson, O'Neill, Leech, Hannigan, Barber, Dixon.
SCHALKE 04: Nigbur; Senger, Wuest, van Haaren, Fichtel, Libuda, Pohlschmidt, Neuser, Wittkamp, Pirkner.

Oct. 1 1969: SCHALKE 04 (1) 3 (Libuda, Pirkner, Wittkamp) SHAMROCK ROVERS (0) 0.

SCHALKE 04: Nigbur; Becher, Senger, Wittkamp, Fitchel, van Haaren, Libuda, Neuser, Wuest (Erlhoff), Pohlschmidt, Pirkner.

SHAMROCK ROVERS: Smith; Gregg, Courtney, Keiran, Mulligan, Richardson, O'Neill, Leech, Hannigan, Barber, Haverty.

Schalke 04 won 4–2 on aggregate.

Sept. 17 1969: ARDS (N. Ireland) (0) 0 A.S. ROMA (Italy) (0) 0.

ARDS: Kydd; McCoy, Crothers, Bell, Stewart, Nixon, Humphries, McAvoy, McAteer, Burke, Welsh.

A.S. ROMA: Ginulfi; Bet, Carpenetti, Spinosi, Cappelli, Santarini, Peiro, Braglia, Landini, Capello, Scaratti.

Oct. 1 1969: A.S. ROMA (1) 3 (Salvori 2, Peiro) ARDS (0) 1 (Crothers).

A.S. ROMA: Ginulfi; Bet, Petrelli, Salvori, Cappelli, Santarini, Bertogna, Capellini, Peiro, Capello, Cordova.

ARDS: Kydd; McCoy, Crothers, Bell, Stewart, Nixon, Humphries, McAvoy, McAteer, Anderson, Welsh.

A.S. Roma won 3–1 on aggregate.

Sept. 17 1969: MJOENDALEN (Norway) (1) 1 (Olsen J.) CARDIFF CITY (Wales) (3) 7 (Clark 2, Toshack 2, Lea, Sutton, King).

MJOENDALEN: Nilsen; Brock (Olsen O.), Jensrud, Loe, Svendsen, Skistad, Brede, Kristiansen, Solberg, Holmen (Larsen), Skistad Boye, Olsen J.

CARDIFF CITY: Davies; Derrett, Carver, Sutton, Murray, Jones, Phillips, Clark, Lea, Toshack, King.

Oct. 1 1969: CARDIFF CITY (4) 5 (King 2, Allen) MJOENDALEN (1) 1 (Sozberg E.).

CARDIFF CITY: Davies; Carver, Bell, Sutton, Murray, Lewis, Jones, Clark, Allan, Toshack (Lea), King.

MJOENDALEN: Larsen; Brock, Jensrud, Loe, Svendsen, Skistad, Olsen O., Kristiansen (Larsen S.), Solberge, Holmen (sub Solberg K.), Olsen J.

Cardiff City won 12–2 on aggregate.

Sept. 17 1969: ATLETICO BILBAO (Spain) (2) 3 (Argoitia, Clemente, Uriarte) MANCHESTER CITY (England) (1) 3 (Young, Booth, Echevarria o.g.)

ATLETICO BILBAO: Iribar; Saez, Echevarria, Aranguren, Igartua, Larrauri, Argoitia, Uriarte, Arieta, Clemente, Rojo.

MANCHESTER CITY: Corrigan; Book, Pardoe, Doyle, Booth, Oakes, Bell, Summerbee, Lee, Young, Bowyer.

Oct. 1 1969: MANCHESTER CITY (0) 3 ATLETICO BILBAO (0)

Oct. 1 1969: MANCHESTER CITY (0) 3 (Oakes, Bell, Bowyer) MANCHESTER CITY: Corrigan; Book, Pardoe, Doyle, Booth, Oakes, Summerbee, Bell, Lee, Young, Bowyer.

ATLETICO BILBAO: Iribar; Zugagaga, Aranguren, Igartua, Echevarria, Larrauri, Argoitia, Betzuen (Ortuzono), Arieta, Clemente, Rojo.

Manchester City won 6–3 on aggregate.

Sept. 17 1969: RAPID VIENNA (Austria) (1) 1 (Bjerregaard) P.S.V.
EINDHOVEN (Holland) (2) 2 (Veenstra, Smith-Hansen).
Oct. 1 1969: P.S.V. EINDHOVEN (2) 4 (Kuylen, Veenstra, Smith-Hansen 2) RAPID VIENNA (1) 2 (Flogel, Bjerregaard)
P.S.V. Eindhoven won 6–3 on aggregate.

Sept. 17 1969: GOEZTEPE IZMIR (Turkey) (1) 3 (Fevzi, Mehet, Fadil)
UNION LUXEMBURG (0) 0.
Oct. 1 1969: UNION LUXEMBURG (0) 2 GOEZTEPE IZMIR (2) 3.
Goeztepe Izmir won 6–2 on aggregate.

Sept. 17 1969: DUKLA PRAGUE (Czechoslovakia) (1) 1 (Hudel)
MARSEILLES (France) (0) 0.
Oct. 1 1969: MARSEILLES (1) 2 DUKLA PRAGUE (0) 0.
Marseilles won 2–1 on aggregate.

Aug. 30 1969: I.B.V. REYKJAVIK (Iceland) (0) 0 LEVSKI SPARTAK
(Bulgaria) (4) 4 (Vassilenovz 2, Pavlov, Asparoukhov).
Oct. 1 1969: LEVSKI SPARTAK (1) 4 (Kotkov 3, Gaidarski) I.B.V.
REYKJAVIK (0) 0.
Levski Spartak won 8–0 on aggregate.

Sept. 17 1969: F.C. MAGDEBURG (E. Germany) (1) 1 (Sparwasser)
M.T.K. BUDAPEST (Hungary) (0) 0.
Oct. 1 1969: M.T.K. BUDAPEST (1) 1 (Takacs) F.C. MAGDEBURG
(0) 1 (Sparwasser).
(After extra time)
F.C. Magdeburg won 2–1 on aggregate.

Sept. 17 1969: DINAMO ZAGREB (Yugoslavia) (1) 3 (Miljkovic,
Novak, Gucmirtk) SLOVAN BRATISLAVA (Czechoslovakia) (0) 0.
Oct. 1 1969: SLOVAN BRATISLAVA (0) 0 DINAMO ZAGREB (0) 0.
Dinamo Zagreb won 3–0 on aggregate.

Sept. 17 1969: I.F.K. NORKOPPING (Sweden) (3) 5 SLIEMA
WANDERERS (Malta) (1) 1 (Bonnet).
Sept. 30 1969: SLIEMA WANDERERS (0) 1 (Griffiths) I.F.K. NOR-
KOPPING (0) 0.
I.F.K. Norkopping won 5–2 on aggregate.

Sept. 17 1969: FREM COPENHAGEN (Denmark) (2) 2 (Hansen H. 2)
ST GALLEN (Switzerland) (1) 1 (Nafziger).
Oct. 1 1969: ST GALLEN (0) 1 (Cornioley) FREM COPENHAGEN
(0) 0.
St Gallen won on away goal.

Sept. 17 1969: OLYMPIAKOS (Greece) (0) 2 (Gioutos, Sideris) GORNIK
ZABRZE (Poland) (2) 2 (Wilczek 2).
Oct. 1 1969: GORNIK ZABRZE (1) 5 (Wilczek, Skowronel, Szoltysik,
Banas 2, 1 pen.) OLYMPIAKOS (0) 0.
Gornik Zabrze won 7–2 on aggregate.

Sept. 17 1969: ACADEMICA COIMBRA (Portugal) (0) 0 PALLO-SEURA KUPIO (Finland) (0) 0.

Oct. 1 1969: PALLOSEURA KUPIO (0) 0 ACADEMICA COIMBRA (0) 1 (Nene).

Academica Coimbra won 1–0 on aggregate.

Sept. 17 1969: LIERSE S.K. (Belgium) (5) 10 (Vermeyen 3, Denul 4, Put, Janssens 2) APOEL (Cyprus) (0) 1 (Agatholleus).

Sept. 24 1969: APOEL (0) 0 LIERSE S.K. (1) 1 (Denul).

(Also played at Lierse)

Lierse S.K. won 11–1 on aggregate.

Second Round

Nov. 12 1969: GOEZTEPE IZMIR (Turkey) (3) 3 (Fevzi, Erkan, Nielsen) CARDIFF CITY (Wales) (0) 0.

GOEZTEPE IZMIR: Mehmet K.; Caglayan, Ozer, Mehmet B., Ihsan, Nevzat, Fevzi, Ertan, Nielsen, Gursel, Mehmet F.

CARDIFF CITY: Davies; Carver, Bell, Sutton, Murray, Harris, Lea, Clark, King, Toshack, Sharp (Allan).

Nov. 26 1969: CARDIFF CITY (0) 1 (Bird) GOEZTEPE IZMIR (0) 0.

CARDIFF CITY: Davies; Carver, Bell, Sutton, Murray, Harris, Allan, Clark, Lea (Bird), Toshack (Coldrick), King.

GOEZTEPE IZMIR: Ali; Mehmet R. Caglayan, Ozer, Mehmet B., Nevzat, Fevzi, Ertan, Nielsen (Hald), Gursel, Mehmet F.

Goeztepe Izmir won 3–1 on aggregate.

Nov. 12 1969: LEVSKI SPARTAK SOFIA (Bulgaria) (2) 4 (Kostov, Panov, Nitkov, Kirilov) ST GALLEN (Switzerland) (0) 0

LEVSKI SPARTAK: Michailov; Peshev, Zhechev, Gaidarski, Ivkov, Kirilov, Vesselinov, Mitkov, Panov, Kotkov, Kostov.

ST GALLEN: Bigaggi; Schwig, Kaspar, Nafziger, Ziehmann, Furer, Frei, Pfirter, Rutti, Brander, Turin.

Nov. 26 1969: ST GALLEN (0) 0 LEVSKI SPARTAK (0) 0.

Levski Spartak won 4–0 on aggregate.

Nov. 12 1969: MARSEILLES (France) (1) 1 (Loubet) DINAMO ZAGREB (Yugoslavia) (0) 1 (Cercek).

MARSEILLES: Escale; Lopez, Hodoul, Zwunka, Djorkaeff, Novi, Merschel, Magnusson, Bonnel, Joseph, Loubet.

DINAMO ZAGREB: Dauthegovic; Cvec, Ramljak, Blaskovic, Gracanin, Belin, Kis, Cercek, Piric, Novak, Rora.

Nov. 26 1969: DINAMO ZAGREB (0) 2 (Novak 2) MARSEILLES (0) 0.

DINAMO ZAGREB: Dauthegovic; Cvec, Gracanin, Belin, Ramljak, Blaskovic, Vabec, Piric, Novak, Gucmirtl, Rora.

MARSEILLES: Escale; Lopez, Hodoul, Zwunka, Djorkaeff, Novi, Merschel, Loubet, Bonnell, Joseph, Destrumelle.

Dinamo Zagreb won 3–1 on aggregate.

Nov. 12 1969: NORKOPPING (Sweden) (0) 0 SCHALKE 04 (West Germany) (0) 0.

NORKOPPING: Andersson; Lafleur Carlsson L., Nordqvist, Pressfeldt, Hutt, Larsson, Jansson, Norblad, Hesselgren, Berglund.

SCHALKE 04: Elting; Slomiany, Rausch, Wittkamp, Fichtel, Van Haaren, Libuda, Scheer, Pirkner, Neuser, Lutkeboehmert.

Nov. 26 1969: SCHALKE 04 (1) 1 (Scheer) NORKOPPING (0) 0.
Schalke 04 won 1–0 on aggregate.

Nov. 12 1969: LIERSE S.K. (Belgium) (0) 0 MANCHESTER CITY (England) (3) 3 (Lee 2, Bell).

LIERSE S.K.: Engelen; Dierickx, Bogaerts, Michielsen, Van Den Eynde, Willens, Vermeyen, Van Opstal, Denul, De Ceulaer, Janssens.

MANCHESTER CITY: Corrigan; Book, Pardoe, Doyle, Booth, Oakes, Summerbee, Bell, Lee, Young, Bowyer.

Nov. 26 1969: MANCHESTER CITY (1) 5 (Lee 2, Bell 2, Summerbee) LIERSKE S.K. (0) 0.

MANCHESTER CITY: Mulhearn; Book, Pardoe, Doyle, Booth, Oakes, Summerbee, Bell, Lee, Jeffries, Bowyer.

LIERSE S.K.: Engelen; Van Der Eynde, Bogaerts, Michielsen, Mertens, Willens, Van Opstal, Jannssens, De Ceulaer, Denul, Min.

Manchester City won 8–0 on aggregate.

Nov. 12 1969: F.C. MAGDEBURG (East Germany) (1) 1 (Sparwasser) ACADEMICA COIMBRA (Portugal) (0) 0.

F.C. MAGDEBURG: Moldenhauer; Sykora (Oelz), Fronzeck, Ohn, Retschlag Kubisch, Seguin, Walter, Sparwasser, Abraham, Hermann.

ACADEMICA COIMBRA: Viegas; Artur, Alhino, Belo, Araujo, Rodriguez, Gervasio, Campos, M, Nene, Campos, V.

Nov. 26 1969: ACADEMICA COIMBRA (0) 2 (Alhinho, Campos) F.C. MAGDEBURG (0) 0.
Academica Coimbra won 2–1 on aggregate.

Nov. 12 1969: A.S. ROMA (Italy) (0) 1 (Capello pen.) P.S.V. EINDHOVEN (Holland) (0) 0.

A.S. ROMA: Ginulfi; Scaratti, Spinosi, Salvori, Bet, Santarini, Cappelini, Landini, Peiro, Capello, Cordova.

P.S.V. EINDHOVEN: Doesburg; Van Den Dungen, Strik, Radovic, Kemper, Van Stippent, Bjerre, Hansen, Van Der Kuylen, Veenstra, Ressel.

Nov. 26 1969: P.S.V. EINDHOVEN (0) 1 (Van Der Kuylen pen.) A.S. ROMA (0) 0.

(After extra time)

P.S.V. EINDHOVEN: Doesburg; Van Den Dungen, Strik, Radovic, Kemper, Van Stippent, Bjerre, Hansen, Mares, Van Der Kuylen, Ressel.

A.S. ROMA: Ginulfi; Bet, Spinosi, Salvori, Cappelli, Santarini, Cappellini, Braglia, Peiro, Cordova, Scaratti.

A.S. Roma won on toss of a disc.

Nov. 12 1969: GORNIK ZABRZE (Poland) (2) 3 (Lubanski 2, Szardynski) GLASGOW RANGERS (Scotland) (0) 1 (Persson).

GORNIK ZABRZE: Kostka; Latocha, Oslizlo, Gorgon, Florenski, Szoltysik, Wilczek, Olek, Banas, Lubanski, Szardynski.

GLASGOW RANGERS: Neef; Johansen, Heron, Greig, McKinnon, Baxter, Henderson, Penman, Stein, Johnston, Persson.

Nov. 26 1969: GLASGOW RANGERS (1) 1 (Baxter) GORNIK ZABRZE (0) 3 (Olek, Lubanski, Skoweronek).

GLASGOW RANGERS: Neef; Johansen, Heron, Greig, McKinnon, Baxter, Henderson, Penman, Stein, Johnston, Persson.

GORNIK ZABRZE: Kostka; Kuchta, Oslizlo, Latocha, Gorgon, Szoltysik, Wilczek, Olek, Banas, Lubanski, Szardynski (Skoweronek).

Gornik Zabrze won 6–2 on aggregate.

Quarter-Finals

Mar. 4 1970: ACADEMICA COIMBRA (Portugal) (0) 0 MAN-CHESTER CITY (England) (0) 0.

ACADEMICA COIMBRA: Cardoso; Artur, Alhino, Rodriguez, Marques, Campos M., Campos V., Jorge, Nene, Serafin.

MANCHESTER CITY: Corrigan; Book, Mann, Doyle, Booth, Oakes, Pardoe, Bell, Summerbee, Lee, Young.

Mar. 18 1970: MANCHESTER CITY (0) 1 (Towers) ACADEMICA COIMBRA (0) 0.

(After extra time. Score at 90 minutes 0–0)

MANCHESTER CITY: Corrigan; Book, Mann, Booth, Heslop (Towers), Oakes, Doyle, Bell, Lee, Young, Pardoe.

ACADEMICA COIMBRA: Cardoso; Artur, Alhino, Rodriguez, Marques, Rocha, Campos M., Campos V., Antonio, Nene, Serafin.

Manchester City won 1–0 on aggregate.

Mar. 4 1970: A.S. ROMA (Italy) (1) 2 (Landini, Capelli) GOEZTEPE IZMIR (Turkey) (0) 0.

A.S. ROMA: Ginulfi; Bet, Spinosi, Salvori, Cappelli, Santarini, Cappellini, Landini, Piero, Capello, Cordova.

GOEZTEPE IZMIR: Ali; Mehmet R., Caglayan, Ozer (Huseyin), Mehmet B., Nevzat, Ihsan, Ertan, Nielsen, Fevzi, Gursel.

Mar. 18 1970: GOEZTEPE IZMIR (0) 0 A.S. ROMA (0) 0.

GOEZTEPE IZMIR: Ali; Mehmet R., Caglayan, Ozer, Mehmet B., Nevzat, Halil, Ertan, Fevzi, Gursel, Mehmet B.

A.S. Roma won 2–0 on aggregate.

Mar. 4 1970: LEVSKI SPARTAK SOFIA (Bulgaria) (2) 3 (Asparoukhov 2, Panov) GORNIK ZABRZE (Poland) (1) 2 (Sozltysik, Lubanski).

LEVSKI SPARTAK: Kamenski; Peshev, Ivkov, Aladjov, Zhechev, Kirilov Y., Kirilov P., Panov, Asparoukhov, Kotkov, Mitkov.

GORNIK ZABRZE: Kostka; Kuchta, Oslizlo, Latocha, Gorgon, Szolty-sik, Wilczek, Olek, Banas, Lubanski, Deia.

Mar. 18 1970: GORNIK ZABRZE (1) 2 (Lubanski, Banas) LEVSKI SPARTAK SOFIA (0) 1 (Kirilov P.).

GORNIK ZABRZE: Gomola; Kuchta, Oslizlo, Gorgon, Latocha, Wilczek, Szoltysik, Olek, Banas, Lubanski, Deja.

LEVSKI SPARTAK: Kamenski; Gaidarski, Peshev, Zhechev, Aladjov, Kirilov Y., Kirilov P., Asparoukhov, Vesselinov.
Gornik Zabrze won on away goals.

Mar. 4 1970: DINAMO ZAGREB (Yugoslavia) (0) 1 (Cercek) SCHALKE 04 (West Germany) (1) 3 (Pirkner, Fichtel, Becher).
DINAMO ZAGREB: Stincic; Cvec, Vales, Belin, Ramljak, Blaskovic, Cercek, Piric, Novak, Gucmirtl, Rora.
SCHALKE 04: Nigbur; Becher, Rausch, Fichtel, Russmann, Saenger (Erlhoff), Pirkner, Sovieray, Pohlschmidt, Van Haaren, Wuest (Lutkeboehmert).
Mar. 18 1970: SCHALKE 04 (0) 1 (Scheer) DINAMO ZAGREB (0) 0.
SCHALKE 04: Nigbur; Becher, Rausch, Russmann, Fichtel, Van Haaren, Libuda, Neuser, Wuest (Scheer), Pohlschmidt, Pirkner.
DINAMO ZAGREB: Dauthegovic; Cvec (Vabec), Gracanin, Belin, Ramljak, Milkovic, Cercek, Piric, Novak, Gucmirtl, Rora.
Schalke 04 won 4–1 on aggregate.

Semi-Finals
April 1 1970: SCHALKE 04 (W. Germany) (0) 1 (Libuda) MAN-CHESTER CITY (England) (0) 0.
SCHALKE 04: Nigbur; Slomiany, Becher, Erlhoff, Fichtel, Van Haaren, Libuda, Neuser, Pohlschmidt, Wittkamp, Pirkner.
MANCHESTER CITY: Corrigan; Book, Pardoe, Doyle, Booth, Oakes, Jeffries, Bell, Summerbee, Lee, Young.
April 15 1970: MANCHESTER CITY (3) 5 (Doyle 2, Young, Lee, Bell) SCHALKE 04 (0) 1 (Libuda).
MANCHESTER CITY: Corrigan; Book, Pardoe, Doyle, Booth, Oakes, Towers, Bell, Summerbee (Carrodus), Lee, Young.
SCHALKE 04: Nigbur; Slomiany, Becher, Russman, Fichtel, Wittkamp, Libuda, Neuser, Pohlschmidt, Erlhoff (sub Scheer), Van Haaren.
Manchester City won 5–2 on aggregate.

April 1 1970: A.S. ROMA (Italy) (0) 1 (Salvori) GORNIK ZABRZE (Poland) (1) 1 (Banas).
A.S. ROMA: Ginulfi; Spinosi, Bet, Salvori, Cappelli, Santarini, Cappellini, Cordova, Peiro, Capello, Landini.
GORNIK ZABRZE: Kostka; Kuchte, Oslizlo, Latocha, Gorgon, Szoltysik, Wilczek, Olek, Banas, Lubanski, Deja.
April 15 1970: GORNIK ZABRZE (0) 2 (Lubanski 2) A.S. ROMA (1) 2 (Capello, La Rosa).
(After extra time. 90-minute score 1–1)
GORNIK ZABRZE: Kostka; Deja, Wilczek, Szoltysik, Banas, Oslizlo, Olek, Lubanski, Latocha, Kuchta, Gorgon.
A.S. ROMA: Ginulfi; Spinosi, Bet, Cappelli, Salvori, Santarini, Capello, Cappellini (Braglia), Peiro, Landini (La Rosa), Franzot.
Play-off
April 22 1970: GORNIK ZABRZE (1) 1 (Lubanski) A.S. ROMA (0) 1 (Capello pen.). Strasbourg.

(After extra time. 90-minute score 1–1)
GORNIK ZABRZE: Kostka; Oslizlo, Florenski, Gorgon, Latocha, Olek, Szardynski (Musiatek), Wilczek (Deja), Szoltysik, Banas, Lubanski.
A.S. ROMA: Ginulfi; Santarini, Bet, Spinosi, Scaratti (Benitez), Salvori, Capello, Peiro, Petrelli, Cappellini (La Rosa), Landini.
Gornik Zabrze won on toss of disc.

Final—Vienna
April 29 1970: MANCHESTER CITY (England) (2) 2 (Young, Lee pen.) GORNIK ZABRZE (Poland) (0) 1 (Oslizlo).
MANCHESTER CITY: Corrigan; Book, Pardoe, Doyle, (Bowyer), Booth, Oakes, Heslop, Bell, Lee, Young, Towers.
GORNIK ZABRZE: Kostka; Gorgon, Oslizlo, Latocha, Florenski (Deja) Szoltysik, Wilczek, N (Skoweronek), Olek, Banas, Lubanski, Szardynski.

Results of Finals

1960–1961	Glasgow Rangers 0 Fiorentina 2	Glasgow
	Fiorentina 2 Glasgow Rangers 1	Florence
1961–1962	Atletico Madrid 1 Fiorentina 1*	Glasgow
	Fiorentina 0 Atletico Madrid 3	Stuttgart
1962–1963	Tottenham Hotspur 5 Atletico Madrid 1	Rotterdam
1963–1964	Sporting Lisbon 3 M.T.K. Budapest 3*	Brussels
	Sporting Lisbon 1 M.T.K. Budapest 0	Antwerp
1964–1965	West Ham United 2 T.S.V. Munich 0	Wembley
1965–1966	Borussia Dortmund 2 Liverpool 1	Glasgow
1966–1967	Bayern Munich 1 Glasgow Rangers 0*	Nuremburg
1967–1968	A.C. Milan 2 S.V. Hamburg 0	Rotterdam
1968–1969	Slovan Bratislava 3 Barcelona 2	Basle
1969–1970	Manchester City 2 Gornik Zabrze 1	Vienna

*After extra time.

Teams in Finals
1960–1961
First leg
May 17 1961: GLASGOW RANGERS (0) 0 FIORENTINA (2) 2 (Milani 2). Glasgow. 80,000
GLASGOW RANGERS: Ritchie; Shearer, Caldow, Davis, Paterson, Baxter, Wilson, McMillan, Scott, Brand, Hume.
FIORENTINA: Albertosi; Robotti, Castelletti, Gonfiantini, Orran, Rimbaldo, Hamrin, Michell, Da Costa, Milani, Petris.
Second leg
May 27 1961: FIORENTINA (1) 2 (Milani, Hamrin) GLASGOW RANGERS (1) 1 (Scott). Florence. 50,000
FIORENTINA: Albertosi; Robotti, Castelletti, Gonfiantini, Orran, Rimbaldo, Hamrin, Michell, Da Costa, Milani, Petris.
GLASGOW RANGERS: Ritchie; Shearer, Caldow, Davis, Paterson, Baxter, Scott, McMillan, Millar, Brand, Wilson.
Fiorentina won 4–1 on aggregate.

1961–1962
May 10 1962: ATLETICO MADRID (1) 1 (Peiro) FIORENTINA (1) 1 (Hamrin). Glasgow. 29,066
(After extra time)
ATLETICO MADRID: Madinbeytia; Rivilla, Calleja, Ramirez, Gonzales, Glaria, Jones, Adelardo, Mendonca, Peiro, Collar.
FIORENTINA: Sarti; Orzan, Casteletti, Ferretti, Gonfiantini, Rimbaldo, Hamrin, Barto, Milani, Dell'Angelo.
Replay
Sept. 5 1962: ATLETICO MADRID (2) 3 (Jones, Mendonca, Peiro) FIORENTINA (0) 0. Stuttgart. 38,120
ATLETICO MADRID: Madinbeytia; Rivilla, Calleja, Ramirez, Griffa, Glaria, Jones, Adelardo, Mendonca, Peiro, Collar.
FIORENTINA: Albertosi; Robotti, Casteletti, Malatrasi, Orzan, Marchesi, Hamrin, Ferretti, Milani, Dell'Angelo, Petris.

1962–1963
May 15 1963: TOTTENHAM HOTSPUR (2) 5 (Dyson 2, Greaves 2, White) ATLETICO MADRID (0) 1 (Collar pen.). Rotterdam. 49,143
TOTTENHAM HOTSPUR: Brown; Baker, Henry, Blanchflower, Norman, Marchi, Jones, White, Smith, Greaves, Dyson.
ATLETICO MADRID: Madinbeytia; Rivilla, Rodriquez, Ramira, Griffa, Glaria, Honez, Adelardo, Chuzo, Mendoza, Collar.

1963–1964
May 13 1964: SPORTING LISBON (1) 3 (Figueiredo 2, Dansky o.g.) M.T.K. BUDAPEST (1) 3 (Sandor 2, Kuti). Brussels. 3,208
(After extra time. 90-minute score 3–3)
SPORTING LISBON: Carvalho; Gomez, Peridsi, Battista, Carlos, Geo, Mendes, Oswaldo, Mascarenhas, Figueiredo, Morais.
M.T.K. BUDAPEST: Kovalik; Keszei, Dansky, Jenei, Nagy, Kovacs, Sandor, Vasas, Kuti, Bodor, Halapi.
Replay
May 15 1964: SPORTING LISBON (1) 1 (Morais) M.T.K. BUDAPEST (0) 0. Antwerp. 13,924
SPORTING LISBON: Carvalho; Gomez, Peridis, Battista, Carlos, Geo, Mendes, Silva (sub Oswaldo), Mascarenhas, Figueiredo, Morais.
M.T.K. BUDAPEST: Kovalik; Keszei, Dansky, Jenei, Nagy, Vasas, Kovacs, Sandor, Kuti, Bodor, Halapi.

1964–1965
May 19 1965: WEST HAM UNITED (0) 2 (Sealey 2) T.S.V. MUNICH (0) 0. Wembley. 97,974
WEST HAM UNITED: Standen; Kirkup, Burkett, Peters, Brown, Moore, Sealey, Boyce, Hurst, Dear, Sissons.
T.S.V. MUNICH: Radenkovic; Wagner, Kohlars, Bena, Reich, Luttrop, Heiss, Kuppers, Brunnenmeier Grosser, Rebele.

1965–1966
May 5 1966: BORUSSIA DORTMUND (0) 2 (Held, Libuda) LIVERPOOL (0) 1 (Hunt). Glasgow. 41,657

(After extra time. 90-minute score 1-1)
BORUSSIA DORTMUND: Tilkowski; Cyliax, Redder, Kurrat, Paul, Aussauer, Libuda, Schmidt, Held, Sturm, Emmerich.
LIVERPOOL: Lawrence; Lawler, Byrne, Milne, Yeats, Stevenson, Callaghan, Hunt, St John, Smith, Thompson.

1966-1967
May 31 1967: BAYERN MUNICH (0) 1 (Roth) GLASGOW RANGERS (0) 0. Nuremburg. 69,480
(After extra time. 90-minute score 0-0)
BAYERN MUNICH: Maier; Nowak, Kupferschmidt, Roth, Beckenbauer, Olk, Na ziger, Ohlhauser, Muller, Koulmann, Brenninger.
GLASGOW RANGERS: Martin; Johansen, Provan, Jardine, McKinnon, Greig, Henderson, Smith A., Hynd, Smith D., Johnston.

1967-1968
May 23 1968: A.C. MILAN (2) 2 (Hamrin 2) S.V. HAMBURG (0) 0. Rotterdam. 53,276
A.C. MILAN: Cudicini; Anquilletti, Schnellinger, Rosato, Trapattoni, Lodetti, Scala, Hamrin, Sormani, Rivera, Prati.
S.V. HAMBURG: Oeczan; Sandmann, Horst, Schulz, Kurbjuhn, Kraemer, Dieckmann, Berndt, Doerfel, Seeler, Hoenig.

1968-1969
May 21 1969: SLOVAN BRATISLAVA (3) 3 (Cvetler, Hrivnak, Jan Capkovic) BARCELONA (1) 2 (Zaldua, Rexach). Basle. 53,000
SLOVAN BRATISLAVA: Vencel; Filo, Hrivnak, Horvath, Zlocha, Josef Capkovic, Hrdlicka, Cvetler, Moder, Jokl, Jan Capkovic.
BARCELONA: Sadurni; Franch (Pereda), Eladio, Rife, Olivella, Zabalza, Pellicer, Castro (Mendoza), Zaldua, Fuste, Rexach.

9 Arsenal Complete British Hat-Trick in the Fairs' Cup

The twelfth edition of the European Fairs' Cup—until last season the competition was known as the Inter-Cities Fairs Cup—brought two newcomers to the two-legged final in Arsenal, of England, and Anderlecht, of Belgium, neither of whom had appeared before in a European final, as the survivors of the 64 clubs who had set out hopefully the previous September.

A spectacular 3–0 victory in the second leg at Highbury after they had finished 3–1 down in Brussels gave Arsenal the trophy and enabled them to follow in the footsteps of Leeds United who had won in 1968 and Newcastle United who had triumphed in 1969.

Curiously this competition, which having been run since its inception in 1955 by Sir Stanley Rous, president of F.I.F.A. and a committee of member clubs is now to be taken over by U.E.F.A., seems to provide fiercer competition than either of the two other major European club tournaments and has more players ordered off the field.

The number of sendings-off reached double figures during the 1969–70 competition—the penalty for marching orders being that a player is not eligible for his club in the following tie—and among the famous players who came under the ban of referees were Johan Cruyff, the Ajax striker valued at £200,000, and Emeric Dembrovski, the Rumanian international who plays for Dinamo Bacau.

But the worst incident of all in the competition occurred at Cagliari in Sardinia in the second leg of the first round tie between the Italians and the Greek team, Aris of Salonika, which the Swiss referee, M. Despand, had to abandon after 80 minutes with Cagliari leading 3–1 because the Greeks refused to continue with the game after there had been fighting between the players.

It seemed that some of the ill-feeling between the players in the first leg which ended in a 1–1 draw had been carried over and right from the start it was an ill-tempered match. During the first half there was fighting between players, shirt pulling and tripping, but the referee had treated the incidents leniently.

Gradually players' tempers became really frayed and the game finally erupted ten minutes from the end when the referee awarded the Greeks a penalty for a foul by a Cagliari defender. But that did not satisfy the Greeks. They started jostling the referee, demanding that the Italian player be expelled from the field as well. That was the signal for a free-for-all. Players started throwing punches, and the Italian police round the touchline not to be outdone rushed on to the field, some 200 of them. Finally after about half an hour order was restored, the pitch was cleared and the referee was ready to restart. But the Greeks found they had only eight players—the police were holding the other three for fighting.

The Greeks refused to continue the game without the three. The police refused to release the three, so the referee had no alternative but to abandon the game.

Later the match was awarded to Cagliari but they were not able to profit by it for in the next round the Italian League leaders were surprisingly beaten by the East German side, Carl Zeiss Jena in both ties losing 2–0 and 1–0. But for the second match in their Amsicora Stadium they were without their 'wonder boy' Luigi Riva, always good for a goal, who was suffering from a leg injury after helping the Italian national side in a World Cup qualifying match.

Carl Zeiss Jena, however, did not progress any further for in the quarter-finals they were put out by Ajax of Amsterdam who pulled back a 3–1 deficit in Jena with a 5–1 victory in Amsterdam.

Irish clubs proved the chopping blocks of the competition. Liverpool led the high scoring in the first round by defeating Dundalk 10–0 and 4–0 while in the second round Anderlecht, on their way to the final, knocked out the unfortunate Coleraine 6–1 and 7–3. But Liverpool had the unlucky experience of going out in the second round to the Portuguese side Vitoria Setubal on the away goals counting double rule by allowing them to score twice at Anfield after holding them at Setubal to a single goal.

Anderlecht, who had taken part in nine European Cup campaigns with one quarter-final as their best achievement, had an easier and luckier path to the final than their less experienced rivals Arsenal, whose only previous experience of European competition was one season in the Fairs' Cup.

In the first round Anderlecht easily accounted for the amateurs of Iceland, F.C. Valur, 6–0 and 2–0, both matches being played in Brussels to cut down expenses, and then dealt summarily with Coleraine. But against Dunfermline they saw a 1–0 home win wiped out by the Scots and Anderlecht got through only by winning the toss; and similar luck attended them against Newcastle United who won 3–1 at St James Park after losing 2–0 at Brussels.

Their best performance however was in the semi-final even though it seemed something of a fluke. Without one of their main strikers,

Paul van Himst, who was suffering from food poisoning, Anderlecht were below form in the first leg against Inter-Milan and were beaten at home by 1–0. Roberto Boninsegna scored the goal in the 48th minute from Mario Corso's free kick just outside the penalty area. With what looked like a winning lead Inter-Milan naturally concentrated on defence.

That goal, however, was not enough. In the return leg the Italians' defence, usually so sound, rather let them down and Anderlecht proved their ability to fight back. Within two minutes of the start in the San Siro Stadium they were on level terms as Bertini failed to clear and Bergholtz, who was in the side only because the Dutch international Jan Mulder had dropped out owing to the death of his father, seized on the ball and shot past Vieri. A second and final goal which put Anderlecht in the final came just before half-time when a free kick taken by Puis was headed past the Inter-Milan defenders on the goalline by Bergholtz.

Arsenal's path to the final contained only two defeats, one fewer than Anderlecht. They began by putting out Glentoran, although they lost 1–0 in Ireland after winning 3–0 at home. They followed with a goalless draw away from home against the Portuguese champions, Sporting Lisbon, and then won 3–0 at Highbury. A goalless draw at Rouen was improved upon by a 1–0 win at Highbury, Jon Sammels scoring the vital goal one minute from the end.

Then came a visit to Rumania to meet Dinamo Bacau where a 2–0 victory was followed by an easy 7–1 success at home. Next on the list for Arsenal were the losing finalists in the previous season's European Cup, Ajax of Amsterdam—and their toughest tie. But they were able to contain Cruyff and his colleagues at Highbury where they gained a 3–0 lead and this proved too much for the Dutch side who could pull back only one goal in the return.

The clubs were given little chance to prepare for the final for the date of the first leg was fixed for only a week after the semi-final matches had been decided; and there was little time for either club to do much 'spying' on the other although Arsenal did get a look at Anderlecht on the Sunday before the first leg. They came to the conclusion that the one weakness in the Belgian side might be their defence.

But Arsenal were unable to take advantage of this when they met Anderlecht in the first leg on April 15 in the Parc Astrid stadium. Their own defence was kept busy by the Anderlecht strikers, Van Himst, Johan Devrindt and Jan Mulder. Although Arsenal had the advantage of playing with the slight slope on the Anderlecht pitch, the Belgians were a goal ahead after 25 minutes when a pass from Nordahl, son of the famous Gunnar Nordahl, was allowed by

Simpson to go to Devrindt who shot under Bob Wilson as he dived.

Five minutes later Mulder volleyed with his left foot a pass by Puis to put the Belgians two up, a lead they retained to half-time, and to which they added after 75 minutes when a fine bout of passing between Devrindt and Mulder ended with the Dutch international again shooting past Wilson. At this point Arsenal brought on Ray Kennedy as substitute for Charlie George and within five minutes he had put them back in the game as he headed a George Armstrong pass into the Belgian net.

For the second leg at Highbury seven days later Arsenal fielded the same side but Anderlecht were able to strengthen their defence with the return of Maurice Maartens who had recovered from the sprained ankle which had kept him out of the first match and Cornelis who had deputised was omitted. Before the match there was some discussion whether away goals would count double in view of the fact that a play-off had been tentatively agreed, but a meeting of the Fairs' Cup committee on the afternoon before play decided that the rules would stand and that away goals would have double value.

Arsenal knew that their only hopes of winning their first major trophy for 17 years rested on attack because it was goals they needed. From the start they went all-out to attack, but their efforts were hurried as they sought that quick but elusive goal which would unsettle the Belgians. But such tactics also left their defence open which was dangerous against such as Devrindt, Van Himst and Mulder.

However, gradually the Arsenal pressure kept the Belgians back and their forwards were needed to help Trappeniers and his defenders. After 25 minutes the Belgian defence was cracked. A corner taken by Armstrong, who had been preferred in both ties to the £100,000 Scot Peter Marinello, was neatly put over for Kelly on the edge of the penalty area to beat Trappeniers.

Anderlecht managed to restrict Arsenal to this single goal lead in the first half and ten minutes after half-time they nearly equalised. Nordahl hit a post and Wilson had to be in his best form to turn Mulder's shot from the rebound for a corner.

Then two goals in a two-minute spell settled the match—and the destination of the trophy. After 72 minutes John Radford headed a great goal from a Bob McNab centre and then Sammels, shooting on the run, made it 3–0 for Arsenal who were able to contain the Belgians for the rest of the game to gain consolation for the loss of successive League Cup finals to Leeds United and Swindon Town.

First Round

Sept. 17 1969: ROSENBORG TRONDHEIM (Norway) (1) 1 (Sunde) SOUTHAMPTON (0) 0

ROSENBORG TRONDHEIM: Fossen; Ronnes, Rime, Eggen, Hvidsand, Christiansen, Naess, Pedersen, Sunde (Haagerud,) Iversen, Loraas, (Diasaeter).

SOUTHAMPTON: Martin; Jones, Kirkup, Fisher, Gabriel, Walker, Paine, Channon, Davies (Saul), Byrne, Stokes.

Oct. 1 1969: SOUTHAMPTON (1) 2 (Davies, Paine) ROSENBORG TRONDHEIM (0) 0.

SOUTHAMPTON: Martin; Kirkup, Hollywood, Kemp, McGrath, Gabriel, Paine, Stokes, Davies, Sydenham, Byrne.

ROSENBORG TRONDHEIM: Fossen; Ronnes, Rime, Eggen, Hvidsand, Christiansen, Naess, Pedersen, Sunde, Iversen, Diasaeter.

Southampton won 2–1 on aggregate.

Sept. 9 1969: ARSENAL (England) (3) 3 (Graham 2, Gould) GLENTORAN (N. Ireland) (0) 0.

ARSENAL: Wilson; Storey, McNab, McLintock, Simpson, Graham, Robertson (Kelly), Gould, Sammels, Armstrong.

GLENTORAN: Finlay; Coyle, McKeag, Stewart, McCullough, Macken, Weatherup, Bruce, Henderson, Morrow, Hill.

Sept. 29 1969: GLENTORAN (1) 1 (Henderson pen.) ARSENAL (0) 0.

GLENTORAN: Finlay; Hill, McKeag, Coyle, McCullough, Macken, Weatherup, Stewart, Henderson, Bruce, Morrow.

ARSENAL: Webster; Rice, Neill, Simpson, McNab, Court, Sammels, Robertson, Gould, George, Radford.

Arsenal won 3–1 on aggregate.

Sept. 15 1969: DUNDEE UNITED (Scotland) (0) 1 (Scott) NEWCASTLE UNITED (England) (0) 2 (Davies 2).

DUNDEE UNITED: Mackay; Rolland, Cameron J., Gillespie, Smith, Markland, Wilson, Reid, Cameron K., Scott, Mitchell.

NEWCASTLE UNITED: McFaul; Craig, Clark, Gibb, Burton, Moncur, Robson, Dyson, Davies, Arentoft, Smith.

Oct. 1 1969: NEWCASTLE UNITED (0) 1 (Dyson) DUNDEE UNITED (0) 0.

NEWCASTLE UNITED: McFaul; Craig, Clark, Gibb, McNamee, Moncur, Robson, Dyson, Davies, Smith, Foggon.

DUNDEE UNITED: Mackay; Rolland, Cameron J., Gillespie, Smith, Markland, Hogg, Reid, Gordon, Scott, Mitchell.

Newcastle United won 3–1 on aggregate.

Sept. 16 1969: LIVERPOOL (England) (5) 10 (Evans 2, Smith 2, Graham 2, Lawler, Thompson, Lindsay, Callaghan) DUNDALK (Rep. of Ireland) (0) 0.

LIVERPOOL: Clemence; Lawler, Strong, Smith, Hughes, Callaghan, Graham, Lindsay, Evans, Thompson.

DUNDALK: Swan; Brennan, O'Reilly, Murray, McConville, Hendricks, Gilmore, Turner, O'Connor, Bartley, Carroll.

Sept. 30 1969: DUNDALK (0) 0 LIVERPOOL (2) 4 (Thompson 2, Graham, Callaghan).

DUNDALK: Swan; Brennan, O'Reilly, Murray, McConville, Millington, Kinsella, Turner, O'Connor, Bartley, Carroll.

LIVERPOOL: Clemence; Lawler, Strong, Smith, Lloyd, Hughes, Boersma, Evans, Graham, St John, Thompson.

Liverpool won 14–0 on aggregate.

Sept. 16 1969: ZURICH (Switzerland) (2) 3 (Volkert, Kunzli, Gruenig) KILMARNOCK (Scotland) (2) 2 (McLean T., Mathie).

ZURICH: Grob; Munch, Hasler, Rebozzi, Kuhn, Gruenig, Winiger, Martinelli, Kunzli, Quentin, Volkert.

KILMARNOCK: McLaughlin; King, Dickson, Gilmour, McGrory, Beattie, McLean T., Strachan, Morrison, McLean J., Mathie.

Sept. 30 1969: KILMARNOCK (1) 3 (McGrory, Morrison, McLean T.) ZURICH (0) 1 (Gruenig).

KILMARNOCK: McLaughlin; King, Dickson, Gilmour, McGrory, Strachan, McLean T., Morrison, Mathie, McLean J., Cook.

ZURICH: Grob; Munch, Hasler, Rebozzi, Kuhn, Gruenig, Winiger, Kyburz, Kunzli, Quentin, Volkert.

Kilmarnock won 5–4 on aggregate.

Sept. 16 1969: DUNFERMLINE (Scotland) (1) 4 (Paton 2, Mitchell, Gardner) BORDEAUX (France) (0) 0.

DUNFERMLINE: Duff; Callaghan, Lunn, McGarty, Baillie, Renton, Mitchell, Paton, Edwards, Gardner, McLean.

BORDEAUX: Montes; Papin, Grabowski, Andrien, Desremaux, Burdino, Dortomb, Simon, Ruiter, Betta, Peyt.

Oct. 1 1969: BORDEAUX (1) 2 (Othily, Wojciak) DUNFERMLINE (0) 0.

Dunfermline won 4–2 on aggregate.

Sept. 18 1969: JEUNESSE ESCH (Luxemburg) (0) 3 (Allamano 3) COLERAINE (N. Ireland) (1) 2 (Curley 2).

Oct. 1 1969: COLERAINE (1) 4 (Wilson 2, Dickson, Jennings) JEUNESSE ESCH (0) 0.

COLERAINE: Hunter; McCurdy, Campbell, O'Doherty, Jackson, Murray, Dunlop, Curley, Wilson, Dickson, Jennings.

JEUNESSE ESCH: Hoffmann R.; Da Grava, Kosmala, Hoffmann J., Morocutti, Drouet, Feyder, Allamano, Di Genova, Langer, Bartolacci.

Coleraine won 6–3 on aggregate.

Sept. 10 1969: ANDERLECHT (Belgium) (5) 6 (Van Himst 4, Nordahl 2) F.C.VALUR (Iceland) (0) 0.

Sept. 16 1969: F.C. VALUR (0) 0 ANDERLECHT (1) 2 (Nordahl, Mulder).

(Played in Ghent by arrangement)

Anderlecht won 8–0 on aggregate.

Sept. 3 1969: T.S.V. MUNICH (West Germany) 2 SKEID OSLO (Norway) 2.

Sept. 16 1969: SKEID OSLO (1) 2 (Sjoeberg 2) T.S.V. MUNICH (1) 1 (Keller).
Skeid Oslo won 4–3 on aggregate.

Sept. 3 1969: S.C. CHARLEROI (Belgium) (2) 2 (Bussot, Boulot) F.C. ZAGREB (Yugoslavia) (1) 1 (Bubanj).
Sept. 24 1969: F.C. ZAGREB (0) 1 (Muttmacher o.g.) S.C. CHARLEROI (1) 3 (Bertoncello, Bussot 2).
S.C. Charleroi won 5–2 on aggregate.

Sept. 16 1969: CARL ZEISS JENA (1) 1 ALTAY IZMIR (Turkey) (0) 0.
Oct. 1 1969: ALTAY IZMIR (0) 0 CARL ZEISS JENA (0) 0.
Carl Zeiss Jena won 1–0 on aggregate.

Sept. 16 1969: LAUSANNE (Switzerland) (1) 1 (Champuisat) VASAS GYOER (Hungary) (2) 2 (Gyoerffy 2).
Oct. 1 1969: VASAS GYOER (0) 2 (Korsos, Somogny) LAUSANNE (0) 1 (Duera).
Vasas Gyoer won 4–2 on aggregate.

Sept. 16 1969: VIENNA SPORTKLUB (Austria) 4 RUCH CHORZOW Poland) 2
Sept. 30 1969: RUCH CHORZOW (2) 4 (Piechniczek, Faber, Marks, Herman) VIENNA SPORTKLUB (0) 1 (Landrup).
Ruch Chorzow won 6–5 on aggregate.

Sept. 17 1969: ARIS SALONIKA (Greece) (1) 1 (Spyridon) CAGLIARI (Italy) (0) 1 (Martiradonna).
Oct. 1 1969: CAGLIARI v. ARIS SALONIKA.
(Abandoned after 80 minutes with Cagliari leading 3–0 because of fighting between police and players; match awarded to Cagliari.)
Cagliari qualified for Second Round.

Sept. 17 1969: V.F.B. STUTTGART (West Germany) (1) 3 (Bjoerklund o.g., Olsson, Haug) MALMOE (Sweden) (0) 0.
Oct. 1 1969: MALMOE (0) 1 (Larsson) V.F.B. STUTTGART (1) 1 (Weidmann).
V.F.B. Stuttgart won 4–1 on aggregate.

Sept. 17 1969: JUVENTUS (Italy) (2) 3 (Veri pen., Leonardi, Castano) LOKOMOTIV PLOVDIV (Bulgaria) (1) 1 (Vasilov).
Oct. 1 1969: LOKOMOTIV PLOVDIV (0) 1 (Vasilov) JUVENTUS (1) 2 (Leonardi, Anastasi).
Juventus won 5–2 on aggregate.

Sept. 17 1969: SABADELL (Spain) (1) 2 (Garzon, Cristo) F.C. BRUGES (Belgium) (0) 0.
Oct. 1 1969: F.C. BRUGES (3) 5 (Carteus, Lambert 2, Turesson 2) SABADELL (0) 1 (Palav).
F.C. Bruges won 5–3 on aggregate.

Sept. 17 1969: LAS PALMAS (Spain) (0) 0 HERTHA BERLIN (West Germany) (0) 0.
Oct. 1 1969: HERTHA BERLIN (0) 1 (Patzke pen.) LAS PALMAS (0) 0.
Hertha Berlin won 1–0 on aggregate.

Sept. 17 1969: DINAMO BACAU (Rumania) (0) 6 (Dembrovski 3, Ene 2, Baluta) FLORIANA (Malta) (0) 0.
Sept. 28 1969: FLORIANA (0) 0 DINAMO BACAU (0) 1 (Baluta).
Dinamo Bacau won 7–0 on aggregate.

Sept. 17 1969: INTER-MILAN (Italy) (0) 3 (Boninsegna 2, Reif) SPARTA PRAGUE (Czechoslovakia) (0) 0.
Oct. 1 1969: SPARTA PRAGUE (0) 0 INTER-MILAN (1) 1 (Boninsegna).
Inter-Milan won 4–0 on aggregate.

Sept. 17 1969: HANSA ROSTOCK (East Germany) (1) 3 (Drews 2, Pankau) PANIONIOS (Greece) (0) 0.
Sept. 30 1969: PANIONIOS (0) 2 (Spyropoulos, Dedes) HANSA ROSTOCK (0) 0.
Hansa Rostock won 3–2 on aggregate.

Sept. 17 1969: METZ (France) (0) 1 (Sczepaniak) NAPOLI (Italy) (1) 1 Bosdaves).
Oct. 1 1969: NAPOLI 2 METZ 1
Napoli won 3–2 on aggregate.

Sept. 17 1969: BARCELONA (Spain) (3) 4 (Ejertsen o.g., Zaldua, Filosia 2) B.K. ODENSE (Denmark) (0) 0.
Oct. 1 1969: B.K. ODENSE (0) 0 BARCELONA (0) 2 (Pellicer, Rexach).
Barcelona won 6–0 on aggregate.

Sept. 18 1969: PARTIZAN BELGRADE (Yugoslavia) (0) 2 (Djordjevic 2) UJPEST DOZSA (Hungary) (0) 1 (Dunai III).
Oct. 1 1969: UJPEST DOZSA (0) 2 (Bene, Dunai III) PARTIZAN BELGRADE (0) 0.
Ujpest Dozsa won 3–2 on aggregate.

Sept. 18 1969: VITORIA SETUBAL (Portugal) (1) 3 (Jacinto Joao, Guerreiro, Jose Maria) RAPID BUCHAREST (Rumania) (0) 1 (Mergue).
Oct. 1 1969: RAPID BUCHAREST (0) 1 (Stelian) VITORIA SETUBAL (2) 4 (Wagner 2 pens, Jose Maria, Lupescu o.g.)
Vitoria Setubal won 7–2 on aggregate.

Sept. 24 1969: HVIDOVRE COPENHAGEN (Denmark) (1) 1 (Soerensen pen.) PORTO (Portugal) (0) 2 (Helder).
Oct. 1 1969: PORTO (1) 2 (Salim, Rolando) HVIDOVRE COPENHAGEN (0) 0.
Porto won 4–1 on aggregate.

Sept. 17 1969: HANOVER (West Germany) (2) 2 (Heyncke, Skoblar) AJAX AMSTERDAM (Holland) (1) 1 (Swart)
Sept. 19 1969: AJAX AMSTERDAM (1) 3 (Cruyff, Swart, Muhren) HANOVER (0) 0.
Ajax Amsterdam won 4–2 on aggregate.

Sept. 24 1969: SPORTING LISBON (Portugal) (1) 4 (Pedras, Goncalves, Peres pen., Lourenco) LINZ A.S.K. (Austria) (0) 0.
Oct. 1 1969: LINZ A.S.K. (1) 2 (Wurdinger, Leitnea II) SPORTING LISBON (1) 2 (Goncalves, Lourenco).
Sporting Lisbon won 6–2 on aggregate.

Sept. 4 1969: VOJVODINA (Yugoslavia) (0) 1 (Dakich) GWARDIA WARSAW (Poland) (1) 1 (Wisniewski).
Sept. 17 1969: GWARDIA WARSAW (1) 1 (Lipinski) VOJVODINA (0) 0.
Gwardia Warsaw won 2–1 on aggregate.

Sept. 9 1969: ROUEN (France) (1) 2 (Senechal, Rustichelli pen.) F.C. TWENTE (Holland) (0) 0.
Sept. 30 1969: F.C. TWENTE (0) 1 (Drost) ROUEN (0) 0.
Rouen won 2–1 on aggregate.

Sept. 10 1969: GUIMARAES (Portugal) (1) 1 (Carlos Manuel) BANIK OSTRAVA (Czechoslovakia) (0) 0.
Oct. 2 1969: BANIK OSTRAVA (0) 1 (Buznik) GUIMARAES (0) 1 (Artur).
Guimaraes won 2–1 on aggregate.

Sept. 17 1969: SLAVIA SOFIA (Bulgaria) (1) 2 (Grigorov, Kolev pen.) VALENCIA (Spain) (0) 0.
Oct. 1 1969: VALENCIA 1 SLAVIA SOFIA 1
Slavia Sofia won 3–1 on aggregate.

Second Round
Nov. 19 1969: PORTO (Portugal) (0) 0 NEWCASTLE UNITED (England) (0) 0.
PORTO: Rui; Gualter, Valdemar, Nunes, Sucena, Colando, Pavao, Salim, Seninho, Pinto, Nobrega.
NEWCASTLE: McFaul; Craig, Clark, Gibb, Burton, Moncur, Robson, Dyson, Davies, Arentoft, Guthrie.
Nov. 26 1969: NEWCASTLE UNITED (1) 1 (Scott) PORTO (0) 0.
NEWCASTLE UNITED: McFaul; Craig, Clark, Gibb, Burton, Moncur, Scott, Robson, Davies, Arentoft, Foggon.
PORTO: Rui (Anibal); Gualter, Valdemar, Nunes, Sucena, Rolando, Salim, Albano, Pavao, Pinto, Nobrega.
Newcastle United won 1–0 on aggregate.

Oct. 29 1969: SPORTING LISBON (Portugal) (0) 0 ARSENAL (England) (0) 0.

Above: Franz Beckenbauer, one of West Germany's midfield stalwarts (centre), busy in defence with Alan Mullery, Francis Lee, Sepp Maier and Berti Vogts. *Below:* Mueller, the Bayern Munich and West German striker, shows his power as he hooks the ball into the England goal during the dramatic quarter final match which ended England's hold on the Cup.

Reinhard 'Stan' Libuda, the West German winger, chased by Guergui
Asparoukhov, the Bulgarian striker, who failed to find his form in Mexico

SPORTING LISBON: Damas; Pedro, Gomes, Calo, Carlos, Hilario, Goncalves, Peres, Morais, Nelson, Lourenco, Marinho.

ARSENAL: Barnett; Storey, McNab, Court, Neill, Simpson, Robertson, Sammels, Radford, Graham, Armstrong.

Nov. 26 1969: ARSENAL (2) 3 (Radford, Graham, McNab) SPORTING LISBON (0) 0.

ARSENAL: Barnett; Storey, McNab, Court, Neill, Simpson, Robertson, Sammels, Radford, Graham, Armstrong.

SPORTING LISBON: Damas; Pedro, Gomes, Celestino, Concalves, Baptista, Calo, Morais (Manaca), Nelson (Lourenco), Marinho, Peres, Dinis.

Arsenal won 3-0 on aggregate.

Nov. 12 1969: VITORIA SETUBAL (Portugal) (1) 1 (Tome) LIVERPOOL (England) (0) 0.

VITORIA SETUBAL: Vital; Conceicao, Cardoso, Alfredo (Arcanjo), Carrico, Tome, Wagner, Jose Maria, Guerriero, Figueiredo, Jacinto Joao.

LIVERPOOL: Lawrence; Lawler, Smith, Yeats, Wall, Graham (St John), Hughes, Callaghan, Ross, Strong, Thompson.

Nov. 26 1969: LIVERPOOL (0) 3 (Smith pen., Evans, Hunt) VITORIA SETUBAL (1) 2 (Wagner pen., Strong o.g.).

LIVERPOOL: Lawrence; Lawler, Strong, Smith, Yeats, Hughes, Callaghan, Peplow (Evans), Graham (Hunt), St John, Thompson.

VITORIA SETUBAL: Vital; Robelo, Cardoso, Moreira, Carrico, Tome, Jose Maria, Wagner, Guerriero, Acanjo, Jacinto Joao.

Vitoria Setubal won on away goals.

Nov. 4 1969: VITORIA GUIMARAES (Portugal) (1) 3 (Mendes 2, Pinto pen.) SOUTHAMPTON (1) 3 (Channon, Davies, Paine).

VITORIA GUIMARAES: Rodriques; Da Velha, Pinto, Jorje, Costeado, Artur, Bilreiro, Manuel, Mendes, Peres, Ademir.

SOUTHAMPTON: Martin; Kirkup, Byrne, Fisher (Hollywood), McGrath, Gabriel, Paine, Channon (Saul), Davies, Walker, Sydenham.

Nov. 12 1969: SOUTHAMPTON (1) 5 (Costeado o.g., Davies 2, 1 pen., Gabriel, Channon) VITORIA GUIMARAES (0) 1 (Ademir).

SOUTHAMPTON: Martin; Kirkup, Byrne, Fisher, McGrath, Gabriel, Paine, Channon, Davies, Walker, Sydenham.

VITORIA GUIMARAES: Rodriques; Da Velha, Pinto, Jorje, Costeado, Artur, Bilreiro, Manuel, Mendes, Peres (Agusto), Ademir.

Southampton won 8-4 on aggregate.

Nov. 5 1969: DUNFERMLINE (Scotland) (1) 2 (McLean, Gardner) GWARDIA WARSAW (Poland) (0) 1 (Marczak).

DUNFERMLINE: Martin; Callaghan, Lunn, McGarty, Baillie, Renton, Mitchell, McKimmie, Edwards, Gardner, McLean.

GWARDIA WARSAW: Pocialik; Jurczak, Kielak, Sroka, Michalik, Dawidczynski, Szmczak, Biernacki, Masztaler, Marczak.

Nov. 18 1969: GWARDIA WARSAW (0) 0 DUNFERMLINE (1) 1 (Renton).

E

GWARDIA WARSAW: Pocialik; Sroka, Jurczak, Michalik, Kielak, Wisniewski, Marczak, Lipinski, Szmczak, Dawidczynski, Masztaler.

DUNFERMLINE: Martin; Callaghan, Lunn, McGarty, Baillie, Renton, Mitchell, Paton, Edwards, Gardner, McLean.
Dunfermline won 3-1 on aggregate.

Nov. 11 1969: ANDERLECHT (Belgium) (3) 6 (Van Himst 2, Mulder 2, Hanon, Devrindt) COLERAINE (N. Ireland) (1) 1 (Murray).

ANDERLECHT: Van Den Bosch; Heylens, Velkeneers, Van Welle, Cornelis, Hanon, Stierli, Van Binst, Mulder, Van Himst, Martens (Devrindt).

COLERAINE: Hunter; McCurdy, O'Doherty, Jackson, Campbell, Murray, Wilson (Irwin), Dunlop, Dickson, Curley, Jennings.

Nov. 20 1969: COLERAINE (0) 3 (Dickson 2, Irwin) ANDERLECHT (6) 7 (Van Himst 3, Puis 3, 2 pens, Devrindt).

COLERAINE: Hunter; McCurdy, Gordon, Campbell, Jackson, Murray, Dunlop, Curley, Dickson, Jennings, Irwin.

ANDERLECHT: Van Den Bosch (Mair); Heylens Velkeneers, Kialunda, Stierli, Hanon, Nordahl, Devrindt, Mulder, Van Himst, Puis.
Anderlecht won 13-4 on aggregate.

Nov. 19 1969: KILMARNOCK (Scotland) (2) 4 (Mathie 2, Cook, Gilmour) SLAVIA SOFIA (Bulgaria) (0) 1 (Shelamanov).

KILMARNOCK: McLaughlin; King, Dickson, Gilmour, McGrory, Beattie, McLean T., Morrison, Mathie, McLean J., Cook.

SLAVIA SOFIA: Zolov; Shalamanov, Christakiev, Alexsiev, Petrov, Davidov, Dimitrov, Georgiev, Michailov, Kolev, Kotzev.

Nov. 26 1969: SLAVIA SOFIA (2) (Michailov, Kotzev) KILMARNOCK (0) 0.

SLAVIA SOFIA: Zolov; Gerov, Alexiev, Davidov, Kolev, Georgiev, Michalov, Grigorov, Dimitrov, Michailov, Kotzev.

KILMARNOCK: McLaughlin; Mathie, Dickson, McLean T., McGrory, King, Strachan, Gilmour, Beattie, Morrison, Cook.
Kilmarnock won 4-3 on aggregate.

Oct. 22 1969: SKEID OSLO (Norway) (0) 0 DINAMO BACAU (Rumania) (0) 0.

Oct. 29 1969: DINAMO BACAU (0) 2 (Dembrovski 2, 1 pen.) SKEID OSLO (0) 0.
Dinamo Bacau won 2-0 on aggregate.

Oct. 21 1969: VASAS GYOER (Hungary) (1) 2 (Varsanyi, Orban) BARCELONA (Spain) (2) 3 (Pellicer, Zaldua 2).

Nov. 26 1969: BARCELONA (1) 2 VASAS GYOER (0) 0.
Barcelona won 5-2 on aggregate.

Oct. 29 1969: CHARLEROI (Belgium) (3) 3 (Bussot 2, Spaute) ROUEN (France) (1) 1 (Villa).

Nov. 19 1969: ROUEN (1) 2 (Rustichelli, Villa) CHARLEROI (0) 0.
Rouen won on away goal.

Oct. 29 1969: BRUGES (Belgium) 5 (Rensenbrink 3, Turesson 2) UJPEST DOZSA (Hungary) 2 (Juhasz, Fazekas).
Nov. 26 1969: UJPEST DOZSA (1) 3 (Fazekas 2, Bene) BRUGES (0) 0.
Ujpest Dozsa won on away goals.

Nov. 12 1969: HANSA ROSTOCK (East Germany) (0) 2 (Hergesell, Sackritz) INTER-MILAN (Italy) (1) 1 (Boninsegna).
Nov. 26 1969: INTER-MILAN (3) 3 (Jair, Suarez, Mazzola) HANSA ROSTOCK (0) 0.
Inter-Milan won 4–2 on aggregate.

Nov. 12 1969: KARL ZEISS JENA (East Germany) (0) 2 (Rock, Irmscher) CAGLIARI (Italy) (0) 0.
Nov. 26 1969: CAGLIARI (0) 0 KARL ZEISS JENA (1) 1 (Stein).
Karl Zeiss Jena won 3–0 on aggregate.

Nov. 19 1969: AJAX AMSTERDAM (Holland) (2) 7 (Cruyff 2, Van Dijk 2, Vasovic 2, 1 pen., Swart) RUCH CHORZOW (Poland) (0) 0.
Nov. 26 1969: RUCH CHORZOW (1) 1 (Piechniczek) AJAX AMSTER-DAM (1) 2 (Muhren, Van Dijk).
Ajax Amsterdam won 9–1 on aggregate.

Nov. 12 1969: HERTHA BERLIN (West Germany) (2) 3 JUVENTUS (Italy) (1) 1.
Nov. 26 1969: JUVENTUS (0) 0 HERTHA BERLIN (0) 0.
Hertha Berlin won 3–1 on aggregate.

Nov. 12 1969: V.F.B. STUTTGART (West Germany) (0) 0 NAPOLI (Italy) (0) 0.
Nov. 26 1969: NAPOLI (0) 1 (Canzi) V.F.B. STUTTGART (0) 0.
Napoli won 1–0 on aggregate.

Third Round
Dec. 17 1969: ROUEN (France) (0) 0 ARSENAL (England) (0) 0.
ROUEN: Rigoni; Largouet, Rio, Senechal, Merelle, Dos Santos, Pospischal, Rustichelli, Villa, Leroy, Bruant.
ARSENAL: Wilson; Storey, Court, Neill, McNab, Sammels, Simpson, Robertson, Radford, Graham (Kelly), Armstrong.
Jan. 13 1970: ARSENAL (0) 1 (Sammels) ROUEN (0) 0.
ARSENAL: Wilson; Storey, Nelson, Court (Graham), Neill, Simpson, Marinello, Sammels, Radford, George, Armstrong.
ROUEN: Rigoni; Largouet, Merelle, Rio, Senechal, Druda, Rustichelli, Dos Santos, Villa, Pospischal, Bruant.
Arsenal won 1–0 on aggregate.

Dec. 17 1969: NEWCASTLE UNITED (England) (0) 0 SOUTHAMP-TON (England) (0) 0.
NEWCASTLE UNITED: McFaul; Craig, Clark, Gibb, Burton, Moncur, Robson, Dyson, Davies W., Arentoft, Scott.

SOUTHAMPTON: Martin; Kirkup, Byrne, Fisher, McGrath (Stokes), Gabriel, Paine, Channon, Davies R., Walker, Jenkins.

Jan. 14 1970: SOUTHAMPTON (1) 1 (Channon) NEWCASTLE UNITED (0) 1 (Robson).

SOUTHAMPTON: Martin; Kirkup, Byrne, Fisher, Gabriel, Walker, Jenkins, Channon, Davies R., Paine, Sydenham.

NEWCASTLE UNITED: McFaul; Craig, Clark, Gibb, McNamee, Moncur, Robson, Smith, Davies W., Young (Guthrie), Ford.

Newcastle won on away goal.

Dec. 17 1969: KILMARNOCK (Scotland) (0) 1 (Mathie) DINAMO BACAU (Rumania) (0) 1 (Baluta).

KILMARNOCK: McLaughlin; King, Dickson, Gilmour, McGrory, Beattie, Cook, Mathie, Morrison, Waddell, McLean T.

DINAMO BACAU: Ghita; Comanescu, Nadelcu, Kis, Vacafu, Velicu, Pana, Dembrovski, Ene, Dutan, Baluta.

Jan. 13 1970: DINAMO BACAU (1) 2 (Ene 2) KILMARNOCK (0) 0.

DINAMO BACAU: Ghita; Comanescu, Nadelcu, Velicu, Kis, Vacafu, Dutan, Pana, Dembrovski, Daniel, Baluta.

KILMARNOCK: McLaughlin; King, McGrory, Strachan, Dickson, Gilmour (Maxwell), McLean T., McLean J., Morrison, Mathie, Shield.

Dinamo Bacau won 3–1 on aggregate.

Dec. 17 1969: ANDERLECHT (Belgium) (1) 1 (Devrindt) DUN-FERMLINE (Scotland) (0) 0.

ANDERLECHT: Van Den Bosch; Heylens, Cornelis, Peeters, Velkeneers, Kialunda, Nordahl, Bergholtz, Mulder, Devrindt, Puis.

DUNFERMLINE: Duff; Callaghan, Lunn, McNicoll, Baillie, McLean, Edwards, McLaren, Mitchell, Gardner, Robertson.

Jan. 14 1970: DUNFERMLINE (1) 3 (McLean 2, Mitchell) ANDER-LECHT (0) 2 (Van Himst, Mulder).

DUNFERMLINE: Duff; Callaghan, Lunn, McNicoll, Baillie, McLean, Edwards, Mitchell, Gardner, Gillespie.

ANDERLECHT: Trappeniers; Heylens, Cornelis, Velkeneers, Kialunda, De Raeve, Nordahl, Peeters, Mulder, Van Himst, Puis.

Anderlecht won on away goals.

Dec. 10 1969: NAPOLI (Italy) (1) 1 (Marservisi) AJAX AMSTERDAM (0) 0.

Jan. 21 1970: AJAX AMSTERDAM (1) 4 (Swart, Suurendonk 3) NAPOLI (0) 0.

(After extra time. Score at 90 minutes Ajax 1–0)

Ajax Amsterdam won 4–1 on aggregate.

Dec. 31 1969: VITORIA SETUBAL (Portugal) (1) 1 (Tome) HERTHA BERLIN (West Germany) (1) 1 (Horn).

Jan. 7 1970: HERTHA BERLIN (0) 1 (Steffenhagen) VITORIA SETUBAL (0) 0.

Hertha Berlin won 2–1 on aggregate.

Jan. 14 1970: KARL ZEISS JENA (East Germany) (0) 1 (Krauss) UJPEST DOZSA (Hungary) (0) 0.

Jan. 21 1970: UJPEST DOZSA (0) 0 KARL ZEISS JENA (2) 3 (Scheitler, Stein, Ducke).

Karl Zeiss Jena won 4–0 on aggregate.

Jan. 14 1970: BARCELONA (Spain) (1) 1 (Fuste) INTER-MILAN (Italy) (2) 2 (Boninsegna, Bertini).

Jan. 28 1970: INTER-MILAN v. BARCELONA. (Abandoned after 33 minutes, fog, Inter-Milan leading 1–0, Boninsegna the scorer.)

Feb. 4 1970: INTER-MILAN (1) 1 (Boninsegna) BARCELONA (1) 1 (Rexach).

Inter-Milan won 3–2 on aggregate.

Quarter-Finals

Mar. 11 1970: DINAMO BACAU (Rumania) (0) 0 ARSENAL (England) (0) 2 (Sammels, Radford).

DINAMO BACAU: Ghita; Comanescu, Nadelcu, Velicu, Kis, Vacafu, Dutan, Neumayer, Pana, Ene, David (Tanaucean).

ARSENAL: Wilson; Storey, McLintock, Simpson, McNab, Sammels, Kelly, Graham, Marinello, Radford, George.

Mar. 18 1970: ARSENAL (4) 7 (Radford 2, George 2, Sammels 2, Graham) DINAMO BACAU (1) 1 (Balutza).

ARSENAL: Wilson; Storey, McNab, Kelly, McLintock, Simpson, Marinello, Sammels, Radford, Graham (Armstrong), George.

DINAMO BACAU: Ghita; Comanescu, Nadelcu, David, Vacafu, Velicu, Pana, Dembrovski, Ene, Dutan, Balutza.

Arsenal won 9–1 on aggregate.

Mar. 11 1970: ANDERLECHT (Belgium) (1) 2 (Desanghere, Puis) NEWCASTLE UNITED (England) (0) 0.

ANDERLECHT: Trappeniers; Heylens, Martens, Nordahl, Velkeneers, Kialunda, Desanghere, Devrindt, Mulder, Van Himst, Puis.

NEWCASTLE UNITED: McFaul; Craggs, Guthrie, Gibb, McNamee, Moncur, Robson, Smith, Davies, Foggon, Dyson.

Mar. 18 1970: NEWCASTLE UNITED (2) 3 (Robson 2, Dyson) ANDERLECHT (0) 1 (Nordahl).

NEWCASTLE UNITED: McFaul; Craig, Clark (Young), Gibb, Burton, Moncur, Robson, Dyson, Davies, Guthrie, Foggon.

ANDERLECHT: Trappeniers; Heylens, Martens, Nordahl, Velkeneers, Kialunda, Desanghere, Devrindt, Mulder, Van Himst, Puis.

Anderlecht won on away goal.

Mar. 4 1970: HERTHA S.C. (West Germany) (0) 1 (Horr) INTER-MILAN (Italy) (0) 0.

HERTHA S.C.: Gross; Patzke, Witt, Wild, Pferschl, Altendorff, Gayer, Steffenhagen, Brungs, Horr, Weber.

INTER-MILAN: Girardi; Landini, Guarneri, Cella, Vecchigedin, Colloani, Jair, Boninsegna, Bertini, Corso.

Mar. 18 1970: INTER-MILAN (0) 2 (Boninsegna 2) HERTHA S.C. (0) 0.
INTER-MILAN: Vieri (Girardi); Bellugi, Facchetti, Bertini, Guarneri,
Landini, Jair, Mazzola, Boninsegna, Suarez, Vanello.
HERTHA S.C.: Fraydl; Patzke, Witt, Wild, Pferschl, Altendorff, Gayer,
Steffenhagen, Brungs, Horr, Weber.
Inter-Milan won 2–1 on aggregate.

Mar. 4 1970: KARL ZEISS JENA (East Germany) (3) 3 (Ducke R.,
Stein, Ducke P.) AJAX AMSTERDAM (Holland) (0) 1 (Vasovic).
KARL ZEISS JENA: Blochwitz; Stein, Rock, Krauss, Werner, Strempel,
Schlutter, Irmscher, Ducke P., Scheitler, Ducke R.
AJAX AMSTERDAM: Bals; Vasovic, Suurbier (Suurendonk), Hulshoff,
Krol, Rijinders, Muhren, Swart, Cruyff, Van Dijk, Keizer.
Mar. 11 1970: AJAX AMSTERDAM (3) 5 (Vasovic, Swart 2, Keizer,
Cruyff) KARL ZEISS JENA (1) 1 (Ducke P.).
AJAX AMSTERDAM: Bals; Suurbier, Hulshoff, Vasovic, Krol, Rijnders,
Muhren, Swart, Cruyff, Van Dijk, Keizer.
KARL ZEISS JENA: Blochwitz; Rock, Stein, Strempel, Werner, Krauss,
Irmscher, Schlutter, Ducke P., Scheitler, Ducke R.
Ajax Amsterdam won 6–4 on aggregate.

Semi-Finals
April 8 1970: ARSENAL (England) (1) 3 (George 2, 1 pen., Sammels)
AJAX AMSTERDAM (Holland) (0) 0.
ARSENAL: Wilson; Storey, McNab, Kelly, McLintock, Simpson,
Marinello (Armstrong), Sammels, Radford, George, Graham.
AJAX AMSTERDAM: Bals; Vasovic, Suurbier, Hulshoff, Krol, Rijnders,
Muhren, Swart, Cruyff, Van Dijk, Keizer (Surrendonck).
April 15 1970: AJAX AMSTERDAM (1) 1 (Muhren) ARSENAL (0) 0.
AJAX AMSTERDAM: Bals; Vasovic, Suurbier, Hulshoff, Krol, Muhren,
Rijnders, Swart, Van Dijk, Cruyff, Keizer.
ARSENAL: Wilson; Storey, Kelly, Simpson, McNab, Armstrong,
McLintock, Sammels, Radford, George, Graham.
Arsenal won 3–1 on aggregate.

April 1 1970: ANDERLECHT (Belgium) (0) 0 INTER-MILAN (Italy)
(0) 1 (Boninsegna).
ANDERLECHT: Trappeniers; Heylens, Velkeneers, Peeters, Martens,
Nordahl, Puis, Desanghere, Devrindt, Mulder, Bergholtz.
INTER-MILAN: Vieri; Burgnich, Facchetti, Bedin, Landini, Cella,
Suarez, Mazzola, Boninsegna, Bertini, Corso.
April 15 1970: INTER-MILAN (0) 0 ANDERLECHT (2) 2 (Bergholtz 2).
INTER-MILAN: Vieri; Burgnich, Bellugi, Bedin, Landini, Cella, Suarez,
Mazzola, Boninsegna, Bertini, Corso.
ANDERLECHT: Trappeniers; Heylens, Martens, Nordahl, Velkeneers,
Kialunda, Desanghere, Bergholtz, Devrindt, Van Himst, Puis.
Anderlecht won 2–1 on aggregate.

Final—Two Legs
April 22 1970: ANDERLECHT (Belgium) (2) 3 (Devrindt, Mulder 2)
ARSENAL (England) (0) 1 (Kennedy).

ANDERLECHT: Trappeniers; Heylens, Velkeneers, Kialunda, Cornelis (Peeters), Desanghere, Nordahl, Devrindt, Mulder, Van Himst, Puis.

ARSENAL: Wilson; Storey, McNab, Kelly, McLintock, Simpson, Armstrong, Radford, Sammels, Graham, George (Kennedy).

April 28 1970: ARSENAL (1) 3 (Kelly, Radford, Sammels) ANDERLECHT (0) 0.

ARSENAL: Wilson; Storey, McNab, Kelly, McLintock, Simpson, Armstrong, Sammels, Radford, George, Graham.

ANDERLECHT: Trappeniers; Heylens, Martens, Nordahl, Velkeneers, Kialunda, Desanghere, Devrindt, Mulder, Van Himst, Puis.

Arsenal won 4–3 on aggregate.

Results of Finals

1955–1958	London 2 Barcelona 2	Stamford Bridge
	Barcelona 6 London 0	Barcelona
1958–1960	Birmingham City 0 Barcelona 0	Birmingham
	Barcelona 4 Birmingham 1	Barcelona
1960–1961	Birmingham City 2 A.S. Roma 2	Birmingham
	A.S. Roma 2 Birmingham City 0	Rome
1961–1962	Valencia 6 Barcelona 2	Valencia
	Barcelona 1 Valencia 1	Barcelona
1962–1963	Dinamo Zagreb 1 Valencia 2	Zagreb
	Valencia 2 Dinamo Zagreb 0	Valencia
1963–1964	Real Zaragoza 2 Valencia 1	Zaragoza
1964–1965	Juventus 0 Ferencvaros 1	Turin
1965–1966	Barcelona 0 Real Zaragoza 1	Barcelona
	Real Zaragoza 2 Barcelona 4	Zaragoza
1966–1967	Dinamo Zagreb 2 Leeds United 0	Zagreb
	Leeds United 0 Dinamo Zagreb 0	Leeds
1967–1968	Leeds United 1 Ferencvaros 0	Leeds
	Ferencvaros 0 Leeds United 0	Budapest
1968–1969	Newcastle United 3 Ujpest Dozsa 0	Newcastle
	Ujpest Dozsa 2 Newcastle United 3	Budapest
1969–1970	Anderlecht 3 Arsenal 1	Brussels
	Arsenal 3 Anderlecht 0	Highbury

Previous Final Teams

1955–1958
First leg

Mar. 5 1958: LONDON (1) 2 (Greaves, Langley pen.) BARCELONA (2) 2 (Tejada, Martinez). Stamford Bridge. 45,466

LONDON: Kelsey (Arsenal); Sillett P. (Chelsea), Langley (Fulham), Blanchflower (Tottenham Hotspur), Norman (Tottenham Hotspur), Coote (Brentford), Groves (Arsenal), Greaves (Chelsea), Smith (Tottenham Hotspur), Haynes (Fulham), Robb (Tottenham Hotspur).

BARCELONA: Estrema; Olivella, Segarra, Gracia, Gensana, Ribelles, Vasora, Everisto, Martinez, Villaverde, Tejada.

Second leg
May 1 1958: BARCELONA (3) 6 (Suarez 2, Martinez, Evaristo 2, Verges)
LONDON (0) 0. Barcelona. 62,000.
BARCELONA: Ramallets; Olivella, Segarra, Verges, Bruges, Gensana,
Tejada, Evaristo, Martinez, Suarez, Basora.
LONDON: Kelsey (Arsenal); Wright (West Ham), Cantwell (West Ham),
Blanchflower (Tottenham Hotspur), Brown (West Ham), Bowen
(Arsenal), Medwin (Tottenham Hotspur), Groves (Arsenal), Smith
(Tottenham Hotspur), Bloomfield (Arsenal), Lewis (Chelsea).
Barcelona won 8–2 on aggregate.

1958–1960
First leg
Mar. 29 1960: BIRMINGHAM CITY (0) 0 BARCELONA (0) 0.
Birmingham. 40, 500
BIRMINGHAM: Schofield; Farmer, Allen, Watts, Smith, Neal, Astell,
Gordon, Weston, Orritt, Hooper.
BARCELONA: Ramallets; Olivella, Rodri, Gracia, Segarra, Gensana,
Coll, Kocsis, Martinez, Ribelles, Villaverde.
Second leg
May 4 1960: BARCELONA (2) 4 (Czibor 2, Martinez, Coll) BIRMING-
HAM (0) 1. (Hooper) Barcelona. 70,000
BARCELONA: Ramallets; Olivella, Gracia, Verges, Rodri, Segarra, Coll,
Ribelles, Martinez, Kubala, Czibor.
BIRMINGHAM: Schofield; Farmer, Allen, Watts, Smith, Neal, Astell,
Gordon, Weston, Murphy, Hooper.
Barcelona won 4–1 on aggregate.

1960–1961
First leg
Sept. 27 1961: BIRMINGHAM CITY (0) 2 (Hellawell, Orritt) A.S.
ROMA (1) 2 (Manfredini 2). St Andrews. 21,000
BIRMINGHAM CITY: Schofield; Farmer, Sissons, Hennessey, Foster,
Beard, Hellawell, Bloomfield, Harris, Orritt, Auld.
A.S. ROMA: Cudicini; Fontana, Corsini, Giuliana, Losi, Carpanesi,
Orlando, Da Costa, Manfredini, Angelillo, Menichelli.
Oct. 11 1961: A.S. ROMA (0) 2 (Farmer o.g., Pestrin) BIRMINGHAM
CITY (0) 0. Rome. 60,000
A.S. ROMA: Cudicini; Fontana, Corsini, Carpanesi, Losi, Pestrin,
Orlando, Angelillo, Manfredini, Lojacono, Menichelli.
BIRMINGHAM CITY: Schofield; Farmer, Sissons, Hennessey, Smith,
Beard, Hellawell, Bloomfield, Harris, Singer, Orritt.
A.S. Roma won 4–2 on aggregate.

1961–1962
First leg
Sept. 9 1962: VALENCIA 6 (Yosu 2, Guillot 3, Nunez) BARCELONA 2
(Kocsis 2). Valencia. 65,000
VALENCIA: Zamora; Verdu, Chicao, Piquer, Mestre, Sastre, Ficha,
Ribeda, Waldo, Guillot, Coll.

BARCELONA: Pesudo; Benitez, Rodri, Olivella, Verges, Gracia, Cubilla, Kocsis, Re, Villaverde, Cams.
Sept. 13 1962: BARCELONA 1 (Kocsis) VALENCIA 1 (Guillot). Barcelona. 60,000
BARCELONA: Pesudo; Benitez, Garay, Gracia, Verges, Fuste, Cubilla, Villaverde, Kocsis, Goyvaerts, Cams.
VALENCIA: Zamora; Verdu, Chicao, Piquer, Mestre, Sastre, Ficha, Urtiaga, Waldo, Guillot, Coll.
Valencia won 7–3 on aggregate.

1962–1963
First leg
June 12 1963: DINAMO ZAGREB (1) 1 (Zambata) VALENCIA (0) 2 (Waldo, Urtiaga). Zagreb. 40,000
DINAMO ZAGREB: Skoric; Belin, Braun, Biscam, Markovic, Perusic, Kobesnac, Zambata, Knez, Matus, Lamza.
VALENCIA: Zamora; Piquer Chicao Paquito Quinoces, Sastre, Mano, Sanchez, Lage, Waldo, Ribelles, Urtiaga.
Second leg
June 26 1963: VALENCIA (1) 2 (Mano, Nunez) DINAMO ZAGREB (0) 0. Valencia. 55,000
VALENCIA: Zamora; Piquer, Chicao, Paquito, Quinoces, Sastre, Mano, Sanchez, Lage, Waldo, Ribelles, Nunez.
DINAMO ZAGREB: Skoric; Belin, Braun, Matus, Markovic, Perusic, Kobesnac, Lamza, Raus, Knez.
Valencia won 4–2 on aggregate.

1963–1964
One leg
June 25 1964: REAL ZARAGOZA (1) 2 (Villa, Marcelino) VALENCIA (1) 1. Urtiaga, Barcelona. 50,000
REAL ZARAGOZA: Yarza; Corino, Santamaria, Reija, Isasi, Pepia, Canario, Duca, Marcellino, Villa, Lapetre.
VALENCIA: Zamora; Arnal, Quinoces, Villegani, Paquito, Roberto, Suco, Guillot, Waldo, Urtiaga, Ficha.

1964–1965
One leg
June 23 1965: JUVENTUS (0) 0 FERENCVAROS (1) 1 (Fenyvesi). Turin. 25,000
JUVENTUS: Anzolin; Gori, Sarti, Bercellini, Castano, Leoncini, Estacchini, Del Sol, Combin, Mazza, Menichelli.
FERENCVAROS: Gerzi; Novak, Horvath, Juhasz, Matrai, Orosz, Karaba, Varga, Albert, Rakosi, Fenyvesi.

1965–1966
First leg
Sept. 14 1966: BARCELONA (0) 0 REAL ZARAGOZA (1) 1 (Canario). Barcelona. 70,000
BARCELONA: Sadurni; Benitez, Eladio, Montesinos, Gallego, Torres, Zabella, Muller, Zaldua, Fuste, Vidal.

REAL ZARAGOZA: Yarza; Irusquieta, Reija, Pais, Santamaria, Violeta, Canario, Santos, Marcellino, Villa, Lapetra.

Second leg

Sept. 21 1966: REAL ZARAGOZA(1) 2 (Marcellino 2) BARCELONA (1) 4 (Pujol 3, Zabella). Zaragoza. 70,000
(After extra time. 90-minute score Barcelona 3–2)

REAL ZARAGOZA: Yarza; Irusquieta, Reija, Pais, Santamaria, Violeta, Canario, Santos, Marcellino, Villa, Lapetra.

BARCELONA: Sadurni; Foncho, Eladio, Montesinos, Gallego, Torres, Zabella, Mas, Zaldua, Fuste, Pujol.

Barcelona won 4–3 on aggregate.

1966–1967
First leg

Aug. 31 1967: DINAMO ZAGREB (1) 2 (Cercek, Rora) LEEDS UNITED (0) 0. Zagreb. 40,000

DINAMO ZAGREB: Skoric; Gracanin, Brncic, Belin, Ramljak, Blaskovic, Cercek, Piric, Zambata, Gucmirtl, Rora.

LEEDS UNITED: Sprake; Reaney, Cooper, Bremner, Charlton, Hunter, Bates, Lorimer, Belfitt, Gray, O'Grady.

Second leg

Sept. 6 1967: LEEDS UNITED (0) 0 DINAMO ZAGREB (0) 0. Leeds. 35,604

LEEDS UNITED: Sprake; Bell, Cooper, Bremner, Charlton, Hunter, Reaney, Belfitt, Greenhoff, Giles, O'Grady.

DINAMO ZAGREB: Skoric; Gracanin, Brncic, Belin, Ramljak, Blaskovic, Cercek, Piric, Zambata Gucmirtl, Rora.

Dinamo Zagreb won 2–0 on aggregate.

1967–1968
First leg

Aug. 7 1968: LEEDS UNITED (1) 1 (Jones) FERENCVAROS (0) 0. Leeds. 25,268

LEEDS UNITED: Sprake; Reaney, Cooper, Bremner, Charlton, Hunter, Lorimer, Madeley, Jones, Giles, Gray.

FERENCVAROS: Geczi; Novac, Pancsics, Havasi, Juhasz, Szucs, Szoke, Varga, Albert, Rakosi, Fenyvesi.

Second leg

Sept. 11 1968: FERENCVAROS (0) 0 LEEDS UNITED (0) 0. Budapest. 76,000

FERENCVAROS: Geczi; Novak, Pancsics, Szucs, Havasi, Juhasz, Rakosi, Szoke (Karaba), Varga, Albert, Katona.

LEEDS UNITED: Sprake; Reaney, Cooper, Bremner, Charlton, Hunter, O'Grady, Lorimer, Jones, Madeley, Hibbitt (Bates).

Leeds United won 1–0 on aggregate.

1968–1969
First leg

May 29 1969: NEWCASTLE UNITED (0) 3 (Moncur 2, Scott) UJPEST DOZSA (0) 0. Newcastle. 60,000

NEWCASTLE UNITED: McFaul; Craig, Burton, Moncur, Clark, Gibb, Arentoft, Scott, Robson, Davies, Sinclair (Foggon).

UJPEST DOZSA: Szentimihalyi; Kaposzta, Nosko, Dunai E., Solymosi, Bankuti, Gorocs, Fazekas, Bene, Dunai A., Zambo.

Second leg

June 11 1969: UJPEST DOZSA (2) 2 (Bene, Gorocs) NEWCASTLE UNITED (0) 3 (Moncur, Arentoft, Foggon). Budapest. 37,000

UJPEST DOZSA: Szentimihalyi; Kaposzta, Solymosi, Bankuti, Dunai E., Nosko, Fazekas, Gorocs, Bene, Dunai A., Zambo.

NEWCASTLE UNITED: McFaul; Craig, Clark, Gibb, Burton, Moncur, Scott (Foggon), Robson, Davies, Arentoft, Sinclair.

Newcastle United won 6-2 on aggregate.

10 Pele Reaches His Thousand with a Penalty

Normally a meeting between Vasco da Gama and Santos, the two Brazilian clubs, even with Edson Arantes Do Nascimento, better known throughout the football world as Pele, playing for Santos, would not arouse any great excitement, particularly as in this case the game was part of the Taca de Prata (Silver Cup) tournament, the national soccer championship, from which both clubs had been practically eliminated.

But their meeting in the giant 150,000 capacity Maracana Stadium in Rio de Janeiro, one of the largest in the world, on November 19 1969, had just that touch of drama which took it out of the ordinary run of the mill. The 28-year-old Pele was 999 not out after a professional career of 13 years—and the excitement of hoping to see him become the first player to score 1,000 goals had been mounting over the past few weeks as the target continued to elude the ebony goalgetter and the tension of the magic milestone was beginning to tell on all.

No wonder that two days before the match was due to take place it was reported that nearly every seat had been sold in the vast stadium which Pele considered one of the friendliest in the world. 'The spectators there have always been one of the best crowds,' he said. 'I received more cheers than boos from them in spite of the fact that I played for a team from another state.'

Surprisingly, on the day of the game the stadium was only about half full, the attendance being returned at 75,157. Most of the spectators in the ground decided to station themselves behind the goal they reckoned they would have the best chance of seeing history made—the net in which Pele would put the ball for his 1,000th goal.

But they had a frustrating and disappointing first half for the best that their great idol could do was to hit a goalpost, shoot straight at Andreade, Vasco's former Argentine international goalkeeper, and then put a good scoring chance wide of the net. Obviously the strain was telling on the player as well.

So the match went into the second half with the majority of the crowd scampering round the ground to take up their positions behind the other goal. Thirty minutes of the second half had gone and still that magic goal was eluding the man who in the past had found no trouble in putting the ball in the net.

Then twelve minutes from the end Pele was streaking through the Vasco defence and the goal looked like coming when he was tripped in the penalty area. The referee, Manoel Amaro de Lima, immediately pointed to the spot and, despite the usual protests of the Vasco players, stuck to his decision.

At first Rildo, of Santos, shaped up to take the kick but that was not what the crowd wanted. 'Pele, Pele,' they yelled. As Rildo hesitated the Santos captain bowed to their wishes, changed his mind, and gave the spot kick to the highest paid footballer in the world. The score at the time was one goal each, Beneti having given Vasco the lead after 17 minutes with Santos equalising through an own goal by Rene after 35 minutes. With a low drive Pele put the ball past Andreade in the Vasco goal and so reached his 1,000—the signal for hundreds of spectators to invade the pitch and hold up the game.

As they raced across the ground to get to their hero Andreade, who had come prepared to be beaten by Pele, tore off his jersey to reveal underneath a silver shirt with the figure 1,000 on it. Pele was carried shoulder high round the ground by his delighted fans. Tears were streaming down the cheeks of the player who had risen from poverty to riches to become a household name in world soccer and to become even better known than the president of his own country.

After the match—Pele's penalty had given Santos a 2–1 victory—the stadium president, Dr Abelard Franca, unveiled a bronze plaque to mark the historic event. Pele was also presented with a diploma from F.I.F.A., signed by Sir Stanley Rous, the president. A few days later Pele made a triumphant tour of Brazil during which he met one of his greatest fans—the president of Brazil. His visit to Brasilia aroused such interest that for the first time the police there were called upon to deal with traffic jams.

But amid all the glamour and glorification there was still soccer and four days after the history-making match the Black Pearl fell from grace—he was dismissed from the field after 20 minutes of Santos's game at Belo Horizonte for 'disrespect' by the referee, Amilcar Ferreira. And less than an hour earlier the State governor had unveiled a monument—an imprint of Pele's right foot—to mark his record.

11 The Four Home Countries 1969–70

ENGLAND

EVERTON HOLD OFF LEEDS

Everton's triumph in the League championship was a continuation of the quiet success they have enjoyed since Harry Catterick, who was once a centre-forward on their books before the war, rejoined them as manager in 1961 after a spell with Sheffield Wednesday.

In Catterick's first season Everton finished fourth in the table, won the Championship the following year, and were third in 1964. In 1965 they were fourth again, and in 1966, although finishing half-way down the table, they beat Sheffield Wednesday in the F.A. Cup Final. They finished sixth in 1967 and in 1968 again reached the F.A. Cup Final only to be beaten in extra time by West Bromwich Albion. That season they were fifth in the table.

In 1969 they were third in the League and lost in the F.A. Cup semi-final to the ultimate winners, Manchester City. Last season their run in the Cup ended rather surprisingly in the third round when they were beaten at Bramall Lane by Sheffield United by 2–1.

At one time during last season it appeared that a loss of form and injuries to key players like Brian Labone and the £80,000 buy from Blackburn Rovers, Keith Newton, would upset their chances of winning the championship for the seventh time, but they came back well.

When it looked as though Leeds United might offer a strong challenge for the Championship the commitments of Don Revie's team in the European and F.A. Cups had their effect of piling up fixtures in the attenuated season and they fell away to leave Everton in undisputed command by the end of March.

Catterick has built an all-round team from his youth side and by judicious buying. In addition to Newton who was acquired in December to strengthen the defence, Catterick bought Alan Ball from Blackpool for £110,000 in 1966 and he has proved more than his value with his work-rate, and also from Blackpool there was Gordon West, the goalkeeper who was bought in May 1962 for £27,500—then a record fee for a goalkeeper. He was one of Catterick's first big buys.

In 1967 Catterick persuaded Preston to part with Howard Kendall for £80,000. The big buying has led to Everton being known as the 'Millionarios'.

Yet in the side are the experienced Labone, Joe Royle, Colin Harvey and Tommy Wright, who were signed as schoolboys and did not cost a penny, as well as newcomers Alan Whittle, of whom Catterick has a high opinion, and Roger Kenyon. A sign of a champion side is the strength of its reserves.

EVERTON'S LEAGUE RECORD
(Everton score first)

	Home	*Away*
Arsenal		1–0
Manchester United		2–0
Crystal Palace	2–1	
Manchester United	3–0	
Manchester City		1–1
Sheffield Wednesday	2–1	
Leeds United	3–2	
Derby County		1–2
West Ham United	2–0	
Newcastle United		2–0
Ipswich Town		3–0
Southampton	4–2	
Wolverhampton Wanderers		3–2
Crystal Palace		0–0
Sunderland	3–1	
Stoke City	6–2	
Coventry City		1–0
Nottingham Forest	1–0	
West Bromwich Albion		0–2
Chelsea		1–1
Burnley	2–1	
Liverpool	0–3	
West Ham United		1–0
Derby County	1–0	
Manchester City	1–0	
Leeds United		1–2
Ipswich Town	3–0	
Southampton		1–2
Newcastle United	0–0	
Wolverhampton Wanderers	1–0	
Arsenal	2–2	
Coventry City	0–0	
Nottingham Forest		1–1
Burnley		2–1
Tottenham Hotspur		1–0
Tottenham Hotspur	3–2	

Liverpool		2-0
Chelsea	5-2	
Stoke City		1-0
West Bromwich Albion	2-0	
Sheffield Wednesday		1-0
Sunderland		0-0

FINAL LEAGUE TABLE (DIVISION ONE), 1969-70

	P	W	D	L	Goals F	A	Pts
Everton	42	29	8	5	72	34	66
Leeds United	42	21	15	6	84	49	57
Chelsea	42	21	13	8	70	50	55
Derby County	42	22	9	11	64	37	53
Liverpool	42	20	11	11	65	42	51
Coventry City	42	19	11	12	58	48	49
Newcastle United	42	17	13	12	57	35	47
Manchester United	42	14	17	11	66	61	45
Stoke City	42	15	15	12	56	52	45
Manchester City	42	16	11	15	55	48	43
Arsenal	42	12	18	11	51	48	42
Tottenham Hotspur	42	16	9	16	53	55	41
Wolverhampton Wanderers	42	12	16	14	55	57	40
Burnley	42	12	15	15	56	61	39
Nottingham Forest	42	10	18	14	50	71	38
West Bromwich Albion	42	14	9	19	58	66	37
West Ham United	42	12	12	18	51	60	36
Ipswich Town	42	10	11	21	40	63	31
Southampton	42	6	17	19	46	67	29
Crystal Palace	42	6	15	21	34	68	27
Sunderland	42	6	14	22	30	68	26
Sheffield Wednesday	42	8	9	25	40	71	25

LEAGUE CHAMPIONS

1889	Preston North End	1902	Sunderland
1890	Preston North End	1903	Sheffield Wednesday
1891	Everton	1904	Sheffield Wednesday
1892	Sunderland	1905	Newcastle United
1893	Sunderland	1906	Liverpool
1894	Aston Villa	1907	Newcastle United
1895	Sunderland	1908	Manchester United
1896	Aston Villa	1909	Newcastle United
1897	Aston Villa	1910	Aston Villa
1898	Sheffield United	1911	Manchester United
1899	Aston Villa	1912	Blackburn Rovers
1900	Aston Villa	1913	Sunderland
1901	Liverpool	1914	Blackburn Rovers

1915	Everton	1948	Arsenal
1915–19	No competition	1949	Portsmouth
1920	West Bromwich Albion	1950	Portsmouth
1921	Burnley	1951	Tottenham Hotspur
1922	Liverpool	1952	Manchester United
1923	Liverpool	1953	Arsenal
1924	Huddersfield Town	1954	Wolverhampton Wanderers
1925	Huddersfield Town	1955	Chelsea
1926	Huddersfield Town	1956	Manchester United
1927	Newcastle United	1957	Manchester United
1928	Everton	1958	Wolverhampton Wanderers
1929	Sheffield Wednesday	1959	Wolverhampton Wanderers
1930	Sheffield Wednesday	1960	Burnley
1931	Arsenal	1961	Tottenham Hotspur
1932	Everton	1962	Ipswich Town
1933	Arsenal	1963	Everton
1934	Arsenal	1964	Liverpool
1935	Arsenal	1965	Manchester United
1936	Sunderland	1966	Liverpool
1937	Manchester City	1967	Manchester United
1938	Arsenal	1968	Manchester City
1939	Everton	1969	Leeds United
1939–46	No competition	1970	Everton
1947	Liverpool		

THE F.A. CUP

CHELSEA COME BACK THREE TIMES TO WIN TROPHY

After promising so much for so long Chelsea at last delivered the goods on April 29 when they beat Leeds United 2–1 to win the F.A. Cup for the first time in their 65-year history. But it was only by sheer persistence that they gained their objective, for not only did they need a replay at Old Trafford and extra time but also they had to come from behind three times in order to win.

Yet, as everyone duly paid tribute to Chelsea for their refusal to be beaten, there was genuine sympathy for Leeds who after playing well for the rest of the season had collapsed too surprisingly in the final month. Just when they looked poised for a history-making treble of League championship, F.A. Cup and European Cup, everything went wrong and their Old Trafford defeat was the final bitter blow for Don Revie's men.

How they lost this gladiatorial struggle, more physical than skilful, even they will never be able to explain to themselves. For an hour they were in complete control of the match, a goal up through Mick Jones after 35 minutes, with Chelsea nervous and hesitant and their goalkeeper, Peter Bonetti, limping from a leg injury.

Suddenly the game switched completely round. For Leeds it turned sour; it became all Chelsea and nothing Leeds could do could stop them. Peter Osgood flew through the air to head an equalising goal with 12 minutes to go and again force the final into extra time. After 12 minutes of the extra period Ian Hutchinson took one of his long throw ins. The ball went to David Webb, the man who had had such a miserable Wembley against Eddie Gray. He jumped to head what proved the winning goal against a team whose spirit seemed to have been completely broken on the wheel of misfortune. The teams were:

CHELSEA: Bonetti; Harris, McCreadie, Hollins, Dempsey, Webb, Baldwin, Cooke, Osgood (Hinton 112 mins), Hutchinson, Houseman.

LEEDS UNITED: Harvey; Madeley, Cooper, Bremner, Charlton, Hunter, Lorimer, Clarke, Jones, Giles, Gray.

The Wembly final—on April 11—produced a more memorable encounter for the 100,000 crowd. Jack Charlton put Leeds into the lead after 21 minutes but Peter Houseman equalised 9 minutes later. Seven minutes from the end Jones again put Leeds ahead with what most people thought would be the winning goal, but Chelsea's fighting spirit stood them in good stead and within three minutes Hutchinson had again levelled the scores. So for the first time in the 47 years' history of Wembley the Cup Final went into extra time.

No further goals were scored and a replay was necessary but this could not take place the following week because of the start of the Home International championship, and was postponed for 18 days. It also raised the question of whether a provincial ground is a suitable setting for a replay. The Football Association might consider having any future replays at Wembley, for without that setting the final seems to lose some of its glamour. The teams at Wembley were:

CHELSEA: Bonetti; Webb, McCreadie, Hollins, Dempsey, Harris (Hinton 90 mins), Baldwin, Houseman, Osgood, Hutchinson, Cooke.

LEEDS UNITED: Sprake; Madeley, Cooper, Bremner, Charlton, Hunter, Lorimer, Clarke, Jones, Giles, Gray.

Leeds' disastrous season did not end with their failure to carry off one of the three trophies for which they had looked such favourites. There was worse to come. A few days after their defeat by Chelsea they were fined a record £5,000 by the Football League for failing to field teams of full strength in League matches towards the end of the season.

Leeds' explanation of why they had put out a depleted side against Southampton and a reserve team against Derby County was that their leading players were mentally and physically exhausted. This was not accepted by the League Management Committee. The previous record fine for this offence was the £2,000 imposed on Everton in 1966.

F.A. CUP 1970 SIXTH ROUND TO FINAL

SIXTH ROUND
February 21 1970

MIDDLESBROUGH (1) 1 (Hickton) MANCHESTER UNITED (1) 1 Sartori. 40,000
QUEEN'S PARK RANGERS (1) 2 (Venables pen., Bridges) CHELSEA (3) 4 (Webb, Osgood 3. 33,572
SWINDON TOWN (0) 0 LEEDS UNITED (2) 2 (Clarke 2). 27,500
WATFORD (0) 1 (Endean) LIVERPOOL (0) 0. 34,047

REPLAY—February 25 1970
MANCHESTER UNITED (1) 2 (Charlton, Morgan pen.) MIDDLES-BROUGH (0) 1 (Hickton). 63,418

SEMI-FINALS
March 14 1970

WATFORD (1) 1 (Garbett) CHELSEA (1) 5 (Houseman 2, Webb, Osgood, Hutchinson). At White Hart Lane, Tottenham. 55,200
MANCHESTER UNITED (0) 0 LEEDS UNITED (0) 1. At Hillsborough, Sheffield. 55,000

REPLAY—March 23 1970
MANCHESTER UNITED (0) 0 LEEDS UNITED (0) 0 After extra time. At Villa Park, Birmingham. 62,500

SECOND REPLAY—March 26 1970
LEEDS UNITED (1) 1 (Bremner) MANCHESTER UNITED (0) 0 At Bolton. 56,000

FINAL
April 11 1970

CHELSEA (1) 2 (Houseman, Hutchinson) LEEDS UNITED (1) 2 (Charlton, Jones). After extra time; 90-minute score 2-2. At Wembley Stadium. 100,000

REPLAY—April 29 1970
CHELSEA (0) 2 (Osgood, Webb) LEEDS UNITED (1) 1 (Jones). After extra time; 90-minute score 1-1. At Old Trafford, Manchester. 62,000

THIRD PLACE PLAY-OFF
April 10 1970

WATFORD (0) 0 MANCHESTER UNITED (0) 2 (Kidd 2). At Highbury London.

PREVIOUS WINNERS

1872	Wanderers	1921	Tottenham Hotspur
1873	Wanderers	1922	Huddersfield Town
1874	Oxford University	1923	Bolton Wanderers
1875	Royal Engineers	1924	Newcastle United
1876	Wanderers	1925	Sheffield United
1877	Wanderers	1926	Bolton Wanderers
1878	Wanderers	1927	Cardiff City
1879	Old Etonians	1928	Blackburn Rovers
1880	Clapham Rovers	1929	Bolton Wanderers
1881	Old Carthusians	1930	Arsenal
1882	Old Etonians	1931	West Bromwich Albion
1883	Blackburn Olympiads	1932	Newcastle United
1884	Blackburn Rovers	1933	Everton
1885	Blackburn Rovers	1934	Manchester City
1886	Blackburn Rovers	1935	Sheffield Wednesday
1887	Aston Villa	1936	Arsenal
1888	West Bromwich Albion	1937	Sunderland
1889	Preston North End	1938	Preston North End
1890	Blackburn Rovers	1939	Portsmouth
1891	Blackburn Rovers	1940–45	No competition
1892	West Bromwich Albion	1946	Derby County
1893	Wolverhampton Wanderers	1947	Charlton Athletic
1894	Notts County	1948	Manchester United
1895	Aston Villa	1949	Wolverhampton Wanderers
1896	Sheffield Wednesday	1950	Arsenal
1897	Aston Villa	1951	Newcastle United
1898	Nottingham Forest	1952	Newcastle United
1899	Sheffield United	1953	Blackpool
1900	Bury	1954	West Bromwich Albion
1901	Tottenham Hotspur	1955	Newcastle United
1902	Sheffield United	1956	Manchester City
1903	Bury	1957	Aston Villa
1904	Manchester City	1958	Bolton Wanderers
1905	Aston Villa	1959	Nottingham Forest
1906	Everton	1960	Wolverhampton Wanderers
1907	Sheffield Wednesday	1961	Tottenham Hotspur
1908	Wolverhampton Wanderers	1962	Tottenham Hotspur
1909	Manchester United	1963	Manchester United
1910	Newcastle United	1964	West Ham United
1911	Bradford City	1965	Liverpool
1912	Barnsley	1966	Tottenham Hotspur
1913	Aston Villa	1967	Everton
1914	Burnley	1968	West Bromwich Albion
1915	Sheffield United	1969	Manchester City
1916–19	No competition	1970	Chelsea
1920	Aston Villa		

INTERNATIONALS

Nov. 5 1969: HOLLAND (0) 0   ENGLAND (0) 1 (Bell). Amsterdam,
ENGLAND: Bonetti (Chelsea); Wright (Everton), Hughes (Liverpool).
Mullery (Tottenham Hotspur), Charlton J. (Leeds United), Moore
(West Ham), Lee (Manchester City), Thompson (Liverpool), Bell
(Manchester City), Charlton R. (Manchester United), Hurst (West
Ham), Peters (West Ham).

Dec. 10 1969: ENGLAND (1) 1 (Charlton J.) PORTUGAL (0) 0.
Wembley. 100,000
ENGLAND: Bonetti (Chelsea); Reaney (Leeds United), Hughes (Liver-
pool), Mullery (Tottenham Hotspur), Charlton J. (Leeds United), Moore
(West Ham), Lee (Manchester City), Bell (Manchester City), Peters
West Ham), Astle (West Bromwich Albion), Charlton R. (Manchester
United), Ball (Everton).

Jan. 14 1970: ENGLAND (0) 0   HOLLAND (0) 0.   Wembley. 75,000
ENGLAND: Banks (Stoke City); Newton (Everton), Cooper (Leeds
United), Peters (West Ham United), Charlton J. (Leeds United),
Hunter (Leeds United), Lee (Manchester City), Mullery (Tottenham
Hotspur), Jones (Leeds United), Hurst (West Ham United), Charlton R.
(Manchester United), Moore I. (Nottingham Forest).

Feb. 25 1970: BELGIUM (0) 1   ENGLAND (1) 3 (Ball 2, Hurst).
Brussels. 36,000
ENGLAND: Banks (Stoke City); Wright (Everton), Cooper, (Leeds
Unted), Moore (West Ham United), Labone (Everton), Hughes,
(Liverpool) Lee (Manchester City), Ball (Everton), Osgood (Chelsea),
Hurst (West Ham United), Peters (West Ham United).

April 18 1970: WALES (1) 1 (Krzywicki) ENGLAND (0) 1 (Lee).
Cardiff. 50,000
ENGLAND: Banks (Stoke City); Wright (Everton), Hughes (Liverpool),
Mullery (Tottenham Hotspur), Labone (Everton), Moore (West Ham
United, Lee (Manchester City), Ball (Everton), Charlton R. (Man-
chester United), Hurst (West Ham United), Peters (Tottenham Hotspur).

April 21 1970: ENGLAND (1) 3 (Peters, Hurst, Charlton R.) NORTH-
ERN IRELAND (0) 1 (Best). Wembley. 100,000
ENGLAND: Banks (Stoke City); Newton (Everton), Hughes (Liverpool),
Mullery (Tottenham Hotspur), Moore (West Ham United), Stiles
(Manchester United), Coates (Burnley), Kidd (Manchester United),
Charlton R. (Manchester United), Hurst (West Ham United), Peters
(Tottenham Hotspur).

April 25 1970: SCOTLAND (0) 0   ENGLAND (0) 0.   Hampden Park.
137,438
ENGLAND: Banks (Stoke City); Newton (Everton), Hughes (Liverpool),
Stiles (Manchester United), Labone (Everton), Moore (West Ham
United), Thompson (Liverpool), Mullery (Tottenham Hotspur), Ball
(Everton), Astle (West Bromwich Albion), Hurst (West Ham United),
Peters (Tottenham Hotspur).

May 20 1970: COLOMBIA (0) 0   ENGLAND (2) 4 (Peters 2, Charlton R., Ball) Bogota. 35,000
COLOMBIA: Quintana; Segovia, Segrera, Lopez D., Lopez O., Hernandez, Paz, Canon, Brand, Gallego, Garcia.
ENGLAND: Banks (Stoke City); Newton (Everton), Cooper (Leeds United), Mullery (Tottenham Hospur), Labone (Everton), Moore (West Ham United), Lee (Manchester City), Ball (Everton), Charlton R. (Manchester United), Hurst (West Ham United), Peters (Tottenham Hotspur).

May 24 1970: ECUADOR (0) 0   ENGLAND (1) 2 (Lee, Kidd). Quito.
ECUADOR: Mejfa; Utreras, Campoverde, Portilla, Valencia, Gardenas, Bolanos, Munoz (Cabreza), Penaherrera, Carrera (Rodriquez), Larrea.
ENGLAND: Banks (Stoke City); Newton (Everton), Cooper (Leeds United), Mullery (Tottenham Hotspur), Labone (Everton), Moore (West Ham United), Lee (Manchester City), Kidd (Manchester United), Ball (Everton), Charlton R. (Manchester United), Sadler, (Manchester United), Hurst (West Ham United), Peters (Tottenham Hotspur).

June 2 1970: RUMANIA (0) 0   ENGLAND (0) 1 (Hurst). Guadalajara.

June 7 1970: ENGLAND (0) 0   BRAZIL (0) 1 (Jairzinho). Guadaljara.

June 11 1970: ENGLAND (0) 1 (Clarke pen)   CZECHOSLOVAKIA (0) 0. Guadalajara.

June 14 1970: WEST GERMANY (0) 3 (Beckenbauer, Seeler, Mueller)   ENGLAND (1) 2 (Mullery, Peters). After extra time at Leon. Score at 90 minutes 2–2.
(World Cup finals in Mexico. See Chapter 4 for teams.)

THE FOOTBALL LEAGUE CUP

TREBLE FOR MANCHESTER CITY

Manchester City completed a treble when they won the Football League Cup at Wembley on March 7, having won the F.A. Cup the previous year and the League Championship the year before that. However, they needed extra time before they beat West Bromwich Albion by two goals to one. Although probably the heavier team, Manchester City outstayed Albion in the muddy conditions of the stadium pitch, which had been cleared of snow, and a goal by Glyn Pardoe after 102 minutes play settled the issue.

Albion had given City a shock when a typically headed goal by Astle had put them in the lead after only five minutes' play and for a time City were fighting desperately to hold off their rivals. Gradually, however, thanks to some tireless work on the wing by Francis Lee, who came out as the man of the match, they equalised almost on the hour with a goal by Mick Doyle when the Albion defence failed to clear a Pardoe corner.

City's performance was all the more remarkable because they had played a European Cup-Winners' Cup-tie in Portugal the previous Wednesday and on their way home late on Thursday had been diverted to Birmingham as Heathrow Airport was closed. This had meant a road journey down the M1 to arrive in London in the early hours of Friday morning.

Wembley officially returned the crowd at the final as 100,000, with receipts of £123,000. Teams:

MANCHESTER CITY: Corrigan; Book, Mann, Doyle, Booth, Oakes, Heslop, Bell, Summerbee (Bowyer 67 mins), Lee Pardoe.

WEST BROMWICH ALBION: Osborne; Fraser, Wilson, Brown, Talbut, Kaye, Cantello, Suggett, Astle, Hartford (Kryzwicki 84 mins), Hope

FOOTBALL LEAGUE CUP—1970 FIFTH ROUND TO FINAL

FIFTH ROUND
October 29 1969

LEICESTER CITY (0) 0   WEST BROMWICH ALBION (0) 0.   35,121
MANCHESTER CITY (3) 3 (Bell 2, Summerbee)   QUEEN'S PARK RANGERS (0) 0   42,058
OXFORD UNITED (0) 0   CARLISLE (0) 0.   17,964

November 12 1969
DERBY COUNTY (0) 0   MANCHESTER UNITED (0) 0.   38,893

REPLAYS
November 4 1969
CARLISLE (0) 1 (Balderstone pen)   OXFORD UNITED (0) 0.   16,303

November 5 1969
WEST BROMWICH ALBION (2) 2 (Astle 2)   LEICESTER CITY (0) 1 (Cross).   25,186

November 19 1969
MANCHESTER UNITED (0) 1 (Kidd)   DERBY COUNTY (0) 0. 57,122

SEMI-FINALS
Two Legs

November 19 1969
CARLISLE (0) 1 (Barton)   WEST BROMWICH ALBION (0) 0.   20,322

December 3 1969
MANCHESTER CITY (1) 2 (Bell, Lee pen)   MANCHESTER UNITED (0) 1 (Charlton R.).   55,799
WEST BROMWICH ALBION (0) 4 (Hope, Suggett, Brown, Martin) CARLISLE (0) 1 (Barton).   32,791 (West Bromwich A. won 4–2 on aggregate).

December 17 1969
MANCHESTER UNITED (1) 2 (Edwards, Law) MANCHESTER
CITY (1) 2 (Bowyer, Summerbee). 63,418 (Manchester City won 4–3
on aggregate).

FINAL
March 7 1970
MANCHESTER CITY (0) 2 (Doyle, Pardoe) WEST BROMWICH
ALBION (1) 1 (Astle). 100,000. £123,000. At Wembley. After
extra time; score at 90 minutes 1–1.

PREVIOUS FINALS
1960–1961

Aug. 22 1961: Rotherham United 2 Aston Villa 0 At Rotherham.
Sept. 5 1961: Aston Villa 3 Rotherham United 0 At Villa Park. After
extra time. Aston Villa won 3–2 on aggregate.

1961–1962
April 26 1962: Rochdale 0 Norwich City 3 At Rochdale.
May 1 1962: Norwich City 1 Rochdale 0 At Norwich. Norwich City
won 4–0 on aggregate.

1962–1963
May 23 1963: Birmingham City 3 Aston Villa 1 At St. Andrew's.
May 27 1963: Aston Villa 0 Birmingham City 0 At Villa Park.
Birmingham City won 3–1 on aggregate.

1963–1964
April 13 1964: Stoke City 1 Leicester City 1 At Stoke.
April 22 1964: Leicester City 3 Stoke City 2 At Leicester. Leicester
City won 4–3 on aggregate.

1964–1965
March 15 1965: Chelsea 3 Leicester City 2 At Stamford Bridge.
April 5 1965: Leicester City 0 Chelsea 0 At Leicester. Chelsea won
3–2 on aggregate.

1965–1966
March 9 1966: West Ham United 2 West Bromwich Albion 1 At
Upton Park.
March 23 1966: West Bromwich Albion 4 West Ham United 1 At
The Hawthorns. West Bromwich Albion won 5–3 on aggregate.

1966–1967
March 4 1967: Queen's Park Rangers 3 West Bromwich Albion 2 At
Wembley.

1967–1968
March 2 1968: Leeds United 1 Arsenal 0 At Wembley.

1968–1969
March 15 1969: Swindon Town 3 Arsenal 2 At Wembley. After
extra time.

NORTHERN IRELAND
GLENTORAN AND LINFIELD TAKE HONOURS

Glentoran won the Irish League championship for the 14th time and the third time in four years, while Linfield were successful in the Irish Cup final for a record thirtieth time, triumphs which put both clubs back into European competition

The big question in Northern Ireland is whether clubs in that part of the world can afford the expense of playing in Europe. Last season it was reported that Linfield's two-legged European Cup ties with Belgrade's Red Star cost the club something in the region of £2,000, while Ards competing in the Cup-Winners' Cup against AS Roma were down by a similar sum.

Neither club got past the first ties—but perhaps the prestige of taking part in European competition is worth it.

Linfield had a big shock before they won a gale-swept incident-packed Cup final at Cliftonville in April. Within two minutes Vic Fleming had the ball in Linfield's net to give Ballymena United a surprise lead.

After a few minutes to regain their balance Linfield got back on level terms after eleven minutes when Phil Scott turned a Bryan Hamilton centre into a goal. Not until five minutes after half-time did Linfield impress their superiority on the game with their second goal—a fine effort by Scott from a corner by Hamilton.

LINFIELD: Stewart; Gilliland, Paterson, Bowyer, Hatton, Andrews, Viollet, Hamilton, Millen, Scott, Pavis.

BALLYMENA UNITED: Platt; Erwin, Richardson, Torrens, Averell, Russell, Porter, McGowan, Fleming, Martin, McFall.

GLENTORAN LEAGUE RECORD
(Glentoran's score first)

	Home	Away
Derry City	1–0	
Linfield		2–0
Ards	1–1	
Crusaders		0–2
Portadown	2–1	
Coleraine	2–1	
Distillery		5–0
Cliftonville	2–0	
Bangor		1–1
Ballymena		3–0
Glenavon	2–0	

Derry City		0–0
Linfield	2–2	
Ards		3–2
Crusaders	7–2	
Portadown		3–1
Coleraine		0–2
Distillery	3–0	
Cliftonville		3–0
Bangor	2–0	
Ballymena	0–0	
Glenavon		2–2

FINAL IRISH LEAGUE TABLE

	P	W	D	L	Goals F	A	Pts
Glentoran	22	14	6	2	46	17	34
Coleraine	22	12	3	7	50	31	27
Ards	22	10	7	5	41	26	27
Linfield	22	11	5	6	48	36	27
Derry City	22	11	5	6	38	31	27
Portadown	22	11	3	8	42	37	25
Glenavon	22	7	8	7	32	36	22
Bangor	22	6	7	9	32	36	19
Crusaders	22	8	3	11	42	52	19
Ballymena United	22	5	6	11	24	42	16
Distillery	22	5	5	12	25	45	15
Cliftonville	22	1	4	17	20	51	6

IRISH LEAGUE CHAMPIONS

1891	Linfield	1909	Linfield
1892	Linfield	1910	Cliftonville
1893	Linfield	1911	Linfield
1894	Glentoran	1912	Glentoran
1895	Linfield	1913	Glentoran
1896	Distillery	1914	Linfield
1897	Glentoran	1915	Belfast Celtic
1898	Linfield	1915–20	No competition
1899	Distillery	1921	Glentoran
1800	Belfast Celtic	1922	Linfield
1901	Distillery	1923	Linfield
1902	Linfield	1924	Queen's Island
1903	Distillery	1925	Glentoran
1904	Linfield	1926	Belfast Celtic
1905	Glentoran	1927	Belfast Celtic
1906	Cliftonville and Distillery	1928	Belfast Celtic
1907	Linfield	1929	Belfast Celtic
1908	Linfield	1930	Linfield

1931	Glentoran	1954	Linfield
1932	Linfield	1955	Linfield
1933	Belfast Celtic	1956	Linfield
1934	Linfield	1957	Glenavon
1935	Linfield	1958	Ards
1936	Belfast Celtic	1959	Linfield
1937	Belfast Celtic	1960	Glenavon
1938	Belfast Celtic	1961	Linfield
1939	Belfast Celtic	1962	Linfield
1940	Belfast Celtic	1963	Distillery
1941–47	No competition	1964	Glentoran
1948	Belfast Celtic	1965	Derry City
1949	Linfield	1966	Linfield
1950	Linfield	1967	Glentoran
1951	Glentoran	1968	Glentoran
1952	Glenavon	1969	Linfield
1953	Glentoran	1970	Glentoran

SEMI-FINALS
March 14 1970

DERRY 1   LINFIELD 2   At the Oval, Belfast.
BALLYMENA 2   COLERAINE 0   At Windsor Park, Belfast.

FINAL
April 4 1970

BALLYMENA 1 (Fleming)   LINFIELD 2 (Scott 2)   At Cliftonville Belfast.

IRISH F.A. CUP WINNERS

1881	Mayola Park	1900	Cliftonville
1882	Queen's Island	1901	Cliftonville
1883	Cliftonville	1902	Linfield
1884	Distillery	1903	Distillery
1885	Distillery	1904	Linfield
1886	Distillery	1905	Distillery
1887	Ulster	1906	Shelbourne
1888	Cliftonville	1907	Cliftonville
1889	Distillery	1908	Bohemians
1890	Gordon Highlanders	1909	Cliftonville
1891	Linfield	1910	Distillery
1892	Linfield	1911	Shelbourne
1893	Linfield	1912	Linfield
1894	Distillery	1913	Linfield
1895	Linfield	1914	Glentoran
1896	Distillery	1915	Linfield
1897	Cliftonville	1916	Linfield
1898	Linfield	1917	Glentoran
1899	Linfield	1918	Belfast Celtic

1919	Linfield	1945	Linfield
1920	Shelbourne	1946	Linfield
1921	Glentoran	1947	Belfast Celtic
1922	Linfield	1948	Linfield
1923	Linfield	1949	Derry City
1924	Queen's Island	1950	Linfield
1925	Distillery	1951	Glentoran
1926	Belfast Celtic	1952	Ards
1927	Ards	1953	Linfield
1928	Willowfield	1954	Derry City
1929	Ballymena	1955	Dundela
1930	Linfield	1956	Distillery
1931	Linfield	1957	Glenavon
1932	Glentoran	1958	Ballymena United
1933	Glentoran	1959	Glenavon
1934	Linfield	1960	Linfield
1935	Glentoran	1961	Glenavon
1936	Linfield	1962	Linfield
1937	Belfast Celtic	1963	Linfield
1938	Belfast Celtic	1964	Derry City
1939	Linfield	1965	Coleraine
1940	Ballymena United	1966	Glentoran
1941	Belfast Celtic	1967	Crusaders
1942	Linfield	1968	Crusaders
1943	Belfast Celtic	1969	Ards
1944	Belfast Celtic	1970	Linfield

INTERNATIONALS

Sept. 10 1969: NORTHERN IRELAND (0) 0   RUSSIA (0) 0   Belfast. 36,000.

Oct. 22 1969: RUSSIA (1) 2 (Nodiya, Byshovets)   NORTHERN IRE-LAND (0) 0   Moscow.   103,000.
(World Cup qualifying matches. See World Cup Group Four.)

April 18 1970: NORTHERN IRELAND (0) 0   SCOTLAND (0) 1 (O'Hare)   Belfast.   31,000
NORTHERN IRELAND: Jennings (Tottenham Hotspur); Craig (Newcastle United), Clements (Coventry City), Todd (Burnley), O'Kane (Nottingham Forest), Neill (Arsenal), Nicholson (Huddersfield), Campbell (Dundee), Dickson (Coleraine), Lutton (Wolverhampton Wanderers), Dougan (Wolverhampton Wanderers), McMordie (Middlesbrough), Best (Manchester United).

April 21 1970: ENGLAND (1) 3 (Peters, Hurst, Charlton R.)   NORTH-ERN IRELAND (0) 1 (Best)   Wembley.   100,000
NORTHERN IRELAND: Jennings (Tottenham Hospur); Craig (Newcastle United), Clements (Coventry City), O'Kane (Nottingham Forest), Neill (Arsenal), Nicholson (Huddersfield), McMordie (Middlesbrough),

Best (Manchester United), Dougan (Wolverhampton Wanderers), O'Doherty (Coleraine), Lutton (Wolverhampton Wanderers).

April 25 1970: WALES (1) 1 (Rees) NORTHERN IRELAND (0) 0
Swansea
NORTHERN IRELAND: McFaul (Newcastle United); Craig (Newcastle United), Nelson (Arsenal), O'Kane (Nottingham Forest), Neill (Arsenal), Nicholson (Huddersfield), Campbell (Dundee), O'Doherty (Coleraine), Best (Manchester United), Dickson (Coleraine), McMordie (Middlesbrough), Clements (Coventry City).

REPUBLIC OF IRELAND

WATERFORD MAKE IT THREE TITLES IN A ROW

Waterford won the League of Ireland championship for the third successive year to equal the feat of Cork United nearly 30 years ago. They clinched the title with a 4–2 away victory over Finn Harps at Ballybofey, only the second time Harps had lost at home in nearly eight months.

Waterford's success was, however, rather overshadowed by their player-manager Alfie Hale putting in a transfer request immediately after the title had been won. Hale had taken over the job in mid-season from Vinny Maguire, and not only had he got together a useful side but was also one of the club's leading goalscorers.

Waterford's goalkeeper, Peter Thomas, became the first English player to be named soccer personality of the year. Thomas joined the club from Coventry City and his outstanding play earned him a place in League of Ireland representative sides.

A move at the annual meeting to increase the size of the League from 14 to 16 clubs was defeated but there are hopes that next season two of the many clubs anxious to get into the League will be more successful.

Bohemians, the last of the amateur clubs to go professional, won the F.A.I. Cup but it took them three games and 300 minutes of football to dispose of Sligo Rovers (who were appearing in their first final since 1940) by two goals to one to inscribe their name on the trophy for the third time in their history.

The two clubs first met at Dalymount Park, Dublin, on April 19 when a colourless game produced only the second goalless draw in nearly half a century of the competition. Few thrills came as both sides seemed more concerned with defence than offence. The teams were:

BOHEMIANS: Lowry; Doran, Fullam, Nolan, Parkes, Conroy, Kelly T., Swan, O'Connell, Hamill, Kelly M.

SLIGO ROVERS: Lally; Turner, Fallon, Pugh, Stenson, Burns, McCluskey, Fagan, Cooke, Mitchell, Brooks.

The first replay took place the following Wednesday (April 22) on the same ground and after 110 minutes of much more enterprising and attacking football defences again held out for a goalless draw with the Rovers' midfield player, the 17-year-old Pat McCluskey, being the outstanding player. Teams:

BOHEMIANS: Lowry; Doran, Parkes, Fullam, Nolan, Conroy, Swan, Kelly T., O'Connell, Hamill, Kelly M.

SLIGO ROVERS: Lally; Turner, Burns, McCluskey, Pugh, Stenson, Cooke, Fagan, Mitchell, Fallon, Brooks.

Bohemians had to come from behind in the second replay on May 3 on the same ground for victory and a place in Europe for the first time. Within 15 minutes Johnny Cooke had beaten two Bohemian defenders to put Rovers ahead, a lead they held until the interval. A tactical move by Bohemians after the break by putting Johnny Fullam, possessor of six Cup medals with Shamrock Rovers, into midfield brought its reward.

Within four minutes he had equalised from a pass by Doran and then O'Connell from 25 yards smashed home the winning goal. The man of the match award, worth £50, went to Tommy Kelly, the Bohemians midfield player. Teams:

BOHEMIANS: Lowry; Doran, Fullam, Nolan, Parkes, Hamill, Kelly T., Swan, O'Connell, O'Sullivan, Kelly M. (Clarke 46 mins).

SLIGO ROVERS: Lally; Fallon, Turner, Pugh, Stenson (McKiernan 12 mins), Burns, Fagan, McCluskey, Cooke, Mitchell, Brooks.

WATERFORD'S LEAGUE RECORD
(Waterford's score first)

	Home	Away
St. Patrick's Athletic	1–0	
Drumcondra		2–0
Drogheda	4–0	
Bohemians		2–1
Athlone	1–0	
Sligo Rovers		5–1
Cork Celtic	4–1	
Shamrock Rovers		1–4
Shelbourne	1–0	
Dundalk		1–6
Limerick		0–1
Finn Harps	3–2	
Cork Hibernians		0–0

St. Patrick's Athletic	4–1
Drumcondra	6–1
Drogheda	1–1
Bohemians	3–2
Athlone	1–1
Sligo Rovers	1–0
Cork Celtic	1–1
Shamrock Rovers	2–4
Shelbourne	3–2
Dundalk	0–0
Limerick	3–1
Finn Harps	4–2
Cork Hibernians	1–1

FINAL LEAGUE OF IRELAND TABLE

	P	W	D	L	Goals F	A	Pts
Waterford	26	16	6	4	55	33	38
Shamrock Rovers	26	14	8	4	55	29	36
Cork Hibernians	26	13	9	4	35	20	35
Limerick	26	12	6	8	35	24	30
Dundalk	26	12	6	8	42	37	30
Shelbourne	26	10	7	9	38	32	27
Finn Harps	26	10	6	10	48	51	26
Sligo Rovers	26	11	4	11	37	41	26
Cork Celtic	26	8	6	12	34	38	22
Athlone Town	26	9	4	13	40	49	22
Bohemians	26	8	4	14	39	45	20
Drogheda	26	5	9	12	26	37	19
St. Patrick's Athletic	26	8	1	17	35	54	17
Drumcondra	26	5	6	15	35	64	16

LEAGUE OF IRELAND CHAMPIONS

1922	St. James's Gate	1937	Sligo Rovers
1923	Shamrock Rovers	1938	Shamrock Rovers
1924	Bohemians	1939	Shamrock Rovers
1925	Shamrock Rovers	1940	St. James's Gate
1926	Shelbourne	1941	Cork United
1927	Shamrock Rovers	1942	Cork United
1928	Bohemians	1943	Cork United
1929	Shelbourne	1944	Shelbourne
1930	Bohemians	1945	Cork United
1931	Shelbourne	1946	Cork United
1932	Shamrock Rovers	1947	Shelbourne
1933	Dundalk	1948	Drumcondra
1934	Bohemians	1949	Drumcondra
1935	Dolphin	1950	Cork Athlteic
1936	Bohemians	1951	Cork Athletic

1952 St. Patrick's Athletic	1962 Shelbourne
1953 Shelbourne	1963 Dundalk
1954 Shamrock Rovers	1964 Shamrock Rovers
1955 St. Patrick's Athletic	1965 Drumcondra
1956 St. Patrick's Athletic	1966 Waterford
1957 Shamrock Rovers	1967 Dundalk
1958 Drumcondra	1968 Waterford
1959 Shamrock Rovers	1969 Waterford
1960 Limerick	1970 Waterford
1961 Drumcondra	

SEMI-FINALS
March 28 1970

BOHEMIANS 1   DUNDALK 0.   Tolka Park Dublin.

March 29 1970

SLIGO ROVERS 0   CORK HIBERNIANS 0.   Dalymount Park, Dublin.

REPLAY—April 1 1970

SLIGO ROVERS 2   CORK HIBERNIANS 1.

FINAL
April 19 1970

BOHEMIANS 0   SLIGO ROVERS 0.   Dalymount Park, Dublin.

REPLAY—April 22 1970

BOHEMIANS 0   SLIGO ROVERS 0.   After extra time.   Dalymount Park, Dublin.

SECOND REPLAY—May 3 1970

BOHEMIANS (0) 2 (Fullam, O'Connell)   SLIGO ROVERS (1) 1 (Cooke).   Dalymount Park, Dublin.

F.A.I.   CUP   WINNERS

1922 St. James's Gate	1938 St. James's Gate
1923 Alton United	1939 Shelbourne
1924 Athlone Town	1940 Shamrock Rovers
1925 Shamrock Rovers	1941 Cork United
1926 Fordsons	1942 Dundalk
1927 Drumcondra	1943 Drumcondra
1928 Bohemians	1944 Shamrock Rovers
1929 Shamrock Rovers	1945 Shamrock Rovers
1930 Shamrock Rovers	1946 Drumcondra
1931 Shamrock Rovers	1947 Cork United
1932 Shamrock Rovers	1948 Shamrock Rovers
1933 Shamrock Rovers	1949 Dundalk
1934 Cork	1950 Transport
1935 Bohemians	1951 Cork Athletic
1936 Shamrock Rovers	1952 Dundalk
1937 Waterford	1953 Cork Athletic

Above: Karol Dobias (No. 2) saves the Czechoslovakian line after goal-keeper Vencel has been beaten by a shot from Rumania's Lucescu, seen falling on the goalkeeper. *Below:* A high leap by Christian Piot, the Belgian goalkeeper, to save during the match against Mexico in the Aztec Stadium

Rumanian goalkeeper Stere Adamache saves from England's Geoff Hurst as Lajos Satmareanu watches

1954	Drumcondra	1963	Shelbourne
1955	Shamrock Rovers	1964	Shamrock Rovers
1956	Shamrock Rovers	1965	Shamrock Rovers
1957	Drumcondra	1966	Shamrock Rovers
1958	Dundalk	1967	Shamrock Rovers
1959	St. Patrick's Athletic	1968	Shamrock Rovers
1960	Shelbourne	1969	Shamrock Rovers
1961	St. Patrick's Athletic	1970	Bohemians
1962	Shamrock Rovers		

INTERNATIONALS

Oct. 7 1969: CZECHOSLOVAKIA (3) 3 (Ademec 3) REP. OF IRELAND (0) 0. Prague. 36,000

Oct. 15 1969: REP. OF IRELAND (1) 1 (Givens) DENMARK (1) 1 (Jensen B.). Dublin. 22,000

Nov. 5 1969: HUNGARY (1) 4 (Halmosi, Bene, Puskas, Kocsis) REP. OF IRELAND (0) 0. Budapest.

(World Cup qualifying matches. See World Cup group two.)

Sept. 21 1969: REP. OF IRELAND (1) 1 (Givens) SCOTLAND (1) 1 (Stein). Dublin. 30,000

REPUBLIC OF IRELAND: Kelly (Preston North End); Brennan (Manchester United), Meagan (Drogheda), Finucane (Limerick), Mulligan (Shamrock Rovers), Conway (Fulham), Rogers (Blackburn Rovers), Giles (Leeds United), Givens (Manchester United), Hale (Waterford), Treacy (Charlton Athletic).

May 6 1970: POLAND (2) 2 (Kozerski Szoltysik) REPUBLIC OF IRELAND (0) 1 (Givens). Poznan. 85,000

REPUBLIC OF IRELAND: Kelly (Preston North End); Kinnear (Tottenham Hotspur), Carroll (Ipswich Town), Brennan (Manchester United), Hand (Plymouth Argyle), Mulligan (Chelsea), Byrne (Southampton), Dunphy (Millwall), Giles (Leeds United), Conway (Fulham), Treacy (Charlton), Conroy (Stoke City), Givens (Luton Town).

May 9 1970: WEST GERMANY (1) 2 (Seeler, Loehr) REPUBLIC OF IRELAND (0) 1 (Mulligan). West Berlin. 55,000

REPUBLIC OF IRELAND: Kelly (Preston North End); Brennan (Manchester United), Carroll (Ipswich Town), Hand (Plymouth Argyle), Dempsey (Chelsea), Mulligan (Chelsea), Byrne (Southampton), Conway (Fulham), Dunphy (Millwall), Giles (Leeds United), Conroy (Stoke City), Givens (Luton Town), Treacy (Charlton).

SCOTLAND

RANGERS LIVE IN SHADOW OF CELTIC LEAGUE SUCCESS

Once again, for the fifth year in succession, Celtic won the Scottish League championship to the dismay of Rangers, who are becoming

F

a little concerned at the dominance of Scottish football by the side that Jock Stein built.

Rangers, who finished 12 points behind their rivals, were in Europe only by courtesy of Celtic. They were beaten Cup finalists and so gained a place in the Cup-Winners' Cup competition as Celtic, the winners, as League champions opted for the more prestigeous European Cup.

When Rangers crashed 3–1 at home to the Polish club, Gornik Zabrze, in the second round of the Cup-Winners' Cup in November drastic action was taken. A board meeting was held the following morning and the decision made to sack their manager, David White, who had been in the job a few days over two years after taking over from Scot Symon.

The last time that Rangers achieved any success was in 1966 when they won the Scottish Cup, and the directors reckoned that in recent years their failure to make progress in European competition had cost the club something in the region of £100,000.

A week after White's dismissal Rangers appointed Willie Waddell, 48, one of their former players and one of Scotland's outstanding internationals of the post-war period, as manager with a mandate to get Rangers back among the trophies. Waddell, who had been out of football for some years, has a reputation for being a disciplinarian, and it was hoped that he could pull Rangers out of the rut.

Scotland's Footballer of the Year was Pat Stanton, the Hibernian captain, who proved a good winner over Celtic's veteran Bertie Auld. In his seven years with Hibernian Stanton played four times for Scotland and five times for the Scottish League, but illness kept him out of the home international championship last season.

CELTIC LEAGUE RECORD
(Celtic score first)

	Home	Away
St. Johnstone	2–2	
Kilmarnock		4–2
Dunfermline		1–2
Hibernian	1–2	
Rangers		1–0
Clyde	2–1	
Raith Rovers	7–1	
Airdrieonians		2–0
Aberdeen		3–2
Ayr United		4–2
Heart of Midlothian	0–2	
Motherwell		2–1
Morton		3–0

St. Mirren	2–0
Dundee	1–0
St. Johnstone	4–1
Dundee United	7–2
Kilmarnock	3–1
Partick Thistle	8–1
Clyde	2–0
Rangers	0–0
Hibernian	2–1
Dunfermline	3–1
Partick Thistle	5–1
Raith Rovers	2–0
Airdrieonians	4–2
Dundee United	2–0
Morton	4–0
Ayr United	3–0
Aberdeen	1–2
Heart of Midlothian	0–0
Motherwell	6–1
Dundee	1–2
St. Mirren	3–2

FINAL SCOTTISH LEAGUE TABLE

	P	W	D	L	Goals F	A	Pts
Celtic	34	27	3	4	96	33	57
Rangers	34	19	7	8	67	40	45
Hibernian	34	19	6	9	65	40	44
Heart of Midlothian	34	13	12	9	50	36	38
Dundee United	34	16	6	12	62	64	38
Dundee	34	15	6	13	49	44	36
Kilmarnock	34	13	10	11	62	57	36
Aberdeen	34	14	7	13	55	45	35
Morton	34	13	9	12	52	52	35
Dunfermline	34	15	5	14	45	44	35
Motherwell	34	11	10	13	49	51	32
Airdrieonians	34	12	8	4	59	64	32
St. Johnstone	34	11	9	14	50	62	31
Ayr United	34	12	6	16	37	52	30
St. Mirren	34	8	9	17	39	54	25
Clyde	34	9	7	18	34	56	25
Raith Rovers	34	5	11	18	32	67	21
Partick Thistle	34	5	7	22	41	82	17

SCOTTISH LEAGUE CHAMPIONS

1891	Dumbarton and Rangers	1894	Celtic
1892	Dumbarton	1895	Heart of Midlothian
1893	Celtic	1896	Celtic

1897	Heart of Midlothian	1931	Rangers
1898	Celtic	1932	Motherwell
1899	Rangers	1933	Rangers
1900	Rangers	1934	Rangers
1901	Rangers	1935	Rangers
1902	Rangers	1936	Celtic
1903	Hibernian	1937	Rangers
1904	Third Lanark	1938	Celtic
1905	Celtic	1939	Rangers
1906	Celtic	1940-46	No competition
1907	Celtic	1947	Rangers
1908	Celtic	1948	Hibernian
1909	Celtic	1949	Rangers
1910	Celtic	1950	Rangers
1911	Rangers	1951	Hibernian
1912	Rangers	1952	Hibernian
1913	Rangers	1953	Rangers
1914	Celtic	1954	Celtic
1915	Celtic	1955	Aberdeen
1916	Celtic	1956	Rangers
1917	Celtic	1957	Rangers
1918	Rangers	1958	Heart of Midlothian
1919	Celtic	1959	Rangers
1920	Rangers	1960	Heart of Midlothian
1921	Rangers	1961	Rangers
1922	Celtic	1962	Dundee
1923	Rangers	1963	Rangers
1924	Rangers	1964	Rangers
1925	Rangers	1965	Kilmarnock
1926	Celtic	1966	Celtic
1927	Rangers	1967	Celtic
1928	Rangers	1968	Celtic
1929	Rangers	1969	Celtic
1930	Rangers	1970	Celtic

ABERDEEN UPSET FAVOURITES IN SCOTTISH CUP

Aberdeen upset all the odds when they stopped Celtic completing a Scottish treble by beating Jock Stein's team 3–1 in the Scottish Cup Final at Hampden Park. This was Aberdeen's second Cup success, their previous victory being in 1947.

An early penalty against Brogan for hands which put Aberdeen in the lead seemed to upset Celtic, who never found the rhythm which had brought them so much success during the season. The further the game went the more frustrated they became with themselves and with the referee.

And so Celtic's twenty-first victory in 34 appearances in the final eluded them, but on the day they did not deserve to win. Aberdeen played mainly a defensive game, but their tactics proved to be right for the occasion, and in Derek McKay they had the man to snap up the scoring chances.

The 19-year-old McKay was given a free transfer by Dundee at the end of the 1968–69 season and he thought that his career in league football was finished. But he was snapped up by Manager Eddie Turnbull for Aberdeen and he has repaid the club by scoring the only goal in the quarter-final and also the semi-final, in addition to the two in the final. He also had a hand in the first goal, for it was his shot which caused Brogan to handle.

ABERDEEN: Clark; Boel, Murray G., Hermiston, McMillan, Buchan, McKay, Robb, Forrest, Harper, Graham.

CELTIC: Williams; Hay, Gemmell, Murdoch, McNeill, Brogan, Johnstone, Wallace, Connelly, Lennox, Hughes (Auld 72 mins).

SCOTTISH CUP—THIRD ROUND TO FINAL

THIRD ROUND
February 21 1970

CELTIC 3 (Lennox, Hay, Johnstone) RANGERS 1 (Craig o.g.).
EAST FIFE 0 DUNDEE 1 (Bryce).
FALKIRK 0 ABERDEEN 1 (McKay).
MOTHERWELL 0 KILMARNOCK 1 (Mathie).

SEMI-FINALS
March 14 1970

ABERDEEN 1 (McKay) KILMARNOCK 0. At Muirton Park, Perth).
DUNDEE 1 (Wallace) CELTIC 2 (Macari, Lennox). At Hampden Park, Glasgow.

FINAL
April 11 1970

ABERDEEN (1) 3 (McKay 2, Harper pen) CELTIC (0) 1 (Lennox).
At Hampden Park, Glasgow. 108,434.

SCOTTISH F.A. CUP WINNERS

1874	Queen's Park	1885	Renton
1875	Queen's Park	1886	Queen's Park
1876	Queen's Park	1887	Hibernian
1877	Vale of Leven	1888	Renton
1878	Vale of Leven	1889	Hibernian
1879	Vale of Leven	1890	Queen's Park
1880	Queen's Park	1891	Heart of Midlothian
1881	Queen's Park	1892	Celtic
1882	Queen's Park	1893	Queen's Park
1883	Dumbarton	1894	Rangers
1884	Queen's Park	1895	St. Bernard

1896	Heart of Midlothian	1933	Celtic
1897	Rangers	1934	Rangers
1898	Rangers	1935	Rangers
1899	Celtic	1936	Rangers
1900	Celtic	1937	Celtic
1901	Heart of Midlothian	1938	East Fife
1902	Hibernian	1939	Clyde
1903	Rangers	1940–46	No competition
1904	Celtic	1947	Aberdeen
1905	Third Lanark	1948	Rangers
1906	Heart of Midlothian	1949	Rangers
1907	Celtic	1950	Rangers
1908	Celtic	1951	Celtic
1909	Cup withheld	1952	Motherwell
1910	Dundee	1953	Rangers
1911	Celtic	1954	Celtic
1912	Celtic	1955	Clyde
1913	Falkirk	1956	Heart of Midlothian
1914	Celtic	1957	Falkirk
1915–19	No competition	1958	Clyde
1920	Kilmarnock	1959	St. Mirren
1921	Partick Thistle	1960	Rangers
1922	Morton	1961	Dunfermline
1923	Celtic	1962	Rangers
1924	Airdrieonians	1963	Rangers
1925	Celtic	1964	Rangers
1926	St. Mirren	1965	Celtic
1927	Celtic	1966	Rangers
1928	Rangers	1967	Celtic
1929	Kilmarnock	1968	Dunfermline
1930	Rangers	1969	Celtic
1931	Celtic	1970	Aberdeen
1932	Rangers		

INTERNATIONALS

Sept. 21 1969: REPUBLIC OF IRELAND (1) 1 (Givens)   SCOTLAND (1) 1 (Stein). Dublin. 30,000.

SCOTLAND: McGarr (Aberdeen); Greig (Rangers), Gemmell (Celtic), Stanton (Hibernian), McKinnon (Rangers), Moncur (Newcastle United), Henderson (Rangers), Bremner (Leeds United), Stein (Rangers), Cormack (Hibernian), Hughes (Celtic).

Oct. 22 1969: WEST GERMANY (1) 3 (Fichtel, Libuda, Mueller) SCOTLAND (1) 2 (Johnstone, Gilzean). Hamburg. 70,000.

Nov. 5 1969: AUSTRIA (1) 2 (Redl 2)   SCOTLAND (0) 0. Vienna. 30,000.

(World Cup qualifying matches.   See World Cup group seven.)

April 18 1970: NORTHERN IRELAND (0) 0 SCOTLAND (0) 1 (O'Hare). Belfast. 31,000.

SCOTLAND: Clark (Aberdeen); Hay (Celtic), Dickson (Kilmarnock), McLintock (Arsenal), McKinnon (Rangers), Moncur (Newcastle United), McLean T. (Kilmarnock), Carr (Coventry City), O'Hare (Derby County), Gilzean (Tottenham Hotspur), Stein (Rangers), Johnston (Rangers).

April 22 1970: SCOTLAND (0) 0 WALES (0) 0. Hampden Park. 35,000.

SCOTLAND: Cruickshank (Hearts); Callaghan (Dunfermline), Dickson (Kilmarnock), Greig (Rangers), McKinnon (Rangers), Moncur (Newcastle United), McLean T. (Kilmarnock), Lennox (Celtic), Hay (Celtic), O'Hare (Derby County), Stein (Rangers), Carr (Coventry City).

April 25 1970: SCOTLAND (0) 0 ENGLAND (0) 0. Hampden Park. 137,438.

SCOTLAND: Cruickshank (Hearts); Gemmell (Celtic), Dickson (Kilmarnock), Greig (Rangers), McKinnon (Rangers), Moncur (Newcastle United), Gilzean (Tottenham Hotspur), Johnstone (Celtic), Hay (Celtic), Stein (Rangers), O'Hare (Derby County), Carr (Coventry City).

SCOTTISH LEAGUE CUP
CELTIC SET RECORD IN LEAGUE CUP

Celtic set up records in beating St Johnstone in the Scottish League Cup Final at Hampden Park, Glasgow, on October 25 1969. It was their seventh victory and their fifth in succession, beating Rangers' record of six and two in succession. The only goal of the game came in the second minute from Bertie Auld, who shot a rebound from the crossbar where Donaldson, the St Johnstone goalkeeper, had pushed Chalmers' header.

Once again Auld proved the schemer of the Celtic side, while the return of Bobby Murdoch added authority to their midfield play. St Johnstone had their chances but seemed shattered by the early goal and were a long time settling to their normal game, but this was not good enough, even for a Celtic side who had yet to find their best form.

CELTIC: Fallon; Craig, Hay, Murdoch, McNeill, Brogan, Callaghan, Hood, Hughes, Chalmers (Johnstone), Auld.

ST JOHNSTONE: Donaldson; Lambie, Coburn, Gordon, Rooney, McPhee, Aird, Hall, McCarry, Connelly, Aitken.

PREVIOUS SCOTTISH LEAGUE CUP WINNERS

1946	Aberdeen	1949	Rangers
1947	Rangers	1950	East Fife
1948	East Fife	1951	Motherwell

1952	Dundee	1962	Rangers
1953	Dundee	1963	Hearts
1954	East Fife	1964	Rangers
1955	Hearts	1965	Rangers
1956	Aberdeen	1966	Celtic
1957	Celtic	1967	Celtic
1958	Celtic	1968	Celtic
1959	Hearts	1969	Celtic
1960	Hearts	1970	Celtic
1961	Rangers		

WALES

A FOURTH SUCCESSIVE CUP WIN
FOR CARDIFF CITY

For the fourth successive year Cardiff City won the Welsh F.A. Cup, a record, and registered their sixth success in the last seven finals, Fourth Division Chester proving little match for the Welsh side in the two-leg game.

The Welsh Cup, although it includes English clubs, is one of the competitions qualifying for the European Cup-Winners' Cup, but clubs who wish to take part in both the F.A. and Welsh competitions have to nominate in advance from which tournament they wish to qualify.

Cardiff opt for the Welsh Cup and the curiosity of the 1969–70 tournament was that whatever happened in the final, they had already qualified for Europe by beating Swansea City in the semi final. This was because Chester, had they won the final, would not have been eligible for Europe through this competition.

The first leg of the final was played at Chester where Cardiff took an early lead through Ronnie Bird, which they held to the end to win 1–0. As the final is decided on results and not goals the number of goals did not matter, but in the second leg Cardiff ran out easy winners by 4–0. Bobby Woodruff and Bird put them two ahead inside ten minutes and before half time Leslie Lea and Brian Clark had added further goals to make the second half little more than a formality.

FIRST LEG
Chester—May 8 1970

CHESTER (0) 0   CARDIFF CITY (1) 1 (Bird).
CHESTER: Carling; Cheetham, Edwards, Ashworth, Turner, Sutton, Tarbuck, Bradbury, Webber, Draper, McMillan.
CARDIFF CITY: Davies; Carver, Bell, Sutton, Murray, Harris, King, Toshack, Woodruff, Clark, Bird.

SECOND LEG
Cardiff—May 13 1970

CARDIFF CITY (4) 4 (Woodruff, Bird, Lea, Clark)   CHESTER (0) 0.
CARDIFF CITY: Davies; Carver, Bell, Sutton, Murray, Harris, Lea, Woodruff, Clark, King, Bird.
CHESTER: Carling; Cheetham, Edwards, Bradbury, Turner, Sutton, Spence, Tarbuck, Webber, Draper, McMillan.

WELSH CUP 1970

SEMI-FINALS
March 11 1970

CARDIFF CITY (1) 2 (Woodruff, Toshack)   SWANSEA CITY (1) 2 (Evans, Williams H.).   18,500.

March 18 1970
HEREFORD UNITED 3 (Punter, Timms, Round)   CHESTER 3 (Dearden 2 Tarbuck).

REPLAY—March 25 1970
CHESTER (1) 3 (Provan, Draper, Dearden)   HEREFORD UNITED (0) 0.

REPLAY—May 2 1970
SWANSEA CITY (0) 0   CARDIFF CITY (0) 2 (Bird, King).   After extra time.   20,479.

FINAL (two legs)
FIRST LEG—May 8 1970
CHESTER (0) 0   CARDIFF CITY (1) 1 (Bird).

SECOND LEG—May 13 1970
CARDIFF CITY (4) 4 (Woodruff, Bird, Lea, Clark)   CHESTER (0) 0.

WELSH CUP WINNERS

1878	Wrexham	1893	Wrexham
1879	Newtown	1894	Chirk
1880	Druids	1895	Newtown
1881	Druids	1896	Bangor
1882	Druids	1897	Wrexham
1883	Wrexham	1898	Druids
1884	Oswestry	1899	Druids
1885	Druids	1900	Aberystwyth
1886	Druids	1901	Oswestry
1887	Chirk	1902	Wellington
1888	Chirk	1903	Wrexham
1889	Bangor	1904	Druids
1890	Chirk	1905	Wrexham
1891	Shrewsbury	1907	Oswestry
1892	Chirk	1098	Chester

1909	Wrexham	1939	South Liverpool
1910	Wrexham	1940	Wellington Town
1911	Wrexham	1941–46	No competition
1912	Cardiff City	1947	Chester
1913	Swansea Town	1948	Lovell's Athletic
1914	Wrexham	1949	Merthyr Tydfil
1915	Wrexham	1950	Swansea Town
1916–19	No competition	1951	Merthyr Tydfil
1920	Cardiff City	1952	Rhyl
1921	Wrexham	1953	Rhyl
1922	Cardiff City	1954	Flint
1923	Cardiff City	1955	Barry Town
1924	Wrexham	1956	Cardiff City
1925	Wrexham	1957	Wrexham
1926	Ebbw Vale	1958	Wrexham
1927	Cardiff City	1959	Cardiff City
1928	Cardiff City	1960	Wrexham
1929	Connahs Quay	1961	Swansea Town
1930	Cardiff City	1962	Bangor City
1931	Wrexham	1963	Borough United
1932	Swansea Town	1964	Cardiff City
1933	Chester	1965	Cardiff City
1934	Bristol City	1966	Swansea Town
1935	Tranmere Rovers	1967	Cardiff City
1936	Crewe Alexandra	1968	Cardiff City
1937	Crewe Alexandra	1969	Cardiff City
1938	Shrewsbury Town	1970	Cardiff City

INTERNATIONALS

July 28 1969: WALES (0) 0   REST OF UNITED KINGDOM (1) 1 (Lee).   Cardiff.   18,000.

WALES: Sprake (Leeds United); Rodriques (Leicester City), Thomas R. (Swindon Town), Hennessey (Nottingham Forest), England (Tottenham Hotspur), Moore G. (Charlton Athletic), Jones B. (Cardiff City), Jones C. (Fulham), Davies R. (Southampton), Toshack (Cardiff City), Rees (Nottingham Forest).

REST OF UNITED KINGDOM: Jennings (Tottenham Hotspur and Northern Ireland); Gemmell (Celtic and Scotland), Cooper (Leeds United and England), Bremner (Leeds United and Scotland), Charlton J. (Leeds United and England), Mullery (Tottenham Hotspur and England), Best (Manchester United and Northern Ireland), Lee (Manchester City and England), Dougan (Wolverhampton Wanderers and Northern Ireland), Charlton R. (Manchester United and England), Hughes (Celtic and Scotland).

Oct. 22 1969: WALES (0) 1 (Powell)   EAST GERMANY (0) 3 (Vogel, Loewe, Frenzel).   Cardiff.   23,409.

Nov. 4 1969: ITALY (1) 4 (Riva, 3 Mazzola) WALES (0) 1 (England).
Rome. 76,000.
(World Cup qualifying matches. See World Cup group three.)
April 18 1970: WALES (1) 1 (Krzywicki) ENGLAND (0) 1 (Lee).
Cardiff. 50,000.
WALES: Millington (Swansea City); Rodrigues (Leicester City), Thomas
(Swindon Town), Hennessey (Derby County), England (Tottenham
Hotspur), Powell (Sheffield United), Krzywicki (Huddersfield Town),
Durban (Derby County), Davies (Southampton), Moore (Charlton
Athletic), Rees (Nottingham Forest).

April 22 1970: SCOTLAND (0) 0 WALES (0) 0. Hampden Park.
35,000.
WALES: Millington (Swansea City); Rodriques (Leicester City), Thomas
(Swindon Town), Hennessey (Derby County), England (Tottenham
Hotspur), Powell (Sheffield United), Krzywicki (Huddersfield Town),
Durban (Derby County), Davies (Southampton), Moore (Charlton),
Rees (Nottingham Forest).

Aprl 25 1970: WALES (1) 1 (Rees) NORTHERN IRELAND (0) 0.
Swansea.
WALES: Millington (Swansea City); Rodriques (Leicester City), Thomas
(Swindon Town), Hennessey (Derby County), England (Tottenham
Hotspur), Powell (Sheffield United), Krzywicki (Huddersfield Town),
Durban (Derby County), Davies (Southampton), Moore (Charlton
Athletic), Rees (Nottingham Forest).

WELSH LEAGUE FINAL TABLE

	P	W	D	L	Goals F	A	Pts
Cardiff City	34	25	8	1	106	35	58
Haverfordwest	34	20	8	6	80	40	48
Ton Pentre	34	18	9	7	61	43	45
Llanelli	34	19	6	9	64	37	44
Swansea City	34	17	8	9	68	49	42
Bridgend	34	16	9	9	79	42	41
Newport	34	16	9	9	60	37	41
Ammanford	34	15	9	10	62	47	39
Abergavenny	34	16	5	13	78	54	37
Caerleon	34	11	10	13	45	43	32
Pembroke	34	10	11	13	61	61	31
Ebbw Vale	34	8	14	11	43	54	30
Ferndale	34	8	12	14	46	57	28
S.W. Switchgear	34	10	6	18	48	60	26
Barry	34	9	7	18	48	70	25
Merthyr	34	7	7	20	33	78	21
Caerau	34	5	3	26	35	126	13
Tredomen	34	3	5	26	38	122	11

12 The European Season

(Note: every effort has been made to ensure that the statistics in this chapter are as comprehensive and accurate as possible, but results from some countries are occasionally difficult to obtain from an authoritative source.)

AUSTRIA

AUSTRIA VIENNA RECOVER TO RETAIN TITLE

Austria Vienna, 1968–1969 champions of the Austrian League, gave the impression at the start of the 1969–1970 season that they were not likely to retain their title. They could not get into their stride and with five League matches played they had surrendered half the points, which put them in the bottom half of the table.

Then came the turning point—and the big revival. Six victories in succession followed and a run of 16 matches without defeat sent them soaring up the table to the championship, even though they finished the season almost as badly as they had begun it.

They were expecting to lose their trainer, Ernst Ocwirk, who felt he could not settle down in Vienna and was being tempted by clubs in Italy, where he was well known as a player and trainer, and Switzerland.

This was Austria Vienna's fifth championship in ten years but, unlike their great local rivals, Rapid Vienna, who are passing through a moderate period, have never been able to make much impact on the European Cup.

A new name appears on the Austrian Cup with the success in May of Wacker Innsbruck. They won the trophy by beating Linz A.S.K. in Vienna with a second-half goal by their inside left Hans Ettmayer.

LEAGUE CHAMPIONS

1927	Sportklub Admira	1934	Sportklub Admira
1928	Sportklub Admira	1935	Rapid Vienna
1929	Rapid Vienna	1936	Sportklub Admira
1930	Rapid Vienna	1937	Sportklub Admira
1931	First Vienna	1938	Wiener S.K.
1932	Sportklub Admira	1939	Rapid Vienna
1933	First Vienna	1940	Wiener S.K.

1941	Rapid Vienna	1956	Rapid Vienna
1942	Rapid Vienna	1957	Rapid Vienna
1943	First Vienna	1958	Wiener S.K.
1944	First Vienna	1959	Wiener S.K.
1945	First Vienna	1960	Rapid Vienna
1946	Not decided	1961	F.K. Austria
1947	Rapid Vienna	1962	F.K. Austria
1948	Wacker	1963	F.K. Austria
1949	F.K. Austria	1964	Rapid Vienna
1950	F.K. Austria	1965	Linz A.S.K.
1951	Rapid Vienna	1966	Admira Vienna
1952	Rapid Vienna	1967	Rapid Vienna
1953	F.K. Austria	1968	Rapid Vienna
1954	Rapid Vienna	1969	Austria Vienna
1955	First Vienna	1970	Austria Vienna

AUSTRIA VIENNA LEAGUE RECORD

	Home	Away
Wacker Vienna	1–0	
Sturm Durisol		3–6
Austria Salzburg	3–0	
F.C. Dornbirn		0–1
Admira Energie		0–0
W.S.G.S. Wattens	3–2	
Rapid Vienna		6–0
Graz A.K.	3–1	
Linz A.S.K.	2–0	
Austria Klagenfurt		2–1
Eisenstadt	1–0	
Voest Linz		0–0
Vienna Sportklub	2–0	
Wacker Innsbruck		2–1
Wacker Vienna		4–2
Vienna	4–1	
Sturm Durisol	1–0	
Austria Salzburg		1–1
F.C. Dornbirn	3–1	
Admira Energie	1–0	
W.S.G.S. Wattens		1–0
Rapid Vienna	2–2	
Graz A.K.		1–2
Austria Klagenfurt	5–1	
Eisenstadt		4–2
Linz A.K.		0–0
Voest Linz	1–1	
Vienna Sportklub		2–4
Wacker Innsbruck	4–1	
Vienna		1–1

FINAL AUSTRIAN LEAGUE TABLE

	P	W	D	L	Goals F	A	Pts
Austria Vienna	30	19	7	4	63	31	45
Vienna Sportklub	30	16	6	8	63	34	38
Sturm-Durisol	30	14	8	8	43	34	36
Linz A.S.K.	30	13	8	9	41	27	34
Wacker Innsbruck	30	14	5	11	52	38	33
Rapid Vienna	30	12	7	11	52	35	31
W.S.G.S. Wattens	30	12	7	11	45	35	31
Austria Salzburg	30	12	7	11	45	38	31
Vienna	30	8	14	8	35	43	30
Admira Energie	30	11	6	13	38	45	28
Wacker Vienna	30	11	6	13	55	69	28
Voest Linz	30	11	6	13	31	48	28
Graz A.K.	30	8	11	11	37	35	27
Eisenstadt	30	7	8	15	40	63	22
Austria Klagenfurt	30	5	11	14	26	51	21
F.C. Dornbirn	30	4	9	17	23	63	17

CUP WINNERS
(AUSTRIA)

1919	Rapid Vienna	1938	W.A.C.
1920	Rapid Vienna	1939–45	No competition
1921	Austria Amateurs	1946	Rapid Vienna
1922	W.A.F.	1947	Wacker Vienna
1923	Vienna Sportclub	1948	Austria Vienna
1924	Austria Amateurs	1949	Austria Vienna
1925	Austria Amateurs	1950–58	No competition
1926	Austria Amateurs	1959	W.A.C.
1927	Rapid Vienna	1960	Austria Vienna
1928	Admira Energie	1961	Rapid Vienna
1929	Vienna .FC.	1962	Austria Vienna
1930	Vienna F.C.	1963	Austria Vienna
1931	W.A.C.	1964	Admira Energie
1932	Admira Energie	1965	Linz A.S.K.
1933	Austria Vienna	1966	Admira Energie
1934	Admira Energie	1967	Austria Vienna
1935	Austria Vienna	1968	Rapid Vienna
1936	Austria Vienna	1969	Rapid Vienna
1937	Vienna F.C.	1970	Wacker Innsbruck

INTERNATIONALS

Sept. 21 1969: AUSTRIA (1) 1 (Pirkner) WEST GERMANY (1) 1 (Mueller). Vienna. 28,000.

AUSTRIA: Fuchsbichler; Gebhart, Sturmberger, N. Hof, Pumm, Schmidradner, Floegel (Geyer), Ettmayer, Paritz, Pirkner, Redl.

Nov. 5 1969: AUSTRIA (1) 2 (Redl 2) SCOTLAND (0) 0. Vienna. 10,000.

(World Cup qualifying match. See World Cup—Group Seven.)

April 8 1970: YUGOSLAVIA (0) 1 (Bajevic) AUSTRIA (1) 1 (Redl). Sarajevo. 6,000.

AUSTRIA: Harreither; Pumm, Sturmberger, Huberts, Schmidradner, Kreiger, Geyer, Pirkner, Paritz, Ettmayer, Redl.

April 12 1970: AUSTRIA (0) 1 (Hrivnak o.g.) CZECHOSLOVAKIA (3) 3 (Albrecht, Hrdlicka, Adamec). Vienna. 30,000.

AUSTRIA: Harreither (Rettensteiner); Pumm, Sturmberger, Schmidradner, Huberts, Geyer, Krieger, Pirkner (Kreuz), Paritz, Ettmayer (Hickensberger), Redl.

April 29 1970: BRAZIL (0) 1 (Rivelino) AUSTRIA (0) 0. Rio de Janeiro. 56,000.

BRAZIL: Fliex; Carlos Alberto, Brito, Piazza, Marco Antonio, Clodoaldo, Gerson, Rivelino, Rogerio (Jairzinho), Tostao (Dario), Pele.

AUSTRIA: Rettensteiner; Pumm, Sturmberger, Schmidradner, Huberts, Geyer, Ettmayer, Hof, Parits, Kreuz, Redl.

BELGIUM
STANDARD LIEGE AGAIN CHAMPIONS

Standard Liege, European Cup semifinalists in 1962 and European Cup-Winners' Cup semi-finalists in 1967, won the Belgian League championship for the fifth time in their history—and the second year running. And the highlight of their season was probably their victory over the fading Real Madrid in the Bernabeu Stadium in Madrid in the European Cup.

Unfortunately they were unable to capitalise on this surprise success because they were drawn against Leeds United in the following round, at a time when Revie's team were at the top of their form, and so failed to reach the semifinals again.

However, their manager, Rene Hauss, known to his players as 'The Chief', was not too disappointed at the result. With the idea of getting some of the glamour away from Anderlecht he has built a team of all the talents by scouting around Europe and on occasions he has included players of five different nationalities in his team.

On the books there are two Jugoslavs, Sylvester Takac—signed from Rennes, the French club, just in time to be eligible for the European Cup competition—and Galic; Louis Pilot, who has played several times for Luxemburg and was in their World Cup team for the qualifying matches; Kostedde, a forward from West Germany; and Rudoiv Cvetler, a Czech who operates on the wing and was signed from Slovan Bratislava after they had won the European Cup-Winners' Cup in the summer of 1969.

In the side there are also Henri Depireux, who can score goals from half-chances, Jackie Beurlet, Nico Dewalque, Leon Jeck, Christian Piot, the No. 1 goalkeeper, Leon Semmeling, Jean Thissen and Wilfred Van Moer, all of whom figured in Belgiums' provisional list of forty for the World Cup in Mexico.

One of the oldest clubs in Belgium—Standard Liege were founded in 1898—it was not until 1938 that they achieved any success, but Hauss seems to have found the right formula at the moment, mostly by hard work and dedication during his two years with the club.

STANDARD LIEGE LEAGUE RECORD

	Home	Away
Beerschot		0–3
Lierse S.K.	1–0	
Ostend		3–0
F.C. Liege	2–1	
Beeringen		2–1
Anderlecht	1–0	
Charleroi	2–1	
Beveren		0–0
Racing White	9–0	
F.C. Bruges		1–1
St. Trond		3–1
Union St. Gilloise	2–0	
Crossing		1–3
Waregem	2–0	
Beerschot	2–2	
La Gantoise		0–0
Ostend	5–0	
F.C. Liege		1–1
Beeringen	5–3	
Anderlecht		2–0
La Gantoise	2–1	
Charleroi		4–2
Lierse S.K.		2–0
Beveren	3–0	
Racing White		1–0
F.C. Bruges	2–0	
St. Trond	2–0	
Union St. Gilloise		2–1
Crossing	0–3	
Waregem		2–0

FINAL BELGIAN LEAGUE TABLE

	P	W	D	L	Goals F	A	Pts
Standard Liege	30	22	5	3	64	24	49

F.C. Bruges	30	20	5	5	75	36	45
La Gantoise	30	16	7	7	49	35	39
Anderlecht	30	15	6	9	64	29	36
Beveren	30	14	8	8	45	29	36
Beerschot	30	14	7	9	42	26	35
Lierse S.K.	30	12	8	10	39	42	32
Racing White	30	10	10	10	36	41	30
Charleroi	30	13	3	14	42	43	29
Waregem	30	8	9	13	35	51	25
F.C. Liege	30	8	7	15	34	44	23
Saint-Trond	30	8	7	15	36	57	23
Crossing	30	8	7	15	29	50	23
Union St. Gilloise	30	6	10	14	26	45	22
Beeringen	30	4	10	16	27	49	18
Ostend	30	4	7	19	24	66	15

LEAGUE CHAMPIONS

1896 F.C. Liege	1931 Antwerp
1897 R.C. Brussels	1932 S.K. Lierse
1898 F.C. Liege	1933 Union St. Gilloise
1899 F.C. Liege	1934 Union St. Gilloise
1900 R.C. Brussels	1935 Union St. Gilloise
1901 R.C. Brussels	1936 Daring Brussels
1902 R.C. Brussels	1937 Daring Brussels
1903 R.C. Brussels	1938 Beerschot
1904 Union St. Gilloise	1939 Beerschot
1905 Union St. Gilloise	1940–41 No competition
1906 Union St. Gilloise	1942 S.K. Lierse
1907 Union St. Gilloise	1943 Malines
1908 R.C. Brussels	1944–45 No competition
1909 Union St. Gilloise	1946 Malines
1910 Union St. Gilloise	1947 Anderlecht
1911 C.S. Bruges	1948 Malines
1912 Daring Brussels	1949 Anderlecht
1913 Union St. Gilloise	1950 Anderlecht
1914 Daring Brussels	1951 Anderlecht
1915–19 No competition	1953 F.C. Liege
1920 F.C. Bruges	1954 Anderlecht
1921 Daring Brussels	1955 Anderlecht
1922 Beerschot	1956 Anderlecht
1923 Union St. Gilloise	1957 Antwerp
1924 Beerschot	1958 Standard Liege
1925 Beerschot	1959 Anderlecht
1926 Beerschot	1960 Lierse S.K.
1927 S.C. Bruges	1961 Standard Liege
1928 Beerschot	1962 Anderlecht
1929 Antwerp	1963 Standard Liege
1930 C.S. Bruges	1964 Anderlecht

1965	Anderlecht	1968	Anderlecht
1966	Anderlecht	1969	Standard Liege
1967	Anderlecht	1970	Standard Liege

CUP WINNERS
(BELGIUM)

1954	Standard Liege	1966	Standard Liege
1955	Antwerp	1967	Standard Liege
1956	Tournaisien	1968	F.C. Bruges
1957–63	No competition	1969	Lierse S.K.
1964	La Gantoise	1970	F.C. Bruges
1965	Standard Liege		

INTERNATIONALS

Oct. 19 1969: YUGOSLAVIA (3) 4 (Belin, Spasovski 2, Dzajic)   BEL-
GIUM (0) 0.   Skopje.   22,000.
(World Cup qualifying match.   See World Cup—Group Six.)
Nov. 5 1969: MEXICO (1) 1 (Velarde) BELGIUM (0) 0.   Mexico
City.   50,000.
MEXICO: Calderon; Alejandrez (Galindo), Pena, Nunez, Perez, Onofre,
Pone (Nunguia), Velarde, Alvarado, Pereda (Borja), Padilla.
BELGIUM: Piot; Heylens, Dewalque, Jeck, Thiessen, Van Moer, Dockx,
Verheyen, Polleunis, Van Puymbroeck, Janssen (Despireux).
Feb. 25 1970: BELGIUM (0) 1 (Dockx) ENGLAND (1) 3 (Ball 2,
Hurst).   Brussels.   36,000.
BELGIUM: Trappeniers; Heylens, Dewalque, Jeck, Thiessen, Van Moer,
Dockx, Polleunis (Verheyen), Semmeling, Devrindt, Van Himst.
(World Cup finals matches.   Mexico City.   See Chapter Four.)

BULGARIA

(Results of Home season not available at time of going to press)

INTERNATIONALS

Sept. 24 1969: BULGARIA (0) 0   WEST GERMANY (1) 1 (Doerfel).
Sofia.   60,000.
Oct. 22 1969: HOLLAND (1) 1 (Veenstra) BULGARIA (0) 1 (Bonev).
Rotterdam.   65,000.
(World Cup qualifying match.   See World Cup—Group Eight.)
Nov. 9 1969: POLAND (1) 3 (Jarosik 2, Dejna) BULGARIA (0) 0.
Warsaw.   80,000.
(World Cup qualifying match.   See World Cup—Group Eight.)
Dec. 7 1969: LUXEMBURG (0) 1 (Phillippe pen) BULGARIA (2) 3
(Dermendjiev, Yakimov, Bonev).   Luxemburg.   2,000.
(World Cup qualifying match.   See World Cup—Group Eight.)
Feb. 15 1970: MEXICO 1   BULGARIA 1.
Feb. 18 1970: MEXICO 2   BULGARIA 0.

Feb. 25 1970: PERU 5 BULGARIA 3. Lima.
Feb. 27 1970: PERU 1 BULGARIA 3. Lima.
April 9 1970: FRANCE (1) 1 (Michel) BULGARIA (1) 1 (Jekov).
Rouen. 20,000.
May 5 1970: BULGARIA (1) 3 (Jekov 2, Bonev) RUSSIA (2) 3 (Yvery-
uzhikhin, Byshoevets, Nodiya). Sofia. 20,000.
May 26 1970: BULGARIA (0) 0 RUSSIA (0) 0. Sofia.
(World Cup finals matches. Mexico City. See Chapter Four.)

CZECHOSLOVAKIA

SLOVAN BRATISLAVA PIP SPARTAK TRNAVA

Slovan Bratislava proved that their success in winning the European
Cup Winners' Cup in May 1969 was no fluke by regaining the
championship of the Czechoslovakia League after a lapse of 15 years,
pushing the champions of 1968 and 1969, Spartak Trnava, into
second place.

They were one of four teams—the others were Spartak Trnava,
Inter-Bratislava, and Union Teplice—who went through the season
with an unbeaten home record during which they conceded only two
goals in fifteen matches, a tribute to the excellent goalkeeping of
Alexander Vencel, who gained a place in Czechoslovakia's World
Cup squad in Mexico.

With such internationals as Vladimir Hvriknak, Alexander
Horvath and Jan Zlocha in the back four, Ivan Hrdlicka in midfield,
and Karel Jokl and Jan Capkovic, one of 22-year-old twins in the
forward line, they were able to play a good all-round game.

Their defence of the European Cup Winners' Cup in which they
were naturally seeded was, however, surprisingly halted in the first
round. They conceded three goals to Dinamo Zagreb in Yugoslavia
and found the deficit too big in the return leg in which they were able
to obtain only a goalless draw.

Spartak Trnava, who were leading the table and looked to have
a good chance of making it a hat-trick of championships, lost their
opportunity in a bad patch during April when they lost seven points
in five games, while Dukla Prague, who used to be the Real Madrid
of Czechoslovakian soccer, were never able to recover from a poor
start to the season which left them in eighth place after the autumn
half of the programme.

The Slovan Bratislava culb is one of the oldest in Czechoslovakia,
having been founded in 1919, and has competed in the League since
1935. Some famous players have turned out for them, including
Adislas Kubala and Jan Popluhar, holder of 63 caps. Most of their
players work at a chemical factory which employs about 7,500
people. Their stadium is capable of holding 65,000.

SLOVAN BRATISLAVA LEAGUE RECORD

	Home	Away
Tatran Presov		1–0
Bohemians	4–0	
Sparta Prague		0–0
T.J. Gottwaldov	2–0	
Lokomotiva Kosice		1–1
Dukla Prague		3–2
Sonp Kladno	0–0	
Union Teplice		1–3
Spartak Trnava	2–0	
Slavia Prague		2–1
ZVL Zilina	1–0	
V.S.S. Kosice		0–1
Inter Bratislava	2–1	
Banik Ostrava		0–0
Jednota Trencin	1–0	
Tatran Presov	0–0	
Bohemians		0–0
T.J. Gottwaldov		2–1
Lokomotiva Kosice	1–0	
Sparta Prague	1–1	
Dukla Prague	3–0	
Sonp Kladno		0–0
Union Teplice	3–0	
Spartak Trnava		1–1
Slavia Prague	1–0	
ZVL Zilina		1–1
V.S.S. Kosice	2–0	
Inter Bratislava		1–2
Banik Ostrava	3–0	
Jednota Trencin		0–0

FINAL CZECH LEAGUE TABLE

	P	W	D	L	Goals F	A	Pts
Slovan Bratislava	30	16	11	3	39	15	43
Spartak Trnava	30	15	10	5	55	23	40
Sparta Prague	30	15	8	7	40	25	38
Inter Bratislava	30	14	8	8	45	32	36
Union Teplice	30	11	11	8	26	19	33
Lokomotiva Kosice	30	12	8	10	36	25	32
Dukla Prague	30	10	12	8	34	31	32
V.S.S. Kosice	30	10	10	10	32	31	30
Tatran Presov	30	9	12	9	22	22	30
Jednota Trencin	30	8	11	11	35	29	27
Banik Ostrava	30	7	12	11	26	32	26

Z.V.L. Zilina	30	9	8	13	34	42	26
Slavia Prague	30	7	12	11	29	42	26
T.J. Gottwaldov	30	8	7	15	28	45	23
Sonp Kladno	30	7	7	16	29	61	21
Bohemians	30	3	11	16	23	59	17

LEAGUE CHAMPIONS

1926	A.C. Sparta	1949	N.V. Bratislava
1927	A.C. Sparta	1950	N.V. Bratislava
1928	Viktoria Zizkov	1951	N.V. Bratislava
1929	Slavia Prague	1952	Sparta Prague
1930	Slavia Prague	1953	U.D.A. Prague
1931	Slavia Prague	1954	Sparta Prague
1932	Sparta Prague	1955	Slovan Bratislava
1933	Slavia Prague	1956	Dukla Prague
1934	Slavia Prague	1957	Dukla Prague
1935	Slavia Prague	1958	Dukla Prague
1936	Sparta Prague	1959	Red Star Bratislava
1937	Slavia Prague	1960	Spartak Prague
1938	Sparta Prague	1961	Dukla Prague
1939	Sparta Prague	1962	Dukla Prague
1940	Slavia Prague	1963	Dukla Prague
1941	Slavia Prague	1964	Dukla Prague
1942	Slavia Prague	1965	Sparta Prague
1943	Slavia Prague	1966	Dukla Prague
1944	Slavia Prague	1967	Sparta Prague
1946	Sparta Prague	1968	Spartak Trnava
1947	Slavia Prague	1969	Spartak Trnava
1948	Sparta Prague	1970	Slovan Bratislava

CUP WINNERS

(CZECHOSLOVAKIA)
(Instituted in 1961)

1961	Dukla Prague	1966	Dukla Prague
1962	Slovan Bratislava	1967	Spartak Trnava
1963	Slovan Bratislava	1968	Slovan Bratislava
1964	Sparta Prague	1969	Dukla Prague
1965	Dukla Prague	1970	P. J. Gottwaldov

INTERNATIONALS

Sept. 10 1969: CZECHOSLOVAKIA (1) 3 (Hagara, Kvasnak, Kuna) HUNGARY (2) 3 (Bene, Dunai, Fazekas). Prague. 40,000.

Oct. 7 1969: CZECHOSLOVAKIA (3) 3 (Adamec 3) REPUBLIC OF IRELAND (0) 0. Prague. 36,000.

Dec. 3 1969: CZECHOSLOVAKIA (1) 4 (Kvasnak pen, Vesely, Adamec, Jokl) HUNGARY (0) 1 (Kocsis pen). Marseilles. 7,000.

(All World Cup qualifying matches.   See World Cup—Group Two.)
April 12 1970: AUSTRIA (0) 1 (Hrivnak o.g.)   CZECHOSLOVAKIA
(3) 3 (Albrecht, Hrdlicka, Adamec).   Vienna.   30,000.
CZECHOSLOVAKIA: Viktor; Dobias, Hrivnak, Migas, Hagara,
Hrdlicka, Vesely B. (Vesely F.), Jurkanin, Adamec, Albrecht.
May 9 1970: LUXEMBURG (0) 0   CZECHOSLOVAKIA (1) 1 (Jur-
kanin) Luxemburg.
May 13 1970: NORWAY (0) 0   CZECHOSLOVAKIA (1) 2 (Olafsen
o.g., Horvath).   Oslo.
CZECHOSLOVAKIA: Viktor; Dobias, Migas, Zlocha, Horvath, Hrd-
licka, Vesely B., Jurkanin, Kuna, Jokl, Capkovic, Jan.
(World Cup finals matches.   Guadalajara.   See Chapter Four.)

DENMARK

At a meeting of the Danish Football Association following the end
of the season in November, an attempt was made to introduce semi-
professional football into the national team with a view to improving
the standard of Danish football in Europe.

Although generally the delegates were in favour of the proposal
that a maximum of five professional players should be included in
the eleven it did not receive the necessary two-thirds majority for a
change in the law, so Denmark will continue on its all-amateur lines.

A lot of Danish players have been enticed away to other European
clubs where their talent has been rewarded, and it was felt that
Denmark could put up a better show on the international front if
some of these players could be included in the national side.

The amateur players in the league will, however, be able to earn
a little extra during the 1970 season when for the first time they are
to be allowed to display advertisements on their shirts.

Denmark's representatives in the 1970-71 European Cup will be
Boldklub 1903, who took the 1969 championship by the wide
margin of five points for the first time since before the war, to the
great delight of their young Swedish coach, Bosse Haakonsson, 27,
who was in only his first year with the club.

But in spite of their success in the league Boldklub had rather a
rude shock in the Cup when they were put out in the quarter-finals
by Ikast Boldklub, a club then occupying a lowly place in the
second division.

The Cup went to Aalborg who beat Lyngby Boldklub, a team
from the Third Division, in the final by 2-1 in Copenhagen on
May 7 – the match being played soon after the start of the following
season. But a crowd of 16,500 saw the First Division side given a
tough fight before they finally gained their second success in the
competition.

They took the lead seven minutes after halftime through one of their midfield players, Boerge Bak, but conceded a penalty 12 minutes from the end. Axel Soerensen equalised the scores from the spot kick but with five minutes to go Bak got his second goal to clinch victory.

FINAL DANISH LEAGUE TABLE

	P	W	D	L	Goals F	A	Pts
Boldklub 1903 Copenhagen	22	15	4	3	50	25	34
K.B. Copenhagen	22	14	2	6	58	38	30
Aalborg	22	12	5	5	52	26	29
Hvidovre	22	11	4	7	35	34	26
Horsens	22	9	6	7	39	36	24
Akademisk Boldklub	22	9	5	8	32	36	23
B. 1913 Odense	22	8	3	11	33	40	19
Vejle	22	6	5	11	33	42	17
Frem Copenhagen	22	5	7	10	33	45	17
Boldklub 1901 Nykopping	22	7	3	12	30	15	17
Boldklub 1909 Odense	22	6	4	12	44	56	16
Esbjerg	22	5	2	15	30	49	12

LEAGUE CHAMPIONS

1913	K.B. Copenhagen	1937	Akademisk
1914	K.B. Copenhagen	1938	B.K. 03
1915	No competition	1939	B.K. 93
1916	B.K. 93	1940	B.K. 93
1917	Boldklub	1941	Frem
1918	Boldklub	1942	B.K. 93
1919	Akademisk	1943	No competition
1920	B.K. 03	1944	Frem
1921	Akademisk	1945	No competition
1922	Boldklub	1946	B.K. 93
1923	Frem	1947	Akademisk
1924	B.K. 03	1948	Boldklub
1925	Boldklub	1948	Boldklub
1926	B.K. 03	1949	Boldklub
1927	B.K. 93	1950	Boldklub
1928	No competition	1951	Akademisk
1929	B.K. 93	1952	Akademisk
1930	No competition	1953	Boldklub
1931	Frem	1954	Koge B.K.
1932	Boldklub	1955	Aarhus G.F.
1933	No competition	1956	Aarhus G.F.
1934	B.K. 93	1957	Aarhus G.F.
1935	B.K. 93	1958	Vejle
1936	Frem	1959	B.K. 09 Odense

1960	Aarhus G.F.	1966	Esbjerg
1961	Odense	1967	Hvidovre Copenhagen
1962	Esbjerg F.K.	1968	A.B. Copenhagen
1963	Esbjerg F.K.	1969	Boldklub 03 Copenhagen
1964	Odense	1970	Boldklub 03 Copenhagen
1965	Odense		

CUP WINNERS
(DENMARK)

1955	G.F. Aarhus	1964	Esbjerg
1956	Frem Copenhagen	1965	G.F. Aarhus
1957	G.F. Aarhus	1966	Aalborg B.K. 1885
1958	Vejle	1967	Randers Freja
1959	Vejle	1968	Randers Freja
1962	G.F. Aarhus	1969	K.B. Copenhagen
1963	B.K. Odense 09	1970	Aalborg

INTERNATIONALS

July 1 1969: DENMARK (2) 6 (Michaelsen, Jensen B. 3 (1 pen), Sorensen L., Sorensen O.). Copenhagen. 12,000.
DENMARK: Engedahl (Rask); Larsen J., Jensen H. M., Moller, Neilsen T., Sorensen L., Michaelsen, Jensen B., Sorensen O., Madsen, Larsen S. K.
Sept. 10 1969: DENMARK (4) 5 (Jensen B. 3, Roemer S. 2) FINLAND (1) 2 (Lindholm, Tolsa). Copenhagen. 22,600.
Sept. 21 1969: NORWAY (2) 2 (Olsen O. D., Sathrang) DENMARK (0) 0. Oslo. 15,054.
DENMARK: Poulsen; Larsen J., Jensen H. M., Moller, Neilsen T., Michaelsen, Neilsen E. (Thorst), Jensen B., Madsen (Jorgensen), Andersen, Roemer.
Oct. 15 1969: REPUBLIC OF IRELAND (1) 1 (Givens) DENMARK (1) 1 (Jensen B.). Dublin. 22,000.
Oct. 22 1969: HUNGARY (2) 3 (Bene 2, Szucs) DENMARK (0) 0. Budapest. 35,000.
(World Cup qualifying matches. See World Cup—Group Two.)
May 19 1970: DENMARK (0) 0 POLAND (1) 2 (Banas, Jarosik). Copenhagen. 17,500.
DENMARK: Hildebrandt; Larsen, Neilsen J., Neilsen T., Andraesen, Moeller, Petersen J., Kjaersgaard, Petersen K., Rasmussen, Wiberg-Larsen.

FRANCE

ST. ETIENNE COMPLETE LEAGUE AND CUP DOUBLE

St. Etienne again proved themselves the best side in France by adding the Cup to the League championship which they won for the fourth successive year. While outstanding in domestic competition, however, they have yet to prove their class in Europe.

Under the 50-year-old Rheims-born Albert Batteux the team have maintained a high standard and played attractive football, which not surprisingly has been reflected at the box office with increased gates.

In goal St. Etienne have the best goalkeeper in the country in George Carnus, now 28, who is an international, and for goals they rely on their twin strikers, the 24-year-old Herve Revelli and the African-born Salif Keita who comes from Bamako in Mali.

But there is a sound back four in Georges Polny, Bernard Bosquier, an experienced international, Wladimir Durkovic, and Robert Herbin, another international. Last season Batteux added to his playing staff the right winger Spasoje Samarsic, 28, from the Dutch club, Feyenoord.

On their way to their Cup success St. Etienne met with stiff resistance only from their first division rivals, Nimes, in a third round tie. The French Cup competition, like the European cups, is played on a two-leg basis and after losing the first match 1–0 at Nimes St. Etienne could not wipe out the goal deficit in the return, winning only by 2–1, so a play-off was necessary.

So great was the interest in this third match that something like 30,000 tried to force their way into the 19,000 capacity Parc des Princes stadium to see it. Many were injured in the stampede to get into the stadium and officials estimated that about 25,000 saw St. Etienne win 2–0 and that about 10,000 did not bother about the formality of paying at the gates.

That was really the only threat to St. Etienne's progress. They crushed Metz 5–0 and removed Valenciennes by a single goal to reach the final. They reserved their best football for this game, which was played in the Colombes Stadium where 32,894 saw them gain a 5–0 victory over Nantes with some splendid attacking football.

Their goal scoring account was opened after 25 minutes by a 19-year-old amateur, Patrick Parizon, a right winger who had made his League debut less than six months earlier, and added to by George Bereta, the only locally born man in the side, to give them a 2–0 interval lead. Robert Herbin added a third seven minutes after half-time and Revelli completed a fine afternoon's work with two goals —in the 73rd and 87th minutes. The teams were:

ST. ETIENNE: Carnus; Durkovic, Herbin, Bosquier, Polny, Larque, Jacquet, Parizon, Revelli, Keita, Bereta.
NANTES: Fouche; Omsan, Lemerre, Esteve, De Michele, Eo (Arribas), Pech, Blanchet, Gondet, Michel, Levavasseur.

FRENCH LEAGUE CHAMPIONS

1933	O.L. Lilloise	1955	Stade de Rheims
1934	F.C. Sete	1956	O.G.C. Nice
1935	F.C. Souchaux	1957	Saint Etienne
1936	Racing Club Paris	1958	Stade de Rheims
1937	O.L. Marseilles	1959	O.G.C. Nice
1938	F.C Souchaux	1960	Stade de Rheims
1939	F.C. Sete	1961	A.S. Monaco
1940–45	No competition	1962	Stade de Rheims
1946	Lille O.S.C.	1963	A.S. Monaco
1947	O.C. Roubaix-Tourcoing	1964	Saint Etienne
1948	F.C. Souchaux	1965	Nantes
1949	O.L. Marseilles	1966	Nantes
1950	Stade de Rheims	1967	Saint Etienne
1951	Girondins Bordeaux	1968	Saint Etienne
1952	O.G.C. Nice	1969	Saint Etienne
1953	Stade de Rheims	1970	Saint Etienne
1954	Lille O.S.C.		

FRENCH CUP
QUARTER-FINALS

(Two Legs.   April 12 and 19)
Metz 1   Saint Etienne 1
Saint Etienne 5   Metz 0
Limoges 1   Rennes 3
Rennes 4   Limoges 0
Angers 2   Nantes 2
Nantes 2   Angers 0
Paris-Neuilly 2   Valenciennes 1
Valenciennes 1   Paris-Neuilly 0
Valenciennes 2   Paris-Neuilly 1   (April 25)

SEMI-FINALS
(Two Legs.   May 9 and 16)
Rennes 0   Saint-Etienne 1
Saint-Etienne 1   Rennes 1
Valenciennes 0   Nantes 2
Nantes 0   Valenciennes 0

FINAL
(May 31)
Saint-Etienne 5   Nantes 0

CUP WINNERS
(FRANCE)

1918	Olympique Pantin	1921	Red Star
1919	C.A.S. Genereaux	1922	Red Star
1920	C.A. Paris	1923	Red Star

1924	Olympique Marseilles		1948	Lille O.S.C.
1925	C.A.S. Generaux		1949	R.C. Paris
1926	Olympique Marseilles		1950	Stade de Rheims
1927	Olympique Marseilles		1951	R.C. Strasburg
1928	Red Star		1952	O.G.C. Nice
1929	S.O. Montpelier		1953	Lille O.S.C.
1930	F.C. Sete		1954	O.G.C. Nice
1931	Club Francais		1955	Lille O.S.C.
1932	A.S. Cannes		1956	Sedan
1933	Excelsior Roubaix		1957	Toulouse
1934	F.C. Sete		1958	Stade de Rheims
1935	Olympique Marseilles		1959	Le Havre
1936	R.C. Paris		1960	A.S. Monaco
1937	F.C. Souchaux		1961	Sedan
1938	Olympique Marseilles		1962	Saint Etienne
1939	R.C. Paris		1963	A.S. Monaco
1940	R.C. Paris		1964	Lyon
1941	Girondins Bordeaux		1965	Rennes
1942	Red Star Olympique		1966	Strasburg
1943	Olympique Marseilles		1967	Lyon
1944	Nancy-Lorraine		1968	Saint Etienne
1945	R.C. Paris		1969	Olympique Marseilles
1946	Lille O.S.C.		1970	Saint Etienne
1947	Lille O.S.C.			

INTERNATIONALS

Sept. 10 1969: NORWAY (0) 1 (Olsen D.) FRANCE (1) 3 (Revelli 2, Michel) Oslo. 23,000.

Oct. 15 1969: SWEDEN (1) 2 (Kindvall 2) FRANCE (0) 0. Stockholm. 51,954.

Nov. 1 1969: FRANCE (3) 3 (Bras 2, Djorkaeff) SWEDEN (0) 0. Paris. 7,916.

(All World Cup qualifying matches. See World Cup—Group Five.)

April 9 1970: FRANCE (1) 1 (Michel) BULGARIA (1) 1 (Jekov) Rouen. 20,000.

FRANCE: Carnus; Djorkaeff, Bosquier, Novi, Rostagni, Michel, Broissart, Bras, Revelli, Loubet, Bereta (Chiesa).

April 28 1970: FRANCE (2) 2 (Loubet, Djorkaeff) RUMANIA (0) 0. Rheims. 11,000.

FRANCE: Carnus; Djorkaeff, Bosquier, Novi, Rostagni, Michel, Huck, Bras, Revelli, Loubet, Bereta.

May 3 1970: SWITZERLAND (1) 2 (Blaettler 2) FRANCE (0) 1 (Revelli). Basle. 24,000.

FRANCE: Carnus; Rostagni, Bosquier, Novi, Djorkaeff, Michel, Mezy, Bras (Lech), Loubet (Chiesa), Revelli, Bereta.

EAST GERMANY

SECOND TRIUMPH FOR CARL ZEISS JENA

Carl Zeiss Jena, under Georges Buschner—also trainer for the national side—proved easily the best equipped team in the East Germany League and became champions three weeks before the season was due to end.

This was their second triumph in three years and they pipped the defending champions F.C. Vorwaerts of East Berlin. For good measure they gave the East Berliners a 5–0 thrashing on their own ground in the final match of the season just to prove their right to the championship.

Their success was based mainly on a strong defence backed by a very sound halfback line with more than one forward able to score goals.

Carl Zeiss Jena's only previous appearance in the European Cup turned out to be a non-appearance. It was at the time of the Russian invasion of Czechoslovakia, which came after the draw for the first round had been made.

U.E.F.A. decided to make a redraw of certain ties because they considered there might be travelling and visa difficulties for some original matches. But the Warsaw Pact countries who had supported the invasion of Czechoslovakia considered this was discrimination and made a wholesale withdrawal which left Red Star Belgrade of Yugoslavia, who were drawn against Carl Zeiss Jena, with a bye.

CARL ZEISS JENA LEAGUE RECORD

	Home	Away
H.F.C. Chemie Halle		1–1
Chemie Leipzig		0–1
F.C. Magdeburg	4–1	
Hansa Rostock		1–0
Wismut Aue	3–1	
Stahl Riesa		1–2
B.F.C. Dinamo	2–0	
Stahl Eisenstadt		0–0
Rotweiss Erfurt	3–1	
Karlmarxstadt		0–1
Sachsenring Zwickau	1–1	
Dynamo Dresden		2–1
F.C. Vorwaerts Berlin	3–1	
H.F.C. Chemie Halle	2–1	
Chemie Leipzig	3–0	
F.C. Magdeburg		3–1
Hansa Rostock	3–0	

Wismut Aue		0–0
Stahl Riesa	3–0	
Dynamo Dresden		1–1
Stahl Eisenstadt	2–0	
Rotweiss Erfurt		3–0
Karlmarxstadt	1–1	
Sachsenring Zwickau		1–1
Dynamo Dresden	2–0	
F.C. Vorwaerts Berlin		5–0

FINAL EAST GERMAN LEAGUE TABLE

	P	W	D	L	Goals F	A	Pts
Carl Zeiss Jena	26	16	7	3	50	16	39
F.C. Vorwaerts Berlin	26	12	8	6	43	34	32
Dynamo Dresden	26	13	5	8	36	26	31
Chemie Leipzig	26	11	8	7	33	27	30
Sachsenring Zwickau	26	9	10	7	25	26	28
B.F.C. Dinamo	26	10	8	8	29	32	28
Wismut Aue	26	10	7	9	31	34	27
F.C. Magdeburg	26	10	4	12	37	37	24
Rotweiss Erfurt	26	8	8	10	32	40	24
Chemie Halle	26	8	6	12	35	34	22
Stahl Riesa	26	9	4	13	31	35	22
Hansa Rostock	26	7	7	12	22	33	21
Karlmarxstadt	26	7	5	14	27	42	19
Stahl Eisenstadt	26	5	7	14	21	36	17

EAST GERMAN LEAGUE CHAMPIONS

1950	Zwickau Horch	1961	Empor Rostock
1951	Leipzig Chemie	1962	A.S.K. Vorwaerts Berlin
1952	Halle Turbine	1963	Motor Jena
1953	Dresden Dynamo	1964	Leipzig Chemie
1954	Erfurt Turbine	1965	A.S.K. Vorwaerts Berlin
1955	Erfurt Turbine	1966	A.S.K. Vorwaerts Berlin
1956	Karl Marx Stadt	1967	Karl Marx Stadt
1957	Karl Marx Stadt	1968	Carl Zeiss Jena
1958	A.S.K. Vorwaerts Berlin	1969	A.S.K. Vorwaerts Berlin
1959	Karl Marx Stadt	1970	Carl Zeiss Jena
1960	A.S.K. Vorwaerts Berlin		

CUP WINNERS
(EAST GERMANY)

1949	North Dessau Waggonworks	1952	Dresden V.P.
1950	Thale E.H.W.	1953	No competition
1951	No competition	1954	A.S.K. Vorwaerts Berlin

1955	Karl Marx Stadt	1963	Motor Zwickau
1956	Leipzig Chemie	1964	Magdeburg Aufbau
1957	Leipzig Lokomotive	1965	Magdeburg S.C.
1958	Dresden Einheit S.C.	1966	Chemie Leipzig
1959	Berlin Dynamo	1967	Motor Zwickau
1960	Motor Jena	1968	Union East Berlin
1961	No competition	1969	F.C. Magdeburg
1962	Halle Chemie S.C.	1970	A.S.K. Vorwaerts Berlin

INTERNATIONALS

July 7 1969: EAST GERMANY (3) 7 (Frenzel 3, Sparwasser 2, Vogel, Loewe) UNITED ARAB REPUBLIC (0) 0. Rostock. 10,000.

EAST GERMANY: Croy (Schneider); Dobermann, Urbanczyk, Zapf, Bransch, Schutze, Seehaus, Kreitsche (Loewe), Sparwasser, Frenzel, Vogel.

UNITED ARAB REPUBLIC: Mokhtar; Yakan, El Sherbini, Abul Ezz, Hany, El Mazati (El Guhari), Tah Visry, Riad, Ali Ismali, El Shazli, El Sayed (Samed).

July 25 1969: EAST GERMANY (1) 2 (Loewe, Frenzel) RUSSIA (1) 2 (Puzach, Khmelnitsky). Leipzig. 90,000.

EAST GERMANY: Blochwitz (Schneider); Fraesdorf, Bransch, Seehaus, Urbanczyk, Koerner, Loewe, Stein, Frenzel, Kreitsche, Vogel (Sparwasser).

Oct. 22 1969: WALES (0) 1 (Powell) EAST GERMANY (0) 3 (Vogel, Loewe, Frenzel). Cardiff. 23,409.

Nov. 22 1969: ITALY (3) 3 (Mazzola, Domenghini, Riva) EAST GERMANY (0) 0. Naples. 92,000.

(World Cup qualifying matches. See World Cup—Group Three.)

Dec. 12 1969: IRAQ (1) 1 (Ammo) EAST GERMANY (1) 1 (Koerner). Baghdad. 20,000.

IRAQ: Saltar; Hassan, Mijbell, Raheem, Majeed, Hazim (Gebrall), Doglas, Falih, Ammo, Nuri, Mudafer (Golbert).

EAST GERMANY: Croy; Fraesdorf, Urbanczyk, Ganzera, Bransch, Stein, Irmscher, Koerner, Sparwasser (Streich), Kreitsche, Vogel.

Dec. 21 1969: UNITED ARAB REPUBLIC (0) 1 (Jacub). EAST GERMANY (1) 3 (Sparwasser, Kreische 2). Cairo. 20,000.

May 16 1970: POLAND (1) 1 (Dejna) EAST GERMANY (1) 1 (Vogel). Cracow. 25,000.

WEST GERMANY

BORUSSIA MUNCHENGLADBACH GAIN FIRST TITLE

Borussia Munchengladbach put a new name on the West German list of League champions as they pipped the previous season's title-holders and Cup winners, Bayern Munich. In only their fifth season in the first division, this team from the north-west industrial town of 150,000, not far from Dusseldorf, took the title and their players earned a bonus of more than £1,000 each, which is something unusual for the German League.

Hans Weisweiler, their 50-year-old coach, believes that a sound defence is halfway towards success and he proved this by the fact that Munchengladbach conceded fewer goals than any of the other 17 teams in the league, their average working out at less than one a match.

In Berti Vogts, 23, he has a world class full back who has shown his ability in the national side and was one of West Germany's squad for the World Cup in Mexico. Gunter Netzer, capped 14 times for West Germany, is a strong midfield player and captain of the side.

Although he lost a little caste with Helmut Schoen, the national team trainer, after the shock defeat by Spain in a warm-up match for Mexico, his temporary loss of form was quickly overcome and he was forgiven and included in the Mexico party.

To help Netzer in midfield there is another World Cup player in Peter Dietrich, 25, whose grafting in the match has caused him to be compared with Alan Ball of England. Star of the forward line is a Dane, Ulrich Le Fevre, an international left winger, always liable to pop in goals.

The club was formed in 1900 and their previous successes included winning the Rhineland regional championship in 1920 and 1965, a triumph which gave them first division status. They were surprise winners of the German Cup in 1960, but their only venture into European competition ended at Hampden Park that year when Glasgow Rangers put them out in their first tie.

Bayern Munich, who finished as runners-up, again provided the leading scorer in the league with Gerd Mueller, who scored 38 of their 88 goals to set a record for the League, beating the 31 by Luther Emmerich in 1966. Munich 1860, who reached the final of the European Cup-Winners' Cup in 1965 when they were beaten by West Ham United, had a season of problems and were one of the two clubs to lose their places in the first division.

BORUSSIA MUNCHENGLADBACH LEAGUE RECORD

	Home	Away
Schalke 04		0–2
Bayern Munich	2–1	
Rotweiss Essen	2–1	
Eintracht Frankfurt		2–1
Kaiserlautern	1–1	
Borussia Dortmund		1–2
Eintracht Brunswick	1–0	
Werder Bremen		0–0

M.S.V. Duisburg	4–1	
Munich 1860		3–0
Alemania Aachen	5–1	
Hertha Berlin		1–1
V.F.B. Stuttgart	3–0	
F.C. Cologne		1–0
Hanover 96	5–0	
Hamburg S.V.		3–1
Rotweiss Oberhausen	6–1	
Eintracht Frankfurt	1–2	
Kaiserlautern		4–1
Borussia Dortmund	4–2	
Werder Bremen	1–0	
M.S.V. Duisburg		1–0
Schalke 04	2–0	
Munich 1860	3–1	
Alemania Aachen		3–0
Eintracht Brunswick		1–0
Hertha Berlin	1–1	
V.F.B. Stuttgart		0–0
F.C. Cologne	2–0	
Bayern Munich		0–1
Hanover 96		0–1
Rotweiss Essen		0–1
Hamburg S.V.	4–3	
Rotweiss Oberhausen		4–3

FINAL WEST GERMAN LEAGUE TABLE

	P	W	D	L	Goals F	A	Pts
Borussia Munchengladbach	34	23	5	6	71	29	51
Bayern Munich	34	21	5	8	88	37	47
Hertha Berlin	34	20	5	9	67	42	45
F.C. Cologne	34	20	3	11	82	37	43
Borussia Dortmund	34	14	8	12	60	67	36
Hamburg S.V.	34	12	11	11	57	54	35
V.F.B. Stuttgart	34	14	7	13	59	62	35
Eintracht Frankfurt	34	12	10	12	54	54	34
Schalke 04	34	11	12	11	43	54	34
F.C. Kaiserlautern	34	10	12	12	43	55	32
Werder Bremen	34	10	11	13	36	44	31
Rotweiss Essen	34	8	15	11	38	52	31
Hanover 96	34	11	8	15	49	60	30
Rotweiss Oberhausen	34	11	7	16	50	62	29
M.S.V. Duisburg	34	9	11	14	35	48	29
Eintracht Brunswick	34	9	10	15	40	49	28
Munich 1860	34	9	7	18	41	56	25
Alemania Aachen	34	5	7	22	31	83	17

Gordon Banks, of England, the world's No. 1 goalkeeper who was awarded the O.B.E., punches clear from Rumania's Dumitrache, with Keith Newton and Brian Labone in support

Above: Aberdeen centre forward Jim Forrest heading past Celtic's international fullback, Tommy Gemmell, during the Scottish Cup Final which Aberdeen surprisingly won. *Below:* Ian Hutchinson heads Chelsea's late equaliser past Gary Sprake of Leeds to force extra time in the F.A. Cup Final at Wembley

WEST GERMAN LEAGUE CHAMPIONS

1948	I.F.C. Nuremburg	1960	S.V. Hamburg
1949	V.I.R. Mannheim	1961	F.C. Nuremburg
1950	V.F.B. Stuttgart	1962	F.C. Cologne
1951	F.C. Kaiserlautern	1963	Borussia Dortmund
1952	V.P.R. Stuttgart	1964	F.C. Cologne
1953	F.C. Kaiserlautern	1965	Werder Bremen
1954	S.V. Hanover 96	1966	T.S.V. Munich 1860
1955	Rot Weiss Essen	1967	Eintracht Brunswick
1956	Borussia Dortmund	1968	F.C. Nuremburg
1957	Borussia Dortmund	1969	Bayern Munich
1958	F.C. Schalke 04	1970	Borussia Munchengladbach
1959	Eintracht Frankfurt		

WEST GERMAN CUP WINNERS

1953	Rot Weiss Essen	1962	F.C. Nuremburg
1954	V.F.B. Stuttgart	1963	Hamburg S.V.
1955	Karlsruhe S.C.	1964	T.S.V. Munich 1860
1956	Karlsruhe	1965	Borussia Dortmund
1957	Bayern Munich	1966	Bayern Munich
1958	V.F.B. Stuttgart	1967	S.V. Hamburg
1959	Rot Weiss Essen	1968	F.C. Cologne
1960	Borussia Munchengladbach	1969	Bayern Munich
1961	Werder Bremen	1970	Offenbach Kickers

INTERNATIONALS

Sept. 21 1969: AUSTRIA (1) 1 (Pirkner) WEST GERMANY (1) 1 (Mueller). Vienna. 28,000.

WEST GERMANY: Wolter; Hottges, Weber (Fichtel), Schultz (Vogts), Overath, Beckenbauer, Doerfel (Libuda), Seeler, Mueller, Held.

Sept. 24 1969: BULGARIA (0) 0 WEST GERMANY (1) 1 (Doerfel). Sofia. 60,000.

WEST GERMANY: Maier; Hoettges, Schultz, Fichtel, Vogts, Beckenbauer, Overath, Doerfel, Seeler, Mueller, Maas.

Oct. 10 1969: WEST GERMANY (1) 3 (Fichtel, Mueller, Libuda). SCOTLAND (1) 2 (Johnstone, Gilzean). Hamburg. 70,000.

(World Cup qualifying match. See World Cup—Group Seven.)

Feb. 11 1970: SPAIN (2) 2 (Arieta 2). WEST GERMANY (0) 0. Seville.

WEST GERMANY: Manglitz; Vogts, Schultz, Weber, Schnellinger, Haller, Netzer, Libuda, Mueller, Seeler, Grabowski.

April 8 1970: WEST GERMANY (1) 1 (Overath). RUMANIA (1) 1 (Neagu). Stuttgart. 73,000.

WEST GERMANY: Maier; Vogts, Beckenbauer, Schnellinger, Hottges, Haller (Lorenz), Grabowski, Weber (Sieloff), Overath, Mueller, Maas (Roth).

May 9 1970: WEST GERMANY (1) 2 (Seeler, Loehr) REPUBLIC OF IRELAND (0) 1 (Mulligan). West Berlin. 55,000.
WEST GERMANY: Wolter; Patzke, Vogts, Beckenbauer, Schultz, Weber, Grabowski (Dietrich), Seeler, Mueller, Overath (Held), Loehr.
May 13 1970: WEST GERMANY (1) 1 (Seeler) YUGOSLAVIA (0) 0. Niedersachen. 71,000.
WEST GERMANY: Manglitz; Vogts, Fichtel, Schnellinger, Hottges, Beckenbauer, Overath, Libuda, Seeler, Mueller, Loehr.
(World Cup finals. See Chapter Four.)

HOLLAND

AJAX BRING OFF LEAGUE AND CUP DOUBLE

Holland's advance in football was shown by the fact that they produced two of the best club sides in Europe in Feyenoord of Rotterdam, who won the European Cup, and Ajax of Amsterdam, who brought off the double of Dutch League championship and Dutch Cup, while the national side after losing to England only by an 84th minute goal in Amsterdam came to Wembley and earned their goalless draw.

Ajax, losing semi-finalists to Arsenal in the European Fairs' Cup and the previous season's beaten European Cup finalists, ran away with the championship from their Rotterdam rivals, who probably found the strain of European competition affecting their League form. Even so, like Ajax, they could point to only one League defeat, but 11 of their matches were drawn as against six and they finished second five points behind.

Ajax's only defeat was against Feyenoord early in the season in Rotterdam, but their attack—with the controversial 23-year-old Johan Cruyff, valued at £150,000, as striker—picked up a century of goals. The power of the attack and the spirit of the side coached by 42-year-old Rinus Michels, their former international centre-forward, was well shown in their return game with Feyenoord in April.

After an hour's play Feyenoord were well on their way to completing the double over Ajax, being 3–1 ahead in Amsterdam. But Ajax then put on continuous pressure, shot in two goals, and gained a three–three draw which gave them a five points lead with six matches to play—a result which almost decided the championship there and then.

A week after the League championship had been decided Ajax beat P.S.V. Eindhoven 2–0 in the Cup final at Denbosch to complete the double for the second time in their history. But they were lucky to get that far. They were beaten by AZ 67 of Alkmaar in the third round, but as one of the losing teams was required to make up the eight for the quarter-finals Ajax happened to be the lucky club drawn from the seven losers.

Surprisingly at the end of the 1968–1969 season Ajax transferred Theo van Duivenbode to Feyenoord but they acquired players like Nico Rijnders and Dick Van Dijk to strengthen the side, and with Gert Bals, 33, in his sixth season as goalkeeper, Wim Suurbier, an attacking back, Barry Hulshoff, one of the back four like the Yugoslav international Velibor Vasovic, who helped Partizan Belgrade become the first club from a Communist club to reach the European Cup final (in 1966), Ajax played some attractive football.

The idea of the club was mooted in the Café East India in Kalverstraat, Amsterdam, 70 years ago. They became members of the First Division in 1911, had several English trainers, including Vic Buckingham, and won the first of their 14 League championships in 1918.

D.O.S. Utrecht, who just escaped relegation in 1968–1969, again escaped in their final match of the season. They managed to beat G.V.A.V. Groningen, a result which sent G.V.A.V. down. G.V.A.V. will be replaced by Volendam, who quickly returned to the First Division after only one season's absence.

AJAX AMSTERDAM LEAGUE RECORD

	Home	Away
G.V.A.V. Groningen		3–1
Go Ahead Deventer	2–0	
Sparta Rotterdam		4–2
N.E.C. Nijmegen	2–1	
AZ 67 Alkmaar		1–0
Haarlem	4–0	
Holland Sport		4–1
P.S.V. Eindhoven	3–0	
F.C. Twente Enschede		3–0
D.O.S. Utrecht	4–0	
Feyenoord Rotterdam		0–1
N.A.C. Breda	2–1	
D.W.S. Amsterdam		2–0
Telstar Velsen	4–1	
S.V.V. Schiedam		6–0
A.D.O. The Hague	2–1	
N.E.C. Nijmegen		0–0
M.V.V. Maastricht		1–1
AZ 67 Alkmaar	4–1	
Go Ahead Deventer		3–1
Sparta Rotterdam	2–1	
Haarlem		1–0

Holland Sport	5–1	
G.V.A.V. Groningen	3–0	
P.S.V. Eindhoven		3–1
F.C. Twente Enschede	3–0	
D.O.S. Utrecht		7–1
Feyenoord Rotterdam	3–3	
M.V.V. Maastricht	2–0	
N.A.C. Breda		1–1
D.W.S. Amsterdam	6–1	
Telstar Velsen		1–1
S.V.V. Schiedam	8–0	
A.D.O. The Hague		1–1

FINAL DUTCH LEAGUE TABLE

	P	W	D	L	Goals F	A	Pts
Ajax Amsterdam	34	27	6	1	100	23	60
Feyenoord Rotterdam	34	22	11	1	81	22	55
P.S.V. Eindhoven	34	19	8	7	70	34	46
F.C. Twente Enschede	34	17	8	9	62	43	42
Sparta Rotterdam	34	16	9	9	56	41	41
A.D.O. The Hague	34	14	12	8	56	33	40
Go Ahead Deventer	34	11	13	10	40	42	35
M.V.V. Maastricht	34	10	14	10	45	45	34
Holland Sport	34	13	7	14	48	63	33
N.A.C. Breda	34	11	10	13	40	54	32
N.E.C. Nijmegen	34	8	15	11	31	39	31
AZ 67 Alkmaar	34	8	12	14	31	48	28
Haarlem	34	6	15	13	23	36	27
Telstar Velsen	34	5	14	15	33	48	24
D.W.S. Amsterdam	34	9	5	19	26	50	23
D.O.S. Utrecht	34	7	9	18	27	64	23
G.V.A.V. Groningen	34	7	8	19	20	45	22
S.V.V. Schiedam	34	5	5	24	31	90	15

DUTCH LEAGUE CHAMPIONS

1898	R.A.P.	1910	H.V.V. The Hague
1899	R.A.P.	1911	Sparta Rotterdam
1900	H.V.V. The Hague	1912	Sparta Rotterdam
1901	H.V.V. The Hague	1913	Sparta Rotterdam
1902	H.V.V. The Hague	1914	H.V.V. The Hague
1903	H.V.V. The Hague	1915	Sparta Rotterdam
1904	H.B.S. The Hague	1916	Willem II Tilburg
1905	H.V.V. The Hague	1917	Go Ahead Deventer
1906	H.B.S. The Hague	1918	Ajax Amsterdam
1907	H.V.V. The Hague	1919	Ajax Amsterdam
1908	Quick The Hague	1920	Quick The Hague
1909	Sparta Rotterdam	1921	N.A.C. Breda

Above: Feyenoord, the European Cup winners from Holland, Standing (*l. to r.*): Treijtel, Haak, Laseroms, Romeyn, Israel, Wery, Veldhoen, Graafland, Front row: Teuns, Kindvall, Hasil, Geels, Van Hanegem, Jensen, Moulijn, Not in picture is Van Duivenbode, who played in the final. *Below:* Ove Kindvall, the Swedish international, toe-ends the ball over the head of Williams, the Celtic goalkeeper, to give Feyenoord the European Cup in Milan

Above: Jubilant Manchester City players with the European Cup-Winner's Cup after beating Gornik Zabrze of Poland in the final in Vienna. *Below:* Gornik Zabrze's goalkeeper Kostka shows his despair after failing to stop a penalty by Francis Lee in the European Cup Winner's Cup Final

1922	Go Ahead Deventer	1947	Ajax Amsterdam
1923	R.C.H. Haarlem	1948	B.V.V. Scheidam
1924	Feyenoord Rotterdam	1949	S.V.V. Scheidam
1925	H.B.S. The Hague	1950	Limburgia
1926	Enschede	1951	P.S.V. Eindhoven
1927	Heracles	1952	Willem II Tilburg
1928	Feyenoord Rotterdam	1953	R.C.H. Haarlem
1929	P.S.V. Eindhoven	1954	P.S.V. Eindhoven
1930	Go Ahead Deventer	1955	Willem II Tilburg
1931	Ajax Amsterdam	1956	Rapid J.C. Haarlem
1932	Ajax Amsterdam	1957	Ajax Amsterdam
1933	Go Ahead Deventer	1958	D.O.S. Utrecht
1934	Ajax Amsterdam	1959	Sparta Rotterdam
1935	P.S.V. Eindhoven	1960	Ajax Amsterdam
1936	Feyenoord Rotterdam	1961	Feyenoord Rotterdam
1937	Ajax Amsterdam	1962	Feyenoord Rotterdam
1938	Feyenoord Rotterdam	1963	P.S.V. Eindhoven
1939	Ajax Amsterdam	1964	D.W.S. Amsterdam
1940	Feyenoord Rotterdam	1965	Feyenoord Rotterdam
1941	Heracles	1966	Ajax Amsterdam
1942	A.D.O. The Hague	1967	Ajax Amsterdam
1943	A.D.O. The Hague	1968	Ajax Amsterdam
1944	Volewijckers, Amsterdam	1969	Feyenoord Rotterdam
1945	No competition	1970	Ajax Amsterdam
1946	Haarlem		

THE CUP
(HOLLAND)

QUARTER-FINALS
(April 22 1970)

G.V.A.V. (Groningen) 1   AZ 67 (Alkmaar) 0
F.C. Twente (Enschede) 2   Elinkwijk (Utrecht) 0
P.S.V. (Eindhoven) 2   A.D.O. (The Hague) 0
D.W.S. (Amsterdam) 1   Ajax (Amsterdam) 2

SEMI-FINALS
(May 13 1970)

Ajax (Amsterdam) 4   F.C. Twente (Enschede) 0
P.S.V. (Eindhoven) 1   G.V.A.V. (Groningen) 0

FINAL
(May 27 1970)

Ajax (Amsterdam) 2   P.S.V. (Eindhoven) 0

CUP WINNERS
(HOLLAND)

1899	R.A.P.	1902	Haarlem
1900	Velcoitas Breda	1903	H.V.V. The Hague
1901	H.B.S. The Hague	1904	H.F.C.

1905	H.F.C.	1935	Feyenoord Rotterdam
1906	Concordia Rotterdam	1936	Roermond
1907	V.O.C.	1937	P.S.V. Eindhoven
1908	Quick The Hague	1938	V.S.V.
1909	H.B.S. The Hague	1939	Wageningen
1910	Quick The Hague	1940–42	No competition
1911	Quick The Hague	1943	Ajax Amsterdam
1912	Haarlem	1944	Willem II Tilburg
1913	H.F.C.	1945–47	No competition
1914	D.F.C.	1948	Wageningen
1915	H.F.C.	1949	Quick Njimegen
1916	R.C.H.	1950	P.S.V. Eindhoven
1917	Ajax Amsterdam	1951–56	No competition
1918	Quick The Hague	1957	F.C. Fortuna
1919	No competition	1958	Sparta Rotterdam
1920	C.V.V.	1959	V.V.V.
1921	Schoten	1960	No competition
1922–24	No competition	1961	Ajax Amsterdam
1925	Z.F.C.	1962	Sparta Rotterdam
1926	Longa	1963	Willem II Tilburg
1927	V.U.C.	1964	F.C. Fortuna Geleen
1928	R.C.H.	1965	Feyenoord Rotterdam
1929	No competition	1966	Sparta Rotterdam
1930	Feyenoord Rotterdam	1967	Ajax Amsterdam
1931	No competition	1968	A.D.O. The Hague
1932	D.F.C.	1969	Feyenoord Rotterdam
1933	No competition	1970	Ajax Amsterdam
1934	Velocitas Groningen		

INTERNATIONALS

Sept. 8 1969: POLAND (0) 2 (Jarosik, Lubanski) HOLLAND (1) 1
(Wery). Chorzow. 80,000.

Oct. 22 1969: HOLLAND (1) 1 (Veenstra) BULGARIA (0) 1 (Bonev).
Rotterdam. 65,000.
(World Cup qualifying matches. See World Cup—Group Eight.)

Nov. 5 1969: HOLLAND (0) 0 ENGLAND (0) 1 (Bell). Amsterdam.
HOLLAND: Treijtel; Drost, Israel, Eykenbroek, Krol, Veenstra (Van
Dijk), Rijnders, Cruyff, Mulder, Van Hanegem (Muhren), Rensenbrink.

Jan. 14 1970: ENGLAND (0) 0 HOLLAND (0) 0. Wembley. 100,000.
HOLLAND: Van Beveren; Drost, Israel, Eykenbroek, Krol, Jansen,
Rijnders, Van Dijk, Cruyff, Van Hanegem, Keizer.

Jan. 28 1970: ISRAEL (0) 0 HOLLAND (1) 1 (Brokamp). Jaffa.
16,000.
ISRAEL: Vissoker; Bar, Rosen, Wallach, Bello, Schum, Shuruk, Spigler,
Ben-Rimok, Romano, Feigenbaum.
HOLLAND: Treijte; Drost, Israel, Strik, Krol, Jansen, Muhren, Pal-
platz, Brokamp, Van Dijk, Rensenbrink.

HUNGARY

UJPEST DOZSA BRING OFF DOUBLE

The decline of the standard of football in Hungary—at national level where the Olympic champions failed for the first time to qualify for the World Cup finals and at club level where little progress was made in the European competitions—was reflected in the public interest in the League competition throughout the season, which ran from March to December with a short break during the summer.

But Ujpest Dozsa, under the splendid coaching of the ex-Hungarian international Lajos Baroti, hope to improve the club scene next season, having fulfilled the promise they have been showing in recent years and benefiting by European experience to win the League championship for the first time in ten years—and the tenth time in their history—by four points from their nearest challengers, Honved, whom they also beat to win the Cup for the very first time.

Their success was not surprising because the previous season they had given notice of their intent by running their great rivals, Ferencvaros, to a photo-finish, ending only a point behind after scoring 102 goals, a remarkable feat in Hungarian football, nearly 40 more than the champions.

Once again Ujpest Dozsa, one of the oldest clubs in Europe, having been formed in 1885, were the highest scorers in the League, thanks to two of their front running forwards Antal Dunai and Ferenc Benes, two internationals and Olympic medal winners, who between them scored more than half their goals.

Ferencvaros, who dropped to third place, had managerial troubles. In November a few weeks before the season ended, Dr. Karoly Lakatm, who took the club to the championship in 1968 and managed the Hungarian team to Olympic titles in Tokyo and Mexico City, resigned saying he wanted to forget the past year as quickly as possible.

He was succeeded by Geza Kalocsay, who had made a big impression on Polish football as manager of the miners' team, Gornik Zabrze, during his stay in the country. A big effort was made to get him to stay in Poland but he wanted to return to his own country. It remains to be seen whether he can revive the flagging spirit of Ferencvaros.

Meanwhile Ujpest Dozsa will make their second appearance in the European Cup competition in 1970–71. Their last was in 1960–61 when after beating Red Star Belgrade they lost 6–2 to Benfica in Lisbon, although they had beaten the Eagles of Lisbon 2–1 at home. Their place in the European Cup-Winners' Cup, of course, will go to the runners-up, Honved. Curiously there were only 15,000 people in the vast Nepstadion in Budapest to see Ujpest gain their first ever Cup success last August.

For the 1970 season the Hungarians decided to fall more in line with the Western European countries. Instead of running their League competition during spring and autumn, they are to have an autumn to spring tournament with a break during the winter when their grounds are unplayable because of snow and ice.

To fill in the spring months a subsidiary competition was run. The sixteen clubs in the League were divided into two groups of eight clubs each, playing home and away matches until June. To give this an added interest for both clubs and players, and to give them something to play for, points were to be awarded on the basis of where clubs finished—eight for top place, seven for second place and so on, and clubs are to carry these points through to the League competition starting later in the year.

UJPEST DOZSA LEAGUE RECORD

	Home	Away
Komlo	2–0	
Csepel		2–0
Donaujvaros	3–1	
Egyetertes		4–0
Honved Budapest	3–3	
Szombathely		4–1
Vasas Goyer	4–2	
Pecs		0–1
Salgotarjan		2–0
Diosgoyer	2–1	
Tatabanya	1–2	
Ferencvaros	2–0	
M.T.K. Budapest		6–0
Raba	5–1	
Eger		4–1
Dunaujvaros		4–0
Egyetertes	4–4	
Honved Budapest		1–1
Szombathely	3–0	
Vases Goyer		6–1
Pecs	2–1	
Diosgoyer		4–1
Salgotarjan	3–1	
Tatabanya		0–0
Ferencvaros	1–1	
Raba		1–1
M.T.K. Budapest	6–1	

Komlo 1–1
Eger 2–0
Csepel 1–1

FINAL HUNGARIAN LEAGUE TABLE

	P	W	D	L	Goals F	A	Pts
Ujpest Dozsa	30	20	8	2	83	27	48
Honved	30	18	8	4	66	28	44
Ferencvaros	30	15	9	6	56	33	39
Vasas	30	18	3	9	72	43	39
Raba	30	12	10	8	53	36	34
Pecs	30	13	6	11	41	38	32
Csepel	30	11	10	9	37	36	32
Tatabanya	30	10	8	12	33	41	28
M.T.K. Budapest	30	9	8	13	43	53	26
Salgotarjan	30	10	5	15	29	39	25
Szombathely	30	7	11	12	26	44	25
Komlo	30	5	14	11	21	37	24
Diosgoyer	30	7	9	14	31	51	23
Donaujvaros	30	9	5	16	26	48	23
Egyetertes	30	6	9	15	36	52	21
Eger	30	5	7	18	23	64	17

HUNGARIAN LEAGUE CHAMPIONS

1901	B.T.C.	1924	M.T.K. Budapest
1902	B.T.C.	1925	M.T.K. Budapest
1903	F.T.C.	1926	F.T.C.
1904	M.T.K. Budapest	1927	Ferencvaros
1905	F.T.C.	1928	Ferencvaros
1906	F.T.C.	1929	Hungaria
1907	F.T.C.	1930	Ujpest Dozsa
1908	M.T.K. Budapest	1931	Ujpest Dozsa
1909	F.T.C.	1932	Ferencvaros
1910	F.T.C.	1933	Ujpest Dozsa
1911	F.T.C.	1934	Ferencvaros
1912	F.T.C.	1935	Ujpest Dozsa
1913	F.T.C.	1936	Hungaria
1914	M.T.K. Budapest	1937	Hungaria
1915–16	No competition	1938	Ferencvraos
1917	M.T.K. Budapest	1939	Ujpest Dozsa
1918	M.T.K. Budapest	1940	Ferencvaros
1919	M.T.K. Budapest	1941	Ferencvaros
1920	M.T.K. Budapest	1942	Csepel
1921	M.T.K. Budapest	1943	Csepel
1922	M.T.K. Budapest	1944	Nagyvarad
1923	M.T.K. Budapest	1945	Ujpest Dozsa

1946	Ujpest Dozsa	1959	Csepel
1947	Ujpest Dozsa	1960	Ujpest Dozsa
1948	Csepel	1961	Vasas Budapest
1949	Ferencvaros	1962	Vasas Budapest
1950	(spring–autumn) Honved	1963	Ferencvaros
1951	(spring–autumn) Bastyn	1964	Ferencvaros
1952	Honved	1965	Vasas Budapest
1953	Voros Lobogo	1966	Vasas Budapest
1954	Honved	1967	Vasas Budapest
1955	Honved	1968	Ferencvaros
1956	Not completed	1969	Ujpest Dozsa
1957	Vasas Budapest	1970	Ujpest Dozsa
1958	M.T.K. Budapest		

HUNGARIAN CUP COMPETITION

QUARTER-FINALS
Csepel 2　Pecs 1
Ozd 0　Honved 4
Szombathely 1　M.T.K. 2
Volan 2　Ujpest Dozsa 4

SEMI-FINALS
Ujpest Dozsa 4　M.T.K. 0
Honved 2　Csepel 1

FINAL
Ujpest Dozsa 3　Honved 1

UJPEST DOZSA: Szentmihaly; Kaposzta, Solymosi, Nosko, Bankuti, Dinai E., Gorocs, Fazekas, Bene, Dunai A., Nagy.

HONVED: Bicskei; Ruzsinki, Kelemen, Marosi, Russinger, Tajti, Komora, Pusztai, Szurgent, Karakas.

Scorers: Ujpest Dozsa—Dunai A., 40 mins; Bene, 43 mins; Nagy, 47 mins.　Honved—Russinger, 80 mins.

CUP WINNERS
(HUNGARY)

1963	M.T.K. Budapest	1967	Vasas Gyoer
1964	Honved	1968	M.T.K. Budapest
1965	Honved	1969	Ujpest Dozsa
1966	Vasas Gyoer	1970	Ujpest Dozsa

INTERNATIONALS

Sept. 14 1969: CZECHOSLOVAKIA (1) 3 (Hagara, Kvasnak, Kuna) HUNGARY (2) 3 (Bene, Dunai, Fazekas).　Prague.
(World Cup qualifyidg match.　See World Cup—Group Two)
Sept. 24 1969: SWEDEN (0) 2 (Nicklasson, Pancsics o.g.) HUNGARY (0) 0.　Stockholm.

HUNGARY: Szentimihalyi; Kaposzta, Pancsics, Ihasz, Meszoly, Juhasz, Fazekas, Gorocs, Bene, Dunai II, Zambo.

Oct. 22 1969: HUNGARY (2) 3 (Bene 2, Szucs) DENMARK (0) 0. Budapest.

Nov. 5 1969: HUNGARY (1) 4 (Halmosi, Bene, Puskas, Kocsis). REPUBLIC OF IRELAND (0) 0. Budapest.

Dec. 3 1969: HUNGARY (0) 1 (Kocsis pen) CZECHOSLOVAKIA (1) 4 (Kvasnak pen, Vesely, Adamec, Jokl). (World Cup qualifying matches. See World Cup—Group Two.)

April 12 1970: YUGOSLAVIA (1) 2 (Pancsics o.g., Gracanjn) HUNGARY (1) 2 (Fazekas, Bene). Belgrade.

HUNGARY: Tamas; Velai, Vidats, Fejes, Halmosi, Pancsics, Pustai, Bene, Fazekas, Somogyl (Karsai), Dunai II.

May 2 1970: HUNGARY (0) 2 (Fazekas, Karsai) POLAND (0) 0. Budapest.

HUNGARY: Tamas; Nosko, Konrad, Pancsics, Fejes, Dunai, Halmosi, Fazekas, Kocsis, Bene, Karsai.

May 16 1970: HUNGARY (1) 1 (Fazekas) SWEDEN (0) 2 (Persson, Ejderstadt). Budapest.

HUNGARY: Tamas; Nosko, Konrad, Pancsics, Fejes, Dunai III, Karsai, Kocsis, Fazekas, Bene, Dunai II.

ICELAND

FINAL LEAGUE TABLE

	P	W	D	L	F	A	Pts
I.B.K. Keflavik	12	7	1	4	20	12	15
I.A. Akranes	12	6	2	4	22	19	14
K.R. Reykjavik	12	4	4	4	24	20	12
I.B.V. Vestmannis	12	3	6	3	20	20	12
Valur Reykjavik	12	4	4	4	18	19	12
Fram Reykjavik	12	2	6	4	8	16	10
Iba Akureyri	12	2	5	5	12	18	9

ITALY

CAGLIARI MAKE LEAGUE HISTORY

A new name appears on the Italian roll of honour. Cagliari, the club from Sardinia, became League champions for the first time in their history, thus fulfilling the promise they had shown the previous season when they finished runners-up to Fiorentina after promising to run off with the title. Not only was it a first time for Cagliari, who were celebrating the 50th anniversary of their foundation, but also the first time a club south of Rome had won the title and the first time the championship had gone outside the mainland.

Cagliari are one of the Italian League's youngest clubs. They gained promotion from the second division in 1963–64 and in their first season among the top clubs in 1964–65 finished sixth. In 1965–66 they were eleventh, sixth the following year, ninth in 1967–68 and second in 1968–69.

Much of their success is due to the scoring efforts of their 25-year-old outside left, Luigi Riva, known as the 'golden boy' of Italian soccer. He has been sought by many clubs and in June of 1969 Inter-Milan were reported to have offered a fantastic £860,000 for his services, which would have made him easily the highest-priced footballer in the world. Cagliari, however, are not parting.

The 5ft. 11in. Riva has that priceless ability—particularly in Italian football, which is inclined to be defensive—of being able to score goals, and he usually manages to get one past opposing goalkeepers in most matches in which he plays. This is shown by the fact that during the season he scored 21 goals in 28 matches, which put him on top of the list of First Division goalscorers.

It also brought him for the third year in succession the Chevron gold trophy, which is awarded to the Italian player with best goal average per match. With an average of 0·75 Riva easily beat his nearest rival, Vicenza's Sandro Vitali, whose 17 goals in 27 matches brought him an average of 0·62.

Cagliari led the table for most of the season. It was not until their 12th game that they met with a setback, and a surprising one at that, because they were beaten 1–0 by bottom of the table Palermo. They quickly recovered and practically made sure of the championship when they drew with Juventus in Turin in March.

This match had all the excitement of an English Cup final, as Juventus were their chief rivals for the championship. All the seats were sold well in advance, and fantastic prices were being offered on the black market for a ticket, including such inducements as a week's holiday all paid in Sardinia. A crowd of 116,138 paid a record £94,447 for a league game to see the match. Such was the tremendous interest in the match that the Italian Football Federation agreed to the whole match being televised—the first time that this had happened in Italy.

Cagliari play at the Amsicora Stadium, which holds about 28,000 people, and they will be carrying Italy's hopes in the European Cup.

Italy's success in qualifying for the World Cup finals helped to increase interest in the game, and attendances at League games during the season were up by 180,000 over the previous season. The Italian Football Federation said that the total number of spectators at League matches during the 1969–70 season was 4,489,990.

Above: Gerrif Muhren of Ajax, scores the only goal in the European Fairs' Cup semi-final against Arsenal in Amsterdam, beating Eddie Kelly (No. 4). However, it was not enough to wipe out Arsenal's 3–0 first leg lead.
Below: Meeting of the giants: Hughes scores for Celtic in the second leg of their European Cup semi-final against Leeds, in spite of Jackie Charlton (centre) and Terry Cooper

Above: Anderlecht's goalkeeper Jean Trappeniers on the ground pushes the ball away from Arsenal's Charlie George in the European Fairs' Cup Final at Highbury. Armstrong is in support. Arsenal won the match 3–0 and the Cup 4–3 on aggregate. *Below:* All action in an Italian League game in which Roberto Boninsegna of Inter-Milan jumps high over Lazio right back Papadopulo. On the left Facchetti of Inter-Milan, on the right, Di Vincenzo, Lazio's goalkeeper

CAGLIARI LEAGUE RECORD

	Home	Away
Sampdoria		0–0
Vicenza	2–1	
Brescia		2–0
Lazio	1–0	
Fiorentina		1–0
Inter-Milan	1–1	
Napoli		2–0
A.S. Roma	1–0	
Juventus	1–1	
Verona		1–1
Bologna	1–0	
Palermo		0–1
Bari		0–0
A.C. Milan	1–1	
Torino	2–0	
Sampdoria	4–0	
Vicenza		2–1
Brescia	4–0	
Lazio		2–0
Fiorentina	0–0	
Inter-Milan		0–1
Napoli	2–0	
A.S. Roma		1–1
Juventus		2–2
Verona	1–0	
Bologna		0–0
Palermo	2–0	
Bari	2–0	
A.C. Milan		0–0
Torino		4–0

FINAL ITALIAN LEAGUE TABLE

	P	W	D	L	F	A	Pts
Cagliari	30	17	11	2	42	11	45
Inter-Milan	30	16	9	5	41	19	41
Juventus	30	15	8	7	43	20	38
A.C. Milan	30	13	10	7	38	24	36
Fiorentina	30	15	6	9	40	33	36
Napoli	30	10	11	9	24	21	31
Torino	30	11	8	11	20	31	30
Vicenza	30	11	7	12	32	31	29
Lazio Roma	30	11	7	12	33	32	29
Bologna	30	6	16	8	22	24	28
A.S. Roma	30	8	12	10	27	36	28
Verona	30	8	10	12	26	30	26

Sampdoria	30	6	12	12	22	37	24
Brescia	30	5	10	15	20	35	20
Palermo	30	5	10	15	23	45	20
Bari	30	5	9	16	11	35	19

ITALIAN LEAGUE CHAMPIONS

1898	Genoa	1935	Juventus
1899	Genoa	1936	Bologna
1900	Genoa	1937	Bologna
1900	A.C. Milan	1938	Ambrosiana-Inter
1901	Genoa	1939	Bologna
1902	Genoa	1940	Ambrosiana-Inter
1903	Genoa	1941	Bologna
1904	Genoa	1942	A.S. Roma
1905	Juventus	1943	Torino
1906	A.C. Milan	1944–45	No competition
1907	A.C. Milan	1946	Torino
1908	Pro Vercelli	1947	Torino
1909	Pro Vercelli	1948	Torino
1910	Internazionale	1949	Torino
1911	Pro Vercelli	1950	Juventus
1912	Pro Vercelli	1951	A.C. Milan
1913	Pro Vercelli	1952	Juventus
1914	Casale	1953	Inter-Milan
1915–19	No competition	1954	Inter-Milan
1920	Internazionale	1955	A.C. Milan
1921	Pro Vercelli	1956	Fiorentina
1922	Pro Vercelli (CCI)	1957	A.C. Milan
1922	Novese (FICG)	1958	Juventus
1923	Genoa	1959	A.C. Milan
1924	Genoa	1960	Juventus
1925	Bologna	1961	Juventus
1926	Juventus	1962	A.C. Milan
1927	Torino	1963	Inter-Milan
1928	Torino	1964	Bologna
1929	Bologna	1965	Inter-Milan
1930	Ambrosiana-Inter	1966	Inter-Milan
1931	Juventus	1967	Juventus
1932	Juventus	1968	A.C. Milan
1933	Juventus	1969	Fiorentina
1934	Juventus	1970	Cagliari

CUP WINNERS
(ITALY)

1922	Vado	1938	Juventus
1936	Torino	1939	Ambrosiana Inter
1937	Genoa	1940	Fiorentina

1941	Venezia	1963	Atalanta
1942	Juventus	1964	A.S. Roma
1943	Torino	1965	Juventus
1944–57	No competition	1966	Fiorentina
1958	Lazio Rome	1967	A.C. Milan
1959	Juventus	1968	Torino
1960	Juventus	1969	A.S. Roma
1961	Fiorentina	1970	Bologna
1962	Napoli		

INTERNATIONALS

Nov. 4 1969: ITALY (1) 4 (Riva 3, Mazzola) WALES (0) 1 (England). Rome. 76,000.

Nov. 22 1969: ITALY (3) 3 (Mazzola, Domenghini, Riva) EAST GERMANY (0) 0. Naples. 92,000.

(World Cup qualifying matches. See World Cup—Group Three.)

Feb. 21 1970: SPAIN (2) 2 (Burgnich o.g., Salvadore o.g.) ITALY (2) 2 (Anastasi, Riva). Madrid. 80,000.

ITALY: Zoff; Burgnich, Facchetti, Cera, Puja, Salvadore, Domenghini, Rivera, Anastasi, De Sisti, Riva.

May 10 1970: PORTUGAL (0) 1 (Humberto) ITALY (1) 2 (Riva 2). Lisbon. 35,000.

ITALY: Albertosi; Burgnich, Facchetti, Bertini, Puja, Ferrante, Domenghini, Rivera, Mazzola, De Sisti, Riva.

(World Cup finals matches. See Chapter Four.)

LUXEMBURG

JEUNESSE ESCH REGAIN THEIR LEAGUE TITLE

Jeunesse Esch won the championship of Luxemburg, where the League season was extended into June—its longest in history, because of the long, cold winter which resulted in grounds being unplayable—although the League consists of only 12 clubs, one of the smallest in Europe.

This was their third League championship in the last four seasons, the sequence being broken by Avenir Beggen, who upset their chance of equalling their feat of a hat-trick from 1958 to 1960.

They will be taking part in their sixth European Cup campaign, but their best effort to date has been to reach the last eight.

Their leading striker was Langer, who scored 18, but a remarkable record for the League was set by Devillet, of Spora, who hit more than half his side's 60 goals in 22 matches.

Red Boys, who hold the record for the number of Cup victories, again reached the final but found Union Luxemburg, the holders, just a little too superior for them. A first half goal by the young international Nicky Braun enabled Union to retain the trophy and notch up their fifth victory in the last 12 years.

JEUNESSE ESCH LEAGUE RECORD

	Home	Away
Spora	3–2	
Red Boys		1–2
Mendorf	6–1	
Tetange		2–0
U.S. Dudelange	4–0	
Avenir Beggen		4–0
Niederkorn		2–2
Union		1–0
Rumelange	1–1	
Aris	3–0	
Stade		3–0
Spora		2–1
Red Boys	4–0	
Mendorf		3–0
Tetange	0–0	
U.S. Dudelange		0–0
Avenir Beggen	1–0	
Aris		3–0
Niederkorn	4–0	
Union	0–0	
Rumelange		2–2
Stade	6–4	

FINAL LUXEMBURG LEAGUE TABLE

	P	W	D	L	Goals F	A	Pts
Jeunesse Esch	22	15	6	1	55	15	36
Rumelange	22	13	5	4	49	24	31
Spora	22	14	2	6	60	32	30
Red Boys	22	12	4	6	56	37	28
Union	22	9	5	8	52	36	23
Aris	22	10	3	9	37	42	23
Avenir Beggen	22	9	4	9	31	31	22
Tetange	22	6	6	10	25	44	18
Stade	22	8	1	13	41	44	17
Niederkorn	22	4	8	10	28	45	16
U.S. Dudelange	22	3	9	10	24	43	15
Mendorf	22	2	1	19	21	86	5

LUXEMBURG LEAGUE CHAMPIONS

1910	Racing Luxemburg	1912	U.S. Hollerich-Bonnevoie
1911	Sporting Luxemburg	1913	No competition

1914	U.S. Hollerich-Bonnevoie
1915	U.S. Hollerich-Bonnevoie
1916	U.S. Hollerich-Bonnevoie
1917	U.S. Hollerich-Bonnevoie
1918	Fola Esch
1919	Sporting Luxemburg
1920	Fola Esch
1921	Jeunesse Esch
1922	Fola Esch
1923	Red Boys Differdange
1924	Fola Esch
1925	Spora Luxemburg
1926	Red Boys Differdange
1927	Union Luxemburg
1928	Spora Luxemburg
1929	Spora Luxemburg
1930	Fola Esch
1931	Red Boys Differdange
1932	Red Boys Differdange
1933	Red Boys Differdange
1934	Spora Luxemburg
1935	Spora Luxemburg
1936	Spora Luxemburg
1937	Jeunesse Esch
1938	Spora Luxemburg
1939	Stade Dudelange
1940	Stade Dudelange

1941–44	No competition
1945	Stade Dudelange
1946	Stade Dudelange
1947	Stade Dudelange
1948	Stade Dudelange
1949	Spora Luxemburg
1950	Stade Dudelange
1951	Jeunesse Esch
1952	National Schifflge.
1953	Progres Niedercorn
1954	Jeunesse Esch
1955	Stade Dudelange
1956	Spora Luxemburg
1957	Stade Dudelange
1958	Jeunesse Esch
1959	Jeunesse Esch
1960	Jeunesse Esch
1961	Spora Luxemburg
1962	Union Luxemburg
1963	Jeunesse Esch
1964	Aris Bonnevoie
1965	Stade Dudelange
1966	Aris Bonnevoie
1967	Jeunesse Esch
1968	Jeunesse Esch
1969	Avenir Beggen
1970	Jeunesse Esch

CUP WINNERS
(LUXEMBURG)

1922	Racing Luxemburg
1923	Fola Esch
1924	Fola Esch
1925	Red Boys Differdange
1926	Red Boys Differdange
1927	Red Boys Differdange
1928	Spora Luxemburg
1929	Red Boys Differdange
1930	Red Boys Differdange
1931	Red Boys Differdange
1932	Spora Luxemburg
1933	Progres Niedercorn
1934	Red Boys Differdange
1035	Jeunesse Esch
1936	Red Boys Differdange
1937	Jeunesse Esch
1938	Stade Dudelange
1939	U.S. Dudelange

1940	Spora Luxemburg
1941–44	No competition
1945	Progres Niedercorn
1946	Jeunesse Esch
1947	Union Luxemburg
1948	Stade Dudelange
1949	Stade Dudelange
1950	Spora Luxemburg
1951	Sport Club Tetange
1952	Red Boys Differdange
1953	Red Boys Differdange
1954	Jeunesse Esch
1955	Fola Esch
1956	Stade Dudelange
1957	Spora Luxemburg
1958	Red Boys Differdange
1959	Union Luxemburg
1960	National Schifflge.

H

1961	Alliance Dudelange	1966	Spora Luxemburg
1962	Alliance Dudelange	1967	Aris Bonnevoie
1963	Union Luxemburg	1968	U.S. Rumelange
1964	Union Luxemburg	1969	Union Luxemburg
1965	Spora Luxemburg	1970	Union Luxemburg

INTERNATIONALS

Oct. 12 1969: LUXEMBURG (1) 1 (Kirchens)   POLAND (0) 5 (Dejna 2, Jaroski pen, Bula, Lubanski). Luxemburg.

Dec. 7 1969: LUXEMBURG (0) 1 (Phillipp pen)   BULGARIA (2) 3 (Dermendjiev, Yakimov, Bonev). Luxemburg. 2,000.

(World Cup qualifying matches. See World Cup—Group Eight.)

May 9 1970: LUXEMBURG (0) 0   CZECHOSLOVAKIA (1) 1 (Jurkanin). Luxemburg. 4,500.

NORWAY

LYN OSLO SLIDE AS ROSENBORG CLIMB

The big surprise of the Norwegian League season, which runs from April to October, was the sudden decline of the very experienced Lyn Oslo side. The champions of the previous year, who were crushed by Leeds United in the European Cup by 10–0 at Elland Road and 6–0 in Oslo, slumped right down to the foot of the table and had the humiliating experience of being relegated. They won only four of their 18 League games.

The championship went to Rosenborg Trondheim by a margin of five points. This is the club who appointed as manager George Curtis, 49, the former Arsenal, Southampton, Sunderland and Hull City player, who had managerial experience with Brighton and also coaching experience in California and is now on his second spell in Norway.

Accompanying Lyn Oslo into the second division were Start of Kristiansand after only one season among the elite, while the other promoted club, Hoedd of Ulsteinvik, just saved their place with a 3–1 victory in their final League game.

A replay was necessary to decide the holders of the Cup, and finally Stroemsgodset of Drammen qualified for the European Cup-Winners' Cup competition. They managed a goal in the final minute to force a draw, two goals each, with Fredrikstad in the first match, and although extra time was played no further goals were scored.

The following week Stroemsgodset made no mistake and won 5–3 to inscribe their name on the King Olav Cup for the first time in their history.

ROSENBORG TRONDHEIM LEAGUE RECORD

	Home	Away
Sarpsborg		1–0
Brann Bergen	5–0	
Start Kristiansand		4–1
Skeid Oslo	4–0	
Stroemgodset		0–0
Lyn Oslo	3–0	
Hoedd Ulsteinvik		2–1
Fredrikstad	2–0	
Viking Stavanger		1–3
Sarpsborg	2–0	
Brann Bergen		1–0
Start Kristiansand	2–0	
Skeid Oslo		0–2
Stroemgodse	3–1	
Fredrikstad		2–4
Hoedd Ulsteinvik	2–1	
Lyn Oslo		2–1
Viking Stavanger	0–1	

FINAL NORWEGIAN LEAGUE TABLE

	P	W	D	L	Goals F	A	Pts
Rosenborg Trondheim	18	13	1	4	36	15	27
Fredrikstad	18	8	6	4	28	15	22
Stroemsgodset Drammen	18	8	6	4	34	22	22
Skeid Oslo	18	9	2	7	29	22	20
Viking Stavanger	18	6	6	6	18	17	18
Brann Bergen	18	6	6	6	20	26	18
Sarpsborg	18	6	5	7	22	22	17
Hoedd Ulsteinvik	18	4	4	10	24	39	12
Start Kristiansand	18	5	2	11	20	35	12
Lyn Oslo	18	4	4	10	21	39	12

NORWEGIAN LEAGUE CHAMPIONS

1938	Fredrikstad	1955	Larvik Turn
1939	Fredrikstad	1956	Larvik Turn
1940–47	No competition	1957	Fredrikstad
1948	Freidig	1958	Kiking
1949	Fredrikstad	1959	Lillestroem
1950	Fram	1960	Fredrikstad
1951	Fredrikstad	1961	Fredrikstad
1952	Fredrikstad	1962	Fredrikstad
1953	Larvik Turn	1963	Lyn Oslo
1954	Fredrikstad	1964	Lyn Oslo

1965 Lyn Oslo	1968 Lyn Oslo
1966 Skeid Oslo	1969 Rosenborg Trondheim
1967 Rosenborg Trondheim	1970 Rosenborg Trondheim

INTERNATIONALS

Sept. 21 1969: NORWAY (2) 2 (Olsen O. D., Sathrang) DENMARK (0) 0. Oslo. 15,054.
NORWAY: Hafthorsen; Egger, Thorsen, Olafsen, Slinning, Borno, Gulbrandsen, Olsen O. D., Iversen, Johansen, Sathrang.
Nov. 11 1969: MEXICO (2) 4 (Onofre, Padilla, Ponce 2) NORWAY (0) 0. Mexico City. 32,000.
MEXICO: Calderon; Alejandrez, Perez, Onofre (Munguia), Pena, Nunez, Ponce, Velardo, Alverado, Pereda (Lopez), Padilla.
NORWAY: Hafthorsen; Eggen, Slinning, Borno, Thorsen, Olafsen, Olsen O. D., Gulbrandsen (Spydevold), Iversen, Johansen, Sathrang (Hestad).
Nov. 16 1969: GUATEMALA (0) 1 (Torres) NORWAY (1) 3 (Spydevold, Hestad 2). Guatemala City. 26,000.
NORWAY: Hafthorsen (Karlsen); Eggen (Wengen), Thorsen, Olafsen, Slinning, Borno, Spydevold, Olsen O. D., Sunde (Mathiesen), Hestad, Sathrang.
May 13 1970: NORWAY (0) 0 CZECHOSLOVAKIA (1) 2 (Olafsen o.g., Horvath). Oslo.
NORWAY: Hafthorsen; Goa, Thorsen, Olafsen, Slinning, Borno, Pettersen P., Olsen O. D., Pettersen S., Pressburg, Olsen.
July 3 1969: NORWAY (2) 3 (Olsen D. B., Iversen 2) BERMUDA (0) 0. Stavenger. 13,000.
NORWAY: Kasperen; Mathiesen, Spydevold, Eggen, Slinning, Borno, Kvla, Hestad, Iversen, Nilsen (Austboe), Olsen O. D.
July 20 1969: NORWAY (2) 2 (Iversen, Nilsen) ICELAND (0) 1 (Schram). Trondheim. 11,000.
NORWAY: Kasperen; Mathiesen, Slinning, Borno, Eggen, Spydevold, Hestad, Nilsen, Iversen, Kvla, Olsen O. D.
ICELAND: Dagsson; Atlasson, Kjartansson, Schram, Fridtiofsson, Bjornsson, Hallgrimsson, Hafsteinsson, Gunnarsson, Thorolfur, Beck.
Aug. 24 1969: FINLAND (2) 2 (Tulsa, Lindholm) NORWAY (2) 2 (Iversen 2). Helsinki. 10,700.
NORWAY: Kasperen; Mathiesen, Spydevold, Olafsen, Slinning, Borno, Kvla (Nilsen), Olsen O. D., Iversen, Johansen, Sathrang.
Aug. 27 1699: POLAND (5) 6 (Lubanski 2, Marks 2, Deyna, Brychezy) NORWAY (1) 1 (Iversen) Lodz. 35,000.
NORWAY: Kasperen (Hafthorsen); Mathiesen (Thorsen), Olafsen, Spydevold, Slinning, Borno, Nilsen, Iversen, Johansen (Kvla), Sathrang, Danielsen.
Sept. 10 1969: NORWAY (0) 1 (Olsen D. B.) FRANCE (1) 3 (Revelli 2, Michel). Oslo. 23,000.

(World Cup qualifying match.   See World Cup—Group Five.)
June 17 1970: NORWAY (0) 2 (Paulsen, Seemann)   FINLAND (0) 0.
Bergen.
NORWAY: Hafthorsen; Pettersen P., Thorsen, Alasker-Noestdal,
Slinning, Borno, Paulsen, Olsen E., Pettersen S., Jensen, Seemann.

POLAND

LEGIA WARSAW RETAIN THE CHAMPIONSHIP

After taking 13 years to win the League championship in 1969,
Legia Warsaw soon made sure that no one would take it from them
last season and with two matches left to play they had an unassailable
lead of five points.

The Polish Army side have been outstanding in the last two seasons
and it was only the Dutch side, Feyenoord, who went on to win,
who put them out of the European Cup.

They have the outstanding young Polish footballer in Dejna,
internationals like Stachurski in the back four, Blaut in midfield,
and Gadocha on the wing.

POLISH LEAGUE CHAMPIONS

1921	Cracovia	1949	Wisla Gwardia
1922	Lwow Pogon	1950	Wisla Gwardia
1923	Lwow Pogon	1951	Ruch Chorzow
1924	No competition	1952	Ruch Chorzow
1925	Lwow Pogon	1953	Ruch Chorzow
1926	Lwow Pogon	1954	Polonia Bytom
1927	Wisla Krakow	1955	Warsaw C.W.K.S.
1928	Wisla Krakow	1956	Warsaw C.W.K.S.
1929	Warta	1957	Gornik Zabrze
1930	Cracovia	1958	Lodz L.K.S.
1931	Garbania	1959	Gornik Zabrze
1932	Cracovia	1960	Ruch Chorzow
1933	Ruch Chorzow	1961	Gornik Zabrze
1934	Ruch Chorzow	1962	Polonia Bytom
1935	Ruch Chorzow	1963	Gornik Zabrze
1936	Ruch Chorzow	1964	Gornik Zabrze
1937	Cracovia	1965	Gornik Zabrze
1938	Cracovia	1966	Gornik Zabrze
1939	Not completed	1967	Gornik Zabrze
1940–45	No competition	1968	Ruch Chorzow
1946	Warsaw Polonia	1969	Legia Warsaw
1947	Warta	1970	Legia Warsaw
1948	Cracovia		

INTERNATIONALS

Aug. 27 1969: POLAND (5) 6 (Marks 2, Lubanski 2, Dejna, Brychezy) NORWAY (1) 1 (Iversen). Lodz. 30,000.

POLAND: Kostka; Szradkowski, Anczok, Brychezy, Wrazy, Blaut, Szoltysik, Marks, Lubanski, Deyna, Faber (Szmidt)

Aug. 31 1969: RUSSIA (0) 0 POLAND (0) 0. Moscow 70,000

Sept. 8 1969: POLAND (0) 2 (Jarosik, Lubanski) HOLLAND (1) 1 (Wery). Chorzow. 60,000.

Oct 12 1969: LUXEMBURG (1) 1 (Kirschens) POLAND (0) 5 (Dejna 2, Jarosik pen, Bula, Lubanski). Luxemburg.

Nov. 9 1969: POLAND (1) 3 (Jarosik 2, Deyna) BULGARIA (0) 0. Warsaw. 80,000.

(World Cup qualifying matches. See World Cup—Group Eight.)

May 2 1970: HUNGARY (0) 2 (Fazekas, Karsai) POLAND (0) 0. Budapest.

POLAND: Szygula; Stachurski, Szradkowski, Winkler, Anczok, Blaut, Bula, Kozerski, Chikoewicz, Jarosik, Gadocha.

May 6 1970: POLAND (2) 2 (Kozerski, Szoltysik) REPUBLIC OF IRELAND (0) 1 (Givens). Poznan. 85,000.

POLAND: Kostka; Latocha, Oslizlo, Anczok, Szradkowski, Bula, Chikoewicz, Soltysik, Lubanski, Soltysik.

May 16 1970: POLAND (1) 1 (Dejna) EAST GERMANY (1) 1 (Vogel). Cracow. 25,000.

May 19 1970: DENMARK (0) 0 POLAND (1) 2 (Banas, Jarosik). Copenhagen. 17,500.

POLAND: Kostka; Stachurski, Winkler, Anczok, Szradkowski, Blaut, Banas, Szoltysik, Dejna, Lubanski, Kozerski (Jarosik).

PORTUGAL

SPORTING LISBON BREAK BENFICA'S MONOPOLY

For the third time in less than a decade Sporting Lisbon broke the grip of Benfica on the Portuguese League championship and easily outpaced their local rivals to make sure of their 13th League title, three weeks before the season ended.

Under coach Fernando Vas, Sporting Lisbon showed that a new approach and new players were needed by the old Lisbon Eagles and with a side captained well by the midfield man Hilario, who did so well against England in the World Cup semi-final of 1966, and containing several players good enough for the international side, they led the table for most of the season.

In goal they have the 23-year-old Damas, who from Under 23 internationals has become Portugal's number one goalkeeper, and the internationals, the experienced John Carlos and Calo as twin stoppers, and the 26-year-old Marinho as a dangerous centre-forward when on the attack.

Original members of the first division of the Portuguese League when it was formed in 1934, Sporting Lisbon are one of the four clubs who have never been relegated and their record to date is: *Played:* 798; *Won:* 535; *Drawn:* 130; *Lost:* 133; *Goals for:* 2,370; *Goals against:* 1,200.

They have had a fair amount of European experience and their best season was in 1963–64 when they won the European Cup-Winners' Cup by a single goal in a replay against M.T.K. Budapest. On their way to the final they beat Manchester United 5–0 in Lisbon after losing 4–1 at Old Trafford.

Last season, however, they were well beaten in the Fairs' Cup by the eventual winners, Arsenal, offering little resistance in the second leg at Highbury.

Benfica had a frustrating season but there were signs that they were getting back to their old form later on when they won their last six League matches and were unbeaten in their last eight games to take them into second place.

During the pre-season weeks they had contract problems with their star player Eusebio, which were finally resolved, and then in January suffered the humiliation of having their ground closed by the Portuguese Football Federation for eight home games following disturbances.

These came after their match with Belenenses, which was abandoned just before halftime when some 5,000 people invaded the pitch to protest at the referee's decision to send off two Benfica players, the international centre-forward Jose Torres and full back Malta Da Silva. The club were fined £100, while Torres was suspended for six matches and Da Silva for five.

The following month Benfica dismissed their Brazilian manager, Gloria, the former trainer of Real Madrid, and their assistant manager, Fernando Canrita, blaming them for the poor display of the team. After they had been turned down by Sir Alf Ramsey, Benfica appointed Jimmy Hagan, 52, the former West Bromwich Albion and Peterborough manager, at £10,000 a year, to take over on August 1, 1970.

Meanwhile another Portuguese club, F.C. Porto, who finished seventh, had snapped up the controversial Tommy Docherty soon after he had lost his job as manager of Aston Villa.

SPORTING LISBON LEAGUE RECORD

	Home	Away
Braga	4–0	

Vitoria Setubal		2–0
Unaio de Tomar	5–0	
Barrierense		3–0
Porto	2–1	
Varzim		0–0
Benfica	1–0	
Guimaraes		2–1
Belenenses	2–1	
Academica Coimbra		0–3
C.U.F.	3–0	
Boavista		0–0
Leixoes	4–1	
Braga		3–1
Vitoria Setubal	3–1	
Unaio de Tomar		3–0
Barrierense	1–0	
Porto		1–0
Varzim	1–1	
Benfica		1–1
Guimaraes	5–1	
Belenenses		2–1
Academica Coimbra	2–1	
C.U.F.		3–1
Boavista	3–0	
Leixoes		5–2

FINAL PORTUGUESE LEAGUE TABLE

	P	W	D	L	Goals F	A	Pts
Sporting Lisbon	26	21	4	1	61	17	46
Benfica	26	17	4	5	58	14	38
Vitoria Setubal	26	16	4	6	58	26	36
Barrierense	26	11	6	9	42	33	28
Varzim	26	10	8	8	31	26	28
Guimaraes	26	12	4	10	38	36	28
F.C. Porto	26	8	6	12	36	36	22
C.U.F.	26	9	4	13	25	37	22
Academica Coimbra	26	8	6	12	42	46	22
Leixoes	26	10	1	15	32	47	21
Belenenses	26	8	5	13	22	35	21
Boavista	26	7	5	14	35	62	19
Braga	26	6	5	15	25	52	17
Unaio de Tomar	26	5	4	17	20	50	14

PORTUGUESE LEAGUE CHAMPIONS

1935	F.C. Porto	1938	Benfica
1936	Benfica	1939	F.C. Porto
1937	Benfica	1940	F.C. Porto

1941	Sporting Portugal	1956	F.C. Porto
1942	Benfica	1957	Benfica
1943	Benfica	1958	Sporting Portugal
1944	Sporting Portugal	1959	F.C. Porto
1945	Benfica	1960	Benfica
1946	Belenenses	1961	Benfica
1947	Sporting Portugal	1962	Sporting Lisbon
1948	Sporting Portugal	1963	Benfica
1949	Sporting Portugal	1964	Benfica
1950	Benfica	1965	Benfica
1951	Benfica	1966	Sporting Lisbon
1952	Sporting Portual	1967	Benfica
1953	Sporting Portugal	1968	Benfica
1954	Sporting Portugal	1969	Benfica
1955	Sporting Portugal	1970	Sporting Lisbon

PORTUGUESE CUP
BENFICA GAIN SOME CONSOLATION

Benfica gained some consolation for their failure to win the League championship by retaining the Portuguese Cup and giving the champions, Sporting Lisbon, a 3–1 thrashing in the final. However, they rather blotted their copybook by having one of their players sent off the field in the second half.

A goal by Artur Jorge after 15 minutes gave Benfica an interval lead in the National Stadium before a 60,000 crowd on June 14. Jose Torres added a second goal after 50 minutes and Simoes a third in the 63rd minute.

Not until the game was in its final ten minutes did Sporting get a goal back when Peres got the ball in the net. So Benfica will be in Europe in the Cup-Winners' competition as a result of their 14th Portuguese Cup success.

QUARTER-FINALS
(Two Legs)
Guimaraes 2   Benfica 0
Benfica 4   Guimaraes 1
Sporting Lisbon 6   Braga 1
Braga 0   Sporting Lisbon 2
Leixoes 2   Uniao de Tomar 0
Uniao de Tomar 0   Leixoes 0
Belenenses 1   Tirsense 0
Tirsense 1   Belenenses 0

SEMI-FINALS
(Two Legs)
Benfica 8   Leixoes 0

Leixoes 1   Benfica 1
Sporting Lisbon 4   Belenenses 2
Belenenses 2   Sporting Lisbon 2

FINAL
(June 14—Lisbon)
Benfica (1) 3   Sporting Lisbon (0) 1

CUP WINNERS
(PORTUGAL)

1939	Academica Coimbra	1955	Benfica
1940	Benfica	1958	F.C. Porto
1941	Sporting Lisbon	1957	Benfica
1942	Belenenses	1958	F.C. Porto
1943	Benfica	1959	Benfica
1944	Benfica	1960	Belenenses
1945	Sporting Lisbon	1961	Leixoes
1946	Sporting Lisbon	1962	Vitoria Setubal
1947	Sporting Lisbon	1963	Sporting Lisbon
1948	Sporting Lisbon	1964	Benfica
1949	Benfica	1965	Vitoria Setubal
1950	Benfica	1966	Sporting Braga
1951	Benfica	1967	Vitoria Setubal
1952	Benfica	1968	F.C. Porto
1953	Benfica	1969	Benfica
1954	Sporting Lisbon	1970	Benfica

INTERNATIONALS

Oct. 12 1969: RUMANIA (1) 1 (Dobrin)   PORTUGAL (0) 0.   Bucharest. 90,000.

Nov. 2 1969: SWITZERLAND (0) 1 (Kunzli)   PORTUGAL (1) 1 (Eusebio).   Berne. 30,000.

(World Cup qualifying matches.   See World Cup—Group One.)

Nov. 10 1969: ENGLAND (1) 1 (Charlton J.)   PORTUGAL (0) 0. Wembley. 100,000.

PORTUGAL: Henrique; Conceicao, Cardoso, John Carlos, Murca, Tome, Toni, Graca (Figueiro), Guerreiro, Antonio (Mario Campos), Jacinto Joao.

May 10 1970: PORTUGAL (0) 1 (Humberto)   ITALY (1) 2 (Riva 2). Lisbon. 35,000.

PORTUGAL: Damas; Pedro Gomes, Humberto, Jose Carlos, Hilario, Rodriques, Jaime Graca, Nelson, Torres, Peres, Simoes. Subs.: Matine and Dinis.

RUMANIA

(Results of Home season not available at time of going to press)

INTERNATIONALS

Sept. 30 1969: YUGOSLAVIA 1 RUMANIA 1. Belgrade.

Oct. 12 1969: RUMANIA (1) 1 (Dobrin) PORTUGAL (0) 0. Bucharest. 90,000.

Nov. 16 1969: RUMANIA (1) 1 (Dembrovski) GREECE (0) 1 (Domazos). Bucharest. 100,000.

Feb. 7 1970: PERU 1 RUMANIA 1. Lima.

April 8 1970: WEST GERMANY (1) 1 (Overath) RUMANIA (1) 1 (Neagu). Stuttgart. 73,000.

April 28 1970: FRANCE (2) 2 (Loubet, Djorkaeff) RUMANIA (0) 0. Rheims. 11,000.

May 7 1970: RUMANIA 0 YUGOSLAVIA 0. Bucharest. (World Cup finals. See Chapter Four.)

RUSSIA

MOSCOW SPARTAK TRIUMPH

Last season the Russians decided on a reform to streamline their League. It was considered that a division of 20 clubs was too unwieldy and it was agreed to reduce this to 14 as being more workable.

To do this the 20 clubs were divided into two groups of ten, and the clubs in each group played each other home and away on a league basis to find the top seven in each group.

It has to be remembered that in Russia clubs travel thousands of miles for matches, probably more than in any other country in the world. For instance, when Tashkent play in Moscow their journey is equivalent to one from London to Moscow.

The group matches were played between March and July, and the top seven clubs went into one group to play off for the championship, which ended with Moscow Spartak breaking the three-year grip which Kiev Dynamo had on the title, and winning the championship for the ninth time, having led the table for most of the season.

But their record showed that their success was mainly on their efforts to prevent their opponents scoring, for they managed only 40 goals in their 26 matches, of which Nikolai Osyanin netted 16.

Their goalkeeper, Anzor Kavazashvili, 29, who was on Russia's World Cup squad, finished as runner-up for 'Soviet Soccer Player of the Year' to Vladimir Muntyan, 23, another international, the Kiev Dynamo half-back.

The big surprise of the season was the success of Lvov Karpates in the Cup competition—the first team from the second division ever to win the competition. In the final they beat the Rostov Army team by 2–1 before 100,000 people. They are trained by a former Kiev Dynamo player, Ernst Jst, and include several players who have been in the national side at junior level.

RUSSIAN LEAGUE

GROUP ONE

	P	W	D	L	Goals F	A	Pts
Dynamo Kiev	18	10	8	0	25	6	28
Central Army Sports Club, Moscow	18	9	6	3	18	8	24
Moscow Dynamo	18	7	4	7	17	18	18
Rostov Army Sports Club	18	7	4	7	20	24	18
Lugansk Zarya	18	6	5	7	19	16	17
Neftchi Baku	18	5	7	6	16	18	17
Cernomoretz Odessa	18	5	7	6	14	17	17
Ararat Erewan	18	6	5	7	18	23	17
U. Swerdlowski	18	4	6	8	9	19	14
K. Kuybyschev	18	3	4	11	16	23	10

GROUP TWO

	P	W	D	L	F	A	Pts
Moscow Spartak	18	14	3	1	29	9	31
Tbilisi Dynamo	18	8	9	1	22	7	25
Shakhtyor Donetsk	18	5	8	5	20	17	18
Moscow Torpedo	18	5	8	5	15	14	18
Minsk Dynamo	18	5	6	7	16	19	16
Leningrad Zenith	18	5	6	7	14	18	16
Kutaisi Torpedo	18	7	2	9	17	27	16
Kairat Alma Ata	18	4	7	7	15	18	15
P. Tashkent	18	6	3	8	16	23	15
Moscow Loko	18	2	6	10	13	25	10

FINAL TABLE

	P	W	D	L	Goals F	A	Pts
Moscow Spartak	26	19	5	2	40	11	43
Kiev Dynamo	26	16	7	3	37	13	39
Tbilisi Dynamo	26	12	11	3	34	17	35
Moscow Dynamo	26	12	7	7	44	28	31
Moscow Torpedo	26	11	9	6	29	19	31
Central Army Sports Club	26	10	9	7	19	14	29
Neftchi Baku	26	6	11	9	26	27	23
Cernomoretz Odessa	26	7	7	12	17	26	21
Leningrad Zenith	26	6	9	11	21	34	21
Shakhtyor Donetsk	26	6	8	12	20	28	20
Lugansk Zarya	26	5	9	12	21	30	19
Rostov Army Sports Club	26	6	7	13	23	37	19
Minsk Dynamo	26	5	9	12	14	31	19
Kutaisi Torpedo	26	4	6	16	20	50	14

RUSSIAN LEAGUE CHAMPIONS

1936	(spring) Moscow Dynamo		1954	Moscow Dynamo
	(autumn) Moscow Spartak		1955	Moscow Dynamo
1937	Moscow Dynamo		1956	Moscow Spartak
1938	Moscow Spartak		1957	Moscow Dynamo
1939	Moscow Spartak		1958	Moscow Spartak
1940	Moscow Dynamo		1959	Moscow Dynamo
1941–44	No competition		1960	Moscow Torpedo
1945	Moscow Dynamo		1961	Kiev Dynamo
1946	Moscow C.D.K.A.		1962	Moscow Spartak
1947	Moscow C.D.K.A.		1963	Moscow Dynamo
1948	Moscow C.D.K.A.		1964	Dynamo Tbilisi
1949	Moscow Dynamo		1965	Moscow Torpedo
1950	Moscow C.D.K.A.		1966	Kiev Dynamo
1951	Moscow C.D.K.A.		1967	Kiev Dynamo
1952	Moscow C.D.K.A.		1968	Kiev Dynamo
1953	Moscow Spartak		1969	Moscow Spartak
			1970	Moscow Spartak

RUSSIAN CUP COMPETITION

SEMI-FINALS
Moscow Dynamo 2   Kiev Dynamo 0
Dynamo Tbilisi 1   Neftchi Baku 0

FINAL
Moscow Dynamo 2   Dynamo Tbilisi 1

CUP WINNERS
(RUSSIA)

1936	Moscow Lokomtiv		1955	Moscow Soviet Army
1937	Moscow Dynamo		1956	No competition
1938	Moscow Spartak		1957	Moscow Lokomotiv
1939	Moscow Spartak		1958	Moscow Spartak
1940–43	No competition		1959	No competition
1944	Leningrad Zenith		1960	Moscow Torpedo
1945	Moscow Soviet Army		1961	Donets Shaktyor
1946	Moscow Spartak		1962	Donets Shaktyor
1947	Moscow Spartak		1963	Dynamo Tbilisi
1948	Moscow Soviet Army		1964	Kiev Dynamo
1949	Moscow Torpedo		1965	Moscow Spartak
1950	Moscow Spartak		1966	Kiev Dynamo
1951	Moscow Soviet Army		1967	Moscow Dynamo
1952	Moscow Torpedo		1968	Moscow Torpedo
1953	Moscow Dynamo		1969	Lvov Karpates
1954	Kiev Dynamo		1970	Moscow Dynamo

INTERNATIONALS

July 7 1969: EAST GERMANY (1) 2 (Loewe, Frenzel) RUSSIA (1) 2 (Puzach, Khmelnitsky). Leipzig. 90,000.

RUSSIA: Rudakov; Ponomarev, Lovchev, Esskov, Shesternev, Kaplichny, Muntyan, Khurtsilava (Kisilev), Khasainov (Metreveli), Puzach, Khmelnitsky.

Aug. 6 1969: RUSSIA (0) 0 SWEDEN (1) 1 (Eklund). Moscow. 90,000.

RUSSIA: Rudakov; Ponomarev, Shesternev, Kaplichny, Lovchev, Kiseley, Osisnine, Tchoumakev, Khousinov (Metreveli), Puzach, Khmelnitsky.

Aug. 31 1969: RUSSIA (0) 0 POLAND (0) 0. Moscow. 70,000.

Sept. 10 1969: NORTHERN IRELAND (0) 0 RUSSIA (0) 0. Belfast. 36,000.

(World Cup qualifying match. See World Cup—Group Four.)

Sept. 24 1969: YUGOSLAVIA (1) 1 (Dzajic) RUSSIA (2) 3 (Asatiani, Nodiya, Byshovets). Belgrade. 10,000.

RUSSIA: Rudakov; Dzodzuashvili (Logofet), Lovchev, Kaplichny, Shesternev, Serebryanikov, Muntyan, Asatiani, Osianine, Byshovets, Nodiya.

Oct. 15, 1969: RUSSIA (1) 3 (Muntyan 2, Nodiya) TURKEY (0) 0. Kiev. 100,000.

Oct. 22 1969: RUSSIA (1) 2 (Nodiya, Byshovets) NORTHERN IRELAND (0) 0. Moscow. 100,000.

Nov. 16 1969: TURKEY (1) 1 (Ender) RUSSIA (2) 3 (Asatiani 2, Khmelnitsky). Istanbul.

(World Cup qualifying matches. See World Cup—Group Four.)

Feb. 14 1970: PERU (0) 0 RUSSIA (0) 0. Lima.

PERU: Ruhinos; Campos, Salinas, Challe, De La Torre, Chumpitaz, Baylon, Cruzado, Leon, Cubillas, Gallardo.

RUSSIA: Rudakov; Dzodzuashvili, Lovchev, Serebryanikov, Shesternev, Khurtsilava, Muntyan, Asatiani, Byshovets, Ghershkovich, Nodiya.

Feb. 20 1970: PERU (0) 0 RUSSIA (0) 2 (Puzach 2). Lima.

PERU: Zagarra; Campos, De La Torre, Chumpitaz, Salinas, Cruzado, Challe, Baylon, Leon, Cubillas, Gallardo.

RUSSIA: Kavazashvili; Logofet, Khurtsilava, Kaplichny, Papayev, Muntyan, Asatiani, Puzach, Byshovets, Khmelnitsky, Nodiya.

Feb. 22 1970: EL SALVADOR (0) 0 RUSSIA (1) 2 (Puzach, Serebryanikov). San Salvador. 75,000.

EL SALVADOR: Magana; Mejia, Cabeza, Castro (Mariona), Ruballo, Cabreram Monge, Martinez, Quintanilla, Acevedo (Aparicio).

RUSSIA: Kavazashvili; Logofet, Khurtsilava, Afonin, Kisilev, Kaplichny, Puzach, Muntyan (Serebryanikov), Ghershkovich (Byshoevets), Asatiani, Khmelnitsky.

Feb. 26 1970: MEXICO (0) 0 RUSSIA (0) 0. Mexico City.

MEXICO: Castrejon; Vantolra, Pulido, Perez, Guzman, Montes, Cisneros (Onofre), Padilla, Hernandez, Basaguren (Valdivia), Lopez.

RUSSIA: Kavazashvili; Logofet, Afonin, Kaplichny, Khurtsilava,

Kisilev, Muntyan (Serebryanikov), Asatiani, Ghershkovich (By-shovets), Puzach, Khmelnitsky.

May 26 1970: BULGARIA (0) 0   RUSSIA (0) 0.   Sofia.

RUSSIA: Rudakov; Logofet, Kaplichny (Shesternev), Khurtsilava, Zykov, Afonin, Serebryanikov (Kisilev), Papayev, Metreveli (Para-kuyan), Puzach (Nodiya), Khmelnitsky.

May 5 1970: BULGARIA (1) 3 (Jekov 2, Bonev)   RUSSIA (2) 3 (Yevri-uzhikhin, Byshoevets, Nodiya)   Sofia.   20,000.

RUSSIA: Kavazashvili; Dzodzuashvili, Shesternev, Lovchev, Kaplichny, Muntyan, Serebryanikov, Kisilev, Parakuyan (Nodiya), Byshovets, Yevriuzhikhin.

(World Cup finals matches.   Mexico City.   See Chapter Four.)

SPAIN

ATLETICO MADRID PREVENT A SPANISH RECORD

Ronnie Allen's bid to become the first English manager to take a team to the Spanish League championship and, incidentally, a European Cup place, failed when Atletico Bilbao were pipped on the post after an exciting struggle with Real Madrid's great rivals, Atletico Madrid, by a single piont.

Under their French coach, Marcel Domingo, 46, Atletico Madrid —who for so long have lived in the shadow of their more famous local rivals—clinched the title for the sixth time on the final day of the season after a see-saw battle with Bilbao.

Curiously, as in 1966 when they last won the title, Atletico Madrid won their last match at Sabadell; and it was fitting that their final goal should have been scored by their international captain, the 31-year-old Ivacio Calleja, who had led the side so well throughout the season.

More than half their goals were scored by their two main strikers, Jose Garate and Aragones Luis, both of whom have played for the national side, with 16 each.

Formed in 1903, Atletico Madrid were original members of the Spanish League when it began in 1929, and moved to their present Manzanares Stadium, which holds 70,000 spectators, in 1966.

They and Atletico Bilbao dominated the 1969–70 championship almost from the start and the lead changed hands several times. The £6,000-a-year Allen looked to have added the League title to the Spanish Cup he had won the previous season when Bilbao beat Madrid to regain the lead with two games to go, but a defeat in Valencia, while Madrid went on to win their two final matches, ended Bilbao's chances.

The loss of two key forwards, José Roco for the last five games, and Anton Arieta, the man who scored the two goals that beat West Germany in February, for two, punishment for being sent off against Real Sociedad, may have upset the balance of Bilbao's play for the final run-in.

The big surprise was the decline of Real Madrid who after winning 12 championships in 16 years finished in sixth position and for the first time since the competition was inaugurated in 1955 failed to qualify for the European Cup. They had the mortification of suffering their worst League defeat for 17 years when they were beaten 5-0 by Atletico Bilbao.

Even so, they managed to finish as second highest goalscorers in the League, with the ageing Amancio showing that he retains the art of goalscoring at the age of 30 by ending as joint top scorer in the League with 16 with Garate and Luis. It seems that Real will need a change of style as well as of players to regain their old place in European football.

Valencia, who finished third three places above Real Madrid, snapped up the former Real player, Alfredo Di Stefano, who returned to Spain after a spell in Argentina with Boca Juniors, as manager and trainer. Di Stefano, capped six times by Argentina and 27 times by Spain, had 11 seasons with Real and played for them in seven European Cup finals.

ATLETICO MADRID LEAGUE RECORD

	Home	Away
Seville		1-0
Las Palmas	1-2	
Valencia	2-0	
Celta		1-1
Majorca	3-1	
Granada		0-0
Real Zaragoza	2-0	
Barcelona		2-1
Elche	4-1	
Real Madrid		1-1
Coruna	2-0	
Pontevedra		2-1
Atletico Bilbao	2-1	
Real Sociedad		1-2
Sabadell	0-1	
Seville	1-0	
Las Palmas		2-2
Valencia		3-2
Celta	4-0	
Majorca		0-1
Granada	5-0	

Real Zaragoza		0–1
Barcelona	1–1	
Elche		1–1
Real Madrid	3–0	
Coruna		1–0
Pontevedra	2–0	
Atletico Bilbao		0–2
Real Sociedad	4–0	
Sabadell		2–0

FINAL SPANISH LEAGUE TABLE

	P	W	D	L	F	A	Pts
Atletico Madrid	30	18	6	6	53	22	42
Atletico Bilbao	30	17	7	6	44	20	41
Valencia	30	15	5	10	35	23	35
Barcelona	30	13	9	8	40	31	35
Seville	30	14	7	9	39	32	35
Real Madrid	30	13	9	8	50	42	35
Real Sociedad	30	15	3	12	47	37	33
Real Zaragoza	30	13	7	10	35	39	33
Las Palmas	30	10	7	13	32	40	27
Celta	30	10	7	13	31	39	27
Elche	30	8	10	12	32	44	26
Granada	30	8	10	12	20	31	26
Sabadell	30	10	5	15	31	37	25
Coruna	30	8	9	13	25	32	25
Majorca	30	7	8	15	33	52	22
Pontevedra	30	4	5	21	20	46	13

SPANISH LEAGUE CHAMPIONS

1929	Barcelona	1947	Valencia
1930	Atletico Bilbao	1948	Barcelona
1931	Atletico Bilbao	1949	Barcelona
1932	Real Madrid	1950	Atletico Madrid
1933	Real Madrid	1951	Atletico Madrid
1934	Atletico Bilbao	1952	Barcelona
1935	Betis	1953	Barcelona
1936	Atletico Bilbao	1954	Real Madrid
1937–39	No competition	1955	Real Madrid
1940	Aviacione (Atletico Madrid)	1956	Atletico Bilbao
1941	Aviacione (Atletico Madrid)	1957	Real Madrid
1942	Valencia	1958	Real Madrid
1943	Atletico Bilbao	1959	Barcelona
1944	Valencia	1960	Barcelona
1945	Barcelona	1961	Real Madrid
1946	Seville	1962	Real Madrid

1963	Real Madrid	1967	Real Madrid
1964	Real Madrid	1968	Real Madrid
1965	Real Madrid	1969	Real Madrid
1966	Atletico Madrid	1970	Atletico Madrid

THE SPANISH CUP

QUARTER-FINALS
(Two Legs)

Real Madrid 2   Barcelona 0
Barcelona 1   Real Madrid 1
Sabadell 2   Atletico Bilbao 0
Atletico Bilbao 2   Sabadell 0
Real Zaragoza 4   Murcia 0
Murcia 1   Real Zaragoza 5
Valencia 1   Ferrol 1
Ferrol 2   Valencia 3

SEMI-FINALS
(Two Legs)

Real Madrid 0   Atletico Bilbao 1
Atletico Bilbao 0   Real Madrid 2
Valencia 2   Real Zaragoza 0
Real Zaragoza 1   Valencia 0

FINAL

Real Madrid 3   Valencia 1

CUP WINNERS
(SPAIN)

1902	Vizcaya Bilbao	1922	F.C. Barcelona
1903	Atletico Bilbao	1923	Atletico Bilbao
1904	Atletico Bilbao	1924	Real Union de Irun
1905	Real Madrid	1925	F. C. Barcelona
1906	Real Madrid	1926	F.C. Barcelona
1907	Real Madrid	1927	Real Union de Irun
1908	Real Madrid	1928	F.C. Barcelona
1909	Ciclista Sebastian	1929	Espanol
1910	Atletico Bilbao	1930	Atletico Bilbao
1911	Atletico Bilbao	1931	Atletico Bilbao
1912	F.C. Barcelona	1932	Atletico Bilbao
1913	F.C. Barcelona	1933	Atletico Bilbao
1914	Atletico Bilbao	1934	Real Madrid
1915	Atletico Bilbao	1935	Seville
1916	Atletico Bilbao	1936	Real Madrid
1917	Real Madrid	1937–38	No competition
1918	Real Union de Irun	1939	Seville
1919	Arenas	1940	Espanol
1920	F.C. Barcelona	1941	Valencia
1921	Atletico Bilbao	1942	F.C. Barcelona

1943	Atletico Bilbao		1957	F.C. Barcelona
1944	Atletico Bilbao		1958	Atletico Bilbao
1945	Atletico Bilbao		1959	F.C. Barcelona
1946	Real Madrid		1960	Atletico Madrid
1947	Real Madrid		1961	Atletico Madrid
1948	Seville		1962	Seville
1949	Valencia		1963	F.C. Barcelona
1950	Atletico Bilbao		1964	Real Zaragoza
1951	F.C. Barcelona		1965	Atletico Madrid
1952	F.C. Barcelona		1966	Real Zaragoza
1953	F.C. Barcelona		1967	Valencia
1954	Valencia		1968	F.C. Barcelona
1955	Atletico Bilbao		1969	Atletico Bilbao
1956	Atletico Bilbao		1970	Real Madrid

INTERNATIONALS

Oct. 15 1969: SPAIN (5) 6 FINLAND (0) 0. La Linea. 22,000.
(World Cup qualifying match. See World Cup—Group Six.)

Feb. 11 1970: SPAIN (2) 2 (Arieta 2) WEST GERMANY (0) 0.
Seville.

SPAIN: Iribar; Sol (Bela), Gallego, Costas, Eladio, Arieta, Lora, Amancio, Garate, Ufarte, Rojo.

Feb. 21 1970: SPAIN (2) 2 (Burgnich o.g., Salvadore o.g) ITALY (2) 2 (Anastasi, Riva). Madrid. 80,000.

SPAIN: Iribar; Sol, Gallego (Violeta), Eladio, Costas (Grosso), Uriarte, Lora, Amancio, Garate, Arieta, Rojo.

April 22 1970: SWITZERLAND (0) 0 SPAIN (1) 1 (Uriarte). Lausanne. 22,000,

SPAIN: Iribar; Sol, Gallego, Violeta, Eladio, Lora, Arieta (Grosso), Uriarte, Amancio, Garate (Asensi), Rojo.

SWEDEN

GOTHENBURG I.F.K. BACK AFTER ELEVEN YEARS

Only occasionally do Swedish soccer followers see their best footballers, for although the national side qualified for the World Cup finals, such internationals as Ove Kindvall (now in Holland), Kurt Axelsson (in Belgium), Orjan Persson (in Scotland), Roger Magnusson (in France), Bo Larsson (who was in Germany but has returned to Malmoe), Ove Grahn (in Switzerland), etc., have emigrated from the amateur game for richer rewards abroad.

Even so, the success of the national side in getting to Mexico helped to increase public interest in the club game and the average at league games went up to 10,364 in 1969 from 10,139 the previous season, giving a total of 1,386,047 spectators.

After a lapse of eleven years Gothenburg I.F.K. became League champions in the 1969 campaign—the Swedish season runs from April to early November because football is not possible owing to the weather in the winter. They went into the lead half-way through the season, were never headed, and clinched the title with one week to go.

They succeeded Oester Vaexjoe, who dropped to sixth place, while the two promoted coubs, Jonkopping and Sirius Uppsala, quickly returned to the second division and will be replaced by Hammarby and Oergryte, the latter coming back after only one season in the lower division.

The Cup Final, which took place in June, was won by Norkopping, who beat A.I.K. Stockholm by the only goal, after struggling to beat Kalmar in a semi-final.

GOTHENBURG I.F.K. LEAGUE RECORD

	Home	Away
Aatvidaberg	2–3	
Djurgaarden Stockholm		4–0
Jonkopping	1–1	
Sirius Uppsala		1–0
Oerebro	1–0	
Norkopping		2–0
A.I.K. Stockholm	2–0	
Malmoe F.F.		0–1
G.A.I.S. Gothenburg	2–0	
Oester Vaexjoe		1–4
Elfsborg Borass	2–0	
Elfsborg Borass		3–2
Djurgaarden Stockholm	0–0	
Aatvidaberg		1–1
G.A.I.S. Gothenburg		1–1
Oester Vaexjoe	1–0	
A.I.K. Stockholm		0–1
Malmoe F.F.	3–1	
Oerebro		1–1
Norkopping	2–1	
Jonkopping		3–0
Sirius Uppsala	6–3	

FINAL SWEDISH LEAGUE TABLE

	P	W	D	L	Goals F	A	Pts
Gothenburg I.F.K.	22	13	5	4	39	20	31
Malmoe F.F.	22	11	6	5	34	27	28
Djurgaarden Stockholm	22	12	3	7	38	25	27

Aatvidaberg	22	11	4	7	38	34	26
Oerebro	22	10	5	7	33	27	25
Oester Vaexjoe	22	9	4	9	37	27	22
Norkopping	22	9	4	9	38	34	22
G.A.I.S. Gothenburg	22	7	6	9	31	36	20
A.I.K. Stockholm	22	5	7	10	21	25	17
Elfsborg Borass	22	6	5	11	21	30	17
Jonkopping	22	5	5	12	19	51	15
Sirius Uppsala	22	4	6	12	16	29	14

SWEDISH LEAGUE CHAMPIONS
CUP SYSTEM

1896	Oergryte I.S. Gothenburg	1911	Stockholm I.A.K.
1897	Oergryte I.S. Gothenburg	1912	Stockholm Djurgaarden
1898	Oergryte I.S. Gothenburg	1913	Oergryte I.S. Gothenburg
1899	Oergryte I.S. Gothenburg	1914	Stockholm A.I.K.
1900	A.I.K. Stockholm	1915	Stockholm Djurgaarden
1901	A.I.K. Stockholm	1916	Stockholm A.I.K.
1902	Oergryte I.S. Stockholm	1917	Stockholm Djurgaarden
1903	Gothenburg I.F.K.	1918	Gothenburg I.F.K.
1904	Oergryte I.S. Gothenburg	1919	Gothenburg G.A.I.S.
1905	Oergryte I.S. Gothenburg	1920	Stockholm Djurgaarden
1906	Oergryte I.S. Gothenburg	1921	I.F.K. Eskilstune
1907	Oergryte I.S. Gothenburg	1922	Gothenburg G.A.I.S.
1908	Gothenburg I.F.K.	1923	Stockholm A.I.K.
1909	Oergryte I.S. Gothenburg	1924	Gothenburg Fassbergs I.F.
1910	Gothenburg I.F.K.	1925	Gavle Brynas I.F.

LEAGUE SYSTEM

1925	Gothenburg G.A.I.S.	1942	Gothenburg I.F.K.
1926	Oergryte I.S. Gothenburg	1943	Norkopping I.F.K.
1927	Gothenburg G.A.I.S.	1944	Malmoe F.F.
1928	Oergryte I.S. Gothenburg	1945	Norkopping I.F.K.
1929	Halsingborgs I.F.	1946	Norkopping I.F.K.
1930	Halsingborgs I.F.	1947	Norkopping I.F.K.
1931	Gothenburg G.A.I.S.	1948	Norkopping I.F.K.
1932	Stockholm A.I.K.	1949	Malmoe F.F.
1933	Halsingborgs I.F.	1950	Malmoe F.F.
1934	Halsingborgs I.F.	1951	Malmoe F.F.
1935	Gothenburg I.F.K.	1952	Norkopping I.F.K.
1936	Boras I.F. Elfsborg	1953	Malmoe F.F.
1937	Stockholm A.I.K.	1954	Gothenburg G.A.I.S.
1938	Norkopping I.K. Sleipner	1955	Stockholm Djurgaarden
1939	Boras I.F. Elfsborg	1956	Norkopping I.F.K.
1940	Boras I.F. Elfsborg	1957	Norkopping I.F.K.
1941	Halsingborgs I.F.	1958	Gothenburg I.F.K.

1959	Stockholm Djurgaarden	1965	Malmoe F.F.
1960	Norkopping I.F.K.	1966	Malmoe F.F.
1961	Elfsborg	1967	Stockholm Djurgaarden
1962	Norkopping I.F.K.	1968	Malmoe F.F.
1963	Norkopping I.F.K.	1969	Oester Vaexjoe
1964	Stockholm Djurgaarden	1970	Gothenburg I.F.K.

INTERNATIONALS

Aug. 6 1969: RUSSIA (0) 0 SWEDEN (1) 1 (Eklund). Moscow. 90,000.

SWEDEN: Petersen; Selander, Christensen, Nordqvist, Grip, Svensen, Larsen, Lindman, Eriksson (Sandberg), Eklund, Olson.

Aug. 25 1969: SWEDEN (2) 3 (Eriksson, Danielsson 2) ISRAEL (1) 1 (Talbi). Stockholm. 11,286.

Sept. 24 1969: SWEDEN (0) 2 (Nicklasson, Grahn) HUNGARY (0) 0. Stockholm. 6,357.

SWEDEN: Hellstroem (Larsson); Selander, Axelsson, Nordqvist (Christensen), Grip, Svensen, Larsen, Eriksson, Grahn, Nicklasson, Johansson.

Oct. 15 1969: SWEDEN (1) 2 (Kindvall 2) FRANCE (0) 0. Stockholm. 51,954.

Nov. 1 1969: FRANCE (3) 3 (Bras 2, Djorkaeff pen) SWEDEN (0) 0. Paris. 17,916.

(World Cup qualifying matches: See World Cup—Group Five.)

May 16 1970: HUNGARY (1) 1 (Fazekas) SWEDEN (0) 2 (Persson, Ejderstadt). Budapest. 26,800.

SWEDEN: Hellstroem (Larsson G.); Selander, Axelsson, Kristansson, Nordqvist, Grip, Nordahl, Svensson, Larsson Bo., Ejderstadt, Eriksson, Persson.

(World Cup finals matches. See Chapter Four.)

SWITZERLAND

BASLE TAKE LEAGUE TITLE
IN FIFTEEN MINUTES

One of the most exciting Swiss League championships was kept alive until the final day of the season when only one point separated Basle and Lausanne as they went into their last games against Wettingen and Young Boys respectively.

But Basle, who 12 days earlier had lost a keen Cup Final to Zurich, settled the destination of the League title within a quarter of an hour of the final game's kicking off. Goals by Hauser in the fourth and seventh minutes and a third by Palmer in the 15th soon shattered the lowly-placed Wettingen, who were finally beaten by 5–0.

After a good start to the season Basle struck a moderate patch and at one time were halfway down the table, but they made a steady climb to the top and were probably the best side in the League. They scored more goals than any of their rivals, and conceded fewer.

But in the Cup Final in Berne on May 18 before 47,500 people, they had to admit second best to Zurich by 4–1 after extra time. Although their international Odermatt gave them the lead after 62 minutes, Quentin equalised 13 minutes later—and so the score remained at the end of ninety minutes.

Three minutes after the start of extra time Kunzli—the League's leading scorer—put Zurich into the lead for the first time and followed with another goal nine minutes later. Corti added a fourth seven minutes from the end to give Zurich a victory by a score which rather exaggerated their superiority.

BASLE LEAGUE RECORD

	Home	Away
St. Gallen		4–1
Bellinzona	2–0	
Lausanne		1–1
La Chaux de Fonds	3–2	
Young Boys		1–2
Zurich	1–1	
Winterthur		0–2
Lugano		1–2
Servette	2–2	
Frieburg		0–0
Bienne	5–1	
Grasshoppers		0–2
Wettingen	6–2	
St. Gallen	2–1	
Lausanne	1–1	
Young Boys	3–1	
Zurich		1–0
Winterthur	4–0	
Bellinzona		4–0
Lugano	4–0	
La Chaux de Fonds		0–0
Servette		2–1
Frieburg	3–0	
Bienne		4–1
Grasshoppers	0–0	
Wettingen		5–0

FINAL SWISS LEAGUE TABLE

	P	W	D	L	Goals F	A	Pts
Basle	26	15	7	4	59	23	37
Lausanne	26	12	12	2	54	36	36

	P	W	D	L	F	A	Pts
Zurich	26	15	4	7	49	29	34
Grasshoppers	26	12	7	7	39	24	31
Young Boys	26	13	5	8	52	41	31
Lugano	26	10	10	6	43	37	30
Servette	26	10	9	7	53	37	29
Winterthur	26	11	5	10	50	41	27
La Chaux de Fonds	26	9	3	14	36	55	21
Bellinzona	26	6	8	12	26	43	20
Frieburg	26	7	5	14	27	37	19
Bienne	26	7	5	14	28	55	19
Wettingen	26	6	3	17	33	62	15
St. Gallen	26	6	3	17	28	57	15

SWISS LEAGUE CHAMPIONS

1898 Grasshoppers	1931 Grasshoppers
1899 F.C. Anglo-Americans	1932 Lausanne
1900 Grasshoppers	1933 Servette
1901 Grasshoppers	1934 Servette
1902 F.C. Zurich	1935 Lausanne
1903 Young Boys Berne	1936 Lausanne
1904 Saint Gallen	1937 Grasshoppers
1905 Grasshoppers	1938 Lugano
1906 Winterthur	1939 Grasshoppers
1907 Servette	1940 Servette
1908 Winterthur	1941 Lugano
1909 Grasshoppers	1942 Grasshoppers
1910 Grasshoppers	1943 Grasshoppers
1911 Grasshoppers	1944 Lausanne
1912 Aarua	1945 Grasshoppers
1913 Montriond	1946 Servette
1914 Aarua	1947 Bienne
1915 F.C. Bruhl	1948 Bellinzona
1916 F.C. Cantonal	1949 Lugano
1917 Winterthur	1950 Servette
1918 Servette	1951 Lausanne
1919 La Chaux de Fonds	1952 Grasshoppers
1920 Young Boys Berne	1953 F.C. Basle
1921 Grasshoppers	1954 La Chaux de Fonds
1922 Servette	1955 La Chaux de Fonds
1923 F.C. Berne	1956 Grasshoppers
1924 F.C. Zurich	1957 Young Boys Berne
1925 Servette	1958 Young Boys Berne
1926 Servette	1959 Young Boys Berne
1927 Grasshoppers	1960 Young Boys Berne
1928 Grasshoppers	1961 Servette
1929 Young Boys Berne	1962 Servette
1930 Servette	1963 F.C. Zurich

1964 La Chaux de Fonds	1968 F.C. Zurich
1965 Young Boys Berne	1969 F.C. Basle
1966 F.C. Zurich	1970 F.C. Basle
1967 F.C. Basle	

SWISS CUP
QUARTER-FINALS

(Two Legs)
Zurich 1 Mendrisiostar 1
Mendrisiostar 1 Zurich 3
Bienne 0 Lugano 5
Lugano 0 Bienne 2
Sion 2 Servette 0
Servette 4 Sion 0
Xamax 0 Basle 2
Basle 5 Xamax 2

SEMI-FINALS
(Two Legs)
Lugano 0 Zurich 2
Zurich 3 Lugano 1
Servette 0 Basle 2
Basle 4 Servette 1

FINAL
(May 18 1970—Basle)
Zurich (0) 4 Basle (0) 1
(After extra time. 90-minute score 1–1.)

CUP WINNERS
(SWITZERLAND)

1926	Grasshoppers	1943	Grasshoppers
1927	Grasshoppers	1944	Lausanne
1928	Servette	1945	Young Boys Berne
1929	Urania Geneva	1946	Grasshoppers
1930	Young Boys Berne	1947	F.C. Basle
1931	Lugano	1948	La Chaux de Fonds
1932	Grasshoppers	1949	Servette
1933	F.C. Basle	1950	Lausanne
1934	Grasshoppers	1951	La Chaux de Fonds
1935	Lausanne	1952	Grasshoppers
1936	Young Fellows Zurich	1953	Young Boys Berne
1937	Grasshoppers	1954	La Chaux de Fonds
1938	Grasshoppers	1955	La Chaux de Fonds
1939	Lausanne	1956	Grasshoppers
1940	Grasshoppers	1957	La Chaux de Fonds
1941	Grasshoppers	1958	Young Boys Berne
1942	Grasshoppers	1959	F.C. Granges

1960	Lucerne	1966	F.C. Zurich
1961	La Chaux de Fonds	1967	F.C. Basle
1962	Lausanne	1968	F.C. Lugano
1963	F.C. Basle	1969	St. Gallen
1964	Lausanne	1970	F.C. Zurich
1965	F.C. Sion		

INTERNATIONALS

Sept. 24 1969: TURKEY (2) 3 (Metin, Nihat, Can) SWITZERLAND (0) 0. Istanbul. 25,000.

SWITZERLAND: Kunz; Michaud, Remseier, Stierli, Tacchella, Odermatt, Vuilleumier, Besson, Kunzli, Khun, Quentin.

Oct. 15 1969: GREECE (3) 4 (Botinos 2, Koudas, Sideris) SWITZERLAND (0) 1 (Kunzli). Salonika. 50,000.

Nov. 2 1969: SWITZERLAND (0) 1 (Kunzli). PORTUGAL (1) 1 (Eusebio). Berne. 30,000.

(World Cup qualifying matches. See World Cup—Group One.)

April 22 1970: SWITZERLAND (0) 0 SPAIN (1) 1 (Uriarte). Lausanne. 22,000.

SWITZERLAND: Grob; Weibel, Citherlet (Vuilleumier), Kuhn, Chapuisat, Loichat, Ramseier, Odermatt, Rutchmann, Blaettler (Kunzli), Quintin.

May 3 1970: SWITZERLAND (1) 2 (Blaettler 2) FRANCE (0) 1 (Revelli). Basle. 24,000.

SWITZERLAND: Kunz; Chapuisat, Ramseier, Citherlet (Weibel), Loichat, Odermatt, Kuhn, Balmer, Kunzli (Vuilleumier), Blaettler, Wenger.

YUGOSLAVIA

(Results of Home season not available at time of going to press)

INTERNATIONALS

Sept. 24 1969: YUGOSLAVIA (1) 1 (Dzajic) RUSSIA (2) 3 (Asatiani, Nodiya, Byshovets). Belgrade. 10,000.

Sept. 30 1969: YUGOSLAVIA 1 RUMANIA 1. Belgrade.

Oct. 19 1969: YUGOSLAVIA (3) 4 (Belin, Spasovski 2, Dzajic) BELGIUM (0) 0. Skopje. 22,000.

(World Cup qualifying match. See World Cup—Group Six.)

April 8 1970: YUGOSLAVIA (0) 1 (Bajevic) AUSTRIA (1) 1 (Redl). Sarajevo. 6,000.

April 12 1970: YUGOSLAVIA (1) 2 (Pancsics o.g., Gracanin) HUNGARY (1) 2 (Fazekas, Bene). Belgrade.

May 6 1970: RUMANIA 0 YUGOSLAVIA 0. Bucharest.

May 13 1970: WEST GERMANY (1) 1 (Seeler) YUGOSLAVIA (0) 0. Niedersachen. 71,000.